# THE CONSTITUTION
## FEDERAL COMMONWI

By analysing original sources and evaluating conceptual frameworks, Nicholas Aroney discusses the idea proclaimed in the preamble to the Constitution that Australia is a federal commonwealth. Taking careful account of the influence which the American, Canadian and Swiss Constitutions had upon the framers of the Australian Constitution, the author shows how the framers wrestled with the problem of integrating federal ideas with inherited British traditions and their own experiences of parliamentary government. In so doing, the book explains how the Constitution came into being in the context of the groundswell of federal ideas then sweeping the English-speaking world.

In advancing an original argument about the relationship between the formation of the Constitution, the representative institutions, configurations of power and amending formulas contained therein, fresh light is shed on the terms and structure of the Constitution and a range of problems associated with its interpretation and practical operation are addressed.

NICHOLAS ARONEY is a Reader in Law at the T. C. Beirne School of Law, University of Queensland, a member of the Australian Association of Constitutional Law and a fellow of the Centre for Public, International and Comparative Law at the University of Queensland.

# THE CONSTITUTION OF A FEDERAL COMMONWEALTH

## THE MAKING AND MEANING OF THE AUSTRALIAN CONSTITUTION

NICHOLAS ARONEY

CAMBRIDGE
UNIVERSITY PRESS

CAMBRIDGE UNIVERSITY PRESS
Cambridge, New York, Melbourne, Madrid, Cape Town, Singapore, São Paulo,
Delhi, Dubai, Tokyo

Cambridge University Press
The Edinburgh Building, Cambridge CB2 8RU, UK

Published in the United States of America by Cambridge University Press, New York

www.cambridge.org
Information on this title: www.cambridge.org/9780521716895

First published 2009
Third printing 2010

Printed in the United Kingdom at the University Press, Cambridge

*A catalogue record for this publication is available from the British Library*

*Library of Congress Cataloguing in Publication data*
Aroney, Nicholas.
The constitution of a federal commonwealth : the making and meaning of the
Australian constitution / Nicholas Aroney.
p.  cm.
Includes bibliographical references and index.
ISBN 978-0-521-71689-5 (pbk.) – ISBN 978-0-521-88864-6 (hardback)
1. Federal government–Australia–History.  2. Constitutional history–Australia.
3. Australia–Politics and government.  I. Title.
JQ4020.S8A7 2009
320.494'049–dc22      2008045144

ISBN 978-0-521-88864-6 hardback
ISBN 978-0-521-71689-5 paperback

[A] Commonwealth of commonwealths, a Republic of republics, a State which, while one, is nevertheless composed of other States even more essential to its existence than it is to theirs.

James Bryce (1889)

# CONTENTS

# PREFACE

My present interest in the federal dimensions of the Australian constitutional system was triggered some years ago when writing on the subject of constitutional implications. At the time I was examining a line of cases in which the High Court of Australia had held that the Constitution contained an implied freedom of political communication. One of the arguments apparently accepted by the Court was that since the Constitution was founded upon the sovereignty of the Australian people, it accordingly made provision for a system of representative democracy and that various political freedoms, such as freedom of speech, were necessary in order to preserve the integrity of the system. My central criticism of this and similar lines of argument was that the more radical of these implications were not warranted because the multiple steps in the reasoning, while individually plausible, had the cumulative effect of producing an outcome far removed from the text and structure of the Constitution.[1]

When considering these arguments, however, it was necessary for me to bear in mind another line of High Court decisions in which constitutional implications had been derived from the federal nature of the Constitution. In these cases it had been held that the Commonwealth Parliament could not enact legislation which would prevent the states from continuing to exist and function as autonomous, self-governing bodies politic. A question I had to face was whether these 'federal' implications – in contrast to the 'democratic' ones I had criticised – were warranted. Moreover, in other important cases decided by the High Court it had appeared that federal and democratic implications were in conflict and it seemed necessary for the Court to determine which would prevail.

---

[1] Nicholas T. Aroney, *Freedom of Speech in the Constitution* (Sydney: Centre for Independent Studies, 1998).

Issues such as these forced me to ask to what extent and in what respects democratic and federal principles were embodied in the Constitution. What is more important, the federal or the democratic aspects of the Constitution, and how do these principles relate to one another? A survey of the Constitution's text suggests that while democratic provisions are very evident, federal principles permeate almost every section. Furthermore, the preamble to the Constitution states that the Commonwealth of Australia is a 'federal commonwealth'. What does this mean? What *kind* of union was envisaged, and why?[2] This book is the result of an extended inquiry into questions such as these.

Throughout this period I have benefited substantially from the encouragement and guidance of many colleagues who have read and commented upon the manuscript, including especially Greg Craven, Jeff Goldsworthy, Donald Kommers, Gabriel Moens, Suri Ratnapala and George Winterton.

The book includes a substantial study of American, Canadian and Swiss federalism, and I have been able to benefit from academic interaction with many scholars in these three countries through the support of the T. C. Beirne School of Law at the University of Queensland, together with a number of overseas research institutions. The Pew Charitable Trusts enabled me in 1998 to participate in a highly stimulating seminar on political theory led by Nicholas Wolterstorff at Calvin College, and I wish to extend my hearty thanks both to him and to the organisers and participants of the seminar. Special thanks in this respect are extended to Bill Brewbaker and Mark Hall for reading and commenting on draft chapters of this book. I am also very grateful to John Witte, Director of the Law and Religion Program at Emory University Law School, who in 1999 provided me with an office, enlightening discussion and the opportunity to present my research to a discerning audience. In particular, I must acknowledge my debts to Johan van der Vyver, Charles Reid and the late Harold Berman, whose encouragement and example will be long remembered. William Buss also at this time very kindly gave me the opportunity to present my research to faculty at the University of Iowa College of Law. Similar hospitality was shown to me by the late Daniel Elazar of the Centre for the Study of Federalism at Temple University. Professor Elazar's passing is a great loss; the 'covenantal' approach to federalism applied in this book owes much to

---

[2] Jed Martin, 'Explaining the Sentimental Utopia: Historians and the Centenary of Australian Federation' (2003) 18(1) *Australian Studies* 211, 219.

him. In this connection I need also to thank Ellis Katz, Donald Lutz and Robert Williams for their comments, advice and encouragement.

In 2000, the United States Supreme Court Historical Society of Washington DC enabled me to present a paper on the colonial origins of US federalism to a seminar led by Jack Rakove, Akhil Amar and Maeva Marcus. My thanks are extended to them and to all the participants for stimulating discussions. Between 2001 and 2003, I again made a number of visits to Switzerland, Germany, the Netherlands and the United Kingdom, and was given very helpful guidance by numerous scholars, among whom I must mention Alexandre Fasel, Thomas Fleiner, Max Frenkel, Anton Greber, Walter Kälin, Wolf Linder, Daniel Thürer, Roland Vaubel, Stephen Weatherill, Dieter Wyduckel and the late Alis Koekkoek. Alis in particular organised for me to present my research at the Schoordijk Institute at Tilburg University; his kindness and integrity will long be remembered. Among Canadians, I also owe particular debts to Peter Hogg, Thomas Hueglin, Victor MacKinnon, Wes Pue and Barry Wright. Others I must mention who have commented on aspects of the argument include Ruben Alvarado, Bob Destro, Daniel Dreisbach, James Hutson, Gordon Hylton, Barry Shain, Ryan Streeter, Graham Walker, Peter Wallace and Todd Zywicki.

I am especially grateful to Finola O'Sullivan at Cambridge University Press, who embraced the idea of this book with great enthusiasm, and to many members of the editorial staff for their attention to detail.

Particular thanks are also due to Colin Hughes and John Nethercote, both of whom read the entire typescript closely and provided me with pages of suggestions for improvement. To these and many others, I must express my gratitude. The book is much better than it would have been because of their helpful advice, although I am of course responsible for its remaining shortcomings.

Most importantly, however, I wish to thank my wife, Lisa, for her love, constancy and support. To her I owe more than I can say.

### A note on terminology

The Commonwealth of Australia came into being when the six self-governing colonies of Australia were united into a federal commonwealth by force of the Commonwealth of Australia Constitution Act 1900 (UK). In this book, I use the term 'colony' to designate the six colonies prior to federation and use the term 'state' to designate them subsequent to federation.

# TABLE OF STATUTES AND EXECUTIVE INSTRUMENTS

## Representative and responsible government in the Australian colonies

### New South Wales and the Australian colonies generally

### Tasmania

## Other statutes

## Foreign constitutions and statutes

### *United States of America*

### *Canada*

TABLE OF CASES

# INTRODUCTION: AUSTRALIA AS A FEDERAL COMMONWEALTH

> WHEREAS the people of New South Wales, Victoria, South Australia, Queensland, and Tasmania, humbly relying on the blessing of Almighty God, have agreed to unite in one indissoluble Federal Commonwealth under the Crown of the United Kingdom of Great Britain and Ireland, and under the Constitution hereby established . . .
>
> Commonwealth of Australia Constitution Act 1900, preamble

The preamble to the Australian Constitution declares that the Commonwealth of Australia is a 'Federal Commonwealth'.[1] What did the framers of the Constitution mean by this, and why did they choose to create such an entity? It was certainly incumbent upon them to choose an expression that would capture the essential meaning and nature of the new polity they wished to see created. And so the framers said that this polity would be formed 'under the Crown' and 'under the Constitution' to be enacted by the Parliament of the United Kingdom. But they named it the 'Commonwealth of Australia', and they designated it a 'Federal Commonwealth'.[2]

Speaking abstractly, the framers of the Constitution might just as easily have created a polity that called for a somewhat different description – perhaps, for example, as a representative democracy or a constitutional monarchy. Indeed it is clear that the Constitution was constructed upon representative, democratic, constitutional and monarchical foundations, so that labels such as these would not necessarily have been out of place. The principles of representative government, responsible government and the rule of law are certainly fundamental features of the commonwealth that the framers wished to create.

---

[1] Strictly speaking, the preamble is part of the Commonwealth of Australia Constitution Act 1900 (UK), which in s. 9 sets out the Constitution of the Commonwealth of Australia, itself consisting of 128 sections.

[2] See also Commonwealth of Australia Constitution Act 1900, s. 3 (see select provisions).

The framers plainly chose to construct a representative legislature, whose office-holders would be chosen by the people.[3] After all, the legitimacy of the Constitution rested, chiefly, on the agreement of the people of Australia to unite in a federal commonwealth.[4] Just as clearly, although the executive power of the commonwealth would be vested in the Queen and exercisable by the governor-general, the financial powers given to the Federal Parliament meant that a system of responsible government was likely to emerge, under which the governor-general would exercise executive power on the advice of ministers having the support of the Parliament.[5] Moreover, the literary structure of the Constitution itself, in particular the treatment of the legislature, the executive and the judiciary in separate chapters, suggested that a modified separation of powers was also intended.[6]

However, the institutions created under the Australian Constitution – legislative, executive and judicial – are just as clearly federal institutions. The bicameral Parliament, partly federal in its structure, has only limited 'federal' powers, the judiciary has a limited 'federal' jurisdiction, and the power vested in the executive is expressed to be 'the executive power of the Commonwealth'.[7] Moreover, the Constitution is structured so as to treat separately of the states,[8] and does not explicitly prescribe the proper relationship between the various branches of the state governments.[9] Indeed, the Constitution presupposes the existence of the states, treating them as autonomous, self-governing bodies politic that are, as James Bryce put it, 'more essential to the existence of the Commonwealth than it is to theirs'.[10] Thus, the Constitution does not establish institutions for the states or confer powers upon them – it rather assumes their existence and confirms that they will continue, subject only to the specific measures adopted under the Constitution.[11]

---

[3] Commonwealth Constitution, ss. 7, 24.    [4] Constitution Act, preamble.

[5] Commonwealth Constitution, ss. 61, 64, 81, 83.

[6] Commonwealth Constitution, chs. I, II and III. On the separation of powers, see *R v. Kirby; Ex parte Boilermakers' Society of Australia* (1956) 94 CLR 254, but compare *Victorian Stevedoring & General Contracting Co. Pty Ltd v. Dignan* (1931) 46 CLR 73.

[7] Commonwealth Constitution, ss. 51, 52, 61, 73–6.

[8] Commonwealth Constitution, ch. V.

[9] But in respect of state courts exercising federal jurisdiction, see *Kable v. Director of Public Prosecutions (NSW)* (1996) 189 CLR 51.

[10] James Bryce, *The American Commonwealth*, 2 vols. (2nd edn, London: Macmillan, 1889), I, 12.

[11] Commonwealth Constitution, ss. 106, 107.

In this connection, it is to be recalled that it was not simply the 'Australian people' who agreed to unite into a federal commonwealth, but the people of the several colonies.[12] It followed for those who drafted the Constitution that the legislative powers of the Commonwealth must be vested in a Federal Parliament, the people of the states being separately and equally represented in one house, the Senate, which would share the legislative power of the Commonwealth with a House of Representatives that represented the people of the Commonwealth.[13] For similar reasons, the framers also thought that the amendment of the Constitution must ultimately rest in the combined hands of a majority of the peoples of the States and the people of the Commonwealth, voting at referendums.[14]

In these, and other more particular ways, all fundamental to the Constitution, the Australian framers decided to create a 'federal commonwealth'. However, until recently, remarkably little has been written about what the framers meant by this, or about what the idea of a federal commonwealth might mean to us today.[15]

## The idea of a federal commonwealth

John Quick and Robert Garran gave the idea of a 'federal commonwealth' an extended analysis in their 1901 classic, *The Annotated Constitution of the Australian Commonwealth*.[16] The term 'federal', they observed, qualifies not only the conception of the Australian Commonwealth as a federal commonwealth, but also its principal governing institutions – the legislature, the executive and the judiciary. This led them to conclude that '[t]he Federal idea ... pervades and largely dominates the structure of the newly-created community, its Parliamentary, executive and judiciary departments'.[17]

---

[12] Constitution Act, preamble.     [13] Commonwealth Constitution, ss. 1, 7, 24.

[14] Commonwealth Constitution, s. 128.

[15] Three studies that have considered Australian federalism in more or less theoretical terms are Michael J. Detmold, *The Australian Commonwealth: A Fundamental Analysis of its Constitution* (Sydney: Law Book Co., 1985); Andrew Fraser, *The Spirit of the Laws: Republicanism and the Unfinished Project of Modernity* (Toronto: University of Toronto Press, 1990); and Brian Galligan, *A Federal Republic: Australia's Constitutional System of Government* (Cambridge: Cambridge University Press, 1995).

[16] John Quick and Robert Randolph Garran, *The Annotated Constitution of the Australian Commonwealth* (Sydney: Angus and Robertson, 1901; reprinted Sydney: Legal Books, 1976), 292–4, 332–42.

[17] *Ibid.*, 332.

Although it is one purpose of this book to subject Quick and Garran's exposition of the federal idea to an extended critique,[18] it must be acknowledged at the outset that their analysis has hardly been surpassed since it was first published. The particular strength of the analysis was its sensitivity to the various opinions about federalism which shaped understandings at the time. With analytical clarity Quick and Garran identified the 'several distinct and separate meanings' that the term 'federal' had then acquired and thoroughly explained how they had been variously incorporated into the Constitution.[19]

The 'primary and fundamental' meaning of federalism, Quick and Garran explained, is the idea of a federal compact between states. Here, they said, the focus is on the *fœdus*, treaty or covenant by which several independent states agree to form a common political system while retaining their separate identities. On this account, federalism is in essence something brought about by a compacting agreement between states. The preamble to the Constitution, when reciting the agreement of the peoples of the colonies to form a federal commonwealth, alludes clearly to this sense of federalism. Certainly, the preamble appeals to the people, but it just as clearly appeals to the peoples of each colony.[20]

The second sense of federalism to which Quick and Garran referred concerns the nature of the new state created by such a union. The reference here was not to the bond of union between the federating states, but to the new state created by that bond: a federal state, which is itself a union of constituent states.[21] The expression 'federal commonwealth', they observed, is used in the Australian Constitution in this sense. It is also the sense in which the expression 'federal state' was used by James Bryce, Edward Freeman and A. V. Dicey – key influences on Australian federalism to be examined in a subsequent chapter.[22] For the moment, however, it is vital to appreciate that the reference here is to the composite entity as a whole: a polity in which the incorporation of states into state is taken to be of the very essence of its nature.

---

[18] See, in particular, ch. 4.    [19] Quick and Garran, *Annotated Constitution*, 332–42.
[20] See chs. 1 and 2, below.
[21] The Constitution Act, s. 6 defines 'the States' as constituent 'parts of the Commonwealth'. Quick and Garran, *Annotated Constitution*, 336–7, pointed out that the states 'are welded into the very structure and essence of the Commonwealth'; 'they are inseparable from it and as enduring and indestructible as the Commonwealth itself'; and they form 'the buttress and support of the entire constitutional fabric'.
[22] See ch. 3.

The third and fourth conceptions identified by Quick and Garran concern the system of governments adopted within a federal system, rather than the underlying polities. Their reference in this respect was not to the state and states which form the federation, but to the governing apparatus adopted therein. The idea is one of a dual system of governments, in which there is a federal government that exercises particular powers over the entire territory and several state governments that exercise their powers over separate, smaller territories. The third sense of 'federal' discerned by Quick and Garran concerns this dual system of governments; the fourth sense of the term refers to the federal government in particular.

Quick and Garran noted that this focus on systems of government, and not the underlying state(s), derived from the theory of federalism promulgated by John Burgess – another important but neglected figure in the story of Australian federalism.[23] Theoretically committed to a unitary conception of the state, Burgess insisted that there could be no such thing as a federal state. A state by its essential nature can only be unitary in character, he claimed. A state may certainly happen to utilise a dual system of government, employing 'two separate and largely independent governmental organisations in the work of government',[24] and dividing its sovereign powers between them. But the fundamental nature of the underlying state, he thought, consisted in its unitary character. Such a theory is clearly contrary to the idea of a federal commonwealth in the second sense referred to above.

Quick and Garran were deeply influenced by Burgess's approach to federalism, believing that it accorded with 'the more modern scope of the word'.[25] However, they could not point to any place in the Constitution in which the term 'federal' was used in this sense of a dual system of government within a unitary state. Certainly, the Australian Constitution frequently uses 'federal' to denote the governing institutions of the Commonwealth, but nowhere is the term federal used to refer specifically to Burgess's idea of a dual system of government in the particular sense in which he meant it.

This is not simply a matter of semantics. The implications are far reaching. In the first two senses of 'federal' just discussed, Quick and Garran identified the conception of federalism that shaped the views of

---

[23] See ch. 3.    [24] Quick and Garran, *Annotated Constitution*, 334.
[25] *Ibid.*, 335; similarly at 341–2.

the overwhelming majority of the framers of the Australian Constitution. Not only was the 'federal commonwealth' of Australia plainly founded on the agreement of the peoples of the colonies, but this fact shaped the institutions of government that were actually adopted under the Constitution. Quick and Garran asserted that the fourth sense of federal, as descriptive of the organs of the 'central' or 'general' government, while used throughout the Constitution, 'has no important bearing on federal history or theory'.[26] However, on the contrary, the structure and composition of Australian institutions of government (fourth sense) were deeply shaped by the fact that they were to be the governing institutions of a federal commonwealth (second sense) which emerged from the agreement of the peoples of the states (first sense). Restated in the terminology used in this book, the formation of the Constitution deeply shaped the representative institutions, configuration of powers, and amending formulas adopted under the Constitution.

## The argument

The central argument of this book is that the idea of a federal commonwealth is essential to the text, structure and meaning of the Australian Constitution, and that the relationship between formation, representation and amendment is fundamental to this conception. As Brian Galligan has argued, federalism – not parliamentary responsible government – is the primary organising theme of the Constitution.[27] And, as Galligan has further pointed out, a careful consideration of the federal convention debates of the 1890s is a powerful aid to understanding the Constitution that emerged.[28] In those debates federalism was the non-negotiable presupposition, not responsible government. Responsible government had to be accommodated within federalism, and not vice versa.[29]

The claim that a study of the formation of the Australian Constitution is essential to an understanding of its federal design very obviously calls for a close examination of the process by which the Constitution came into being. This process was a highly complicated one, multifaceted, elaborately interwoven and inherently susceptible to a wide variety of interpretations. Among these interpretations, an approach which seeks to

[26] *Ibid.*, 334.    [27] Galligan, *Federal Republic*, 7, 38.
[28] *Ibid.*, 7, noting decisions of the High Court of Australia to this effect.    [29] See chs. 7 and 8.

draw out the fundamental ideas at stake cannot afford to ignore three important dimensions of the process: the philosophical, the institutional and the deliberative. The argument advanced in this book takes account of each of these three.

The philosophical context of Australian federation is not easy to identify. In the first place, the contending ideas and sources are more diverse than has generally been recognised.[30] And in appraising the relative importance and weight of particular writings, difficult questions of judgement and historical sensitivity are inevitably involved. Still, such a task is integral to identifying the philosophical influences and thus obtaining a clear view of the making and meaning of the Constitution.

Some will say that the attempt to uncover the philosophical basis of Australian federation is misconceived. It has sometimes been asserted that other forces – especially the economic and the political – were the key factors.[31] However, a close reading of the documents and the debates has led me to the conviction that Australian federation involved real theoretical discussion, and was not merely a smokescreen for a deeper controversy between social groups concerned to advance their own material interests.[32] Economic and political interests were certainly involved, but the terms of debate and the outcome (the text of the Constitution) cannot be understood without an appreciation of the philosophical arguments invoked. Competing philosophical ideas cast a powerful explanatory light on the debate and outcome, as it is hoped the

[30] James Warden's study, *Federal Theory and the Formation of the Australian Constitution* (unpublished doctoral thesis, Australian National University, 1990), for example, does not address the views of Edward Freeman and John Burgess.

[31] E.g. Leslie F. Crisp, *Australian National Government* (5th edn., Melbourne: Longman Chesire, 1967), 14–20; R. S. Parker, 'Australian Federation: the Influence of Economic Interests and Political Pressures' (1949) 4(13) *Historical Studies, Australia and New Zealand* 1; Ronald Norris, *The Emergent Commonwealth: Australian Federation: Expectations and Fulfilment 1889–1910* (Melbourne: Melbourne University Press, 1975); Peter Botsman, *The Great Constitutional Swindle: A Citizen's View of the Australian Constitution* (Sydney: Pluto Press, 2000). But compare, e.g. Geoffrey Blainey, 'The Role of Economic Interests in Australian Federation' (1950) 4(15) *Historical Studies, Australia and New Zealand* 235; A. W. Martin, 'Economic Influences in the "New Federation Movement"' (1953) 6(21) *Historical Studies, Australia and New Zealand* 64; Jed Martin, *Australia, New Zealand and Federation, 1883–1901* (London: Menzies Centre for Australian Studies, 2001).

[32] See further Helen Irving, *To Constitute a Nation: A Cultural History of Australia's Constitution* (Cambridge: Cambridge University Press, 1997), 214–15; John Hirst, *The Sentimental Nation: The Making of the Australian Commonwealth* (Oxford: Oxford University Press, 2000), 265–71; Bob Birrell, *Federation: The Secret Story* (Sydney: Duffy & Snellgrove, 2001), ch. 5.

pages that follow serve to demonstrate. Indeed, as will be seen, understanding the Australian Constitution in terms of the federal commonwealth idea enables us to understand how the document can simultaneously be understood as the product of both philosophical speculation and pragmatic bargaining.

In chapters 1–4, I seek to reconstruct the philosophical context of Australian federation. Chapter 1 lays a foundation by critically analysing the three leading conceptual frameworks that have been proposed for the analysis of federal systems and by introducing the particular interpretive framework that will be advanced in this book. Chapter 2 then works out the analytical implications of the conceptual framework sketched in chapter 1, drawing on several features of the American, Canadian and Swiss Constitutions, and suggesting how conceptions about the formation of federal constitutions in each of these countries appear to have influenced the representative institutions and configurations of power adopted therein, and how all of these affected, and were in turn shaped by, the amending process. Chapter 3 then turns from constitutional texts to philosophy, considering again the American, Canadian and Swiss Constitutions as centrally important models, but touching also upon the influence of the leagues of the ancient Greek city-states, the Holy Roman empire, the Dutch United Provinces and the later German empire. In particular, chapter 3 focuses upon the various contending interpretations of these systems, and considers those interpretations in the context of more abstract ideas about the nature of federalism circulating throughout the English-speaking world in the late nineteenth century. Chapter 4 concludes the consideration of conceptual frameworks and theoretical ideas by examining how these models and theories were appropriated by leading Australian figures, and how the Australians used these ideas when formulating specific arguments about the kind of federal system that should be adopted by the Australian colonies. In this way, chapters 1–4 are intended to uncover the conceptions and theories which shaped the discussions and debates that ensued during the composition and ratification of the Australian Constitution.

Federal theory accords an important place to the institutional process by which federal systems come into being. According to Quick and Garran, the notion of a compact between states is the 'primary and fundamental' idea. But in so far as the idea of federalism patently involves a compacting agreement, the notion also suggests that, ideally, the constituent states are independent and autonomous parties to such an agreement. By the same reasoning, agreement between parties also implies specific terms of union, and to arrive at these terms, discussion is essential. However, effective discussion requires rules to control debate and define how decisions will be made. The notion of a federal compact implies that several autonomous states will agree to a decision-making procedure through which the terms of union are discussed and finally agreed. A study of the making and meaning of the Australian Constitution must take careful account of this formative process.

Federal theory is fundamentally historical and empirical in orientation, and this is so for several reasons. First of all, the 'ideal' conditions just described do not necessarily obtain in the real world. Particular political communities may be little more than subordinate administrative divisions of a unitary state; they may be self-governing colonies (as were the Australian colonies prior to federation); or they may be fully autonomous nation-states. The nature and terms of a more or less 'federal union' of such communities will be shaped fundamentally by their initial constitutional status. And this is but another way of saying that the formative basis of a 'federal system' – understood now in institutional terms – will have a profound influence on the kind of system that emerges from the federating process.

The historically contingent circumstances in which a federal arrangement comes into being imply that the terms of the federal compact will themselves depend on contingencies. Especially in so far as the peoples of the constituent states freely agree to terms of union, it is essential to the classical idea of federation that the terms of union will vary from one federal system to another, depending on the particular institutional conditions under which it is formed and the aspirations and interests which motivate those who conduct the negotiations.

In order to understand the drafting of the Australian Constitution it is therefore necessary to examine not only the philosophical context within which the federation took shape, but also the institutional conditions under which the debate was conducted. It is this question which is addressed in chapters 5 and 6. These chapters investigate the legal preconditions and institutional arrangements that were the context in which the Constitution came into being. The investigation involves an inquiry into the roles played by the governing institutions of the Australian colonies and the structure of the federal conventions at which the terms of the Constitution were debated and agreed, as well as the popular referendums at which the Constitution was approved by the voters of the colonies and the process by which the imperial Parliament enacted the Constitution into law.

The final aspect of an inquiry into the making and meaning of the Australian Constitution must concern the actual debates and drafting undertaken within the institutional and philosophical contexts just described. The idea of a union of states achieved through agreement requires specific terms, arrived at through negotiation. In chapters 7–11 I therefore examine the course of deliberation through which the Constitution was drafted. I do this through a close analysis of the formal records of debate within the federal conventions, the colonial legislatures and the imperial Parliament, and a survey of the wider public debate. In these chapters I focus, in particular, upon the drafting of the Australian Constitution through the course of the federal conventions of 1891 and 1897–8, read in the context of the institutional framework identified in chapters 5 and 6 and the theoretical context identified chapters 1–4. The objective here is to demonstrate the influence of the philosophical, institutional and deliberative dimensions of the formation of the Constitution on the federal structures embodied in it.

More specifically, chapters 7 and 8 examine the debate about the representative structures embodied in the Constitution: in particular, the House of Representatives, the Senate and the executive government. The first of these chapters focuses on the debate about the fundamental principles of federal representation that should govern the roles, composition and powers of these institutions. The second focuses on how these principles were embodied in the specific terms of the Constitution related to these institutions.

Chapters 9 and 10 then turn to the continuing functions and powers of the states *vis-à-vis* the new functions and powers conferred on the Commonwealth. These chapters are especially concerned with the scope of, and the relationship between, these two sets of polities, governments and powers. Conventionally referred to as the 'division of powers' between the Commonwealth and the states, I argue that such a conception does not do justice to the specific way in which the competences of the Commonwealth and the states are in fact structured. It is better, I suggest, to conceive of it as a 'configuration', 'distribution' or 'allocation' of power, rather than as a 'division'.

Chapter 11 finally examines the debate about the amendment of the Constitution itself. In a sense, this chapter is concerned with the representation of the people(s) of the Australian federation in the institutions designed for the amendment of the Constitution. It shows how general principles of federal representation were adapted to the question of constitutional amendment.

In each of these chapters the deliberations are analysed in the context of the relevant institutional framework and the philosophical background. Thus, another way of drawing the chapters together is to say that chapters 1–6 are concerned with the formative basis of the Australian federal system; chapters 7 and 8 are concerned with its representative institutions; chapters 9 and 10 are concerned with the configuration of power; and chapter 11 is concerned with mechanisms for constitutional amendment. Chapters 1–6 place the Australian federal system into an appropriate theoretical and institutional context so that the connections between formation, representation and amendment can be recovered, and chapters 7–11 demonstrate the existence of these connections in specific terms.

## Theory and interpretation

The methodology of this study is primarily historical and empirical. Specific terms and structures in the Constitution are explained by reference to the philosophical, institutional and deliberative conditions under which it came into being. However, there is also an important theoretical, as well as a practical, dimension to the study. On the basis of the foregoing chapters, in chapter 12 I construct a federal theory of the Australian constitutional order and, in so doing, seek to lay the groundwork for an approach to its interpretation.

The theory of federal constitutionalism in Australia constructed in chapter 12 naturally emerges from the inquiry into the formation of the Constitution undertaken in the chapters that go before, read in the light of recent insights into the origins, development and theory of federalism, and supported by a comparison with the Swiss, American and Canadian federal systems. I argue, especially in chapter 12, that the four elements of formative basis, representative structures, configuration of power and amendment processes can be brought together to provide a coherent and compelling account of the relationships between these loci of authority in the Australian Constitution. This is not to suggest that there are no inconsistencies and tensions but rather that, notwithstanding the tensions, there is a powerful coherence in these elements – a coherence that emerges especially when the text is read in the light of its formation and recent insights into federal theory and practice. The result is a federal theory of the Australian constitutional order in which the linked ideas of formation, representation and amendment are central to the meaning of the Australian Commonwealth, the so-called 'division' of legislative powers between the Commonwealth and the states being interpreted in this light. Chapter 12, in other words, presents a theory of the Commonwealth of Australia, understood as a federal commonwealth.

Chapter 12 also applies this conception of a federal commonwealth to the resolution of a range of current problems of interpretation of the Australian Constitution.[33] The interpretive questions addressed are primarily concerned with the formation of the Constitution, and with the representative institutions and amendment processes adopted thereunder, as well as with approaches to the interpretation of federal legislative power. As explained, each of these represent particular loci of authority in the Australian federal constitutional system. But what are the relationships between these concentrations of authority? As locations of power, theoretical and practical questions arise as to their individual features and the hierarchy between them. A wide range of critical problems in constitutional interpretation involve such questions. Thus, it has been asked: why is the Australian Constitution legally binding? What is the relationship between democracy and federalism in the Australian constitutional system? What is the hierarchy of institutional design? Is there a locus of ultimate legal authority in Australia and, if so, where is it?

For present purposes, these matters may be reduced to a single question concerning the locus or loci of 'sovereignty'[34] in the Australian constitutional order. This is a question that involves issues of federalism and democracy and the hierarchy between them; differently configured, it

---

[33] Such an approach to interpretation might be justified by reference to its capacity to explain textual detail, its structural coherence, its normative attractiveness or the evidence it supplies of the framers' enactment intentions. But such arguments lie beyond the scope of this book.

[34] 'Sovereignty' is used in this context because proponents of the various views continue to refer, sometimes loosely and uncritically, to 'dual sovereignty', 'state sovereignty' and 'popular sovereignty'. More precisely, it is a question of which institution can do what, in respect of whom, in which circumstances, and how. See ch. 2.

involves competing conceptions of federalism itself. The question in turn intrudes into issues concerning the more substantive and regular features of constitutional law, such as the representative structure of the Commonwealth Parliament and the formation of the federal government. The interpretation of the formative basis of the Constitution, the representative structures of the Commonwealth and the available amending procedures thus involve issues of federalism and democracy. Is it possible to reconstruct a coherent theory of the Australian constitutional system that can account for and answer these interconnected questions?

Members of the High Court of Australia have on occasion expressed the view that the Australian Constitution is now to be regarded as something in the nature of a 'social compact' whereby the Australian people, in exercise of their inherent sovereignty, agreed to form and to submit to a new Commonwealth government under the Australian Constitution – providing the basis and justification for the political order thereby created.[35] Sovereignty within the Australian constitutional order is said to lie with the Australian people; the Constitution is binding because the Australian people originally ratified it by 'popular' referendum and continue to possess ultimate power to amend the Constitution through the referendum procedure contained in section 128.[36]

Justice William Gummow, however, has called attention to some of the problems raised by this point of view. In *McGinty* v. *Western Australia*, his Honour noted, in particular, what he called the 'adaptation of representative democracy to federalism by the framers of the Constitution,'[37] and he asked: 'given the special adaptation of principles of representative government to federalism, where in such a case does ultimate sovereignty reside?' Observing that Bryce had maintained that 'ultimate authority resides with the authority or body which ... may amend the constitution', his Honour pointed out that the authority to alter the Constitution itself 'is reposed by section 128 in a combination of a majority of all the electors and a majority of the electors in a majority of States'. He also noted that the initiative lay with Parliament and that there was provision

---

[35] E.g. *Nationwide News Pty Ltd* v. *Wills* (1992) 177 CLR 1, 70 (Deane and Toohey JJ); *Australian Capital Television Pty Ltd* v. *Commonwealth* (1992) 177 CLR 106, 136 (Mason CJ), 210–11 (Gaudron J).

[36] See Geoffrey Lindell, 'Why is Australia's Constitution Binding? The Reasons in 1900 and Now, and the Effect of Independence' (1986) 16 *Federal Law Review* 29.

[37] (1996) 186 CLR 140, 274–5.

for resolution of deadlocks between the Houses. Even more importantly for present purposes, his Honour noticed the special provision in the fifth paragraph of section 128 for safeguarding particular interests of the states considered individually, particularly regarding the states' representation in Parliament and the territorial boundaries of the states.[38] Most significantly, he concluded:

> Broad statements as to the reposition of 'sovereignty' in 'the people' of Australia, if they are to be given legal rather than popular or political meaning, must be understood in the light of the federal considerations contained in s. 128. Those statements must also allow for the fact that none of the *Australia Acts*, Imperial, Commonwealth or State, followed approval at a referendum, in particular, any submission to the electors pursuant to s. 128 of the Constitution. Moreover, in s. 15 thereof, the *Australia Acts* provide their own mechanism for amendment or repeal by statute and without submission to the electors at State or Commonwealth level.[39]

The wider significance this book depends on the approach to the interpretive problems that it seeks to illuminate. In particular, this book seeks to provide an answer to Justice Gummow's challenge to do justice to the federal dimensions of 'popular sovereignty' in Australian constitutionalism. The final objective of the book is to lay the groundwork for an approach to the resolution of interpretive problems such as these.

[38] *Ibid.*    [39] *Ibid.*, 275. Cf. *Kruger* v. *Commonwealth* (1997) 189 CLR 1, 41–2, 63–4.

# PART 1

Federalism

# 1

# Conceptualising federalism

SOVEREIGNTY. I do not know how it has happened, that this word has crept into our political dialect, unless it be that mankind prefer mystery to knowledge; and that governments love obscurity better than specification.

John Taylor of Caroline (1820)

## The conventional approach

Conceptualising federalism is contentious and difficult. The conventional approach, particularly popular among constitutional lawyers and students of comparative government, states that the defining feature of a federal system is the existence of a 'division of power' between central and regional governments. The basic idea is that of a political system in which governmental power is divided between two territorially defined levels of government, guaranteed by a written constitution and arbitrated by an institution independent of the two spheres of government, usually a court of final jurisdiction.

The popularity of this approach among constitutional lawyers is in large measure due to its legalistic cast, particularly in the form initiated by prominent scholars such as A. V. Dicey, James Bryce and K. C. Wheare.[1] The approach is also popular among leading writers on comparative politics, such as S. E. Finer and Vernon Bogdanor, apparently on account of its simplicity and scope.[2] While parsimonious in its essential elements,

---

[1] Albert Venn Dicey, *Introduction to the Study of the Law of the Constitution* (8th edn, London: Macmillan, 1920), 134–67, 476–80; James Bryce, *The American Commonwealth*, 2 vols. (new edn, London: Macmillan, 1914), I, 432; Kenneth C. Wheare, *Federal Government* (4th edn, New York: Oxford University Press, 1967), ch. 1.

[2] S. E. Finer, Vernon Bogdanor and Bernard Rudden, *Comparing Constitutions* (Oxford: Clarendon Press, 1995), 6, 372–6.

the conventional definition is thought to capture an important set of features of a wide range of political systems that are commonly regarded as being 'federal' in nature.

There are a number of significant limitations in the conventional approach, however.[3] First, as political scientists have often pointed out, the idea of a division of power fails to describe sufficiently the way in which living federal systems actually operate. Rather than displaying a strictly defined distribution of responsibility between two or more 'coordinate' levels of government, federal systems tend in practice to resemble something more like a 'marble cake', in which governmental functions are shared between various governmental actors within the context of an ever-shifting set of parameters shaped by processes of negotiation, compromise and, at times, cooperation.[4]

Moreover, even when understood in strictly juristic terms – that is, as a description of a legal framework and a body of judicially determined case law – the conventional definition of federalism still has only limited explanatory power. It can be granted that, by virtue of its abstraction, the conventional approach captures the formal, constitutionally entrenched and judicially enforced allocation of legislative and other governmental competences that is typical of modern federal constitutions. However, the definition of itself provides no explanation of precisely which competences will be allocated to which level of government and, even more fundamentally, it does not explain the various ways in which this distribution may be effected. Thus, conceiving federalism simply to involve a 'division of powers' provides no insight into the question of whether the competences possessed by each level of government are 'enumerated' or 'residual', and nor does it explain whether the competences are best understood as 'delegated', 'transferred', 'reserved' or, indeed, 'divided'.[5]

---

[3] For critiques, see e.g. William S. Livingston, *Federalism and Constitutional Change* (Oxford: Clarendon Press, 1956), ch. 1; Maurice J. C. Vile, *The Structure of American Federalism* (London: Oxford University Press, 1961), 193–201; Preston King, *Federalism and Federation* (Baltimore: Johns Hopkins University Press, 1982), 133–45; S. Rufus Davis, *Theory and Reality: Federal Ideas in Australia, England and Europe* (Brisbane: University of Queensland Press, 1995), ch. 2.

[4] Morton Grodzins and Daniel J. Elazar, 'Centralization and Decentralization in the American Federal System', in R. A. Goldwin (ed.), *A Nation of States* (2nd edn, Chicago: Rand McNally, 1974).

[5] See e.g. Wheare, *Federal Government*, 12–14, who regards this question as concerning merely 'superficial' and 'non-essential' matters – compared, that is, to the essential and important question of whether the powers of government are divided between coordinate, independent governments.

To refer simply to a 'division of power' is tacitly to presuppose a particular view of the configuration of governmental power within a federal system. To speak in this way is to assume that the 'power' in question was originally a kind of 'unity', which has subsequently been 'divided'. This presupposition of an original unity of power betrays the relationship between the idea of a division of power and theories of sovereignty, understood as a unitary locus of putatively supreme, unlimited governmental power.[6] Thus Dicey formulated his influential theory of federalism against the backdrop of his account of the sovereignty of the United Kingdom Parliament (and his concerns about Irish claims to independence), and it comes as little surprise to find that Bryce, Wheare, Finer and Bogdanor, all of them writing from a fundamentally British perspective, likewise defined the federal principle in terms of a division of power.

To suggest that all federal systems must logically be understood in this way is to underplay the distinction between those cases in which previously independent or, at least, autonomous political communities have been integrated into a federal system and those in which a formerly unitary state has devolved governmental powers upon a number of regions within that state.[7] Indeed, as will be seen, the way in which governmental competences are defined and structured in a particular federal system (i.e. enumerated, residual or reserved, etc.) tends to reflect the process by which the federal system came into being (i.e. through a process of either integration or disintegration).

Another weakness of the 'division of powers' approach to defining federalism is its failure to shed light upon the distinction that is often drawn between 'federation' (federal state, *Bundesstaat*) and 'confederation' (*Staatenbund*).[8] As usually conceived, at least five factors distinguish a

---

[6] Note the correspondence between this approach and the third sense of the word 'federal' identified by Quick and Garran, *Annotated Constitution*, 334. Burgess's definition of federalism as a dual system of government was based on the assumption that all states are necessarily founded upon a unitary locus of sovereign power.

[7] For the distinction, see Alfred Stepan, *Arguing Comparative Politics* (Oxford: Oxford University Press, 2001), 320–3; Ronald Watts, *Comparing Federal Systems* (2nd edn, Montreal: McGill-Queens University Press, 1999), 29–31; Ivo Duchacek, *Comparative Federalism: The Territorial Dimension of Politics* (New York: Holt, Rinehart and Winston, 1970), 113–15, 120–8.

[8] See Kenneth C. Wheare, *Modern Constitutions* (Oxford: Oxford University Press, 1951), 32–4; Livingston, *Federalism and Constitutional Change*, 3–5; William H. Riker, *Federalism: Origin, Operation, Significance* (Boston: Little, Brown and Co., 1964), 5–8; Max Frenkel, *Federal Theory* (Canberra: Centre for Research on Federal Financial Relations, 1986), 62–8.

federation from a confederation: (1) formation – the foundation upon which the federal system originally came into being; (2) representation – the structural features of the representative institutions of the general government; (3) configuration of power – the manner in which governmental power is allocated as between the general and regional governments; (4) operation of federal law – the capacity of the federal government to make laws directly binding upon, and to execute those laws directly against, individual citizens; and (5) amendment – the manner in which the entire federal constitutional arrangement can be altered in the future.[9] However, the conventional definition deals with only one of these dimensions (the allocation of power), and does so in very general terms. It provides no explanation of the other aspects and therefore sheds no light on the problematic distinction between federation and confederation.[10]

Accordingly, there are a number of features that are typical of federal constitutions which the conventional definition simply overlooks and for which it provides no systematic explanation.[11] Discussions of federalism that are premised on the conventional definition usually refer (as they must) to these aspects of federal systems, but the discussion is unrelated to the general definition and hence devoid of a general explanatory framework.[12]

---

[9] See Walter Haller and Alfred Kölz, *Allgemeines Staatsrecht* (Basel: Helbing und Lichtenhahn, 1999), 146–7.

[10] See e.g. Wheare, *Federal Government*, 2–5. Wheare was adamant that the 'federal principle' existed only where the general and regional governments were 'co-ordinate' and 'independent' of one another. In a confederation, he stipulated, the general or federal government was in fact 'subordinate' to the regional or state governments, and for this reason a confederation was not a genuine embodiment of the federal principle. However, when making this very claim, Wheare had to acknowledge the anomaly that, as originally drafted, the United States Constitution (which Wheare took to be the paradigm of federal states) provided that members of the Senate were to be chosen by the legislatures of the several states, in a manner reminiscent of the 'confederal' Articles of Confederation of 1781. Wheare naturally found refuge in the fact that in 1913 the Constitution was amended to provide that senators would be elected by the people of each state.

[11] See Duchacek, *Comparative Federalism*, 207–8; Arendt Lijphart, *Democracies: Patterns of Majoritarian and Consensus Government in Twenty-one Countries* (New Haven: Yale University Press, 1984), 170–1; Watts, *Comparing Federal Systems*, 6–7.

[12] See e.g. Vernon Bogdanor, 'Federalism and the Nature of the European Union', in Kalypso Nicolaidis and Stephen Weatherill (eds.), *Whose Europe? National Models and the Constitution of the European Union* (Papers of a Multi-Disciplinary Conference, Oxford University Press, 2003). Bogdanor adopts Wheare's definition of federalism. However, when analysing the formation of the European Union, the representation of the Member States and the amendment of the constituent treaties, the discussion is introduced with words such as 'oddly', 'strangely' and so on, suggesting the inability of the conventional definition to account for these features of the Union.

## Federal or national?

In 1788 James Madison sought in the famous *Federalist* no. 39 to respond to the criticism voiced by its opponents that the proposed Constitution of the United States was neither genuinely 'federal' nor 'republican' in nature. Madison's analysis of the federal features of the American Constitution in that essay is of abiding relevance to our understanding of the Australian Constitution for two reasons. First, as will be argued in the remainder of this chapter, the analysis provides a particularly insightful starting point for the study of federal systems. Second, as will be seen in subsequent chapters, the United States Constitution itself, as well as Madison's particular interpretation of it, had a profound influence upon Australian conceptions of federalism and thus on the design of the Australian Constitution.

In *Federalist* no. 39, Madison argued that:

> In order to ascertain the real character of the Government, it may be considered in relation to the foundation on which it is to be established; to the sources from which its ordinary powers are to be drawn; to the operation of those powers; to the extent of them; and to the authority by which future changes in the Constitution are to be introduced.[13]

In approaching the question in this way, Madison organised the various federal characteristics of the Constitution into five useful categories. Madison's 'foundation on which it is established' corresponds to what I have so far called the formative basis of the Constitution – the process by which the Constitution was drafted, ratified and enacted into law. By 'the sources from which the ordinary powers [of government] are to be derived' Madison referred to what I have called the representative institutions adopted under the federation – in particular the structure of the federal legislature, as well as the executive and the judiciary. Madison's 'operation of those powers' had to do with the direct authority of the federal government over individual citizens, an important feature of the proposed Constitution which distinguished it from the more 'confederal' Articles of Confederation of 1781. Madison's reference to 'the extent of

---

[13] James Madison, *Federalist* no. 39 [1788], in Clinton Rossiter (ed.), *The Federalist Papers* (New York: New American Library of World Literature, 1961), 243–4.

them' had to do with the supremacy of the federal government within its 'sphere' of 'enumerated objects', in contrast to the 'residuary and inviolable sovereignty over all other objects' enjoyed by the several states – the so-called division of powers. Finally, for Madison, the 'authority by which future changes . . . are to be introduced' referred to the means of amendment of the Constitution. Notably, Madison gave equal weight to each of these five aspects: formation, representation, operation of federal power, distribution of power and amendment.

When Madison sought to classify these aspects of the Constitution, he was constrained by terminology. In Madison's day, the terms 'federal' and 'confederal' were used more or less interchangeably, and were contrasted with 'national' or 'consolidated' systems of government. Current usage, however, furnishes us with at least three separate categories: confederal, federal and unitary, with modern federations, such as the United States, Switzerland and Australia, falling into the second of these categories.[14] However, Madison had to rely solely on the distinction between 'federal' and 'national', and he did so by identifying both national and federal characteristics in the proposed Constitution, concluding that it was 'neither a national nor a federal Constitution, but a composition of both'.[15]

According to Madison, 'federal' referred, in the first place, to an act by which several 'distinct and independent states' would 'unanimously assent' to the proposed Constitution. A genuinely federal government will therefore 'derive its powers' from those states 'as political and co-equal societies', and these societies will be equally represented in the federal government. A federal government will, moreover, operate only on the states in their 'political capacities'; its laws will not operate directly on individual citizens, but will operate only through the states. A federal system will be marked, moreover, by a limited jurisdiction over 'certain enumerated objects only', the several states retaining a 'residuary and inviolable sovereignty over all other objects'. And, finally, a federal Constitution will only be amended with the 'concurrence of each state', that is, unanimously.[16]

---

[14] For more categories, see Daniel J. Elazar, *Exploring Federalism* (Tuscaloosa: University of Alabama Press, 1991), 38–64.

[15] Madison, *Federalist* no. 39, 243–4. But note Madison's apparently inconsistent statement in *Federalist* no. 51, 323. On Madison's (shifting) views, see Jack N. Rakove, *Original Meanings: Politics and Ideas in the Making of the Constitution* (New York: Alfred A. Knopf, 1996).

[16] Madison, *Federalist* no. 39, 243–6.

For Madison, these were the five key characteristics of a federal system. In modern terms, they generally capture the idea of a confederation or *Staatenbund*.[17] Delegates to the Philadelphia Convention of 1787 such as Luther Martin strongly supported this model.[18] For Martin the governing idea was that of a compact between sovereign and independent states, a view of federalism that reflects the etymological derivation of 'federal' from the Latin *fœdus*, which in its technical meaning in Roman law meant 'treaty' or 'alliance'. Older dictionary definitions of 'federal' reflect this understanding of federalism as grounded in a compactual formative process.[19]

On the other hand, Madison considered that a genuinely 'national' Constitution, if 'republican' in character, would be 'founded on the assent and ratification of the people' of 'one aggregate nation': the decision of a majority of individual citizens aggregated into an entire people. A national government, moreover, would be composed of representatives of the entire population. Its laws would operate directly on individual citizens, not the states, and the scope of such laws would be over 'all persons and things'. Its authority, therefore, would be 'supreme', and all local authorities would be 'subordinate' rather than 'independent'. The supreme authority under a national Constitution would therefore rest with the 'majority of the people of the Union' as a whole, and they would 'be competent at all times' to amend the Constitution in any particular.[20]

---

[17] See Martin Diamond, '*The Federalist*'s View of Federalism', in G. S. C. Benson *et al.* (eds.), *Essays in Federalism* (Claremont: Institute for Studies in Federalism, 1961); Martin Diamond, 'What the Framers Meant by Federalism', in R. A. Goldwin (ed.), *A Nation of States* (2nd edn, Chicago: Rand McNally, 1974). For critiques, see Vincent Ostrom, *The Meaning of American Federalism: Constituting a Self-Governing Society* (San Francisco: San Francisco Institute for Contemporary Studies, 1991), ch. 4; Jean Yarbrough, 'Rethinking "*The Federalist*'s View of Federalism"' (1985) 15 *Publius: The Journal of Federalism* 31.

[18] Luther Martin, 'The Genuine Information', in Bernard Bailyn, *The Debate on the Constitution: Federalist and Antifederalist Speeches, Articles, and Letters During the Struggle over Ratification*, 2 vols. (New York: Library of America, 1993), I, 631–61; James Madison, *Notes of Debates in the Federal Convention of 1787*, Adrienne Koch (ed.) (New York: W.W. Norton and Co., 1966), 153, 201–4, 217, 232, 289–90, 309, 564.

[19] Adolf Berger, *Encyclopedic Dictionary of Roman Law* (Philadelphia: American Philosophical Society, 1953), 474; Samuel Johnson, *A Dictionary of the English Language in which Words are Deduced from their Originals* (10th edn, London: Rivington *et al.*, 1810), *s. v.* 'federal'; J. A. Simpson and E. S. C. Weiner (eds.), *The Oxford English Dictionary* (2nd edn, Oxford: Clarendon Press, 1989), *s. v.* 'federal (1)'; Wolfgang Kunkel, *An Introduction to Roman Legal and Constitutional History*, J. M. Kelly (trans.) (2nd edn, Oxford: Clarendon Press, 1973), 38.

[20] Madison, *Federalist* no. 39, 243–6.

According to Madison, these are the five characteristics of a national system. They contrast neatly with the compactualist idea of a federal system, and they generally correspond to the modern idea of the unitary state. Delegates at Philadelphia such as James Wilson strongly supported this model.[21] Central to the conception is the idea of an originally unitary, sovereign, aggregate of individual citizens constituting a particular nation-state. These individuals may well choose to create a federal form of government. But 'federal' in this context only means that there is a 'division' of power between the national and state governments. Apart from this, representation in the national legislature must be proportionate to the national population and amendments to the Constitution must be determined by majority vote as an expression of national sovereignty.

## Compact or constitution?

Neither James Wilson nor Luther Martin was entirely successful at Philadelphia in 1787. The Constitution that emerged was, in Madison's words, a 'composition' of both federal and national characteristics. The foundation of the system was compactual and therefore federal, he said, because the 'assent and ratification of the people of America' was given by the people 'not as individuals composing one entire nation, but as composing the distinct and independent States'. Similarly, federal elements were to be seen in the equal representation of the states in the Senate and the role of the states in the amendment of the Constitution. However, significant consolidating or national elements were also evident: the House of Representatives was a national house, federal laws prevailed over inconsistent state laws and – perhaps most significantly – the federal government had power to enforce its laws directly against individuals. In our day, we usually call this kind of system a 'federation' or *Bundesstaat*, as distinct from both 'confederations' and 'national'

---

[21] Madison, *Debates*, 40, 42, 48–9, 74, 90, 153, 287; Jonathan Elliot (ed.), *The Debates in the Several State Conventions, on the Adoption of the Federal Constitution, as Recommended by the General Convention at Philadelphia in 1787*, 4 vols, (2nd edn, Washington: Jonathan Elliot, 1836), II, 455–6; Max Farrand (ed.), *The Records of the Federal Convention of 1787* (New Haven: Yale University Press, 1911), I, 127, 322, 324; *Chisholm v. Georgia* 2 US (2 Dall.) 419 (1793), 453–7. See Mark Hall, *The Political and Legal Philosophy of James Wilson 1742–1798* (Columbia: University of Missouri Press, 1997), chs. 4 and 6.

systems. Today, the American, Swiss and Australian Constitutions are said to fit into this intermediate category.[22]

Despite Madison's careful classification in *Federalist* no. 39,[23] many later writers sought to interpret such federations in either compactual or nationalistic terms. Writing in the nineteenth century, for example, St George Tucker and John C. Calhoun sought to explain the United States Constitution in terms that did justice to its varied features, but which ultimately fell back on the idea of compact between sovereign states as determinative.[24] According to them, the American Constitution was a 'federal compact' in which 'several sovereign and independent states' formed a confederacy in which each remained a 'perfect state'. Each state was therefore represented as a sovereign agent in the Senate and retained all sovereign power not explicitly delegated to the federal government. As possessors of ultimate sovereignty, the people of each state therefore had a residual power to nullify unconstitutional federal laws, to interpose to prevent their execution and to secede if necessary. Interpretations of the Constitution by the Supreme Court and alterations to the Constitution under the amending formula were not of final authority.

Certainly Tucker and Calhoun had to accept that there were important differences between the American Constitution and the more confederal Articles of Confederation. Adopting Madison's analysis, Tucker conceded that the Constitution was partly in the nature of a national 'social compact' and Calhoun accepted that the Constitution provided for a

---

[22] Madison, *Federalist* no. 39, 243–6. For the more recent terminology, see Wheare, *Federal Government*, 1; Carl J. Friedrich, *Trends of Federalism in Theory and Practice* (London: Pall Mall Press, 1968), ch. 2; Geoffrey Sawer, *Modern Federalism* (London: Watts, 1969), ch. 1.

[23] In publishing the essay Madison had an overarching objective of convincing New York voters to support the ratification of the Constitution. At Philadelphia, he had favoured the more 'nationalist' model promoted by Wilson, but his rhetorical objectives in *The Federalist* called for a close analysis that would underscore both the 'federal' and 'national' features of the Constitution.

[24] St George Tucker (ed.), *Blackstone's Commentaries: With Notes of Reference, to the Constitution and Laws, of the Federal Government of the United States; And of the Commonwealth of Virginia*, 5 vols. (Philadelphia: Birch and Small, 1803); John C. Calhoun, *A Discourse on the Constitution and Government of the United States* [1853] and *A Disquisition on Government* (1853), both in R. M. Lence (ed.), *Union and Liberty: The Political Philosophy of John C. Calhoun* (Indianapolis: Liberty Fund, 1992). See also John Taylor, *Construction Construed, and Constitutions Vindicated* (Richmond: Shepherd and Pollard, 1820; reprinted New York: Da Capo Press, 1970); Alexander H. Stephens, *A Constitutional View of the Late War between the States; Its Causes, Character, Conduct and Results*, 2 vols. (Philadelphia: National Publishing Co., 1868); Senator Robert Hayne in Elliot, *Debates*, IV, 509–16.

'federal government' and not just a 'confederacy'.[25] But for both the fundamental idea remained one of a compact between sovereign states. The strength of this approach was its capacity to explain those features of the Constitution that Madison identified as federal in nature: the formative basis, the Senate, the delegation of powers and the role of the states in the amendment process. Its weakness lay in its explanation of the national aspects: the House of Representatives, the direct federal authority over individuals, the authority of the Supreme Court and the consolidating implications of the amendment formula.

Others attempted to explain the United States Constitution in nationalist terms. Joseph Story and John Burgess, for example, argued that the Constitution was not established by the state governments or by the people of each state, but by the people of the United States understood 'in the aggregate'.[26] As Story put it, the American document was in its nature a 'supreme law', a genuine 'constitution', rather than a 'compact', for the Constitution was 'ordained' by 'We, the people of the United States'.[27] According to Burgess, when choosing which 'form of government' to institute, it was true that the people of the nation decided to constitute a federal system – meaning a division of powers between the general government and the state governments – but a federal form of government for Burgess meant absolutely no more than this.[28] As in the writings of Dicey and Wheare who followed, the 'division of power' theory was thus premised on the idea of an original sovereignty or unitary power that was subsequently divided or distributed.

On this view the national features of the system were easily explained, but the federal features identified by Madison presented difficulties. Story therefore recognised that his nationalism needed to be moderated by at least some aspects of Madison's 'partly national, partly federal'

---

[25] Tucker, Notes of Reference, V, 31, 85–6, 91–2, 126, 142; Calhoun, Discourse, 82.

[26] Joseph Story, Commentaries on the Constitution of the United States with a Preliminary Review of the Constitutional History of the Colonies and States before the Adoption of the Constitution, M. M. Bigelow (ed.) (5th edn, Boston: Little, Brown and Co., 1891), I, 264.

[27] Ibid., I, 252, 254, 352. Compare the Constitution of the Confederate States of America (1861): 'We, the people of the Confederate States, and each State acting in its sovereign and independent character'.

[28] John W. Burgess, Political Science and Comparative Constitutional Law, 2 vols. (Boston: Ginn and Co., 1890), II, 5–9. Other exponents of this general approach include Marshall CJ in McCulloch v. Maryland 17 US (4 Wheat.) 316 (1819), 402–5; Senator Daniel Webster in Elliot, Debates, IV, 496–509.

analysis.[29] He had to address, for example, Madison's observation that the Constitution rested on a compact and was federal as to its foundation. Story admitted that the Constitution was ratified by 'the people in each of the States', but rejected the inference that it was for that reason a mere compact or league. Burgess tried to explain how this could be the case, dogmatically insisting that the movement from confederation to federation necessarily involved legal discontinuity. Empirically, the peoples of the several states may have ratified the Constitution, but when the Constitution came into being, sovereignty mysteriously shifted from the 'peoples' to the 'people'.[30]

At the level of abstract theory Burgess's nationalist argument was coherent. But it could not adequately explain the federal aspects of the scheme identified by Madison, such as the Senate, the configuration of power and the amending formula. The best explanation that he could give was that these features were 'relic[s] of confederatism' and undemocratic 'errors'.[31] By contrast Story followed Madison in recognising that the structure of the government was 'partly federal and partly national', as appropriate to a 'compound republic'. He stated:

> Admitting, then, that it is right among a people thoroughly incorporated into one nation that every district or territory ought to have a proportional share of the government, and that among independent states bound together by a simple league there ought, on the other hand, to be an equal share in the common councils whatever might be their relative size or strength ... it would follow that a compound republic partaking of the character of each ought to be founded on a mixture of proportional and equal representation.[32]

Both nationalists and compactualists thus had to confront Madison's carefully empirical analysis of the American Constitution and to address

---

[29] Story criticised Tucker at length, but admitted that his views were not extreme: Story, *Commentaries*, I, 221–8, 230.

[30] Burgess, *Political Science*, I, 101–8.

[31] *Ibid.*, II, 49. See, likewise, Georg Jellinek, *Allgemeine Staatslehre* (1900) (3rd edn, Berlin: O. Häring, 1914), 762–87 and the discussion in Walter H. Bennett, *American Theories of Federalism* (Tuscaloosa: University of Alabama Press, 1964), chs. 6 and 7.

[32] Story, *Commentaries*, I, 518–19. Compare James Kent, *Commentaries on American Law* (7th edn, New York: James Kent, 1851), I, 231, 235, and see Michael Burgess, *Comparative Federalism: Theory and Practice* (London: Routledge, 2006), ch. 7; Thomas Hueglin and Alan Fenna, *Comparative Federalism: A Systematic Inquiry* (Toronto: Broadview Press, 2006), ch. 7.

its 'partly national, partly federal' character. Yet, in their extreme forms, neither nationalist nor compactual approaches could adequately account for the institutional details embodied in a modern federal constitution.

The fundamental reason for this is that in both approaches the idea of an indivisible sovereignty is either explicitly or tacitly in operation. In the compactual theory, the several states are separately sovereign; in the nationalist theory, the nation as a whole is sovereign. However, in their empirical details, federations persistently resist analysis in terms of sovereignty. To avoid the problem compactual approaches tend to focus on the formative process, while nationalist approaches are typically concerned with outcomes, forms and purposes of government. Compactual approaches tend to treat the formative process as determinative; nationalist approaches tend to treat the division of powers as decisive. The result, in either case, is a disjunction between the formation of federations on the one hand, and the representative institutions and amendment clauses on the other. Thus both approaches fail to provide complete accounts of modern federations in their 'partly federal, partly national' character.

### Federation or confederation?

The period between the late eighteenth century and the mid-twentieth century witnessed a general decline in compactual approaches to federalism. It also saw the general displacement of confederation by federation as a form of inter-state organisation.[33] Thus, in 1787–9, the US Constitution supplanted the Articles of Confederation of 1781 due to perceived weaknesses in the confederal system. The Swiss Constitution of 1848, partially modelled on the US Constitution, replaced the more confederal Pact of 1815 for ostensibly similar reasons. The Australian Constitution of 1900, itself modelled on the Constitutions of the United States and Switzerland, likewise supplanted the loose confederation established under the Federal Council of Australasia Act (1885). Moreover, the American Civil War of 1861–65 involved a conflict between the compactual interpretations of the southern Confederacy and the nationalist

---

[33] But see Elazar, *Exploring Federalism*, 52–3, who observes that 'in the postmodern epoch, as notions of absolute national sovereignty diminish in the face of . . . international interdependence and . . . multiethnic polities . . . new conceptions of political order which allow conceptual and operational space for confederation are emerging'.

interpretations of the Union, so that the resolution of the war in favour of the latter reinforced the nationalist interpretation.[34] On first glance, the British North America Act (1867) represented a decentralising movement away from the Union Act (1840), which had united Upper and Lower Canada into one province. Yet, fearful of civil war, the Canadians in 1867 went out of their way to avoid any suggestion of state sovereignty.[35] And, while in 1900 the Australians were relatively more concerned to protect 'states' rights', they too wished to create an 'indissoluble' federation.[36]

As a result of these developments, nationalist interpretations of modern federalism have tended to prevail, while compactual interpretations have generally come to be regarded as nothing much more than 'discarded constitutional curiosities'.[37] Thus, compactual theories have generally been relegated to the old confederations of 1781, 1815 and 1885, whereas nationalist approaches have been associated with the modern idea of federation as embodied in the Constitutions of 1789, 1848, 1867 and 1900. The result is an asserted empirical dichotomy between confederation and federation – even though the dichotomy, on analysis, actually derives from *a priori* nationalist presuppositions.[38]

According to the nationalist interpretation,[39] a confederation is formed by a unanimous compact between the governments of several sovereign states, whereas a federation is formed under a constitution to which the people of the nation as a whole consent. Under a confederation, it is said, the several states retain their separate sovereign status, whereas in a federation sovereignty inheres in the nation as a whole. In a confederation, the states delegate particular, limited powers to the federal legislature and other branches of government, retaining for themselves an

---

[34] Forrest McDonald, *States' Rights and the Union: Imperium in Imperio, 1776–1876* (Lawrence: University Press of Kansas, 2000), ch. 9.

[35] G. P. Browne (ed.), *Documents on the Confederation of British North America* (Toronto: McClelland and Stewart, 1969), xxvi–xxvii.

[36] Quick and Garran, *Annotated Constitution*, 292–4, discussing the reference to 'one indissoluble federal commonwealth' in the preamble to the Constitution.

[37] Gregory J. Craven, *Secession: The Ultimate States Right* (Melbourne: Melbourne University Press, 1986), 73. The *Oxford English Dictionary*, *s.v.* 'federal', treats the compactual definition of 'federal' as obsolete. See also Friedrich, *Trends of Federalism*, 22.

[38] The fact that the Canadian system is usually called a 'confederation' reflects the older usage in which no sharp distinction was drawn between 'federation' and 'confederation', both terms being used to refer loosely to a federally organised system of government.

[39] E.g. Samuel Beer, *To Make a Nation: The Rediscovery of American Federalism* (Cambridge: Belknap Press, 1993).

inviolable sphere of reserved powers, whereas in a federation the sovereign people divide or distribute the plenitude of sovereignty between the
federal and state governments. In a confederation, moreover, individuals
are solely or primarily citizens of their respective states, whereas in a
federation, individuals are primarily citizens of the federation. Under a
confederation the states are equally represented in the federal legislature
or congress and members of the federal congress are delegates of the state
governments and bound by state instructions. Under a federation, by
contrast, members of the federal legislature are elected on a proportional
basis in order to represent the people as a whole. In a confederation, the
federal assembly will usually make decisions by unanimous vote; amendment of the compact will almost certainly require unanimity, whereas in a
federation, voting in the legislature is by majority, although the process
for amendment of the constitution will be relatively more rigid. Moreover,
a confederal government has no executive power over individuals and the
cooperation of each state is required for the implementation of federal
decisions, whereas the laws of a federal government are executed directly
on individuals by that government.

This dichotomy between federation and confederation overlooks a
number of important continuities and similarities between the successive
confederations and federations of the United States, Switzerland, Canada
and Australia.[40] And, notably, these continuities mirror the 'partly federal' features of the American Constitution that Madison had identified in
1787. In the first place, contrary to nationalist interpretations, integrative
federations such as the United States, Switzerland and Australia[41] – like
confederations – are typically formed out of pre-existing, relatively
independent states, which consent to the formation of a federation.
Certainly, unlike typical confederations, in federations such consent usually involves the consent of 'the people' – a decidedly non-compactual
feature; however, this is usually expressed by several 'peoples' organised
into their respective states – a feature which is more confederal or

---

[40] A point observed by Henry Sidgwick, *Elements of Politics* (1st edn, London: Macmillan, 1891),
507. It is significant that having made this observation Sidgwick went on (at 508) to emphasise the
importance of representation, configuration of power and amendment in the analysis of federal
systems. H. R. G. Greaves, *Federal Union in Practice* (London: George Allen & Unwin, 1940), 11,
made a similar point. See the discussion in Burgess, *Comparative Federalism*, 21–4, 26–7.

[41] Canada is a partial anomaly on a number of these points – and was regarded as such by most
of the framers of the Australian Constitution.

compactual than national. Further, as has been seen, federations often provide for the distinct representation of (the people of) the states – usually on the basis of equality of each state – in one house of the federal legislature (a compactual feature), and at the same time provide for the representation of the people of the entire federation – on the basis of proportionality to population – in the other house (a federal or national feature). Similarly, the amendment of federal constitutions typically involves the consent of both (the people of) the states (a confederal feature) and the people of the federation as a whole (a federal or national feature). Finally, in such federations the 'distribution' of legislative powers is implemented in terms consistent with the idea that such powers are a delegation or grant by the pre-existing states, which reserve or retain the ungranted or unexercised residue – rather than as a division of unitary, sovereign power.

Thus, the matter is much more complicated than a simple dichotomy between confederation and federation suggests. There are important continuities between confederations and federations, in particular as regards their formation, representative structures and amending procedures.

Nationalist approaches to federalism inadequately account for the nature of modern federations. Such accounts maintain that the federal system ultimately derives from a unitary sovereign people of the nation as a whole – or, perhaps, as in the case of Australia and Canada, from the overarching sovereignty of an imperial Parliament. However, the Australian, Swiss, Canadian and American federations were in fact predicated on the agreement of the peoples of the several constituent states, expressed through meetings of delegates, special assemblies and popular referendums.[42] Nationalist approaches to federalism hold that a unitary people divide or distribute sovereign power between the federal and state governments. But, with the important exception of Canada, the language and structure of federal constitutions such as these actually suggests the idea of a delegation of powers by (the people of) the states to the federal government.

---

[42] See Thomas Fleiner, 'Federalism in Australia and in Other Nations', in Gregory J. Craven (ed.), *Australian Federation: Towards the Second Century* (Melbourne: Melbourne University Press, 1992), 20. Even in Canada, despite its imperial origin and nationalist orientation, delegates of the several colonies initially negotiated the basic idea and form of the federation that was subsequently drafted and enacted in the United Kingdom.

At the same time, earlier compact theories of federalism have also been inadequate to the task of explaining modern federalism, and for similar reasons. Compact theories partially accept the same dichotomy between 'national' and 'confederal', but then try to force modern federations into a more confederal or compactual mould, again failing to do justice to many of the specific characteristics of contemporary federal states which distinguish them from confederations. Thus compact theories of federation underplay the degree to which modern federations provide for a unified people, governed by a consolidated federal government, itself subordinate to a binding constitution. A more balanced and nuanced conception of modern federalism is therefore necessary.

## Avoiding sovereignty

The shortcomings of both compactual and nationalist accounts of federalism are rooted in a common commitment to the idea of sovereignty. The way out of the impasse is to reconceive federal systems in a way that avoids the use of sovereignty as a conceptual device.

The modern use of the idea of sovereignty is usually traced to Thomas Hobbes and Jean Bodin, and was widely disseminated in the English-speaking world by John Austin.[43] For these writers sovereignty involved an internal sovereignty over all domestic institutions, corporate bodies and regional powers, and an external sovereignty against imperial, papal and other national authorities. It entailed an ultimate, absolute, indivisible and inalienable power of making law, exercised over a particular political community by a discrete political institution, and a freedom from any other law-making power.[44]

As used by both nationalist and compactual theorists, I propose that the three most important elements of this conception of sovereignty are

---

[43] Jens Bartelson, *A Genealogy of Sovereignty* (Cambridge: Cambridge University Press, 1995), ch. 5; F. H. Hinsley, *Sovereignty* (2nd edn, Cambridge: Cambridge University Press, 1986), ch. 4; Quentin Skinner, *The Foundations of Modern Political Thought*, 2 vols. (Cambridge University Press, 1978), II, 286–301.

[44] Thomas Hobbes, *Leviathan* [1651] Richard Tuck (ed.) (Cambridge University Press, 1991), §2: XVIII, XX, XXVI; Jean Bodin, *Six Livres de la République* [1576], in J. H. Franklin (ed. and trans.), *On Sovereignty, Four Chapters from The Six Books of the Commonweale* (Cambridge: Cambridge University Press, 1992), §I: 8; John Austin, *The Province of Jurisprudence Determined* (London: John Murray, 1832; reprinted London: Weidenfeld and Nicolson, 1954), ch. 6.

unity, autonomy and ultimacy.[45] By 'unity' is meant the idea that sovereignty has a unitary or singular quality; it resides in a particular person or institution; it is indivisible. If that institution consists of various parts, nevertheless sovereignty is unitary in nature, and it must reside in an entire institution, a singular or unitary entity composed of those parts. The concept of 'autonomy' involves the idea of 'self-law' or 'self-rule'. It implies something about the sovereign institution and about the persons or things subject to its authority and those outside its authority. The idea is that a sovereign governs all things within its jurisdiction ('internal' sovereignty), and does so independently of others ('external' sovereignty). The idea of 'ultimacy' is that the sovereign is thus the original, absolute and continuing source of all rule within its jurisdiction. All other authority within the jurisdiction is derived from the sovereign and is subject thereto.[46]

The idea of sovereignty has constrained the way in which federal systems have been understood. Sovereignty had to reside in some discrete political body and be exercised over a particular political community. For Austin, for example, federal arrangements could only be of two kinds: a mere league or confederation among fully sovereign states, or a unitary, fully sovereign state that happened to allow local governments significant freedom in the exercise of delegated powers.[47] Even natural rights theorists such as Hugo Grotius, Samuel Pufendorf and John Locke were not able to conceive of a federal state in the sense of a 'state composed of states'.[48] The natural rights of individuals opposed the 'absolute sovereignty' of the state, but the political community of rights-bearing individuals was still conceived by them in fundamentally unitary terms.[49]

In the particular context in which the US Constitution came into being, the Lockean idiom of a social compact[50] and the Blackstonian

---

[45] Other ways of 'unpacking' the idea of sovereignty are of course possible. Compare Louis Henkin, *International Law: Politics and Values* (Dordrecht: Martinus Nijhoff, 1995), 8–12.

[46] See Herman Dooyeweerd, 'The Contest over the Concept of Sovereignty', in D. F. M. Strauss (ed.), *Essays in Legal, Social and Political Philosophy*, Series B, vol. II: *The Collected Works of Herman Dooyeweerd* (Lewiston: Edwin Mellen Press, 1997), 104 (the idea of sovereignty entails a 'monopoly' over 'the creation of law').

[47] Austin, *Province of Jurisprudence*, 245–6.

[48] Otto von Gierke, *The Development of Political Theory* (New York: Howard Fertig, 1966), 130, n. 77, 263–5, 268.

[49] Patrick Riley, 'Three 17th Century German Theorists of Federalism: Althusius, Hugo and Leibniz' (1976) 5(3) *Publius: The Journal of Federalism* 7, 10–14.

[50] John Locke, *Two Treatises of Government* [1690] Peter Laslett (ed.) (Cambridge: Cambridge University Press, 1992).

doctrine of parliamentary sovereignty[51] influenced the conceptions of nationalists such as James Wilson and Luther Martin. For them the question was whether sovereignty inhered in the United States as a whole or in the several states independently. Later scholars, such as Georg Jellinek, Westel Willoughby and John Burgess, reasoned along similar lines, distinguishing between confederation and federation by reference to whether sovereignty was located in either the federation as a whole or the member states.[52] But, as explained, such approaches have consistently failed to account fully for the institutional details of actual federations.

The way out of the impasse is to reconceptualise integrative federal systems in a way that avoids the ascription of sovereignty to a particular political community, be that the individual states or the federation or nation as a whole.[53] In positive terms, this means conceiving of a political community in which there are multiple loci of partly independent and partly interdependent political communities, bound together under a common legal framework that has been adopted by covenant.

Approaching the question in this manner enables us in principle to account for the many diverse features of modern federal systems, thus avoiding the reductive tendencies of the compactualist and nationalist approaches. It also corresponds to the way in which federalism was positively conceived by those responsible for designing both the American and the Australian Constitutions. Baron de Montesquieu, whose account of federalism influenced the conceptions of James Madison, Alexander Hamilton and others,[54] defined what he called the 'confederate republic' as an 'assemblage of societies' which was itself a 'society'.[55] James Bryce, whose account of the American system decisively shaped the conceptions of Samuel Griffith, Edmund Barton and many other framers of the Australian Constitution, likewise defined a federation as 'a community

---

[51] William Blackstone, *Commentaries on the Laws of England* (Oxford: Oxford University Press, 1765), I, 48–9.

[52] See Sobei Mogi, *The Problem of Federalism: A Study in the History of Political Theory* (London: Allen and Unwin, 1931), I, 192–9, 434–50, 455–524.

[53] On the incompatibility of sovereignty and federalism, see Friedrich, *Trends of Federalism*, ch. 2; S. Rufus Davis, *The Federal Principle: A Journey through Time in Quest of a Meaning* (Berkeley: University of California Press, 1978), 215; Harold J. Laski, *Studies in the Problem of Sovereignty* (London: Allen and Unwin, 1968), 268.

[54] See e.g. *Federalist* nos. 9, 47.

[55] Charles-Louis de Secondat, Baron de Montesquieu, *The Spirit of Laws* (1748) T. Nugent (trans.) (New York: Hafner, 1949), §I: IX:1.

made up of communities'.[56] Both definitions underscore the idea that a federal system is grounded in a founding compact or agreement (corresponding to the first sense of the word 'federal' identified by Quick and Garran, as noted earlier), as well as the notion that what is created through such a compact is a federal state which is itself a union of constituent states (Quick and Garran's second sense of the word 'federal'). Moreover, the two definitions refer to the constituent states as subsisting political communities, a reference which implies that each state will continue to exist as a (partially) independent self-governing political community, but at the same time form part of a wider federal state which is also a (partially) independent self-governing political community. This in turn implies that a federation will involve a dual system of government (Quick and Garran's third sense of 'federal') consisting of both state and federal governments (Quick and Garran's fourth sense). Such an approach is therefore able to account, in principle, for the 'division of powers', but it can also shed light, as will be seen, upon the specific way in which governmental power is distributed in federal systems, and it likewise provides the foundation for an account of the way in which representative institutions and amendment procedures are typically constructed in federations.

For the roots of such an approach – an approach that avoids the extremes of nationalism and compactualism – it is instructive to take account of the way in which political society was conceived prior to the emergence of state-sovereignty theory. The systematic, federalist account of politics that we find in the writings of Johannes Althusius (1557–1638), Professor of Law at the University of Herborn and later Syndic of the City of Emden, is particularly helpful in this respect. Althusius' *Politica Methodice Digesta*, first published in 1603,[57] is widely regarded as the most significant early modern statement of federal theory.[58] It represents a tradition that indirectly influenced modern federal systems,[59] and it

---

[56] Bryce, *The American Commonwealth*, I, 14.

[57] Johannes Althusius, *Politica methodice digesta atque exemplis sacris et profanis illustrata* (3rd edn, 1614; Carl Friedrich (ed.), republished New York: Arno Press, 1979).

[58] See e.g. von Gierke, *Development of Political Theory*, 16–19, 102, 266; Friedrich, *Trends of Federalism*, 12–13; Daniel J. Elazar, *Covenant and Commonwealth: From Christian Separation through the Protestant Reformation* (New Brunswick: Transaction Publishers, 1996), 331.

[59] von Gierke, *Development of Political Theory*, 267 (referring to Althusius' 'epochal' role in the development of the modern 'federal state' conception); Carl Friedrich, 'Introduction,' *Politica methodice digesta*, xix (stating that Althusius 'anticipates' and influences the future development of American federalism); John N. Figgis, *Studies of Political Thought from Gerson to Grotius*

furnishes a distinctive approach to interpreting federalism.[60] In Althusius'
work one meets with a political community that is composed of smaller
communities, both public and private, bound together in a common legal
framework, created by covenant, and a categorical rejection of Bodin's
absolutist theory of sovereignty.[61] Althusius' starting point, rather, is the
governing proposition that:

> Politics is the art of associating men for the purpose of establishing,
> cultivating, and conserving social life among them. Whence it is called
> 'symbiotics'. The subject matter of politics is therefore association
> [*consociatio*], in which the symbiotes pledge themselves each to the other,
> by explicit or tacit agreement, to mutual communication of whatever
> is useful and necessary for the harmonious exercise of social life.[62]

According to Althusius, this proposition applies to all kinds of association,
including, in the order in which he addresses them, family, corporation,
city, province and commonwealth. Each of these is an association, either
private or public, and each is concerned with politics. Associations are
formed by 'the bond of an associating and uniting agreement' among the
'symbiotes', the symbiotes in each case being the smaller associations of
which each larger association is composed. Althusius says that:

> human society develops from private to public association by the definite
> steps and progressions of small societies. The public association exists
> when many private associations are linked together for the purpose of
> establishing an inclusive political order. It can be called a community,
> an associated body, or the pre-eminent political association.[63]

---

*1414–1625* (Cambridge: Cambridge University Press, 1923), 181 (claiming that Althusius
'prepared the ground' for modern federalism). See also Burgess, *Comparative Federalism*, 170–2;
Hueglin and Fenna, *Comparative Federalism*, 89–97.

[60] See e.g. Donald Livingston, *Philosophical Melancholy and Delirium: Hume's Pathology of
Philosophy* (Chicago: University of Chicago Press, 1998), 345–7; Donald Livingston, 'The
Founding and the Enlightenment: Two Theories of Sovereignty', in Gary Gregg (ed.), *Vital
Remnants: America's Founding and the Western Tradition* (Wilmington: ISI Books, 1998).

[61] Althusius, *Politica*, §IX: 20–1, XVIII: 69; 71–2, 105; see Hinsley, *Sovereignty*, ch. 4; Thomas
O. Hueglin, *Early Modern Concepts for a Late Modern World: Althusius on Community and
Federalism* (Waterloo: Wilfrid Laurier University Press, 1999), ch. 4; Thomas O. Hueglin,
'Federalism at the Crossroads: Old Meanings, New Significance' (2003) 36 *Canadian Journal of
Political Science* 275, 277–80.

[62] Althusius, *Politica*, §I: 1–2, 17. The translation is taken from Frederick Carney, *An Abridged
Translation of Politics Methodically Set Forth and Illustrated with Sacred and Profane Examples*
(Indianapolis: Liberty Fund, 1995).

[63] *Ibid.*, §V: 1.

In turn, public associations can exist at a number of levels. What Althusius calls the 'universal association' arises when 'many cities and provinces obligate themselves to hold, organize, use, and defend ... the right of the realm'.[64] It is:

> [the] people united in one body by the agreement of many symbiotic associations and particular bodies, and brought together under one right. For families, cities and provinces existed by nature prior to realms, and gave birth to them.[65]

An Althusian commonwealth therefore consists of one people composed of many peoples, a community of communities, or a *consociatio consociationum*.[66] Every smaller society, such as a city or province, is a genuine political community, with its own communal life and sphere of rights; but the societies are united by covenant to form a wider political community that is equally authentic. While Althusius ascribes *majestas* to the 'entire associated body of the realm', this is always expressed in the 'consent and concord of the associated bodies'. Moreover, he explicitly holds that even the highest governing institutions are subject to divine, natural and civil laws, particularly the *lex fundamentalis* of the commonwealth. The constitutive status of the provinces and cities, and their reserved sphere of rights presents, therefore, 'an insuperable barrier' of fundamental law against any exercise of sovereign authority within the commonwealth.[67]

## Conclusion

A rejection of the idea of sovereignty clears the way to a closer analysis of the empirical characteristics of federal systems. In particular, circumventing sovereignty enables a more precise identification of the many different ways in which formative processes can be structured, and of the influence of those processes on the representative institutions, configurations of power and amending formulas actually adopted under federal constitutions. Assumptions of alternatively 'state' or 'national' sovereignty

---

[64] *Ibid.*, §IX: 1.   [65] *Ibid.*, §IX: 3.

[66] *Ibid.*, §VI: 16, 41–5, 52; VII: 1–2; VIII: 3, 40, 53–4; IX: 7, XVIII. See Elazar, *Exploring Federalism*, ch. 1.

[67] Althusius, *Politica*, §IX: 3–4, 7, 13, 15–24; XVIII: 69, 85, 105; XIX: 7–8, 49; XXXVIII: 7, 53, 71–3, 76, 110–14.

generally serve to drive a wedge between formation, representation and amendment, and to obscure and obfuscate historical and institutional details. Abandoning the extreme compactualist and nationalist theories of federalism derived from the idea of sovereignty enables a more specific and nuanced analysis to be undertaken along the lines pioneered by Madison. This opens up the possibility of analysing the great variety of ways in which federal systems can be constituted, and it also enables a number of more general hypotheses about the formation and nature of federal systems to be advanced.

# Reframing the analysis

[W]e the Inhabitants and Residents of Windsor, Hartford and Wethersfield...do...associate and conjoin ourselves to be as one Public State or Commonwealth; and do for ourselves and our successors and such as shall be adjoined to us at any time hereafter, enter into Combination and Confederation together.

*Fundamental Orders of Connecticut* (1639)

In America, the township was organised before the county, the county before the State, and the State before the Union.

Alexis de Tocqueville (1835)

The manner and context in which a federal system comes into being has a distinct and pervasive influence on the kinds of governing institutions and decision-making processes that are adopted within that system. Every federal constitution establishes a particular set of representative institutions, configurations of power and amending processes. A close analysis of the formative basis of a federal constitution – understood as a complex set of political mores, institutions and laws – sheds significant light on the terms and structure of that constitution.[1] Thus, the various kinds of federal system can be classified by reference to their peculiar formative processes, as well as by reference to the influence of those processes on the representative structures, configuration of powers and amending processes adopted under the federal pact – and not by reference only to those outcomes in abstraction from the processes that led to them. As will be seen, the lines of influence generally move from formative basis to representative institutions and configurations of power, and then, in turn, to the amendment processes adopted thereunder.

---

[1] Compare, generally, John Kincaid and G. Alan Tarr (eds.), *A Global Dialogue on Federalism.* Vol. I: *Constitutional Origins, Structure, and Change in Federal Countries* (Montreal: McGill-Queen's University Press, 2005).

In order to analyse and trace these relationships it is necessary to identify the different ways in which a federal system can come into being and to show how different constitutive foundations tend to imply different representative institutions, configurations of power and amendment processes.

## Integrative and disintegrative federalism

It is vital at the outset to recognise two fundamentally different ways in which a formally 'federal' system of government can come into being. A federation can be formed either through the integration of previously independent political communities or through the disintegration of a consolidated nation-state or empire. Thus, while the American and Swiss federal systems, for example, were clearly integrative, the Australian and Canadian systems were, according to legal orthodoxy, disintegrative to the extent that they involved a devolution of imperial power. For present purposes it is particularly helpful to compare these four systems, not only because they represent a variety of ways in which federal systems can come into being, but because the American, Swiss and Canadian systems were the chief models relied upon by the framers of the Australian Constitution.[2]

When federalism is primarily understood as a particular form or type of government (e.g. a dual system of government in which power is divided), very little difference between integrative and disintegrative federal systems is likely to be discerned. This is because structures very similar to those of integrative federations sometimes emerge out of formative processes that are almost entirely disintegrative or devolutionary, as in modern Belgium and Spain.[3] However, the constitutive foundations of integrative and disintegrative federal constitutions are radically different, and this difference can in practice lead to very different approaches to constitutional interpretation, so that nearly identical constitutional provisions are construed in widely divergent ways.[4] The formative basis of a federal system is thus a vital influence on the way in which a federal constitution can be interpreted.

---

[2] See ch. 3.

[3] Eric M. Barendt, *An Introduction to Constitutional Law* (Oxford: Oxford University Press, 1998), ch. 3; Friedrich, *Trends of Federalism*, 177.

[4] In Australia, for example, variously 'imperial', 'federal' and 'popular' accounts of the formative basis of the Constitution have been utilised in the cases, with very different results. For a brief discussion, see ch. 12.

However, the Australian and Canadian federal systems were not simply disintegrative or devolutionary. They were also integrative in the sense that the constituent states and provinces, each possessing a degree of political independence, severally agreed to federate. The political substance was integrative, especially in Australia, and this political reality has been given increasing legal expression as the 'imperial veil' has been removed.[5] Moreover, in Australia at least, the idea of integrative federalism was taken to be the normative ideal.[6] The two models that most influenced the Australian framers (the United States and Switzerland) were strongly integrative, and most of the authorities upon which the Australians relied considered integrative federalism to be a normative ideal.[7] The Australians accordingly debated the representative structures, configuration of power and amending processes they would adopt for their own federation in strongly integrative terms, on the presupposition of the mutually independent, self-governing status of the pre-existing colonies.[8] The political reality of state independence, as well as the normative ideal of integrative federalism, was an unavoidable premise in Australian federation, as it was in the United States, Switzerland and (to a lesser extent) in Canada.

Through a careful analysis of the precise mix of integrative and devolutionary formative processes that underlie a federal system it is possible to trace the distinct influence of these processes on the representative institutions, configuration of power and amending provisions that emerge from those processes.

## The formation of integrative federations

Within the context of substantially integrative federal systems (and here I include the Canadian and Australian examples), a number of possible

---

[5] This is particularly seen in the amendment processes introduced in Canada and Australia following the abdication of imperial authority in the 1980s. See Constitution Act 1982 (Can.), Pt V and Australia Act 1986 (UK) and (Cth), s. 15.

[6] On integrative federalism generally, see Davis, *Federal Principle*, 215–16; Friedrich, *Trends of Federalism*, 8, cf. 177; Riker, *Federalism*, 12; Elazar, *Exploring Federalism*, 34–8. On Australian attitudes to integrative federalism, see chs. 3, 4 and 5.

[7] E.g. Edward A. Freeman, *History of Federal Government in Greece and Italy* (2nd edn, London: Macmillan, 1893), 70; Albert Venn Dicey, *Introduction to the Study of the Law of the Constitution* (5th edn, London: Macmillan, 1897), 132–3; Francis O. Adams and C. D. Cunningham, *The Swiss Confederation* (London: Macmillan, 1889), ix–x, 22–5.

[8] See the analysis in chs. 7–11.

modes of 'formation' may be distinguished. Practically, formation has typically involved at least four separable processes: what I call structuring, drafting, ratification and enactment of the federal arrangement. These processes may in fact be dealt with simultaneously where one institution is responsible for all four aspects, but their separability is demonstrated by the American, Swiss, Canadian and Australian experience when viewed a whole.

As to the structuring aspect, it is particularly evident that each of these federations was constructed out of pre-existing, relatively independent bodies politic. Because the framers of each constitution wished to preserve a degree of legal continuity,[9] the formative process had to occur with the consent and under the authority of the governing institutions of the constituent states. Decisions had to be made as to how the federal pact would be drafted, ratified and enacted into law, and such decisions were made under the authority and with the consent of the governing institutions of those constituent bodies politic. The governments and legislatures of the constituent states and provinces thus substantially dictated the formative process – hence, the structuring aspect of the formative process.

Accordingly, the simple idea that the American, Swiss, Canadian or Australian federations derived their authority directly from either 'the people', 'the nation' or 'the states' must be qualified.[10] In the United States, the continental Congress and the state legislatures shared in the structuring process, the state legislatures in particular nominating delegates to draft a revision to the existing arrangement and later providing for the ratification of the proposed Constitution in specially elected state conventions.[11] The revolutionary idea of providing for ratification by

---

[9] The preservation of legal continuity in Canada and Australia has been strict. See e.g. Jean Chretian, *The Role of the United Kingdom in the Amendment of the Canadian Constitution* (Ottawa: Government of Canada, 1981), 5; R. D. Lumb, 'The Bicentenary of Australian Constitutionalism: The Evolution of Rules of Constitutional Change' (1988) 15 *University of Queensland Law Journal* 3.

[10] See e.g. Gordon S. Wood, *The Creation of the American Republic, 1776–1787* (New York: W. W. Norton and Co, 1993), 355 and Jack N. Rakove, 'The First Phases of American Federalism', in Mark Tushnet (ed.), *Comparative Constitutional Federalism: Europe and America* (New York: Greenwood Press, 1990), 2 (referring to the 'inherent complexity – or messiness – of the American federal system and the circumstances that led to its creation').

[11] For the relevant records and documents, see Farrand, *Records*; Madison, *Debates*; Merrill Jensen, J. P. Kaminski, and G. J. Saladino (eds.), *The Documentary History of the Ratification of the Constitution*, 29 vols. (Madison: State Historical Society of Wisconsin, 1976–).

conventions in only nine of the thirteen member states was instigated by the delegates at Philadelphia, but the process had to be carried through by the state legislatures or it would not have progressed any further.[12] Furthermore, it is certainly true that the process involved a legal discontinuity as regards the prescribed method of amending the Articles of Confederation;[13] and yet the Constitution only bound those states which ratified it, and hence proceeded on the basis of unanimous agreement as regards the new arrangement.[14] In Switzerland in 1848, likewise breaking with the rule of unanimity under the Federal Pact of 1815, a majority in the Federal Diet nominated a committee to draft a revised Constitution and the legislatures of the cantons provided for varying methods of ratification. Further, since only a majority of cantons actually ratified the Constitution, the new Constitution was in a sense 'imposed' on the dissenting cantons.[15] In Canada, by comparison, the provincial legislatures and governments structured the conferences that were held in Charlottetown, Quebec and London, at which conference delegates nominated by the governments drafted resolutions describing the kind of constitution under which the provinces were prepared to unite, and forwarded the resolutions to the imperial Parliament for drafting and enactment.[16] In Australia, moreover, the entire formative process was structured by the governments and legislatures of the colonies, while elected delegates drafted the Constitution, the peoples of the several colonies ratified the Commonwealth Bill and the imperial Parliament enacted the Constitution into law.[17]

The formative process by which a federal system comes into being can therefore take a number of forms. As to the structuring aspect, classically

[12] Commentators often emphasise the initiative taken by the Philadelphia Convention, but they rarely take note of the essential role of the state legislatures. See e.g. William H. Riker, 'The Lessons of 1787' (1987) 55 *Public Choice* 5, 15–19.

[13] See Richard S. Kay, 'The Illegality of the Constitution' (1987) 4 *Constitutional Commentary* 57.

[14] US Constitution, Art. VII.

[15] See Jean-François Aubert, *Traité de Droit Constitutionnel Suisse* (Neuchâtel: Ides et Calendes, 1967), 30–2. Ironically, despite the deeply entrenched traditions of Swiss confederalism semi-mythically traced to the pact of 1291, of the four federations under consideration, Switzerland is the only one in which there was in this specific sense a 'revolution'.

[16] For the Quebec and London Resolutions, as well as the successive drafts of the British North America Act, see Browne, *Documents*, 154–65, 217–28, 230–8.

[17] As previously mentioned, the *Commonwealth of Australia Constitution Act 1900* (UK) consists of nine sections (often called 'covering clauses'), the last of which contains what is styled as the 'constitution of the Commonwealth', which itself consists of 128 sections. For the relevant records, see Gregory J. Craven (ed.), *The Convention Debates 1891–1898: Commentaries, Indices and Guide* (Sydney: Legal Books, 1986).

integrative federations generally depend upon the political and legal authority of the pre-existing states and thus it is without exception the case that the formative process as a whole is dependent upon enabling legislation and similar action taken by the governing institutions of the constituent states in accordance with their respective state constitutions. This gives the states a very important guiding influence over the entire process and, in this respect, underscores an underlying continuity between confederations and federations. In modern federations, however, the formative process that is actually adopted has usually involved a commitment to a decision-making procedure in which the state governments relinquish immediate control over drafting, ratification and enactment in favour of institutions of a more directly representative or even democratic character. In looser confederations, by contrast, voting on instructions or voting in blocs is often maintained, both at the point of drafting a proposed arrangement as well as within the representative institutions of confederation once formed.[18]

Thus, as to the drafting aspect, while it is readily conceivable that a federal pact might be drafted by (or on the instructions of) the executive governments of the constituent states (as is typically the case in the formation of transnational organisations by international treaty),[19] in the federations under consideration this task was conferred upon a convention consisting either of delegates of the governments[20] or legislatures[21] of the constituent states or representatives directly elected by the peoples of the constituent states.[22] Likewise, as to the ratification aspect, while it is similarly conceivable that a federal pact might be ratified by the executive governments of the several constituent states or by the legislatures of the several constituent states (as is the case in typical international arrangements),[23] in the federations under consideration this task was performed

---

[18] Riker argues that the detachment of 'state' representatives from instructions was the crucial 'centralising' step in the United States, which has prevented the Senate from effectively representing the states: William H. Riker, 'Senate and American Federalism' in *The Development of American Federalism* (Boston: Kluwer, 1987).

[19] Vienna Convention on the Law of Treaties (1969), Art. 7(2).

[20] As in Canada in 1864 (Quebec Conference).

[21] As in the United States in 1787 (Philadelphia Convention), Switzerland in 1848 (Committee of the Swiss Diet), and Australia in 1891 (First National Australasian Convention).

[22] As in Australia in 1897–8 (Second National Australasian Convention).

[23] Compare Vienna Convention on the Law of Treaties, Art. 11. See Arnold Duncan McNair, *Law of Treaties* (Oxford: Clarendon Press, 1961), 129–30, 136.

either by specially elected conventions[24] or through direct, popular referendums held in each constituent state.[25]

Broadly speaking, then, it appears that treaties, alliances and international conventions are characteristically formed primarily by executive agreement; confederations usually depend mostly upon legislative agreement; and integrative federations are typically agreed to, in ultimate terms, by popular agreement through specially elected conventions or direct referendums. Yet despite these very important differences, one similarity binds the American and Australian, and to a lesser extent the Canadian and Swiss Constitutions,[26] namely that the processes of formation were structured by each of the participating states and ratified on the basis of unanimous agreement of all of the states, voting as equals,[27] expressed either through their state governments, state legislatures, state conventions or the people voting in direct referendums. Only in respect of the drafting process is something less than unanimity likely to be involved (i.e. debate about the precise terms of the proposed constitution is usually resolved by majority vote within the relevant conference or convention). But even here, in Australia at least, the actual drafting process was structured by legislation enacted by the constituent colonies, on the basis of unanimity. Notably, the colonies agreed to a drafting or ratification process based on majority vote and committed themselves to the outcome, so that a crucial step was taken at this point: the previously independent colonies were legislatively committed to the possibility of federal union, contingent on the outcome of the drafting or ratification process. And yet this decision was taken unanimously.

To the degree that unanimity and equality do not exist substantially at the point of formation, the process may be said to be less than 'federal' in

---

[24] As in the United States in 1787–9.

[25] As in Switzerland in 1848 (that is, in respect of all cantons except Fribourg and Grisons), and in Australia in 1898–1900. In Canada there was no process of ratification distinct from the process by which provincial delegates agreed upon a series of general resolutions that were subsequently forwarded to the imperial Parliament for detailed drafting and ultimate enactment.

[26] The Swiss Constitution of 1848 was initially approved by delegates of the cantons in the Federal Diet by 13½ cantonal votes in favour and 8½ votes against or abstaining, and was positively ratified in only 15½ cantons: Aubert, *Traité de Droit Constitutionnel Suisse*, 30–2.

[27] Even in British North America, where each of the maritime provinces was represented in the pivotal Quebec Conference of 1864 by fewer delegates than those for Upper and Lower Canada, it was resolved that each provincial delegation would have an equal vote: see Browne, *Documents*, 57–9.

the fully integrative sense. The federal arrangement will begin to resemble a case of imposition of terms on subordinate parts by a larger, more powerful body: a case of consolidation at the formative stage. Devolution of power may nevertheless occur, and real degrees of participation in centralised decision-making, autonomy and constitutional self-determination may be conferred.[28] But such rights are 'granted', not 'asserted' or 'exercised' as a matter of original legal or constitutional entitlement. While representative structures that are approximately federal in form may also be created, the formative basis of the constitutional system remains 'devolutionary' rather than federal in the integrative sense. And such a formative process is likely, at the margin, to have an impact on the terms and interpretation of the constitution. An operative 'federation' may be created, but this will depend on the degree of autonomy that is constitutionally entrenched and thus irrevocably conferred.[29]

In summary, then, unanimity is a typical characteristic of the structuring and ratification aspects of the formative process of integrative federations – as it is for confederations and looser alliances, treaties and international conventions. Alliances, confederations and federations are, however, often distinguished by the means in which the agreement to federate is expressed: either by the several executive governments, the legislatures, specially convened conventions or by direct referendums. This suggests that the distinction between federations and confederations can be rooted at the formative level, as well as by reference to the kind of system that comes into being.

## Representation and amendment in federal constitutions

A second way of examining formation, representation and amendment is to regard each aspect as a means of making 'law' of one kind or another. At the formative stage, the law being made is the federal pact – the *lex fundamentalis* or constitutional law that binds (the people of) the constituent states according to its terms. Unanimity is typically the fundamental decision-making rule in fully integrative federations, particularly

---

[28] Compare Belgian Constitution, Arts. 1, 33, 35, 61, 67 and 195; Spanish Constitution, Arts. 1, 2, 66, 69, 137, 167–8; Scotland Act 1998 (UK), ss. 28–9. Note also the dominating position enjoyed by Prussia under the Constitution of the German Empire (1871). See Watts, *Comparing Federal Systems*, 29–31; Wheare, *Federal Government*, 6.

[29] Duchacek, *Comparative Federalism*, 114, 120–8.

for the structuring and ratifying aspects of the formative process. However, as far as representative institutions within a federal system are concerned, what is at issue is not the constitution itself but rather the making and enforcement of the ordinary, statutory law of the federation and the states. Being ordinary law, the means by which such statutes are to be enacted and amended may be expected to be relatively easier than the processes required for the formation of the entire system under the constitution. In other words, the level of political integration is necessarily higher than that which prevailed during the formative process: a new federal body politic exists. Typically, something approaching majority rule will be the fundamental decision-making procedure for the representative institutions adopted under a typical federation.[30]

In further contrast to the enactment of ordinary legislation, prescribed amendment processes involve fundamental changes to the federal constitution itself. It is therefore to be expected that the means of amendment will be significantly more difficult than the means of enactment of ordinary law. One might even expect the method to be as stringent as the original formative process itself, since what is at stake in constitutional amendment is the federal pact itself, unanimously agreed to by (the people of) the constituent states. However, there is a federation in existence, and (the people of) the states have committed themselves to a joint constitutional destiny. Accordingly, we might do best to expect an amending process that is more majoritarian than the formative process, but less majoritarian than the ordinary law-making process,[31] which is indeed what we find in the four constitutions under consideration.

In this respect Dicey was generally correct to say that the 'rigidity' of the constitution is essential to the integrity of a federal system.[32] However, the precise way in which federal constitutions usually provide for their own rigidity is itself specifically 'federal' in character. For example, a constitution can be made relatively rigid simply by requiring a special

---

[30] On the significance of unanimity and majority rule as decision-making processes, see James M. Buchanan and Gordon Tullock, *The Calculus of Consent: Logical Foundations of Constitutional Democracy* (Ann Arbor: University of Michigan Press, 1962).

[31] Compare Ivo Duchacek, 'Consociational Cradle of Federalism' (1985) 15(2) *Publius: The Journal of Federalism* 35, 40–1.

[32] See Dicey, *Law of the Constitution*, 142–5. For a recent discussion which analyses amendment formulas in federal systems almost entirely in terms of rigidity, see Watts, *Comparing Federal Systems*, 101–4.

majority of, say, 66 per cent or 75 per cent of the national vote for its amendment. However, the American, Swiss, Canadian and Australian federations provide for the rigidity of their respective constitutions by giving the peoples and governments of the constituent states, cantons and provinces a distinct voice in questions of constitutional amendment. The concern, therefore, is not only with rigidity, but also with the representation of the peoples and governing institutions of the constituent states in the amendment process – a specifically 'federal' concern. Indeed, a similar analysis can also be made of the ordinary law-making institutions of federations. These are often analysed in terms simply of the degree to which the system imposes 'conservative' limits on the will of a democratic majority.[33] In this sense, the framers of a constitution can render the legislative system relatively more conservative through the simple expedient of establishing a bicameral legislature. In the four federal constitutions under consideration, however, the actual composition of the two houses of the federal legislature is dictated by specifically 'federal' considerations: the Senate is not just a conservative 'upper house' or 'house of review', but is designed to be a 'states house'.[34]

The similarities and differences between loose alliances, confederations and federations clearly emerge at this point. In the loosest of confederations, unanimity – the agreement and cooperation of all the constituent states – often remains an important decision-making rule for the passage and execution of ordinary laws intended to apply throughout the entire confederation.[35] In relatively tighter confederations, while the constituent states are usually represented on an equal basis,[36] there is a shift towards rule by special majority and even ordinary majority on less controversial matters, as under the Articles of Confederation of 1781,[37] the Swiss Pact

---

[33] See e.g. Robert A. Dahl, 'Federalism and the Democratic Process' in Robert Dahl, *Democracy, Liberty and Equality* (Oslo: Norwegian University Press, 1986), 114–26; Stepan, *Comparative Politics*, 333–7.

[34] On the (problematic) idea of a 'states house', see chs. 7, 8 and 12 below.

[35] E.g. the Treaty Establishing the European Community (Consolidated Version) 2002, Arts. 13, 19, 22, 42, 47, etc.

[36] E.g. US Articles of Confederation 1781, Art. V.

[37] US Articles of Confederation 1781, Art. IX. See Merrill Jensen, *The Articles of Confederation: An Interpretation of the Social-Constitutional History of the American Revolution 1774–1781* (Madison: University of Wisconsin Press, 1940), 140–5 and Randall G. Holcombe, 'Constitutions as Constraints: A Case Study of Three American Constitutions' (1991) 2 *Constitutional Political Economy* 303.

of 1815,[38] and the European Community today.[39] In federations, in turn, the movement towards majority rule is even more emphatic, particularly in the representative structures, although the possibilities are complex and widely variable, and are usually subject to particular federal imperatives. Members of the federal legislature may be chosen in a variety of ways, which typically include appointment by the executive governments[40] or legislatures[41] of the states or by the voters directly.[42] In the latter case, moreover, the voters may themselves be organised into localities, separate states or (in theory) a national electorate. And in bicameral systems, the two houses may be constituted by any combination of these forms, and one house may be elected by the other. However, in federations the structure of the two chambers usually reflects distinctly federal considerations. Thus, typically, the second chamber is structured so as to represent the peoples of the states, either directly (as through direct popular election)[43] or indirectly (as through election by the state legislatures),[44] and this representation of the states is often (but not always) on the basis of equality.[45] It is important to note, moreover, that while in most federations the first chamber is structured so as to represent the people of the entire federation, this is usually achieved through a system of direct popular election on the basis of local electorates, in proportion to population.[46] And, even here, the electoral system is often constitutionally structured at least to some extent along state lines, and thus the constitution may still refer to the members of the first chamber as representing 'the people of the several states'[47] or, where the chamber is to represent 'the people' or 'the people of the [entire] Commonwealth', the mechanism by which representation is made proportionate to population still divides the people up into their respective states or cantons.[48]

---

[38] *Le Pacte fédéral de 1815*, Art. 8.
[39] Treaty Establishing the European Community, Art. 205.
[40] German Basic Law, Art. 51(1).    [41] US Constitution, Art. 1, s. 3.
[42] US Constitution, Art. 1, s. 2, Am. XVII; Swiss Constitution, Art. 149, Art. 150; Australian Constitution, ss. 7, 24; German Basic Law, Art. 38.
[43] US Constitution, Am. XVII; Swiss Constitution, Art. 150; Australian Constitution, s. 7.
[44] US Constitution, Art. 1, s. 3. Compare Canadian Constitution, s. 22.
[45] US Constitution, Am. XVII; Australian Constitution, s. 7. Contrast Canadian Constitution, s. 22; German Basic Law, Art. 51(2) and note the special case of the half cantons under the Swiss Const. Art. 150(2).
[46] US Constitution, Art. 1, s. 2; Swiss Constitution, Art. 149; Canadian Constitution, s. 37; Australian Constitution, s. 24; German Basic Law, Art. 38.
[47] US Constitution, Art. 1, s. 2. See, likewise, Canadian Constitution, s. 37.
[48] Swiss Constitution, Art. 149(3)–(4); Australian Constitution, s. 24.

Similar possibilities abound for the composition of the executive government within a federation, with the additional possibility of responsible government or some other means by which the executive is formally or informally elected by or responsible to the legislature. For example, in Switzerland the Federal Council consists of seven members elected by both houses of the federal legislature, but this is subject to the condition that no more than one member from the same canton can be elected.[49] Similarly, in the United States the president is elected through an electoral college consisting of electors for each state, the number of which is to correspond to the total number of members of Congress to which each state is entitled, thus striking a balance between the 'federal' and 'national' characteristics of the Senate and the House of Representatives.[50] By contrast, the Westminster system as it operates in both Canada and Australia has the tendency to nationalise the executive government because, under the conventions of parliamentary responsible government, the Queen (or her representative, the governor-general) appoints as prime minister a member of the 'lower house' (the House of Representatives) who is able to secure the support of a majority of members in that house and is therefore in a position to guarantee supply.[51] None the less, the framers of the Australian Constitution (following to an extent the Swiss and American Constitutions, but guided also by their experience of colonial self-government) qualified this principle by granting the Senate power to reject or refuse to pass financial bills,[52] enabling it to refuse supply to the government. This capacity the Senate in fact exercised in 1975, setting in train a course of events that led to the dismissal of the prime minister in highly controversial circumstances.[53] Thus, in Canada, the conventions of Westminster responsible government, in conjunction with a relatively weak, non-elected 'upper house' have in formal terms a nationalising effect on the executive government, whereas in Australia this nationalising effect, while clearly in evidence, is

---

[49] Swiss Constitution, Art. 175.    [50] US Constitution, Art. II, s. 1, Am. XII.

[51] George Winterton, *Parliament, the Executive and the Governor-General: A Constitutional Analysis* (Melbourne: Melbourne University Press, 1983), 71–85.

[52] Australian Constitution, s. 53. Under the Canadian Constitution, s. 53, the Senate also has the legal power to refuse supply; however, the fact that it is not a directly elected body has underscored the firm convention that the power will not be exercised. See Peter W. Hogg, *Constitutional Law of Canada* (3rd edn, Toronto: Carswell, 1992), 262–5.

[53] On the dismissal of the Whitlam Labor government in 1975, see ch. 12 below.

subject to important limits imposed by the substantial formal powers possessed by the Australian Senate as a directly elected body.[54]

At the amendment level, a similar variety of structural possibilities emerge. Here, as noted earlier, the degree of integration will typically be greater than that for the formative basis, but less than that for the representative institutions, since the amendment process can potentially alter the entire bargain, including the representative structure itself. Thus, in federations the standard decision-making rule usually falls somewhere between unanimity (among the states) and a simple majority (of the people of the entire nation).[55] Moreover, a distinction between different kinds of changes is often made, so that the amending process requires an especially high level of consensus (i.e. a special majority approaching unanimity) for changes to aspects of the federal pact or constitution regarded as particularly vital. Such provisions can be very revealing about those aspects of a federal constitution that the framers considered to be of greatest importance. Thus, in the United States the amendment clause requires two-thirds of both houses of Congress or two-thirds of the state legislatures to propose a change, and then ratification by either three-quarters of the state legislatures or by conventions in three-quarters of the states.[56] Equal representation of each state in the Senate is further protected by the rule that this cannot be altered without the consent of the state (or states) concerned.[57] Likewise, in Switzerland and Australia the general amendment process requires ratification through a referendum in which a majority of voters in the entire nation, together with a majority of voters in a majority of states or cantons, approve of the proposed change, with the proviso in Australia that representation of each state in the two houses of the Federal Parliament cannot be altered unless a majority of voters in the state concerned approve of the proposed change,[58] and, in Switzerland, that the status of a canton cannot be altered without the consent of the cantonal population concerned, the

---

[54] In practice, however, Canadian prime ministers have to be even more attentive to the federal character of their cabinets than their Australian counterparts.

[55] In confederations, the amendment process usually requires unanimity: see e.g. US Articles of Confederation, Art. XIII; Treaty on European Union, Art. 48.

[56] US Constitution, Art. V.

[57] US Constitution, Art. V. The German imperial Constitution of 1871, Art. 78, similarly provided that the fixed rights of each state could not be altered without that state's consent.

[58] Swiss Constitution, Arts. 138–42; Australian Constitution, s. 128.

government of the canton, the Swiss people as a whole and the cantons generally.[59] Moreover, as will be seen, in both Australia and Canada certain fundamental changes to the constitutional order cannot be altered unless there is unanimous agreement of the state or provincial legislatures.[60]

## Formation, representation and amendment

So far, the analysis of formation, representation and amendment has adopted the concepts of unanimity–majority and flexibility–rigidity, and it has been noted that where rigidity has been desired, federal systems adopt specifically 'federal' structures to secure this objective. It has also been suggested that there are a great variety of ways in which these imperatives may be embodied in a federal constitution. The next observation to be made is that the specific processes by which a federation is formed also seem to have a significant, although more contingent, influence on the particular representative structures and amendment procedures that are adopted.

As noted earlier, the patterns of 'influence' seem to be that the formative process tends to influence conceptions of representation, and the way in which questions about formation and representation are approached seems to influence ideas about an appropriate amendment formula. One interpretation of this influence is that, as a matter of practical politics and entrenched interests, those whose interests happen to be favoured by the formative basis of the constitution will tend to use that power to insist on preservation of their interests. A second line of interpretation is that particular normative perspectives motivating a majority of the framers tend to dictate similar structural features for the formative processes, representative structures and amendment procedures.

Both interpretations appear to be supported by evidence relating to the formation of the federal constitutions under consideration, and it is not my intention to adjudicate between them.[61] For present purposes, the point

---

[59] Swiss Constitution, Art. 53(2). See also the similar protection accorded to the territorial integrity of each canton in Art. 53(3).

[60] See Australia Act 1986 (UK and Aust.), s. 15; Constitution Act 1982 (Can.), s. 41.

[61] For example, advocates of 'states' rights' at the American and Australian federal conventions argued that the separate states were morally entitled to equal representation in at least one house of the federal legislature, but were also very prepared to point out that they had the weight of numbers on their side. They were successful both because of the appeal of this normative claim and because a majority of delegates wished to preserve and advance their interests in this way. On the general point, see Riker, 'Lessons of 1787', 17–18.

is that on either interpretation, representative structures and amendment procedures tend to mirror the formative basis of the federal constitution in question. In skeletal form, the point can be illustrated by reference once again to the American, Canadian and Australian constitutions.

The American debate, as well as its outcome, is particularly instructive. The Virginia plan, as advanced by Edmund Randolph at Philadelphia in 1787 and supported by delegates such as James Wilson, called for ratification of the proposed constitution by the entire people of the United States. As explained in the previous chapter, this scheme was thought by its proponents to provide a sound and legitimate basis for a genuinely national government that would itself be representative of the entire populace and would justifiably exercise supreme legislative and executive power over the entire nation. By contrast, the New Jersey plan proposed by William Paterson and supported by Luther Martin presupposed that the constitution would be ratified by the governments of the constituent states on a state-by-state basis. Proponents of the New Jersey plan accordingly rejected national supremacy and called, as has been seen, for equality of representation of the several states as the constituent members of the union.[62]

The Virginia and New Jersey plans thus gave expression to radically different views about the locus of sovereignty within the system, corresponding to the nationalist and compactualist approaches to federalism discussed in the previous chapter. They also illustrate how reasoning about the formative basis of the proposed constitution was related to reasoning about the representative structures and configuration of power to be adopted. And yet the clash of diametrically opposed positions led to a stalemate and crisis that was only resolved through an apparent compromise, proposed by John Dickinson and others, under which the people

---

[62] Madison, *Debates*, 36–41, 82–3, 94–104, 123, 126; Bennett, *American Theories of Federalism*, 78–85; Herbert J. Storing (ed.), *The Anti-Federalist: Writings by the Opponents of the Constitution, An Abridgment by Murray Dry, of The Complete Anti-Federalist* (Chicago: University of Chicago Press, 1985), 296–7. Other plans were proposed by John Dickinson, James Madison and Alexander Hamilton. Hamilton was the most nationalist: he wanted to transform the states into wholly subordinate, 'municipal' governments. Madison was more moderate, yet he wished to create a national power to veto any state law. The Virginia plan was more moderate still: federal powers, although broad in scope, were enumerated, and the 'national veto' was limited to state laws 'contravening the articles of Union'. See Michael Zuckert, 'Federalism and the Founding: Toward a Reinterpretation of the Constitutional Convention' (1986) 48 *Review of Politics* 166.

would be represented in proportion to population in the House of Representatives, while the states would be equally represented in the Senate.[63]

In settling these questions, the American framers effectively rejected the implications of the idea that sovereignty had to exist in either the nation or the states.[64] As Michael Zuckert has pointed out:

> There were some – notably Luther Martin on the federal side, Hamilton and perhaps Gouverneur Morris on the national side – who clung to the view that sovereignty must reside somewhere, in one government or the other. These few delegates insisted that one or the other must be sovereign, but the main thrust of the delegates' thought was away from such a drastic either/or. Madison, both at the Convention and later, felt that too much was made of the abstract issue of sovereignty . . . 'a compleat supremacy somewhere is not necessary in every society'.[65]

The compromise over representation reflected an older tradition in American politics, reflected in various ways in the constitutions of the American states.[66] The Constitution of Connecticut, for example, had its origin in a kind of federation of three separate town-based settlements under the Fundamental Orders of Connecticut of 1639.[67] Under the Constitution, the 'supreme power of the Commonwealth' was vested in the General Court of Connecticut (a body that undertook both legislative and judicial functions). The citizens of the entire state elected the governor and magistrates, which later evolved into the upper house of the General Court, while the citizens of each town chose four deputies to represent them in what became the lower house. Neither 'town' nor

---

[63] See e.g. Jack N. Rakove, 'The Great Compromise: Ideas, Interests, and the Politics of Constitution Making' (1987) 44 *William and Mary Quarterly* 424.

[64] Dickinson in fact generally avoided the language of sovereignty, and anticipated the need for a 'dual' system of representation in the two houses of the federal legislature from very early on in the proceedings. See Madison, *Debates*, 56–7, 77–8, 84–5, 98–9, 103, 238; Farrand, *Records*, III, 304.

[65] Zuckert, 'Federalism and the Founding', 185–6. See also Peter S. Onuf, 'Reflections on the Founding: Constitutional Historiography in Bicentennial Perspective' (1989) 46(2) *William and Mary Quarterly* 341; Farrand, *Records*, I, 463–4.

[66] Donald S. Lutz, *The Origins of American Constitutionalism* (Baton Rouge: Louisiana State University Press, 1988), 64–6.

[67] Anticipating the language of the United States Constitution, the Fundamental Orders of Connecticut of 1639 recited: 'we the Inhabitants and Residents of Windsor, Harteford and Wethersfield . . . doe therefore assotiate and conioyne our selues to be as one Publike state or Commonwelth; and doe . . . enter into Combination and Confederation together'. See Donald S. Lutz (ed.), *Colonial Origins of the American Constitution: A Documentary History* (Indianapolis: Liberty Fund, 1998), 210–20.

'state' was absolutely 'sovereign' under this system. The foundation of the unified colony had rested in an agreement among the constituent towns, and the towns continued to govern their own internal affairs, subject to the overarching government of the General Court. In turn, the lower house was representative of the several towns, just as the upper house was representative of the citizens of the state as a whole. Town and state were thus mutually independent in certain respects, and interdependent in others. Neither was absolutely sovereign over the other.

While the circumstances of each American colony were unique,[68] as Jack Greene has observed, relations within and between the several colonies, as well as relations between the colonies and the British empire, were generally shaped by a limited conception of 'sovereignty' as the exercise of 'independent authority' within different domains. Within the several colonies, power was dispersed among multiple loci of authority, a diversity of partly independent and partly interdependent towns, counties and colonies, each possessing different, sometimes overlapping and often disputed jurisdictions. Authority, or at least legitimate authority, was 'negotiated' rather than imposed or granted. Larger jurisdictions or bodies politic were typically composed of several smaller corporations that were separately represented in the legislative assemblies or congresses of the wider institutions. So, when it came to declaring independence, establishing the state constitutions, composing the Articles of Confederation and drafting the federal Constitution, 'power and legitimacy... flowed reciprocally from one level...to another' in a complex interrelationship of mutual interdependence and independence.[69] The picture, according to Daniel Elazar, was of 'states as compounds of towns, just as the towns were compounds of individuals or families', echoing the

---

[68] For more detail, see Jack R. Pole, *Political Representation in England and the Origins of the American Republic* (New York: Macmillan, 1966); Michael Kammen, *Deputyes & Liberties: The Origins of Representative Government in Colonial America* (New York: Knoff, 1969).

[69] Jack P. Greene, *Negotiated Authorities: Essays in Colonial Political and Constitutional History* (Charlottesville: University Press of Virginia, 1994), 11; Rakove, *Original Meanings*, 164. See generally, Jack P. Greene, *Peripheries and Center: Constitutional Development in the Extended Politics of the British Empire and the United States, 1607–1788* (Athens: University of Georgia Press, 1986); Peter S. Onuf, *The Origins of the Federal Republic: Jurisdictional Controversies in the United States, 1775–1787* (Philadelphia: University of Pennsylvania Press, 1983); Rosemarie Zagarri, *The Politics of Size: Representation in the United States, 1776–1850* (Ithaca: Cornell University Press, 1987).

federative 'model commonwealth' of Johannes Althusius.[70] The United States Constitution developed out of this institutional context, and was necessarily and profoundly shaped by the institutional experience and political assumptions that it engendered.

M. E. Bradford has pointed out that the structure of the Philadelphia Convention as 'an assembly representing the people of the states' structurally informed the substantive provisions of the Constitution, including its representative institutions, configurations of power and prescribed amendment procedure:

> [T]he political theory built into the original American regime is a doctrine that structurally informs the very sequence by which they arrived at the Constitution 'as it was' – a theory embodied in the process by which the Constitution was ratified, and the method still employed when it is revised by amendment.[71]

Simply put, the Philadelphia Convention was composed of delegates appointed by the legislatures of the several American states and, in turn, the Constitution was ratified in state conventions, authorised by the state legislatures. Moreover, in most of the ratifying conventions the towns and counties of each state were equally represented.[72] In this context, it is important to note, the framers of the Constitution provided that the Senate would be chosen by the legislatures of the several states, each of them equally represented,[73] whereas the House of Representatives would be directly chosen by the people of the United States as a whole. The collegial system of electing the president, in turn, combined the structural design of both houses. Similarly, Article V of the Constitution provided a dual mechanism for the amendment of the Constitution requiring special majorities of either the legislatures of the several states or specially elected

---

[70] Daniel J. Elazar, 'Republicanism, Representation and Consent in the Founding Era' (1979) 9 *Publius* 1, 2. Madison and Hamilton recognised this of the Dutch Confederation: *Federalist* no. 20 in Rossiter, *Federalist Papers*, 134. There is no direct evidence that the Americans read or knew about Althusius, although the second edition of *Politica* was published in the Netherlands at a time when some of the pilgrim fathers had stayed there in exile before sailing to the New World. On circumstantial evidence connecting Althusius with Samuel Rutherford, John Milton and Montesquieu, see Hueglin, *Early Modern Concepts*, 16–18.

[71] Melvin E. Bradford, *Original Intentions on the Making and Ratification of the United States Constitution* (Athens: University of Georgia Press, 1993), 9–10.

[72] Jensen *et al.*, *Documentary History*, III, 59–61, 90–1, 167–8, 171, 227, 266–8, 365–8, 405–52.

[73] That is, until the constitutional amendment of 1913 which provided for the election of senators by the people of each state. See US Constitution, Am. XVII.

conventions in the several states. While there was a movement from unanimity and state equality to majoritarian or popular rule, the formative, representative and amendment aspects of the American constitutional system consistently placed fundamental decision-making power in the hands of the legislatures and specially elected conventions of the several states. Good government, in other words, was understood to be best achieved through deliberation within representative institutions, rather than through a direct, popular vote.

In Canada a similar relationship between formation and amendment is to be observed. The Canadian Constitution originally came into being in the form of a statute of the imperial Parliament, the British North America Act 1867 (UK). The terms of union between the Canadian colonies had been first debated and agreed upon in Canada by delegates of the various North American colonies under British jurisdiction. These debates culminated in the Quebec Resolutions of 1864, prepared by delegates of the provinces of Upper Canada (Ontario), Lower Canada (Quebec), New Brunswick, Prince Edward Island, Nova Scotia and Newfoundland. Unlike the situation in the United States and Switzerland, Upper and Lower Canada entered the debate as a single, formally consolidated province, and a 'legislative union' of the maritime colonies into one province had also been contemplated.[74] It was recognised, however, that the substantial support of each province ought to be secured and that this could only be achieved through a form of 'federal union' in which 'the separate provincial organizations would be in some degree preserved'.[75] In this context, 'federal union' was conceived to represent a compromise between a fully consolidated 'legislative union' on the one hand and a more decentralised 'federation' on the other.

Three features thus characterised the formative process in Canada: (1) recognition of the separate provinces as pre-existing, relatively independent

---

[74] Pursuant to The Union Act 1840 (UK), the distinct colonies of Upper and Lower Canada (under The Constitutional Act 1791 (UK)) were merged into one province under a governor, a nominated council and an elected assembly. In the assembly, the two regions were represented by an equal number of representatives, and continued to regard themselves as substantially distinct political communities. On the other hand, a legislative union limited to New Brunswick, Prince Edward Island and Nova Scotia, was in fact the official business of the Charlottetown Conference of 1864. See Browne, *Documents*, 11–13, 22, 32–49.

[75] Speech of John A. MacDonald, Legislative Assembly, Canada, 6 February 1865, in Janet Ajzenstat, Paul Romney and Ian Gentles (eds.), *Canada's Founding Debates* (University of Toronto Press, 2003), 279–80.

bodies politic, combined with a desire to create a more unified system than that of the United States; (2) the inequality of the individual provinces, noting the treatment of the maritime colonies as a single bloc, as well as the special issues presented by the French-speaking majority in Lower Canada; and (3) the overarching authority of the imperial Parliament. In the outcome, each province was recognised in the British North America Act as a separate, self-governing body politic entitled to separate representation in the Senate. The inequality of the maritime provinces was reflected in the fact that their individual representation in the Senate was numerically weaker than that enjoyed by Upper and Lower Canada, and they were treated as a distinct 'division' under the constitution for the purposes of representation.[76] Further, Canada's colonial status was reflected in the fact that no local power of constitutional amendment was conferred by the imperial Parliament in 1867.

As the Canadian federation expanded throughout the course of the late nineteenth and early twentieth centuries, additional provinces joined the federation,[77] each on specifically negotiated terms as to representation within the Federal Parliament and other matters, which were in turn embodied in imperial legislation.[78] Progressively, Canada was transformed from its colonial origins and centralist logic into an independent nation organised in increasingly federalist terms. This remarkable evolution of Canadian federalism was recognised by the Supreme Court of Canada, first in the Patriation Reference of 1981 and later in the Quebec Secession Reference of 1998.[79] When, in the early 1980s, the federal government and nine out of ten provincial governments agreed to a formal amendment procedure, it is noticeable that the amendment processes adopted for various purposes depended upon widespread legislative approval at both federal and provincial level and in some respects allowed provinces to 'opt out' of proposed changes, and in other respects required unanimous approval.[80] The Charlottetown Accord of

---

[76] Canadian Constitution, s. 22.    [77] Compare Canadian Constitution, ss. 146, 147.

[78] See e.g. Order in Council, 16 May 1871 (British Columbia); Order in Council, 26 June 1873 (Prince Edward Island); Manitoba Act 1870 (Can.); Alberta Act 1905 (Can.); Saskatchewan Act 1905 (Can.); Newfoundland Act 1949 (UK). See also Rupert's Land Act 1868 (UK); Order in Council, 23 June 1870 (Rupert's Land).

[79] *Reference re Amendment of the Constitution of Canada (Nos. 1, 2 and 3)* [1981] 1 SCR 753; *Reference re Secession of Quebec* [1998] 2 SCR 217.

[80] Constitution Act 1982 (Can.), Pt V. On the protracted and often acrimonious political debate leading up to and following this decision, see Alan Cairns, 'The Politics of

1992 even proposed an elected Senate in which each province would be equally represented (by six senators each), and failed only when rejected in a nationwide referendum sponsored by the Dominion and Quebec governments. As Peter Hogg has observed, it was widely understood at the time that, notwithstanding the fact that section 41 of the Constitution empowered the provincial legislatures to ratify such a change, no provincial legislature would be willing to ratify a constitutional amendment that had been rejected by the voters in that province.[81] As with the United States and Australia, therefore, the foundations upon which the Canadian Constitution was originally constructed, as well as the processes through which it was progressively 'federalised', decisively shaped the representative structures and amending formulas that were ultimately adopted. Initially, an imperial formative basis led to an imperial method of amendment; but thereafter an increasingly provincially oriented formative process led to stronger forms of provincial representation within the Canadian Parliament and provincially oriented methods of constitutional amendment.

Finally, as will be seen in more detail in the chapters to follow, in contrast to both the American and Canadian schemes the Australian Constitution was drafted in 1897–8 by a federal convention that was directly elected by the people of the several Australian colonies and was ratified in direct referendums held in the several colonies. Notably, the outcome was a Senate that is directly elected and an amendment procedure which turns on popular referendums held in each of the states. The persistent theme in Australia, therefore, has been one of fundamental decisions being made by direct elections and popular referendums rather than by legislatures and special conventions. Direct democracy and popular participation was thus favoured, at least at the critical points of formation and amendment, over the more 'refined' conception of deliberation by representative delegates in specially elected conventions. As will be seen, however, delegates to the earlier Australian federal convention held in 1891 were chosen by the legislatures of the several states and the convention of 1891 accordingly produced a draft constitution in which the senators were chosen by the state legislatures and the constitution was

---

Constitution-Making: The Canadian Experience' in Keith Banting and Richard Simeon (eds.), *Redesigning the State: The Politics of Constitutional Change in Industrial Nations* (Toronto: University of Toronto Press, 1985).

[81] Hogg, *Constitutional Law of Canada*, 70, n. 45.

to be amended by conventions held in the several states – a formative process, representative system and amendment procedure referable to if not exactly derivative from the American precedent. In each federal convention the Australian framers self-consciously reflected on the formative basis of the federation, and considered both normatively and practically that the representative institutions and amendment processes must be 'consistent with' the formative basis of the Constitution.

Moreover, when the UK Parliament terminated its authority to legislate for Australia in 1986, the legislative process used was guided by the Statute of Westminster 1931 (UK), as well as section 51(38) of the Australian Constitution. Under the Statute of Westminster, the UK Parliament had undertaken not to legislate for a dominion of the Crown (such as Australia) without first obtaining the consent of the dominion concerned.[82] Such consent was therefore obtained,[83] and on that basis the Australia Act 1986 (UK) was enacted. Under section 51(38), however, the Australian Commonwealth Parliament, 'at the request or with the concurrence' of all the state Parliaments, also had the capacity to 'exercise within the Commonwealth [of Australia]' any power which could at the establishment of the Constitution 'be exercised only by the parliament of the United Kingdom'.[84] Pursuant to this provision, the Australian state Parliaments requested the Australian Parliament to exercise this power by enacting the Australia Act 1986 (Cth).[85] Now, the substantive provisions of the UK and Australian versions of the Australia Act were in identical terms. And, given that they were both enacted in accordance with pre-existing law, it is arguable that both statutes were effective to terminate the legislative authority of the UK Parliament over Australia.[86] The particular point of relevance to the present discussion is that section 15 of the Australia Acts provides that the Australia Acts, as well as the Statute of Westminster, can only be repealed or amended by an Act of the Australian Parliament 'passed at the request or with the concurrence of the Parliaments of all the states'.[87] Hence, the means by which the Australia Act (Aust.) came into being (unanimous agreement of the Commonwealth and state Parliaments) was in turn

---

[82] Statute of Westminster 1931 (UK), s. 4.
[83] Such consent was expressed through the Australia (Request and Consent) Act 1986 (Aust.).
[84] Australian Constitution, s. 51(38).
[85] Such request was expressed through state enactments such as the Australia Acts Request Act 1985 (NSW).
[86] See *Sue* v. *Hill* (1999) 199 CLR 462.      [87] Australia Act 1986 (UK and Aust.), s. 15.

adopted as the means by which that Act could be amended. The Australia Acts thus depend upon unanimous legislative agreement as their fundamental principle, and in this way the formative basis of the Australia Act scheme shaped the amendment formula adopted in those Acts.

## Formation, representation and configuration of power

Finally, there is also an intelligible relationship between the way in which federal systems come into being, the representative structures that they adopt and the way in which governmental power is allocated between the various levels of government.

It was explained in chapter 1 that the idea of a 'division of power' inadequately explains the precise way in which power is allocated in various federal systems. In the United States, Switzerland and Australia, the federal constitution presupposes the states and their powers, conferring specific heads of legislative power on the representative institutions of the federal government and affirming that the powers of the States are 'reserved' and shall 'continue'.[88] The Tenth Amendment to the US Constitution provides that 'the powers not delegated to the United States by the Constitution, nor prohibited by it to the states, are reserved for the states respectively, or to the people'. The picture, it seems, is of several pre-existing self-governing states agreeing to form a federation to which specific powers are conferred. And, indeed, when the debate over federation in Australia is examined, it is quite clear that the delegates of the several states very explicitly understood the formative basis of the federation (a compact among states) to dictate such a configuration of power.[89] By comparison, the Canadian Constitution confers specific powers on the provinces and general power, together with specific powers for greater certainty, upon the federation.[90] Here, the picture is of an overarching imperial power distributing power, rather than of self-governing political communities agreeing to federate. And while there was certainly a real sense in which the Canadian union came into being through the agreement of the several provinces, the debate about union very clearly presupposed the overarching sovereignty of the imperial Parliament.

---

[88] US Constitution, Art. I, s. 8; Am. X; Swiss Constitution, Arts. 3, 42–3. Australian Constitution, ss. 51, 52, 106, 107, 109.

[89] See chs. 9 and 10.    [90] Canadian Constitution, ss. 91, 92.

As a consequence, just as formative processes have an impact upon representative institutions and amendment formulas, it is also possible to point to ways in which assumptions embedded in the formative process shape the way in which legislative and other government powers are distributed or configured between the federation and the states within a federal system. Commentators have also observed that, at least in the context of the fundamental principles of the European Union, the extent to which the interests of Member States are secured through representative institutions influences the kinds of competences the states are willing to confer upon the institutions of the government of the Union as a whole.[91] A close analysis of the debate over the making of the Australian Constitution, as will be seen, shows the framers of the Australian Constitution to have been alive to this issue as well, many of them being content to confer significant and wide-ranging legislative powers upon the Federal Parliament so long as each state enjoyed equality of representation in a Senate with powers broadly comparable to those of the House of Representatives.

## Conclusion

These illustrations suggest a recurrent, systemic relationship between the contingent modes of formation of federal constitutions, and the representative and amendment formulas that emerge, as well as the method of allocating governmental power as between the federation and the states. These illustrations also suggest that there is a persistent tendency for the formative processes of federal systems to be grounded in unanimity, representative systems to approach majority vote as a decision-making rule and amending procedures to fall somewhere between unanimity and simple majority. In specific terms, the systematic relationship between formation, representation and amendment means that the particular way in which a federal constitution comes into being has a distinct impact on the specific representative institutions and amendment formulas that are adopted thereunder. In more general terms, the same relationship

---

[91] See e.g. Koen Lenaerts, 'Constitutionalism and the Many Faces of Federalism' (1990) 38 *American Journal of Comparative Law* 205. In Germany, the competence of the federation to enact framework laws on a very wide range of topics is similarly balanced by the representation of the *Länder* governments in the *Bundesrat*: see Hueglin and Fenna, *Comparative Federalism*, 147, 161.

between formation, representation and amendment explains why relatively 'federative' formative processes consistently produce constitutions in which a balance of both generically 'federal' and generically 'national' features – such as those identified by Madison – are frequently embodied in the representative institutions and amendment procedures adopted under constitutions produced in this way.

The Australian federation is no exception to these generalisations. The formative basis of the Australian federal system – understood as a complex mix of philosophical beliefs, received practices and established institutions – had a profound influence upon the specific terms and structure of the Constitution that emerged from that process, particularly in terms of representative institutions, the configuration of power and amendment procedures. Through analysis of these processes, institutions and procedures it is possible to construct a general theory of the Australian Constitution, a theory which presents that document as quintessentially the constitution of a federal commonwealth.

# PART II

Federating Australia

# 3

## Models and sources

> What makes the Union between any States Federal is not the manner
> of its action, but the *Fœdus*, the Covenant, the Convention, the
> Compact upon which it is founded!
>
> Alexander Stephens (1868)

When the political leaders of the Australian colonies turned their minds
to nation-building in the latter half of the nineteenth century, there was
little doubt that a union of the colonies would have to be federal in
form.[1] The reasons for this were both practical and philosophical.

On the practical side, the colonies had enjoyed the benefits of local
self-government and representative institutions since the 1850s.[2] Having
recently acquired such powers, local politicians and voters were not about
to acquiesce in the loss of those rights to a consolidated national government. Samuel Griffith, then premier of the colony of Queensland, observed
that the Australian colonies had been 'accustomed for so long to self-
government' that they had 'become practically almost sovereign states, a
great deal more sovereign states, though not in name, than the separate
States of America'.[3] Josiah Symon, a prominent South Australian delegate
to the federal convention of 1897–8, similarly asserted: 'We all represent
what are really sovereign states – sovereign states in essence, if not in form.'[4]

---

[1] The several Enabling Acts passed by the colonial legislatures establishing the Australian federal
conventions held in the 1890s stipulated that the Constitution must be federal in form.

[2] See Australian Constitutions Act (No. 2), 1850 (UK), and the discussion in W. G. McMinn, *A
Constitutional History of Australia* (Melbourne: Oxford University Press, 1979), chs. 2–3;
A. C. V. Melbourne, *Early Constitutional Development in Australia* (Brisbane: University of
Queensland Press, 1963), pt V, ch. 6 and 443–5; R. D. Lumb, *The Constitutions of the Australian
States* (5th edn, Brisbane: University of Queensland Press, 1992), chs. 1–2, 4.

[3] *Official Record of the Proceedings and Debates of the Australasian Federation Conference,
Melbourne* (Melbourne: Government Printer, 1890), 10.

[4] *Official Record of the Debates of the National Australasian Convention, Second Session: Sydney,
2nd to 24th September 1897* (Sydney: Government Printer, 1897), 294.

In this context, the formation of a unitary nation-state was neither possible nor thinkable. As Griffith put it, the 'essential' and 'preliminary' condition of federation would be that:

> the separate states are to continue as autonomous bodies, surrendering only so much of their powers as is necessary to the establishment of a general government to do for them collectively what they cannot do individually for themselves, and which they cannot do as a collective body for themselves.[5]

Only a compromise would suffice to unify the separate colonies – and even this would depend on months, even years, of meticulous negotiation in a series of conventions held during the 1890s. Compromise was essential, and the federating process provided ample opportunity for a negotiated settlement, fundamentally along federal lines.

The theories and scholarship of the day reinforced the practical considerations. 'Late-Victorian constitutionalists', as one historian has put it, 'were intoxicated by the possibilities of federalism.'[6] Leading contemporary authors could write of 'the absolute perfection of the Federal ideal' and observe that 'the full ideal of Federal Government ... in its highest and most elaborate development, is the most finished and the most artificial production of political ingenuity'.[7] Prominent figures such as James Bryce and A. V. Dicey undertook extensive studies of federations such as the United States, Canada and Switzerland.[8] Distinguished historians such as Henry Maine, Edward Freeman and Otto von Gierke were also drawing attention to a kind of 'federalism' among the Greek city-states and within the Holy Roman empire.[9] Celebrated theorists such as Baron

---

[5] *Official Report of the National Australasian Convention Debates, Sydney, 2 March to 9 April, 1891* (Sydney: Acting Government Printer, 1891), 31–2; see, likewise, Samuel Walker Griffith, *Notes on Australian Federation: Its Nature and Probable Effects* (Brisbane: Government Printer, 1896), 6–7, 10.

[6] Hugh Tulloch, *James Bryce's 'American Commonwealth': The Anglo-American Background* (Woodbridge, Suffolk: Boydell Press, 1988), 103.

[7] Freeman, *Federal Government*, 1–3, 7–8. Freeman continued: 'It is hardly possible that federal government can attain its perfect form except in a highly refined age, and among a people whose political education has already stretched over many generations.'

[8] Dicey, *Law of the Constitution*; Bryce, *American Commonwealth*; John Bourinot, *A Manual of the Constitutional History of Canada* (Montreal: Dawson, 1888); Adams and Cunningham, *Swiss Confederation*.

[9] Henry Sumner Maine, *Ancient Law: Its Connection with the Early History of Society, and its Relation to Modern Ideas* (London: John Murray, 1861), 109; Freeman, *Federal Government*; James Bryce, *The Holy Roman Empire* (4th edn, London: Macmillan, 1895).

de Montesquieu and Alexis de Tocqueville had long argued that federalism enjoyed the strengths, and avoided the weaknesses, of small, independent republics and large, consolidated empires.[10] Perhaps Althusius' federative commonwealth had passed from living memory. But luminaries as diverse as Thomas Jefferson, David Hume and Pierre-Joseph Proudhon had championed very similar, federalist ideals.[11] Images and symbols such as these profoundly shaped late nineteenth-century conceptions of federalism.

Certainly, there were reasons why federalism might not be so popular. The United States of America – then, as now, the world's most prominent federation – had experienced a devastating civil war that some considered referable to inherent defects in its 'federal design'.[12] To many British minds the American disaster emphatically underscored the countervailing benefits of a unitary system of government involving undivided parliamentary sovereignty and responsible government.[13] Yet federalism remained an enticing ideal, a system of government apparently well suited to the government of diverse peoples inhabiting the scattered territories of the New World. Indeed, so attractive was the federal idea that even the loyalist colonists of British North America sought a (modified) federal solution to the problem of accommodating anglophone and francophone communities not long after the close of the American civil war.[14] As Manning Clark put it, federations had come to enjoy 'the warm approval of important writers on political theory' and were 'the fashion for communities in the New World'.[15] Given the fact that the several Australian colonies likewise inhabited a vast, sparsely populated continent, they necessarily looked to

---

[10] Montesquieu, *Spirit of Laws*; Alexis de Tocqueville, *Democracy in America* [1835–43], Henry Steele Commager (ed.) (London: Oxford University Press, 1959).

[11] Letter Jefferson to Cabell (2 February 1816), cited in Story, *Commentaries*, I, 200; David Hume, 'The Idea of a Perfect Commonwealth' [1777] in *Essays, Moral, Political, and Literary*, Eugene F. Miller (ed.) (Indianapolis: Liberty Fund, 1987); Pierre-Joseph Proudhon, *The Principle of Federation* [1863], Richard Vemon (ed.) (Toronto: University of Toronto Press, 1979).

[12] E.g. Dicey, *Law of the Constitution*, 141–2.

[13] See e.g. Walter Bagehot, *The English Constitution* [1867] (London: Fontana, 1963), 34; compare Bryce, *American Commonwealth*, I, 295, 333–4.

[14] British North America Act 1867 (UK). See Browne, *Documents*, 55–152; Ajzenstat, *Founding Debates*, 261–353, especially 299–314. For an influential account of the state of the Canadian colonies midway through the nineteenth century, see John George Lambton, First Earl of Durham, *Lord Durham's Report* [1839], C. P. Lucas (ed.), 3 vols. (Oxford: Clarendon Press, 1912).

[15] C. M. H. Clark (ed.), *Select Documents in Australian History 1851–1900* (Sydney: Angus and Roberston, 1955), 443.

federal models when considering how, in Barton's memorable phrase, a 'nation for a continent'[16] might be governed.

For the Australians, the United States Constitution was undoubtedly the paradigm of federal constitutions.[17] When prominent writers like Bryce, Dicey and Freeman wrote about federalism and the federal state, it was the American system that they had pre-eminently in mind. Central to the lessons that the American Constitution provided for the Australians were the formative processes by which the separate American states integrated themselves into a 'federal republic', the institutions that enabled the peoples of the states and the people of the nation to be represented in the federal legislature, the manner in which federal legislative power was distributed, and the means by which the entire arrangement could be amended. The Swiss Constitution reinforced these lessons, for it showed that these aspects of the American system could be reproduced elsewhere.

Switzerland also contributed ideas of its own. In particular, it provided an example of a non-presidential model of executive government suitable to a federation, and it demonstrated how federalism could be integrated with direct, popular participation by way of referendum. As it happened, the Australians would reproduce many of the most conspicuous features of the American and Swiss Constitutions, including the general structure of the federal legislature (the Senate and House of Representatives) and the pattern of distributing only specific powers to the federal legislature, as well as the peculiarly Swiss idea of the dual referendum as the stipulated mechanism for ratifying constitutional amendments.

The United States and Switzerland were, however, republics,[18] and the Australians recognised that a federation of the Australian colonies would have to be instituted under the imperial Crown and the authority of the Parliament at Westminster. The Australians naturally drew on their own political experience when it came to the exercise of representative and

---

[16] Robert Randolph Garran, *Prosper the Commonwealth* (Sydney: Angus and Robertson, 1958), 101; Geoffrey Bolton, *Edmund Barton* (Sydney: Allen and Unwin, 2000), 172–3; see also Richard Chaffey Baker, *Federation* (Adelaide: Scrymgour and Sons, 1897), 6; John Alexander Cockburn, *Australian Federation* (London: Horace Marshall and Son, 1901), 70.

[17] Sir Owen Dixon, Chief Justice of the High Court of Australia, 1952–1964, observed that the American Constitution was for the Australians an 'incomparable model' which both 'fascinated' them and 'damped the smoldering fires of their originality': Owen Dixon, 'The Law and the Constitution' in *Jesting Pilate* (Melbourne: Law Book Co., 1965), 44.

[18] See James H. Hutson, *The Sister Republics: Switzerland and the United States from 1776 to the Present* (Washington: Library of Congress, 1991).

responsible government within the context of the British empire. Canada's importance was that it showed the Australians how a specifically federal system might be adapted to a monarchical and parliamentary system operating within the British empire.

The Australians thus made use of a wide variety of fundamental ideas, some of them derived from a rather eclectic range of sources. The Australians were aware of, and discussed, a wide range of other systems that were also understood to be broadly federal in nature, including the leagues of the ancient Greek city-states, the Holy Roman empire, the Dutch United Provinces of the seventeenth century, and the German empire of 1871. Moreover, in seeking to amalgamate apparently antithetical ideas such as responsible government, the separation of powers and federalism, a number of autochthonous modifications had to be made. Nevertheless, most of the fundamental features of the Australian Constitution – especially the federal ones – can be traced to structures and institutions embodied in the American, Canadian and Swiss constitutions; and it was the American and Swiss systems that provided the most decisively important guidance.

In order to understand and make use of these models, the Australians had to rely on a wide range of works that explained their intricacies. Here the analyses of Bryce, Freeman and Dicey were critically influential, together with those of other British writers such as John Stuart Mill, Henry Sidgwick and John Austin. The Australian framers also learned a great deal from the writings of leading framers of the American Constitution, such as James Madison and Alexander Hamilton, as well as James Wilson. The *Federalist Papers*, although published more than a hundred years earlier, were decisively influential in several respects. Indeed, an impressively large number of American writers were frequently cited by the Australians, including Andrew Baker, John Burgess, John C. Calhoun, Thomas Cooley, Roger Foster, James Kent, John Marshall, Joseph Story, Westel Willoughby and Woodrow Wilson. The Australians also learnt about the framing of the American Constitution and the later development of American institutions from leading historians of the day such as George Bancroft and John Fiske, as well as from the primary sources edited by Jonathan Elliot and Benjamin Perley Poore.[19]

[19] For citations, see the bibliographies in John A. La Nauze, *The Making of the Australian Constitution* (Melbourne: Melbourne University Press, 1972), 355–61; Craven, *Convention Debates*, VI, 253–4; Leslie F. Crisp, *Federation Fathers*, J. Hart (ed.) (Melbourne: Melbourne

The Australians learned about the constitutions of Switzerland and
Canada through another important set of authors, which included
Francis Adams and C. D. Cunningham, Bernard Moses, John Bourinot,
Goldwin Smith and Charles Borgeaud. Also, the Canadian and US
Constitutions had been progressively interpreted (and reinterpreted) by
the Supreme Courts of those two countries, not to mention the decisively
important interpretations of the British North America Act by the
Judicial Committee of the Privy Council. The better-educated lawyers
among the Australians demonstrated at times extensive knowledge of a
wide range of cases, not all of them as well known, for example, as
*Marbury* v. *Madison* (1803), *McCulloch* v. *Maryland* (1819) or *Hodge* v.
*The Queen* (1883). Although the decided cases often concerned points of
relatively esoteric detail, as the Australians found themselves having to
discuss specific drafting issues and questions of likely interpretation, they
increasingly looked to these decisions for guidance. And, because federalism had to be adapted to the circumstances of a British colony, the
Australians drew on leading expositions of English common law, the
Westminster system and the law of the British empire, such as those of
Walter Bagehot, A. V. Dicey, W. E. Hearn, Thomas Erskine May, David
Syme, Alpheus Todd and others. The Australians even occasionally cited
classic works of political philosophy and analysis, such as those of John
Locke, James Harrington, Thomas Hobbes, Jeremy Bentham, Montesquieu, Tocqueville and John Stuart Mill.[20] Nineteenth-century scholarship on federalism is far richer than is sometimes recognised. While
many of the Australians were far from particularly well read in this
diverse body of literature, the range of material drawn upon by the
better-educated participants in the debate has generally been overlooked.

Each interpreter of federalism injected into his description of each
system his own particular orientations, conceptions and theories. As far
as ideas about federalism were specifically concerned, a close analysis of

University Press, 1990), 400–35; Irving, *Constitute a Nation*, 240–3; George Winterton *et al.*,
*Australian Federal Constitutional Law* (Sydney: LBC Information Services, 1999), 906–10.

[20] See, e.g., Richard Chaffey Baker, *A Manual of Reference to Authorities for the use of the Members
of the National Australasian Convention* (Adelaide: E. A. Pethenick and Co., 1891), 45, 68–9;
Robert Randolph Garran, *The Coming Commonwealth: An Australian Handbook of Federal
Government* (Sydney: Angus and Robertson 1897), 13; Robert Randolph Garran, *Commentaries
on the Constitution of the Commonwealth of Australia* (Sydney: Angus and Robertson, 1901),
313–15, 324.

the debates in the federal conventions of the 1890s as well as the writings of the most influential participants in the debate about federation[21] suggests that the most significant influences upon the Australians were the writings of James Madison, James Bryce, Edward Freeman, A. V. Dicey and John Burgess. Within the federal conventions, Bryce, Freeman and Dicey were quantitatively the most frequently cited scholars on questions of federalism; qualitatively, it is also important to take Madison and Burgess into account. In order to appreciate the leading ideas about the nature of the federal state that demonstrably influenced the Australian framers, it is therefore necessary to examine the writings of each of these authors in turn, and then to examine the way in which the Australians appropriated their ideas for their own purposes. The first of these tasks will be the concern of the remainder of this chapter; the second will be the focus of the succeeding one.

## James Madison

It has been argued that James Madison's examination of the federal features of the United States Constitution undertaken in *Federalist* no. 39 provides the empirically most accurate framework against which to understand the nature and structure of the modern federal state. Not only is his account analytically useful in this general sense, it was a direct and very important influence upon the framers of the Australian Constitution in particular.[22] As Madison's analysis has already been considered in some detail, there is no need to cover the same ground again. The historical focus of the present chapter, however, makes it helpful to contextualise and restate Madison's main theses.

Thinking about federalism in late eighteenth-century America, including that of James Madison, was deeply shaped by the views expressed in

---

[21] I refer here to the published records of the federation conference and federal conventions held in 1890, 1891 and 1897–8, and include the Hansard records of the imperial Parliament and the several colonial legislatures, as well as the numerous Australian books, articles and speeches published outside these formal venues.

[22] For Australian citations of the *Federalist Papers*, including Madison's *Federalist* no. 39, see *Official Report of the National Australasian Convention Debates, Adelaide, March 22 to May 5, 1897* (Adelaide: Government Printer, 1897), 321 (Gordon), 664–5 (Glynn), 666 (Higgins), 943 (Glynn), 950, 961 (Symon); Quick and Garran, *Annotated Constitution*, 336–40.

Montesquieu's classic *De l'esprit des lois*. According to Montesqueiu, what he called a 'confederate republic' arises when:

> several smaller *States* agree to become members of a *larger* one, which they intend to form. It is a kind of assemblage of societies, that constitutes a new one, capable of increasing by means of new associations till they arrive at such a degree of power as to be able to provide for the security of the united body . . . As this Government is composed of small Republics, it enjoys the internal happiness of each, and with respect to its external situation, it is possessed, by means of the association, of all the advantages of large Monarchies.[23]

For Montesquieu, the confederate republic is a 'state' composed of 'states', a 'society' formed when several 'societies' chose to be united, yet retain their own separate identities. Such an 'assemblage of societies', thought Montesquieu, serves to combine the liberty, happiness and virtue of the small republic with the defensive strengths of an extended kingdom.

At around the same time, the celebrated English jurist, Sir William Blackstone, taught many Americans to think that in all forms of government there must be 'a supreme, irresistible, absolute, uncontrolled authority, in which the *jura summi imperii*, or the rights of sovereignty, reside'.[24] This proposition, while arguably contradicted by the realities of the American situation, caused a number of the leading American framers to believe that an *imperio in imperium* was impossible, so that within a federal system sovereignty would either have to be located separately in the several states or else be attributed to the people of the nation as a whole.[25] In other words, many conceived that there were only two ways in which a large territory could be governed: either by a loose confederation of separate sovereign states, or by a single, unitary nation-state. Such a conception became very popular in elite circles, but it was a conception that served to obscure Montesquieu's idea of an assemblage of states that is itself a state.

Following Blackstone, Alexander Hamilton argued at the Philadelphia convention that a genuinely 'national' government was needed, invested with 'complete sovereignty' and the 'power to pass all laws whatsoever'. The implication was that the American state governments, if they were to

---

[23] Montesquieu, *Spirit of Laws*, 183–4.    [24] Blackstone, *Commentaries*, I, 48–9.
[25] For the American reliance on the passage from Blackstone, see Robert McCloskey (ed.), *The Works of James Wilson* (Cambridge: Harvard University Press, 1967), I, 168–9.

continue to exist, must be reduced to complete dependency upon and subordination to the government of the American nation as a whole.[26] Hamilton's objective, in line with other strong nationalists, was a fully consolidated national government. The extreme nationalists were not, however, entirely successful at Philadelphia. Even Hamilton had to admit that the Constitution that actually emerged in 1787 was fundamentally 'federal' in nature because, as he put it, the Constitution assumed the states to be 'constituent parts of the national sovereignty', allowing them 'a direct representation in the Senate' and leaving in their possession 'certain exclusive and very important portions of the sovereign power'.[27] Hamilton would clearly have preferred national consolidation, but at least the proposed Constitution – in comparison with the Articles of Confederation – was a step in the right direction as far as he was concerned. When it came to defending the proposed Constitution in the *Federalist Papers*, therefore, Hamilton argued that the 'federal' nature of the Constitution was indeed one of its virtues.[28]

On the other hand, those opposed to ratification – so-called anti-federalists such as Samuel Adams and Patrick Henry – argued that the proposed Constitution was not genuinely federal in character because it was purportedly derived from 'the people' of the United States as whole, as well as because the states were not equally represented in both houses of Congress. Interrogating the preamble to the proposed Constitution, for example, Henry had thundered:

> what right had they to say, *We, the People . . .* who authorised them to speak the language of, *We, the People*, instead of *We, the States*? States are the characteristics, and the soul of confederation. If the States be not the agents of this compact, it must be one great consolidated National Government of the people of all the States.[29]

---

[26] Farrand, *Records*, I, 283–7; see also Zuckert, 'Federalism and the Founding', 197–9; Raoul Berger, *Federalism: The Founders' Design* (Norman: University of Oklahoma Press, 1987), 33. On the belief that an *imperium in imperio* was a kind of 'political solecism', see Madison, *Debates*, 133; Madison and Hamilton, *Federalist* no. 20 in Rossiter, *Federalist Papers*, 138; Bernard Bailyn, *The Ideological Origins of the American Revolution* (Cambridge: Belknap Press, 1967), 206–7, 223; Forrest McDonald, *Novus Ordo Seclorum: The Intellectual Origins of the Constitution* (Lawrence: University Press of Kansas, 1985), 277; Wood, *American Republic*, 345–54, 527–9.

[27] Hamilton, *Federalist* no. 9.    [28] *Ibid.*

[29] Patrick Henry, 'Speech in the Virginia Ratifying Convention, 4 June 1788' in Storing, *Anti-Federalist*, 296–7. Samuel Adams likewise stated: 'I stumble at the threshold. I meet with a

In *Federalist* no. 9, however, Hamilton responded that the Constitution was fully federal in terms of Montesquieu's definition of a 'confederate republic'. He stated:

> The definition of a Confederate Republic seems simply to be 'an assemblage of societies,' or an association of two or more States into one State. The extent, modifications, and objects of the Federal authority are mere matters of discretion. So long as the separate organisation of the members be not abolished, so long as it exists by a constitutional necessity for local purposes, though it should be in perfect subordination to the general authority of the Union, it would still be, in fact and in theory, an Association of States of a Confederacy. The proposed Constitution, so far from implying an abolition of the State Governments, makes them constituent parts of the National Sovereignty, by allowing them a direct representation in the Senate, and leaves in their possession certain exclusive and very important portions of the sovereign power. This fully corresponds, in every rational import of the terms, with the idea of Federal Government.[30]

Despite his nationalism,[31] Hamilton remarkably now appeared to support the idea of a confederate republic as 'an assemblage of societies' or 'an association of two or more States into one State'. A little more than a hundred years later, Australians such as Thomas Just would cite Hamilton's arguments in support of the idea that a true federation is based upon the agreement of constituent states, and that it provides for equal representation of the states in one house of the federal legislature, together with proportional national representation in the other, as appropriate in a 'compound republic'.[32]

---

National Government instead of a foederal Union of Sovereign States': Bailyn, *Debate on the Constitution*, I, 446. See *Convention Debates, Sydney* (1897), 296 (Symon quoting Adams).

[30]  Hamilton, *Federalist* no. 9.

[31]  Hueglin, 'Federalism at the Crossroads', 280–4, argues that in *Federalist* no. 9 Hamilton subtly adjusted Montesquieu's theory by presenting the states as subordinate to the Union. Hueglin does not, however, cite or discuss Hamilton's reference to the states as 'constituent parts of the National Sovereignty' and as possessing 'certain exclusive and very important portions of the sovereign power'. Nationalists such as Hamilton certainly wished to create a more consolidated federation than Montesquieu's federal republic, and they were to some extent successful; but they also had to acknowledge the degree to which they had been forced to compromise with their opponents.

[32]  Thomas C. Just, *Leading Facts Connected with Federation* (Hobart: The Mercury Office, 1891), 37, reproducing Hamilton, *Federalist* no. 9. Note also Patrick Glynn's use of *Federalist* no. 62: *Convention Debates, Adelaide* (1897), 664–5; *Convention Debates, Sydney* (1897), 276–82, discussed in ch. 8.

At Philadelphia, Madison had also been a supporter of a strong national government. Although he did not support Hamilton's radical consolidation, he argued for representation in proportion to population in both houses of Congress, an extensive federal legislative power and a veto on all state laws.[33] Having failed on these points, when Madison later defended the proposed Constitution as a decided improvement on the Articles of Confederation he, like Hamilton, was acutely aware of its continuing 'federal' features and could describe it quite accurately as such, especially in *Federalist* no. 39.[34]

Due to the accuracy and influence of Madison's analysis, it is worthwhile restating its central theses. James Wilson had wished to ground the formation of the American Constitution on the sovereignty of the people of the entire nation, and the appeal to 'We, the People' in the preamble to the proposed Constitution might be adduced to suggest that this was in indeed the case.[35] On this vital question Madison observed that the Constitution was 'federal' rather than 'national' because, first, the peoples of the several states under warrant of the state legislatures – not 'the whole people' of the United States – were to ratify the Constitution and, second, ratification would depend on the unanimous consent of those states that would agree to become members of the federation – it would not depend upon a vote of the majority.[36] In turn, the representative structures, he said, were 'partly federal, and partly national' because, first, the Senate would 'derive its powers from the States, as political and co-equal societies', represented equally – a federal aspect; second, the people of the United States as a whole would choose members of the House of Representatives, apportioned in proportion to population – a 'national' aspect; and, third, the president would be elected on a state by state basis, the votes of the states being apportioned partly as co-equal societies, partly in proportion to population – thus a 'compound' of federal and national elements. Finally, he added, the amending clause was

[33] Zuckert, 'Federalism and the Founding', 187–97.

[34] On the accuracy and importance of *Federalist* no. 39, see Rakove, *Original Meanings*, 161–2, 181–202. But note Madison's references to 'the people' in *Federalist* nos. 22 and 51 in Rossiter, *Federalist Papers*, 152, 323.

[35] Wilson would thus be cited by Australian nationalists to the effect that an Australian federation ought to be assemblage of individuals, not states: see e.g. *Convention Debates, Adelaide* (1897), 645 (Higgins).

[36] Compare Wilson, in Bailyn, *Debate on the Constitution*, I, 801–3, 835–7 and cf. *Federalist* no. 43 in Rossiter, *Federalist Papers*, 280.

also partly federal and partly national. If it were wholly national, amendments would be made by national majorities; if it were wholly federal, amendments would be made by the unanimous vote of the states. Madison, however, argued that 'in requiring more than a majority, and particularly in computing the proportion by States, not by citizens', the proposed Constitution 'departs from the national and advances towards the federal character', whereas 'in rendering the concurrence of less than the whole number of States sufficient', the Constitution 'loses again the federal and partakes of the national character'.[37]

Madison's analysis of the Constitution would be treated as paradigmatic by many later commentators, compactualist and nationalist, secessionist and unionist alike, as well as by the Australians. In this context it is worth noting that as late as 1830 Madison repeated essentially the same analysis, invoking his own *Federalist* no. 39 in support. As Madison pointed out, the interpretation of the United States Constitution he had advanced in *Federalist* no. 39 had been 'the prevailing view then taken of it' and that the same view had 'continued to prevail', notwithstanding 'eminent exceptions to it'.[38]

## James Bryce

Regius Professor of Civil Law at Oxford between 1870 and 1893, James Bryce was the most prominent of the influences on the Australian framers.[39] Alfred Deakin, an intellectual leader among the Australians, considered the debt they owed to Bryce to be 'almost incalculable'. The remarks of Charles Kingston, then premier of South Australia, were not untypical; he referred to Bryce as 'one of the highest constitutional authorities'.[40] J. A. La Nauze has remarked that Bryce's *The American Commonwealth* was 'the compulsory reading of the framers of the Constitution' and the 'bible' of the 1891 Convention. He observed that

---

[37] *The Federalist* no. 39, as cited in Just, *Leading Facts*, 38 and in Quick and Garran, *Annotated Constitution*, 336–40.

[38] Madison to Edward Everett, 28 August 1830, in Story, *Commentaries*, I, 299–303.

[39] On Bryce, see H. A. L. Fisher, *James Bryce*, 2 vols. (London: Macmillan, 1927); Edmund Ions, *James Bryce and American Democracy, 1870–1922* (London: Macmillan, 1968); Tulloch, *Bryce's American Commonwealth*.

[40] *Conference Debates, Melbourne* (1890), 25–6; *Convention Debates, Adelaide* (1897), 288; *Convention Debates, Sydney* (1897), 287; cf. William Harrison Moore, *The Constitution of the Commonwealth of Australia* (2nd edn, Melbourne: Maxwell, 1910), 66; Andrew Inglis Clark, *Studies in Australian Constitutional Law* (1st edn, Melbourne: Maxwell, 1901), 384.

'[i]n the years ahead the cleverest and the dullest of the men of the Conventions would quote Bryce to add weight to their words'.[41] The importance of Bryce is undoubted, but it is possible to overestimate his influence. Sir John Downer was perhaps more candid than most when he stated 'I humbly follow Mr Bryce when Mr Bryce happens to agree with my own views'.[42] None the less, the citations from Bryce within the federal conventions were extensive, unparalleled and usually deferential.[43]

Bryce's classic work, *The American Commonwealth*, first published in 1888, was widely read and reviewed, passing through numerous editions. His descriptive approach, largely free of abstract 'theorising',[44] presented the United States as a living federation in which the great variety of its features – 'compactual' and 'national' – were highlighted. While the limited theoretical musings in which he did engage occasionally suggested a nationalist conception of federalism,[45] his descriptive and historical approach meant that he drew attention to the many aspects of the American federation that were also compactual in orientation.[46]

Alexis de Tocqueville had said that 'the principle of the sovereignty of the people governs the whole political system of the Anglo-Americans'.[47] For Bryce, 'the most striking and pervading characteristic' of the American Commonwealth was 'the existence of a double government, a double allegiance, a double patriotism'. The Constitution of 1789 was a compromise', he wrote, and 'a compromise arrived at by allowing contradictory propositions to be represented as both true, namely national and state sovereignty.'[48] The states may have given up a measure of

---

[41] La Nauze, *Making of the Constitution*, 18–19; cf. Irving, *Constitute a Nation*, 76, 122.

[42] *Convention Debates, Adelaide* (1897), 209; cf. 176 (Isaacs), 704 (Barton).

[43] On issues of federalism, as indeed on most issues, Bryce was the most cited author in the convention debates. See e.g. *Convention Debates, Adelaide* (1897), 30 (Baker), 98–102 (Higgins), 135 (Symon), 158 (Lyne), 209 (Downer), 243–4 (Fysh), 288–9, 293 (Deakin), 325 (Gordon), 536–8 (Glynn), 582 (Deakin), 646 (Higgins), 665 (Glynn), 704 (Deakin), 963 (Glynn), 965 (Symon), 1015 (Barton); *Convention Debates, Sydney* (1897), 56 (Deakin), 287–8 (Kingston), 536 (Glynn), 584 (Deakin), 588 (O'Connor), 637 (Dobson), 663 (Isaacs).

[44] James Bryce, *The American Commonwealth* (2nd edn, London: Macmillan, 1889), I, 4; cf. I, 25–8, 31–4.

[45] See Galligan, *Federal Republic*, 191; Warden, *Formation of the Australian Constitution*, 66.

[46] On the sources of ideas in *The American Commonwealth* see the 'Preface to the First Edition' and Tulloch, *Bryce's American Commonwealth*, 234–42.

[47] Tocqueville, *Democracy in America*, 61; cf. Bryce, *American Commonwealth*, I, 3–4; James Bryce, *Studies in History and Jurisprudence*, 2 vols. (Oxford: Clarendon Press, 1901), I, 381–429 for Bryce's critique of Tocqueville.

[48] Bryce, *American Commonwealth*, I, 409; see also 306, 311–12.

'sovereignty', he thought, but they tenaciously retained their original powers of independent government and organisation.[49] Accordingly, for Bryce, an understanding of federalism was 'the first and indispensable step to the comprehension of the American institutions'.[50] In Bryce's estimation, the Constitution embodied neither a loose compactual league nor a unitary national government, but rather:

> a Commonwealth of commonwealths, a Republic of republics, a State which, while one, is nevertheless composed of other States even more essential to its existence than it is to theirs.[51]

Bryce was thus critical of 'metaphysical' theories of sovereignty developed in the United States by those seeking to locate ultimate sovereignty in either the whole people or the peoples of the several states.[52] Since the American Commonwealth was a 'Commonwealth of commonwealths', both the 'nation' and the 'states' were represented to be 'sovereign' – an apparently contradictory proposition according to the classical theorists of indivisible sovereignty, such as Jean Bodin, Thomas Hobbes and, more recently, John Austin. But the American Commonwealth did not fit this mould, so Bryce rejected the theories of Bodin and those who followed him, contrasting them with the mediating position of Johannes Althusius.[53] By rejecting abstract theories of sovereignty Bryce thus avoided a whole range of nationalist and compactualist definitions and distinctions. In particular, the defining characteristic of a 'federation' was, thought Bryce, the existence of federal executive authority over individual citizens, not the ultimate sovereignty of the people of the entire nation.[54] In this respect, his approach was a mediating one, reminiscent of both Montesquieu and Madison.

Bryce accordingly recognised both compactual and nationalist features in the American Constitution. It is true that when explaining how it was that the states and the federal government could remain supreme in their own spheres, he drew attention to the American idea that '[a]ll authority

---

[49]  *Ibid.*, I, 314.    [50]  *Ibid.*, I, 15.    [51]  *Ibid.*, I, 12–15, 332.

[52]  Bryce, *History and Jurisprudence*, II, 105.

[53]  *Ibid.*, II, 84–5, alluded to in Bryce, *American Commonwealth*, I, 315, referring to 'the growth of a mass of subtle and, so to speak, scholastic metaphysics regarding the nature of the government it created'.

[54]  Bryce, *American Commonwealth*, I, 13–14; Bryce, *History and Jurisprudence*, I, 470, 489.

flows from the people'.[55] But this need not necessarily mean the people of the nation as an undifferentiated whole, as appears from his discussion of the formative basis of the American system. The federal Constitution, Bryce said, was 'to be considered ratified neither by Congress' (the nationalist interpretation), 'nor by the State legislatures' (the compactualist interpretation), 'but by the peoples of the several States' (the Madisonian interpretation).[56] Moreover, he noted, the governmental structures adopted under the Constitution reflected its essential nature as a Commonwealth constructed out of smaller commonwealths.[57] Hence, the 'most conspicuous' and 'most important' feature of the Senate was that it 'represents the several States of the Union as separate commonwealths, and is thus an essential part of the Federal scheme'.[58]

It is also true that Bryce's empirically accurate depiction of the American system was sometimes at odds with his theorising. He recognised that the composition of the Senate was dictated by the formative idea of a 'Commonwealth of commonwealths', but he held that this was 'not very conformable to democratic theory', apparently meaning national democracy.[59] Further, while Bryce praised the American Senate, this was for conservative, not federal, reasons.[60] The Senate, he thought, had failed to achieve its federal objectives: there had 'never, in point of fact, been any division of interest or consequent contests between the great states and the small ones'.[61] The Senate did not secure the rights of the states simply 'because the extent of State rights has been now well settled'.[62] To say this presupposed that 'states' rights' were nothing more than the legislative powers retained by or distributed to the states – which was to adopt, as will be seen, a more or less Diceyan interpretation of the American system.

Bryce's philosophical commitments also led him to be thoroughly critical of the House of Representatives, contrasting it to the House of Commons and the practice of responsible government in Britain.[63] But such evaluations did not prevent him from accurately describing the

[55] Bryce, *American Commonwealth*, I, 314.
[56] *Ibid.*, I, 17–22; cf. Bryce, *History and Jurisprudence*, II, 105.
[57] Bryce, *History and Jurisprudence*, I, 489. [58] Bryce, *American Commonwealth*, I, 93.
[59] *Ibid.*, I, 94, note 1, remarking that the state of Nevada was 'really a sort of rotten borough for and controlled by the great silver men', an expression echoed by H. B. Higgins: *Convention Debates, Adelaide* (1897), 101–2.
[60] Bryce, *American Commonwealth*, I, 95, 110–12. [61] *Ibid.*, I, 94, 120, 182.
[62] *Ibid.*, I, 120. [63] *Ibid.*, I, 138–44, 147–9, 155–60, 160–70, 171–9.

compactual imperatives that had dictated the form that the House of
Representatives had taken. 'The House of Representatives', he said –

> represents the nation on the basis of population, as the Senate rep-
> resents the States . . . But even in the composition of the House the
> States play an important part. The Constitution . . . leav[es] [each]
> State to determine the districts within its own area for and by which
> the members shall be chosen.[64]

A tension between description and theory runs its way throughout
Bryce's book. It would emerge again in his discussion of the requirement
that members of Congress be resident in the state and district from which
they were elected.[65] Bryce saw the explanation in strong state, district,
county and town loyalties, and in the related commitment to the
'republican' quota for the House, so that every district would have its voice
heard. '[I]t was a matter of course that the people of each township or city
sent one of themselves to the assembly of the State.' Thus 'local self-
government' was 'fully developed and rooted in the habits of the people':

> It is from their local government that the political ideas of the
> American people have been formed: and they have applied to their
> State assemblies and their national assembly the customs which grew
> up in the smaller area.[66]

Bryce despaired that this local orientation was 'assumed to be part of the
order of nature', yet he noted that English practice had once required
members of the House of Commons to be residents of their counties or
boroughs.[67] Adopting a narrow definition of 'federalism' that limited it
to a 'nation-state' schema, he commented:

> So far as the restriction to residents in a State is concerned it is
> intelligible. The senator was – to some extent is still – a sort of
> ambassador from his State. He is chosen by the legislature or collective
> authority of his State. He cannot well be a citizen of one State and
> represent another. Even a representative in the House from one State
> who lived in another might be perplexed by a divided allegiance . . .
> But what reason can there be for preventing a man resident in one part
> of a State from representing another part . . . ?[68]

---

[64] *Ibid.*, I, 121–2, 195; cf. I, 128, 555, 560.    [65] *Ibid.*, I, 186.    [66] *Ibid.*, I, 189.
[67] *Ibid.*, I, 188, n. 2, 189.    [68] *Ibid.*, I, 189–90; see also I, 110, 192–3.

Bryce could not accept that the case for residency could apply at the local, as well as a state, level. For him, federalism was concerned with 'national-state interests'. He therefore adopted Thomas Cooley's view that '[t]he power of a State over all communities within its limits is absolute. It may grant or refuse local government as it pleases.'[69] Yet Bryce also accurately depicted features of American localism which did not fit into the nation-state paradigm.

To a significant degree, this perspective would be shared by the Australian framers: they, too, would focus on 'states' rights' versus 'national rights', treating 'municipalities' as subordinate governments.[70] But the representation of local electorates, an abiding feature of the British, American and Australian systems, continued to point to the original importance of local communities.

Bryce recognised that the American federal system had evolved from the earlier trading corporations, to colonies, to independent states, to confederation, to full federation; and that these derived their existence from the consent of their people.[71] He preferred not to think of the states as being composed of federating counties, however, even though he noticed that the state of Connecticut had been a federation of constituent towns, each of which had demanded a guarantee of local representation in the state legislature.[72] Rather, Bryce criticised the 'rotten boroughs' resulting from the minimum representation of each town or county in the state legislatures and the 'strength of local feeling' in New England state elections. Instead of 'the best men of the whole State', he maintained, the legislatures were composed of lesser lights, 'the leading men of the districts'.[73] This was because 'local feeling was . . . intensely strong, and every little town wanted to have its member'.[74]

Bryce classified the states according to their basic unit of government. The town was the basic unit in the New England states; the county was

---

[69] *Ibid.*, I, 407; see also 405–8, 428–31, relying on Thomas M. Cooley, *A Treatise on the Constitutional Limitations which rest upon the Legislative Power of the States of the American Union* (Boston: Little, Brown and Co., 1868).

[70] See *Federated Municipal and Shire Council Employees' Union of Australia v. Melbourne Corporation* (1919) 26 CLR 508 (per Barton and Isaacs JJ). Compare Chris Aulich and Rebecca Pietsch, 'Left on the Shelf: Local Government and the Australian Constitution' (2002) 61 *Australian Journal of Public Administration* 14.

[71] Bryce, *American Commonwealth*, I, 413–18.      [72] *Ibid.*, I, 415.

[73] *Ibid.*, I, 434–47, 462–4, 505 and 514.      [74] *Ibid.*, I, 166.

basic to the southern states; and the middle states embodied a mixture of both approaches. As to New England:

> [The towns] are to this day the true units of political life . . . the solid foundation of that well-compacted structure of self-government which European philosophers have admired and the new States of the West have sought to reproduce. Till 1821 the towns were the only political corporate bodies in Massachusetts, and till 1857 they formed, as they still form in Connecticut, the basis of representation in her Assembly, each town, however small, returning at least one member. Much of that robust, if somewhat narrow, localism which characterizes the representative system of America is due to this originally distinct and self-sufficing corporate life of the seventeenth century towns. Nor is it without interest to observe that although they owed much to the conditions which surrounded the early colonists . . . they owed something also to those Teutonic traditions of semi-independent local communities, owning common property, and governing themselves by a primary assembly of all free inhabitants, which the English had brought with them from the Elbe and the Weser, and which had been perpetuated in the practice of many parts of England down till the days of the Stuart kings.[75]

Bryce further attributed the local government orientation in the New England states to Puritan church and town meetings, republicanism and direct democracy. The 'northern township', he said:

> is an English parish . . . the Town meeting is the English vestry, the selectmen are the churchwardens, or select vestrymen, called back by the conditions of colonial life into an activity fuller than they exerted in England even in the seventeenth century, and far fuller than they now retain.[76]

These 'miniature commonwealths', self-governed in regular town meetings in which all citizens participated, were 'admittedly the best' of the American systems of local government, he thought. The towns remained 'the true political units' even as they gradually aggregated into counties, colonies and then states: the county, he said, was originally 'an aggregation of towns for judicial purposes'. The towns, therefore, were the basic units of local government and the basis of representation in the

---

[75] *Ibid.*, I, 562–3.    [76] *Ibid.*, I, 583; cf. 565–9.

state assemblies. Members of the town openly debated issues, directly legislated, elected officials and approved taxes.[77]

According to Bryce, very different circumstances led the southern states to centre on the county as the basic unit of local government – a 'less instructive' and 'less successful' arrangement, he thought. Often Episcopalian, mostly rural, slave-holding and propertied, the southerners fixed on the county, a much larger unit, as the basis of local government. They also preferred representative government to the direct democracy of the New England towns. The system often followed the English system of county, parish and hundred – although the hundred later died out, the parish became a purely ecclesiastical division and the county was subordinated to the state.[78]

The middle states, observed Bryce, contained a varying mixture of these two approaches. Typically, they had begun on the county system, but with industrialisation, population growth and New England influence, they had moved towards the town system. Bryce even suggested that the 'town' system seemed 'destined to prevail over the whole North-West', with a consequent decline in the counties. And he here compared the town system to the rural commune within the Swiss cantons.[79] Bryce likewise drew attention to 'home rule' provisions in state constitutions which guaranteed fiscal self-sufficiency, local control over a number of substantial topics, and that state and congressional electoral divisions respect the integrity of local government boundaries.[80] He concluded:

> Local government is so fully developed that many functions, which in Europe would devolve on a central authority, are in all American States left to the county, or the city, or the township, or the school district. These minor divisions narrow the province of the State, just as the State narrows the province of the central government.[81]

In writing this, Bryce remarkably drew attention to the way in which American federalism operated not only at the nation-state level, but also

---

[77] *Ibid.*, I, 418–21, esp. 419–20, n. 2, 561–3, 566–7, 591.
[78] *Ibid.*, I, 563–4, 570–71, 583. Bryce cited Jefferson's desire to see New England 'ward democracy' transplanted into Virginia: I, 567.
[79] *Ibid.*, I, 564–5, 571–81, 577–8, 578, n. 1, 582, 583, n. 2. Bryce noted, however, the problems for the traditional town system presented by the very large cities: I, 581.
[80] Bryce appended a copy of the California Constitution to illustrate these developments: *ibid.*, I, 683–724; see also I, 470, 490, 565, 568–9, 583, 585–9.
[81] *Ibid.*, I, 508.

incorporated the localities as partly independent, partly dependent
political communities. In this way, as in others, there was a tension between
Bryce's empirical observations and his abstract theorising. When it came
to features such as the independence of the American judiciary, the separation of judicial power and the institution of judicial review, Bryce
adopted an explanation which, as will shortly become clear, mirrored
rather closely the views of A. V. Dicey. According to both authors, judicial
review was the means by which the federal Constitution was enforced
against infractions by either the state or federal governments.[82] Unlike
Dicey, however, Bryce insisted that judicial review was not essential to
federalism. The constituent states of a federation might be satisfied to
leave the adjudication of federal issues to a federal council, either alone or
in combination with a federal court, as in Switzerland.[83]

In conclusion, Bryce considered that the merits of American federalism
were the 'counterpart and consequence' of its defects and that, ultimately,
American federalism was well adapted to 'the temper and circumstances'
of the people. Its problems were manifold: the weakness of federal authority
over internal matters, a lack of coherent policy direction, unprincipled local
resistance to national intervention, liability to secession and civil war,
liability to faction, undue complexity of law and administration, and subordination of merit to local popularity. But, according to Bryce, the
blemishes were outweighed by the merits and suitability of the system.

Foremost in Bryce's defence of federalism was the idea of a 'Commonwealth of commonwealths'. Federalism was appropriate in the United
States because federalism was a 'means of uniting commonwealths into one
nation under one national government without extinguishing their separate administrations, legislatures and local patriotisms'. It was the best
means of developing a vast country and it prevented the development of a
'despotic central government'. Second, local self-government stimulated
popular involvement in political life and secured the 'good administration
of local affairs'. Noting that the states were remarkably homogeneous in
culture and legal institutions, Bryce concluded that American federalism
was not an outworking of geographical, racial, cultural or other intrinsic
differences, but was the consequence of a belief in local self-government
and the fact that the states antedated the national government.[84] Third,

---

[82] *Ibid.*, I, 225–8, 235–6, 237–43, 247.    [83] *Ibid.*, I, 253–4.    [84] *Ibid.*, I, 398–405.

there was opportunity for experimentation in government policy, diminishing the risks of social disorders or governmental errors.[85]

Bryce therefore presented the Australian framers with an account of the American 'Commonwealth of commonwealths' which, despite his philosophical leanings, accurately described its many and varied features, including its local, state and national dimensions.[86] The Australians could therefore use him to support many different ideals, such as local self-government, federal representation, responsible government and democracy. For example, Bryce had been critical of the separation of powers and the lack of leadership in the American House of Representatives. He favoured responsible government but praised the American Senate for its executive functions in relation to the ratification of treaties and confirmation of judicial appointments.[87] He also thought that deadlocks between the houses could be disastrous under responsible government.[88] These sentiments were remarkably consistent with the determination of a majority of the framers of the Australian Constitution to find some way of adapting responsible government to federalism. The framers saw in Bryce the benefits of both the Westminster system and federalism. Charles Kingston at one stage sent a copy of the draft Australian Constitution to Bryce and could report Bryce's warm support for a number of their proposals. The Australians seemed well-pleased.[89]

## Edward Freeman

Edward Augustus Freeman's *History of Federal Government in Greece and Italy*, first published in 1863, has been called the 'classic nineteenth-century exposition' of ancient Greek and Roman 'federalism', and remains to this day a remarkably well-cited work of Victorian scholarship.[90] Freeman, who succeeded Bishop William Stubbs in the Regius Chair of Modern History at Oxford, profoundly shaped late nineteenth-century conceptions of

---

[85] *Ibid.*, I, 333–4, 339–40, 342–9.    [86] *Ibid.*, I, 299.

[87] *Ibid.*, I, 182, 213–24, 271–90, 291–304, 525.    [88] *Ibid.*, I, 184.

[89] *Convention Debates, Sydney* (1897), 287–8 (Wise). See also Bryce, *History and Jurisprudence*, I, 468–551.

[90] Jakob A. O. Larsen, *Greek Federal States* (Oxford: Oxford University Press, 1968), 3; Frenkel, *Federal Theory*, 97; Mogi, *Problem of Federalism*, I, 290–7.

federalism.[91] Andrew Inglis Clark spoke for many of the framers of the Australian Constitution when he described Freeman as that 'eminent historian' who had 'studied most closely, and written the most exhaustively on federal government'.[92] John Quick and Robert Garran relied on Freeman extensively, as did Richard Baker and Thomas Just.[93] John Cockburn and Isaac Isaacs referred to Freeman as a great 'authority' on the topic,[94] and in one of their characteristic exchanges, Barton and Isaacs traded scholarship derived from Freeman's *Growth of the English Constitution*.[95] A survey of citations in the convention debates suggests that in issues of federalism Freeman was second in importance only to Bryce.[96] Yet studies of Australian federalism have tended to neglect his influence.[97]

Like Bryce, Freeman's methods were historical and empirical, and his working definition of federal government was consequently broader than those of lawyers and political scientists such as A. V. Dicey and John Burgess (to be discussed shortly).[98] For Freeman, federal government was a 'compromise between two opposite political systems' or 'two widely distant extremes'. It was a 'union of component members'; more than an alliance, less than a consolidated state. In its 'perfect form', the

---

[91] On Freeman, see John Fiske, 'Edward Augustus Freeman' (1893) 71(423) *The Atlantic Monthly* 99; William M. A. Clarke, 'Edward Augustus Freeman' (1892) 12(5) *The New England Magazine* 607; H. A. Cronne, 'Edward Augustus Freeman, 1823–1892' (1943) 28 *History* 78.

[92] *Convention Debates, Sydney* (1891), 243; cf. Andrew Inglis Clark, 'Australian Federation (Confidential)' (Hobart: Attorney-General's Office, 1891), [Wise Papers, MS 1708], 13.

[93] Garran, *Coming Commonwealth*, 13–21, 39–54; Quick and Garran, *Annotated Constitution*, 4, 333; Richard Chaffey Baker, *Executive in a Federation* (Adelaide: C.E. Bristow, Government Printer, 1897), 13; Just, *Leading Facts*, 110–12.

[94] *Convention Debates, Adelaide* (1897), 346, 544.

[95] Edward A. Freeman, *The Growth of the English Constitution from the Earliest Times* (3rd edn, London: Macmillan, 1898); *Convention Debates, Adelaide* (1897), 388. See also Edward A. Freeman, *The History of the Norman Conquest of England*, 6 vols. (3rd edn, Oxford: Clarendon Press, 1867–79).

[96] See e.g. *Convention Debates, Sydney* (1891), 243 (Clark); *Convention Debates, Adelaide* (1897), 73 (Glynn), 180 (Isaacs), 244 (Fysh), 316 (Gordon), 346 (Cockburn), 388, 391 (Barton), 394, 544 (Isaacs), 663–4 (Glynn); *Convention Debates, Sydney* (1897), 292–5 (Symon), 305 (Isaacs), 348 (Higgins), 673 (Cockburn), 793 (Fysh).

[97] For occasional references to Freeman, see John Reynolds, 'A. I. Clark's American Sympathies and his Influence on Australian Federation' (1958) 32 *Australian Law Journal* 62, 64; Frank M. Neasey, 'Andrew Inglis Clark Senior and Australian Federation' (1969) 15(2) *Australian Journal of Politics and History* 1, 9; Davis, *Federal Principle*, ch. 2; James A. Thomson, 'Andrew Inglis Clark and Australian Constitutional Law' in Marcus Haward and James Warden (eds.), *An Australian Democrat: The Life, Work and Consequences of Andrew Inglis Clark* (Hobart: Centre for Tasmanian Historical Studies, University of Tasmania 1995), 59.

[98] Wheare, *Federal Government*, 16–17, contrasted his 'political science' definition with Freeman's 'historical' one.

component 'members' would be 'wholly independent' or 'sovereign' in the 'sphere' which concerned them alone, but 'subject to a common power in those matters which concern the whole body of members collectively'. '[T]his complete division of sovereignty [is] essential', Freeman said, 'to the absolute perfection of the Federal ideal.'[99] Freeman plainly adopted an 'integrative' model of federalism: 'to be of any value', a federal system must, he insisted, arise out of the union of independent states, rather than the division of a united territory.[100] Following Dicey, Freeman accepted that 'federal government' involved a 'division of powers' between the federation and the states. But the idea of a 'Commonwealth of commonwealths' remained central to his account.

Following the famous Swiss scholar, Johann Bluntschli, Freeman subdivided the different kinds of federal system in terms of their treatment of federal executive power, rather than in terms of sovereignty. In a 'system of confederated states' (the German *Staatenbund*), he wrote, the 'federal power' represents and applies only to the governments of the member states. In a 'composite state' or 'supreme federal government' (*Bundesstaat*), the government of the federation both represents and acts directly upon individual citizens. According to Freeman, the American system as constructed under the Constitution was a composite state; under the Articles of Confederation it had been a system of confederated states; yet under both it was a 'real federal government'.[101] Thus, Freeman's definition of 'federal government' did not exclude 'confederation' – unlike the more extreme nationalist interpretations expounded, as will be seen, by John Burgess and Georg Jellinek. Indeed, writing before the cessation of the war between the American states, Freeman was careful to remain neutral as between the positions of Presidents Abraham Lincoln and John Jefferson Davis.[102]

Freeman's historical research was highly influential for a number of reasons. First, he reinforced a belief in the 'federal ideal' – what he called a 'perfect federal government', 'a delicate and artificial structure' and

---

[99] Edward A. Freeman, *Federal Government in Greece and Italy* (2nd edn, London: Macmillan, 1898), 1–3, 7–8.

[100] *Ibid.*, 70.

[101] *Ibid.*, 8–13, 69, 77–8, 156. Cf. Johann K. Bluntschli, *The Theory of the State* [1875], D. G. Ritchie, P. E. Matheson and R. Lodge (trans.) (Oxford: Clarendon Press, 1885), 252–3. Freeman also drew upon Henry Wheaton, Austin, Calhoun, Hamilton, Madison, Mill and Tocqueville.

[102] Freeman, *Federal Government*, 70–1, 91–2. Freeman expressed doubt concerning the constitutional arguments of the Confederate states, but was sympathetic to their arguments from expediency.

'a late growth of a very high state of political culture'. Freeman believed such a form of government to have been embodied in the Achaean League of Ancient Greece, the Swiss Confederation, the United States of America and, with less 'perfection', the United Provinces of the Netherlands. Freeman's influential expression of this 'ideal' stimulated the Australian captivation with the notion of an ideal federal government. Partly under Freeman's influence, the Australian framers were concerned to avoid a constitution in which the federal idea was embodied 'less perfectly' – as in Canada, Germany and the Netherlands. Like Montesquieu before him, Freeman argued that federal government had the distinctive merit of uniting the strengths of systems of independent states with the strengths of large states.[103] This reinforced the sense in which a federal form of government represented an ideal to which the Australians might aspire, but it did so in a concrete way by identifying a number of specific 'benefits', such as the enhancement of political participation and public virtue (associated with the ideal of the small republic),[104] a decrease in local prejudice and party strife, and the increased military capacities of a large territorial state. In this way, Freeman's writings supported what would prove to be three vital principles of Australian federation: local self-government, open markets and mutual defence.

Second, Freeman drew the attention of his readers to many diverse examples of federalism, as well as to older understandings of the idea. Freeman argued that true federations could be found among the Greeks,[105] yet these were unions of city-states rather than nation-states, and they were created by treaties. This reinforced the idea of integrative federalism and made it clear that federal structures could be formed at the scale of towns or cities. Bryce had drawn attention to the localism of American political culture, but resisted the idea that federal principles could apply to local–state relations. Freeman showed that federalism could be embodied at a local–state as well as a state–national level. Freeman's wider genus of 'federal government' included 'confederal' arrangements, such as the Achaean League, the United Provinces, the Articles of Confederation and the secessionist Confederate States of America – as well as the strictly 'federal' American and Swiss Constitutions.[106]

---

[103] *Ibid.*, 4–5, 69.     [104] Cf. Clark, *Australian Constitutional Law*, 13, citing Freeman to this effect.
[105] See Frenkel, *Federal Theory*, 97, citing Freeman, *Federal Government*, 202.
[106] See Freeman, *Federal Government*, 211.

By expanding the genus ('federalism') and identifying two separate species ('confederation' and 'federation'), he underscored the continuities between federation and confederation, a mediating approach akin to Madison's perspective.

Third, Freeman favourably compared the Swiss system with the British and the American systems in a way that challenged a number of standing assumptions. In an essay cited by Andrew Inglis Clark and Richard Baker in Australia, Freeman argued that the 'sort of negative wisdom which the Swiss Government shows, and which is what the position of this country especially needs, is displayed both in the theory and the practice of the Swiss Federal System'.[107] And, in another of Freeman's important works, *The Growth of the English Constitution*, he aimed to demonstrate the influence of 'the earliest institutions of England and of other Teutonic lands' – such as Switzerland – on present English institutions. Edmund Barton would in 1897 quote a lengthy passage from this work in support of parliamentary representation in preference to the use of direct referendums.[108] Despite the hyperbole, the passage warrants reproduction at length:

> In the institutions of ... the Swiss Cantons ... we may see the institutions of our own [English] forefathers... The [Swiss] Commonwealth of Uri, by the peculiar circumstances of its history, grew into an independent and sovereign State. But in its origin it was not a nation; it was not even a tribe. The Landesgemeiden of which I have been speaking are the assemblies, not of a nation, but of a district; they answer in our own land, not to the assemblies of the whole kingdom, but to the lesser assemblies of the shire or hundred. But they are not, on that account, any the less worthy of our notice ... [T]he local divisions are not simply administrative districts traced out for convenience on the map. In fact, they are not divisions at all; they are not divisions of the kingdom, but the earlier elements out of whose union the kingdom grew. Yorkshire by that name is younger than England, but Yorkshire by its elder name of Deira is older than England; and Yorkshire or Deira itself is younger than the smaller districts of which it is made up, Craven, Cleveland, Holderness, and others ... [T]he greater aggregate was simply organised after the model of the lesser

---

[107] Edward A. Freeman, 'Presidential Government' in *Historical Essays*, First Series (4th edn, London: Macmillan, 1886), 416, cited in Clark, *Australian Constitutional Law*, 7.
[108] *Convention Debates, Adelaide* (1897), 388.

elements, out of whose union it was formed. In fact, for the political
unit, for the atom which joined with its fellow atoms to form the
political whole, we must go to areas yet smaller . . . That unit, that
atom, the true kernel of all our political life must be looked for . . . in
England – smile not while I say it – in the parish vestry.[109]

Whether or not Freeman's scholarship was sound,[110] Edmund Barton
was clearly influenced by this idea that political societies are properly
formed by the federation of constituent societies and that the structure of
representation – even within England – should reflect that fact. The
framers of the Australian Constitution drew on a rich tradition of federal
thought, which included the idea of a federative 'Commonwealth of
commonwealths', in which towns and cities, as well as provinces, were
constituent elements of successively larger bodies politic. Edward Freeman was an important conduit of that tradition.

## A. V. Dicey

Writing towards the end of his life, Robert Garran observed that during
the 'pre-natal years' of the Australian Commonwealth the 'idea of federalism' had begun in 'too academic' a way and from an 'ultra-legalistic'
point of view.[111] One of the most important influences in this legalistic
vein was Albert Venn Dicey's *Lectures Introductory to the Study of the Law
of the Constitution*, first published in 1885.[112] Dicey's impact on Australian
conceptions of federalism is widely acknowledged.[113] He was cited in the
convention debates by Isaacs and extensively by Quick and Garran.[114]

---

[109]  Freeman, *English Constitution*, 9–10, 37, 60, 66; cf. Freeman, *Norman Conquest*, I, 79–99; V, 461.

[110]  Compare Brian Tierney, *Religion, Law and the Growth of Constitutional Thought* (Cambridge:
Cambridge University Press, 1982), 55; Blackstone, *Commentaries*, I, 64–6. See also Frederic
W. Maitland, *The Constitutional History of England* (Cambridge: Cambridge University Press,
1955), 363; Bailyn, *Ideological Origins*, 164.

[111]  Garran, *Prosper the Commonwealth*, viii.

[112]  Quotations are from the fifth edition, published in 1897. See also Albert Venn Dicey, *Lectures
on the Relation between Law and Public Opinion in England During the Nineteenth Century*
(London: Macmillan, 1905).

[113]  For background, see Richard A. Cosgrove, *The Rule of Law: Albert Venn Dicey, Victorian Jurist*
(London: Macmillan, 1980); Trowbridge H. Ford, *Albert Venn Dicey, the Man and his Times*
(Chichester: Barry Rose Publishers, 1985).

[114]  E.g. *Convention Debates, Sydney* (1897), 312–13, (Isaacs); *Convention Debates, Adelaide*
(1897), 910–12, 952 (Barton), 307 (Clarke); John Quick, *A Digest of Federal Constitutions*
(Bendigo: J. B. Young, 1896), 12–14; Garran, *Coming Commonwealth*, 15–16, 76; Quick and

Most studies of federal aspects of the Australian Constitution from within the discipline of law (including Garran's own) have followed Dicey's lead in regarding the 'division of powers' between the federation and the states as the defining characteristic of the Australian federation and the most significant aspect of the High Court's interpretive task.[115]

For Dicey, the study of federalism was a counterpoint to his famous thesis about the sovereignty of the British Parliament at Westminster. Thus, Dicey regularly contrasted the 'unitarianism' of the 'exercise of supreme legislative authority by one central power' in the British Parliament with the principle of the 'division of sovereignty' in the American federal system. Dicey's central claim was that the reconciliation of unity and diversity in a federation is achieved through a division of powers between the national and state governments. In a classic federation, he insisted, the terms of this division of powers must be set out in a supreme, rigid, written constitution, which binds both the national and state governments alike and is conclusively interpreted by an independent and tenured judiciary. As a result, the federal legislature is a 'subordinate law-making body', he said, whose statutes are invalid if they go beyond constitutional authority. The 'tendency of federalism', therefore, is 'to limit on every side the action of government and to split up the strength of the state among co-ordinate and independent authorities'. Indeed, this is the 'essential distinction between a federal system . . . and a unitarian system of government'.[116]

Bryce generally agreed with Dicey that judicial review in the United States was the means by which the federal Constitution was enforced against infractions by either the state or federal governments.[117] But, as Bryce continued, the difficulty was to explain the apparent anomaly of Switzerland, where federal legislation was not subject to judicial review. Unlike Dicey, Bryce insisted that judicial review was not essential to federalism. The cantons (or states) might be satisfied to leave the maintenance of the 'federal balance' to a federal executive council and legislature in which the cantons were adequately represented.[118]

---

Garran, *Annotated Constitution*, 325–8. See also Clark, 'Australian Federation', 4; Adams and Cunningham, *Swiss Confederation*, 22–4.

[115] E.g. Wheare, *Federal Government*, ch. 1; Davis, *Theory and Reality*, 24. But cf. Sawer, *Modern Federalism*, 1–2; Galligan, *Federal Republic*, 199–202, 244.

[116] Dicey, *Law of the Constitution*, 130–55, 410–13.

[117] Bryce, *American Commonwealth*, I, 225–8, 235–6, 237–43, 247.   [118] *Ibid.*, I, 253–4.

While Dicey treated the division of powers as definitive of federalism, he also recognised the integrative, compactual origins of federal systems and the influence of those formative processes on the governmental institutions and amending processes adopted thereunder. Dicey held that federations arise when previously existing independent countries are capable of union, and have a desire to federate, but wish to retain their own independence. This 'federal sentiment', he wrote, 'fixes the essential character of federalism', for the foundations of a federal state are a 'complicated contract' and a federal constitution 'partakes of the nature of a treaty'.[119] Accordingly, there were two aspects to Dicey's theory of federalism. One aspect emphasised the integrative idea of a commonwealth constructed out of smaller commonwealths. The other emphasised the division of a conceptually unitary sovereign power into smaller units, the federation and the several states.[120]

Dicey's theory of parliamentary sovereignty was not a universal theory of law but an account of the British system of law in particular. While he held that there was a 'sovereign power' in federations, he regarded it as a 'monarch who slumbers and sleeps', and 'a monarch who slumbers for years', he wrote, 'is like a monarch who does not exist'.[121] Indeed, Dicey concluded that federal governments were 'weak' precisely because 'there exists no person or body of persons possessed of legal sovereignty in the sense given by Austin'.[122] None the less, Dicey's theory was often received on the basis of Austin's universal theory of sovereignty.[123] As will be seen, Australians like Quick and Garran certainly seemed to make the connection, drawing lines between Austin and Dicey at critical points in their discussion.[124] Austin, for example, sought for a sovereign institution or person in every 'independent political society', a problematic quest in the case of federations. For Austin, 'law properly so called' is the 'command of a sovereign', and the sovereign is the institution to which the subjects of a particular political society render habitual obedience and which does not itself render habitual obedience to any other institution.[125] Austin

---

[119] Dicey, *Law of the Constitution*, 137–8, 139, n. 1. 'It is quite conceivable', he continued, 'that the authors of a federal Constitution may intend to provide no constitutional means of changing its terms except the assent of all the parties to the treaty.'

[120] *Ibid.*, 135, 141.    [121] *Ibid.*, 141.    [122] *Ibid.*, 139, n. 1; cf. 68–9, 162–4.

[123] Dicey accepted some of Austin's theoretical arguments: *ibid.*, 58; Cosgrove, *Rule of Law*, 70, 103.

[124] Quick and Garran, *Annotated Constitution*, 285, 324–8.

[125] See Austin, *Province of Jurisprudence*, 193–5.

struggled, however, to identify any such institution in the United States, Canada or Switzerland. In a telling passage, he addressed the 'embarrassing' question of the minimum size of an independent political society:

> Supposing that the term *political* applied to independent societies whose numbers are extremely minute, each of the independent families which constitute the given society would form of itself a political community: for the bulk of each of those families renders habitual obedience to its own peculiar chief. And, seeing that each of those families would form of itself an independent political community, the given independent society could hardly be styled with strictness a natural society. Speaking strictly, that given society would form a congeries of independent political communities.[126]

How did this apply to federations? According to Austinian dogma, there could be only one sovereign in an independent political society. The choice had to be between an alliance or confederation of sovereign states (what Austin called a 'system of confederate states') and a consolidated union under a sovereign government (a 'composite state').[127] And Austin saw clearly the reason why he was forced into this dichotomy:

> I advert to the nature of a composite state, and to that of a system of confederated states, for the following purposes:- It results from positions which I shall try to establish hereafter, that the power of a sovereign is incapable of legal limitation. It also results from positions which I have tried to establish already, that in every society political and independent, the sovereign is *one* individual, or *one* body of individuals: that unless the sovereign be *one* individual, or *one* body of individuals, the given independent society is either in a state of nature, or is split into two or more independent political societies.[128]

More clearly than most, Austin demonstrated how a universal theory of sovereignty forces theorists into conceiving federal systems in terms of a rigid dichotomy between federation and confederation. The United States and Switzerland, however, posed difficulties. Austin was forced to admit that in a composite state the '*one* sovereign body ... is not conspicuous and easily perceived'. For neither the 'common or general government',

---

[126] Austin, *Province of Jurisprudence*, 210–11.     [127] *Ibid.*, 245.

[128] *Ibid.*, 245–6. Dicey would echo the idea of a sovereign 'incapable of legal limitation': Dicey, *Law of the Constitution*, 37–67, 82–6; putting aside 'non–legal' limitations: 73–82.

nor any of the 'several governments' is 'sovereign or supreme'. Austin's solution was that 'the several united governments ... and the general government ... [as one aggregate body] ... are *jointly sovereign* ... [according to] the joint pleasure of a majority of their number, agreeably to the mode or forms determined by their federal compact'.[129] This may have been accurate, but it was also clumsy and forced.

Dicey differed from Austin in his analysis of federalism largely because he was not firmly committed to a universal theory of sovereignty. Dicey could therefore write of the distribution of 'limited ... authority among bodies each co-ordinate with and independent of the other' and could draw attention to the pre-existence of 'independent' states and the integrative, 'compactual' origin of federations.[130] Yet a conception of 'sovereignty' emerged in his definition of federalism. In federations, he said, 'the ordinary powers of sovereignty are elaborately divided', so that the federal and state governments are 'subordinate' to a supreme constitution.[131] The controlling idea here remained that of sovereignty and its corollary, subordination. It was this concept that led Dicey to define federalism by reference to the division of powers, a supreme constitution and judicial review.

Dicey therefore bequeathed a mixed inheritance to his readers. Australian nationalists cited him against equal representation of the states in the Senate, but others could find in Dicey a recognition of the compactual origins of federal systems.[132]

## John Burgess

If Dicey's approach to federalism contained both nationalist and compactual elements, John William Burgess's approach was exclusively and rigorously nationalist.[133] Burgess was Professor of Political Science and Constitutional Law at Columbia University between 1876 and 1912. His most important book, *Political Science and Comparative Constitutional*

[129] Austin, *Province of Jurisprudence*, 246–7, 249, emphasis added. See, likewise, William Edward Hearn, *The Theory of Legal Duties and Rights: An Introduction to Analytical Jurisprudence* (Melbourne: Government Printer, 1883), 36–7. Isaac Isaacs, Henry Bournes Higgins and Alfred Deakin were taught by Hearn at the University of Melbourne.

[130] Dicey, *Law of the Constitution*, 131–8.    [131] *Ibid.*, 135, 141.

[132] *Convention Debates, Sydney* (1897), 312–13; Moore, *Constitution of the Commonwealth*, 78; Adams and Cunningham, *Swiss Confederation*, 22–4; Baker, *Manual of Reference*, 7.

[133] For background, see Bernard E. Brown, *American Conservatives: The Political Thought of Francis Lieber and John W. Burgess* (New York: Columbia University Press, 1951).

*Law* (1890), had a significant influence in its time, but has since been neglected in studies of the making of the Australian Constitution.[134] Admittedly, his influence in Australia was limited to those who interpreted federalism in strongly nationalist terms, such as the largely dissentient voices of Isaacs and H. B. Higgins, and to a lesser extent, those of Quick and Garran.[135] But despite a narrower span of influence, his views furnished an important counterweight to the more prevalent opinion. His importance lies in the systematic nationalist theory of federalism that he expounded against relatively more compactual approaches.

Burgess's political philosophy was deeply influenced by nineteenth-century German state theory. Prior to his appointment at Columbia, he had studied at Göttingen, Leipzig and Berlin, and some time later he was appointed the first Roosevelt Professor at the University of Berlin. At the foundation of Burgess's political philosophy was the idea of the 'nation' as a 'population of an ethnic unity, inhabiting a territory of a geographic unity'. The nation-state is 'the strongest and most perfect form of modern political organisation', he wrote. Within the context of modern international law, it embodies a balance between the despotism of 'universal empire' and the antagonisms of diverse communities. Internally, it strikes an appropriate balance between central and local government. According to Burgess, '[a]lmost every question concerning governmental system and organization of state' sprang out of the relations of ethnicity, geography and statehood. A coincidence of ethnicity and geography indicates that a simple consolidated state is appropriate; federalism is usually indicated where there is ethnic variety.[136]

---

[134] John W. Burgess, *Political Science and Comparative Constitutional Law*, 2 vols. (Boston: Ginn and Co., 1890). See also John W. Burgess, 'The Ideal American Commonwealth' (1895) 10 *Political Science Quarterly* 404.

[135] Westel Woodbury Willoughby, *An Examination of the Nature of the State: A Study in Political Philosophy* (New York: Macmillan, 1896) and Woodrow Wilson, *The State: Elements of Historical and Practical Politics* (Boston: Heath, 1898), were cited to similar effect. See *Convention Debates, Adelaide* (1897), 181, 698, 1022 (Isaacs); *Convention Debates, Sydney* (1897), 306–9, 426, (Isaacs), 433 (O'Connor's reply), 862 (Isaacs), 913 (Glynn's reply); Henry Bournes Higgins, *Essays and Addresses on the Australian Commonwealth Bill* (Melbourne: Atlas Press, 1900), 73; Quick and Garran, *Annotated Constitution*, 325, 333–4; Moore, *Constitution of the Commonwealth*, 68, 598.

[136] Burgess, *Political Science*, I, 1–2, 21, 38–9. A number of his definitions, such as those of 'ethnicity' and 'geography', were slightly unusual, but a precise exposition is not necessary to the present discussion. Burgess defended a policy of ethnic homogeneity and Teutonic domination: *ibid.*, I, 42–8.

Repeating arguments of Jean Bodin, Thomas Hobbes and Georg Hegel, Burgess further maintained that the state is an all-comprehensive, exclusive and sovereign organisation. It embraces 'all persons, natural or legal, and all associations of persons'. It does not recognise any *imperium in imperio*, for it possesses 'original, absolute, unlimited, universal power' over all individuals and associations within its territory. In its highest form, the democratic state is 'the people in political organization', the 'citizens in sovereign organization', democratically embodied in 'the sovereignty of the majority'. The state creates its government, said Burgess, under a constitution, but the state is not itself subject to a constitution, for the state is necessarily sovereign in essence and unitary in form. Accordingly, a state may 'constitute two or more governments', but there cannot be two organisations of the state within the same territory. A 'confederation', therefore, is in essence a union of sovereign states created by treaty, whereas a 'federation' is a 'dual system of government under a common sovereignty'. Burgess recognised that such federations are usually 'previously divided into several independent states', which agree to form a kind of unified state. But, following Georg Jellinek, he held that the process by which federations come into being – as distinct from confederations – inevitably involves a revolutionary transfer of sovereignty from many states to a unitary state. Consequently, while the new sovereign state may allow a residue of powers to the old governments, it will necessarily retain the capacity to make further alterations in that distribution of power.[137]

Sovereignty was therefore as central to Burgess's theory of federalism as it had been for Austin. The idea of the necessarily sovereign state controlled the way in which he defined and understood the relationships between the formation of federal constitutions, the governing institutions adopted thereunder and the amendment of such constitutions. According to Burgess, these referred respectively to 'the revolutionary organization of the state back of the constitution', 'the government created in the constitution' and 'the organization of the state within the constitution'. Drawing a distinction between the constitutional law of a state and the

---

[137] *Ibid.*, I, 51–5, 57–8, 72–6, 79–80 (criticising Bluntschli), 88, 101; II, 4–9, 184. Burgess drew extensively on Jellinek, Bluntschli and other European authors, but differed from Bluntschli in firmly adhering to the indivisible sovereignty of the unitary nation-state: I, 74–82. Georg Jellinek's relevant works included *Die Lehre von den Staatenverbindungen* (Vienna: Alfred Holder, 1882) and *Allgemeine Staatslehre* (1st edn, Berlin: O. Häring, 1900).

'historical and revolutionary forces' which usually underlay its formation, Burgess held that the formal amending process could always be bypassed by an appeal to the 'revolutionary organization of the state'. Given his dogmatic insistence on a revolutionary transformation from a multiplicity of sovereigns to a unitary sovereignty, he could not, however, admit the connections between formative bases, governmental structures and amending formulas that the less dogmatic Bryce and Freeman had identified.[138]

For Burgess, the American Constitution had been formed through a revolutionary repudiation of the Articles of Confederation effected by the entire people of the United States, organised in the Philadelphia Convention. Burgess argued that this gave effect to the political principle that 'the undoubted majority of the political people of any natural political unity possess the sovereign constituting power, and may ... act for the whole people'. But he could not, as a consequence, explain the governmental structures or amending processes provided for by the Constitution. Under the American Constitution, the Senate is composed of an equal number of senators for each state; the amending formula requires the support of two-thirds of both houses and three-fourths of conventions in the several states, and it prevents amendments to the representation of the states in the Senate without their individual consent. In the face of these institutional details, Burgess had to concede that 'we become confused ... as to whether the sovereignty is in the United States or in the commonwealths [i.e. the several states]'. As for Austin, the premise of an undivided, unitary sovereignty brought about this dilemma; the conclusion that the people as a whole were sovereign was more dogmatic than scientific. Glaring anomalies, such as the Senate and the amending formula, had therefore to be dismissed as 'relic[s] of confederatism', and undemocratic 'error[s]'.[139] Nor could Burgess's national principle account for the fact that separate ratifying conventions were held in each of the states.[140] Features such as these made no sense because Burgess radically rejected the idea of federation as a kind of 'Commonwealth of commonwealths'. As such, in a later article cited by

---

[138] *Ibid.*, I, 101–8.
[139] *Ibid.*, I, 90, 107, 142–5, 151–4; II, 49, 115. The latter explanation was cited in Quick and Garran, *Annotated Constitution*, 415–16.
[140] Burgess, *Political Science*, I, 106. See, likewise, I, 109–24, 155–67; II, 78–81.

Isaacs to this effect, Burgess conceded the compactual standpoint that the Constitution rested on its ratification by the peoples of the several states, but argued that the national interpretation was ultimately vindicated by the military imposition of reconstruction amendments after the civil war.[141]

Unlike Madison's careful, empirical analysis, Burgess's scheme could not account for the formative basis and amending procedures of federations. It was difficult to identify any 'unitary sovereignty' in the formative process, or in the representative structures and amending formula actually adopted. Nevertheless, Burgess's nationalist theory deeply influenced Australians such as Isaacs, Quick and Garran. If Dicey's contribution to the nationalist argument was the idea of a 'division of powers', Burgess's contribution was rigorously to apply nationalist theory to the formative processes, representative institutions and amendment procedures of federations. His theory was, therefore, an important nationalist counterpoint to the mediating position adopted by most of the framers of the Australian Constitution. Indeed, it was the integrative nature of Australian federation that made it difficult for the proponents of Burgess's theory to have much influence on the terms of the Australian Constitution. Burgess had argued that a federation was formed through the assertion of sovereignty by the people of the entire nation. It was, however, the voters of the several Australian colonies who in fact 'ratified' the Australian Constitution, and this formative context enabled them and their elected representatives to insist on a Constitution that defied analysis in Burgess's terms. A majority of the Australians, as will be seen, opted for Bryce's 'Commonwealth of commonwealths' over Burgess's unitary conception of the 'federal state'.

---

[141] Burgess, 'Ideal American Commonwealth', 418; *Convention Debates, Sydney* (1897), 306–9.

# 4

## Australian appropriations

[T]he word 'federal' is applied to the composite state, or political community, formed by a federal union of States. It thus describes, not the bond of union between the federating States, but the new State resulting from that bond. It implies that the union has created a new State, without destroying the old States; that the duality is in the essence of the State itself that there is a divided sovereignty, and a double citizenship. This is the sense in which Freeman, Dicey and Bryce speak of a 'Federal State'; and it is the sense in which the phrase 'a Federal Commonwealth' is used in [the Australian Constitution].

John Quick and Robert Garran (1901)

Five key 'authorities' on federalism – James Madison, James Bryce, Edward Freeman, A. V. Dicey and John Burgess – transmitted unique understandings of federalism to their readers, Australian and otherwise. And yet every reader brings to a text his or her own concerns, questions, assumptions and values. How, in particular, did the Australians read these writers? What lessons did they think they had learned, and what did these lessons mean for the federation of the Australian colonies in the late nineteenth century?

Only a relatively small number of Australians – the delegates to the federal conference and conventions of the 1890s – had a direct say concerning the specific content of the Australian Constitution. It can be said with some justification that there were at least as many Australian interpretations of federalism as there were framers of the Australian Constitution. Each participant in the conventions of the 1890s brought to the debate his own conceptions of federalism and of the kind of federation that should be adopted by the Australian colonies. Moreover, although the delegates to the conventions were directly elected or else appointed by popularly elected assemblies in each of the colonies, outside the conventions there was an even broader range of views on the question. And yet – such is the nature of political theory – this stunning diversity of opinion, particularly on matters of specific detail, none the less tended to congeal around a relatively definite set of general perspectives.

An adequate appreciation of the full texture and diversity of the Australian convention debates can best be grasped through personal reading of the debates themselves. In the chapters that follow it is hoped that some sense of this diversity will be conveyed. But for the moment anticipating the results of that account, this chapter will focus on the writings of a select group. For, as the chapters which follow are intended to demonstrate, the full range of approaches to federalism adopted by the Australian framers are well represented by ten leading figures – Andrew Inglis Clark, Samuel Griffith, Richard Baker, Edmund Barton, John Quick, Robert Garran, Charles Kingston, Alfred Deakin, Isaac Isaacs and H. B. Higgins. These individuals relied on the various approaches to federalism canvassed in the previous chapter, they contributed significantly to the Australian debate, and their writings and speeches are significant both as statements of their own views and as influences on others. This does not mean that there were not other delegates of equal standing or of similar influence. What is meant is that the finite number of general perspectives around which the debate tended to consolidate are well represented in the contributions of these particular individuals. As will be seen, not all of these figures were entirely successful in having their views embodied in the Constitution. The process of federating necessarily called for discussion, debate and, at times, heated disagreement. Sometimes differences were resolved by compromise, at other times a majority simply imposed their views on a minority. On some important issues, a kind of synthesis emerged, on others the views of the majority simply prevailed. But to appreciate these processes of compromise and deliberation, it is first necessary to understand the intellectual context in which the debates occurred.

Among this select group of Australian framers, Baker, Just, Quick and Garran wrote 'handbooks' of reference specifically for the edification of delegates to the conventions of 1891 and 1897–8; Clark and Kingston prepared draft constitutions; Baker, Griffith, Kingston and Higgins wrote short monographs addressing many of the key issues; and Clark, Quick and Garran soon thereafter published important commentaries on the constitution. In order to place the convention debates in their proper intellectual context, therefore, in this chapter a selection of documents produced by these individuals will be surveyed in order to identify the way in which the various available models and interpretations of federalism were appropriated by the Australian framers. Each of the documents surveyed was specifically formulated to help prepare, and influence, the delegates to the federal conventions of the 1890s. Space precludes a detailed discussion of a number of other important Australian writings,[1] but, as successive chapters will demonstrate, the particular works addressed are sufficiently representative to provide a fair survey of the principal influences and perspectives that ultimately shaped the terms and structure of the Constitution.

## Thomas Just

One of the most important studies of federalism written specifically for the edification of delegates to the federal convention of 1891 was Thomas Just's *Leading Facts connected with Federation* (1891). It is likely that Just compiled this work on the instructions of the influential Tasmanian Attorney-General, Andrew Inglis Clark,[2] so the arguments advanced and the sources reproduced by Just are of utmost significance.

*Leading Facts* was in the first place descriptive and empirical. Just provided his readers with an extended description of the United States Constitution, together with shorter descriptions of the constitutional systems of Canada, Switzerland, Mexico and the Leeward Islands. He drew on a wide variety of materials, including official dispatches, reports, statistics, statutes, conference proceedings and extracts from newspaper articles, scholarly journals and books. He also provided an extensive bibliography in which most of the crucial authors appeared, including Bryce, Dicey, Freeman, Adams and Cunningham, Poore, Bancroft, Fiske, Smith and Todd.[3] But *Leading Facts* was not only descriptive. It contained a variety of statements of both political principle and practical necessity, and the extracts that it reproduced were organised in a way that

---

[1] Other relevant contemporary writings include Cockburn, *Australian Federation*; Alfred Deakin, *The Federal Story: The Inner History of the Federal Cause* (Melbourne: Melbourne University Press, 1944); Moore, *Constitution of the Commonwealth*; Howard Willoughby, *Australian Federation: Its Aims and Its Possibilities: With a Digest of the Proposed Constitution, Official Statistics, and a Review of the National Convention* (Melbourne: Sands and McDougall, 1891); Bernhard Ringrose Wise, *The Commonwealth of Australia* (London: Isaac Pitman, 1909); Wise, *The Making of the Australian Commonwealth 1889–1890: A Stage in the Growth of Empire* (London: Longmans, Green and Co., 1913).
[2] La Nauze, *Making of the Constitution*, 23.     [3] Just, *Leading Facts*, 83–103, 110–14.

was apparently calculated to guide the reader in a certain direction. Most conspicuous among these were a number of extracts from the *Federalist Papers*. In Just's presentation, these extracts seemed to provide appropriate guidance on almost all important issues relating to Australian federation, apparently on the premise that 'the Constitution of the United States was framed under similar circumstances to those which should mark the formation of the Constitution of United Australasia'.[4]

This was a remarkable claim for Just to make, given that the Australian colonies were still subject to imperial sovereignty. That republican implications may indeed have been intended is suggested by Just's reproduction of the arguments of the Rev. Dr John Dunmore Lang, head of the Presbyterian College in Sydney and a member of the New South Wales Parliament. Lang – whom Charles Duffy said had 'reared a generation of students destined to become public men' – fervently believed that the Australian colonies should be accorded 'complete independence' as 'separate and independent communities' under 'the law of nature and the ordinance of God'. As presented by Just, Lang particularly derived inspiration from the 'American Union as exemplified in the New England States', a system under which the states enjoyed 'complete independence; that is, the entire control of all matters affecting their interests, as men and as citizens, in every possible way'. Lang urged that the Australian colonies should 'combine' into a similar form of federation in order to secure a greater 'weight or influence in the family of nations'. He further desired that the constituent states not merely retain a 'municipal independence' in 'little matters', but should actively secure 'the entire control of all matters affecting their interests'.[5]

Just was centrally concerned to explain how the American example could instruct Australians, and he did so by posing three important questions. These questions were: (1) 'How [should] the question [of federation] ... be approached?' (2) What are the possible 'modes of federation'? (3) What is the true 'character of the American Constitution'? In addressing these questions, Just sought to integrate the leading ideas of the *Federalist Papers* with current discussions about federalism within the

---

[4] *Ibid.*, 33. On Just's use of *The Federalist*, see *ibid.*, 33–4, 37–8, 44, 49–57.

[5] *Ibid.*, 35–7, reproducing John Dunmore Lang, *The Coming Event, or Freedom and Independence for the Seven United Provinces of Australia* (Sydney: J. L. Sherriff, 1870). See also Charles Gavan Duffy, *My Life in Two Hemispheres* (London: Fisher Unwin, 1898), 145–7; Quick and Garran, *Annotated Constitution*, 92.

Australian colonies. In so doing, he introduced his Australian readers to the views of Montesquieu, Hamilton, Jay and Madison, and sought to show how their perspectives could be applied to Australian conditions.

Commencing with Hamilton's *Federalist* no. 1 and Jay's *Federalist* nos. 2 and 4, Just underscored the advantages of 'one strong government' that was able to 'move on uniform principles of policy' and to 'harmonise, assimilate, and protect the several parts and members' of a federal commonwealth, extending 'the benefits of its foresight and precautions to each'. According to Just, the need for a government of such 'efficiency' and 'rigour' arose from the fact that inter-colonial negotiations and arrangements in Australia had frequently broken down in the face of the requirement that decisions be made unanimously and executed separately in each colony. Reproducing papers by William Foster, Agent-General for New South Wales, and a reply published by the *Sydney Morning Herald*, Just presented an analysis of the decision-making rules that had led to this problem, and proposed an alternative set of rules that would prevail under a more rigorous and efficient federal government.

Fearing excessive centralisation, Foster had been concerned that if majority voting was adopted at a federal level 'the interests and feelings of remote and insignificant portions of the [proposed] Federation' would be 'sacrificed to those of the dominant majority'. The *Herald* replied that federation rested on an 'agreement among a group of coterminous Colonies'; and that questions of '*common* concern' would be addressed by '*joint* action', while 'purely local matters' would remain 'exclusively under the jurisdiction of the Colonial Legislatures'. Moreover, the *Herald* argued, inter-colonial conferences had failed because 'the minority ... are not bound by the decisions of the majority' and the 'decisions of the majority are not binding on their respective legislatures'. In the same way, federation would fail unless majority vote was adopted 'in matters of common concern.' In short, the 'almost hopeless condition of unanimity' must, under federation, be replaced by 'majority'.[6]

Putting these points together, Just apparently sought to show that it was necessary to have a strong federal government in which the will of the majority prevailed, but that such a government must first be formed with the consent of each of the several colonies as independent bodies politic. As the *Herald* had maintained, a federation comes into being by unanimous

---

[6] Just, *Leading Facts*, 34, 38–41.

agreement of the constituent bodies politic, and they agree to confer limited functions on a central government that makes its decisions by majority rule, but with the remainder of their constituent powers retained.

In support of this conclusion, Just next reproduced Montesquieu's classic definition of the 'Confederate Republic', together with Hamilton's famous exposition of that definition in *Federalist* no. 9. As noted in the previous chapter, in Montesquieu's day conventional political reflection suggested that large, territorial monarchies had the advantage of external security, but they also suffered the internal disadvantage of a tendency to despotism, whereas small republics had the advantage of a virtuous citizenry actively participating in the government, but suffered the external disadvantage of susceptibility to assimilation by larger powers. Montesquieu suggested, however, that the advantages of each might be secured in what he called the confederate republic, a 'state' composed of 'states'.[7]

As has been seen, Hamilton followed Montesquieu in proposing that a 'Confederate Republic' or 'Federal Government' is best understood as 'an assemblage of societies' or 'an association of two or more States into one State'. So long, Hamilton maintained, that the 'separate organisation of the members be not abolished', but rather existed 'by a constitutional necessity for local purposes', then, despite their 'subordination' to an additional 'general authority' or national government created for specific purposes, the scheme remained 'an Association of States or a Confederacy'. Indeed, Hamilton pointed out, the proposed United States Constitution treated the states as 'constituent parts' of the union, allowing them 'direct representation in the Senate' and leaving them with 'certain exclusive and very important portions of the sovereign power'.[8] In this way, Thomas Just used Montesquieu and Hamilton to present the idea that a federation is essentially an 'assembly of States' which is at the same time itself a 'State', and in which the several states are constituent members, entitled to separate representation in the institutions of the federal government and an exclusive sphere of 'sovereign' power over their own internal affairs.[9]

---

[7] Montesquieu, *Spirit of Laws*, as reproduced in Just, *Leading Facts*, 37.

[8] Hamilton, *Federalist* no. 9, as reproduced in Just, *Leading Facts*, 37.

[9] As noted in ch. 3, despite Hamilton's personal preference for a fully consolidated national government, he was at pains in the *Federalist Papers* to present the distinctively federal features of the proposed Constitution so as to avoid the criticisms of antifederalists that the Constitution was not genuinely 'federal'. That Hamilton was in fact opposed to equality of representation for the states was not apparent from the way in which Just presented his arguments.

Just then turned to Madison's description of the true 'character of the American Constitution' in *Federalist* no. 39.[10] Here Just was careful to reproduce Madison's analysis of the Constitution into its five essential components, these being the formative basis of the federation, the system of representation, the scope of federal power, the execution of federal power and the provision for constitutional amendment.[11] Just then made clear through his explanation of Madison's views that Madison had identified both 'national' and 'federal' characteristics in these aspects of the American system and had concluded that the proposed constitution was best understood as 'a composition of both'.[12] Notably, however, Just only decided to reproduce Madison's analysis of the formative basis of the proposed constitution – that a 'federal' system arises when several 'distinct and independent States' 'unanimously assent' to a proposed union.[13] The lesson for the readers of Just's *Leading Facts*, it seems, was that a federation of the Australian colonies ought to proceed likewise. It is therefore noticeable that a number of Australians would later cite Hamilton and Madison on the American 'compromise' between 'pure federation' and 'national union', using their writings to support equal representation in the Senate and representation in proportion to population in the House as appropriate to what Joseph Story had called 'a compound republic'.[14]

In the remainder of *Leading Facts*, Just included a brief sketch of the events which led to the formation of each of the American state and federal constitutions. For example, he described the representative structure of the federal government and the use of counties as the basis of apportionment of electoral districts. He also reproduced opinions concerning the appropriate powers to be 'transferred to the Federal Parliament from the Colonial Legislatures'.[15] The American model, interpreted in the light of Madison's no. 39, thus loomed large in Thomas Just's analysis.[16] It is likely that Just's book set forth the basic perspective from which Andrew Inglis Clark prepared a draft constitution for the federal convention of 1891.

---

[10] Just, *Leading Facts*, 38.
[11] Madison, *Federalist* no. 39, 243–4, as cited by Just, *Leading Facts*, 38.    [12] *Ibid.*    [13] *Ibid.*
[14] Story, *Commentaries*, I, 518–19. See e.g. Quick and Garran, *Annotated Constitution*, 336–40; *Convention Debates, Adelaide* (1897), 171 (Isaacs), *Convention Debates, Sydney* (1897), 325–6 (Wise), 340 (Barton). For further discussion, see Erling M. Hunt, *American Precedents in Australian Federation* (New York: AMS Press, 1963), 108; Warden, *Formation of the Australian Constitution*, 28–33.
[15] Just, *Leading Facts*, 42–4.    [16] *Ibid.*, 58–83.

## Andrew Inglis Clark

Andrew Inglis Clark's draft constitution was one of two such documents prepared specifically for 1891 convention.[17] Although Just's book undoubtedly sheds light on Clark's draft, a confidential memorandum, written by Clark himself at the time, elaborated the reasoning that lay behind the drafting.[18]

Throughout the memorandum, Clark adhered to his well-known preference for the American over the Canadian model of federalism.[19] At the outset, however, he also drew attention to Switzerland, which, he said, 'present[ed] several unique and very instructive features in the purely democratical organisation of society'.[20] Clark pointed out that in contrast to the later Canadian model, the American federation was 'brought about by the voluntary union of thirteen independent communities', and that this made 'inevitable' the scheme by which 'a limited number of specific powers' were 'delegated' to the federal government, while the powers 'not delegated' were 'reserved' to the states and to the people. In Australia, he argued, while the colonies were not 'sovereign', they performed more functions than the American states had done, and so it was most appropriate for the Australians to follow the American scheme, at least in its federal aspects. In particular, what Clark called the 'provinces' were to be equally represented in the Senate, whereas the House of Representatives was to be 'chosen by the people of the provinces strictly on the basis of population'. Specific powers should be delegated to the federal legislature, with all powers not delegated remaining 'vested in the provincial parliaments'. The federal judiciary was, following the American example, made distinct from the provincial judicial systems, but with the 'innovation' of a general appellate jurisdiction to replace the Privy Council. Moreover, unlike the Canadian system, the state governors were to be appointed separately from the federal government, this being 'essential to

---

[17] La Nauze, *Making of the Constitution*, 24. The other draft was prepared by Charles Kingston.

[18] Andrew Inglis Clark, 'Australian Federation (Confidential)' (Hobart: Attorney-General's Office, 1891).

[19] See Neasey, 'Andrew Inglis Clark Senior and Australian Federation'; Reynolds, 'Clark's American Sympathies'; Williams, "With Eyes Open': Andrew Inglis Clark and our Republican Tradition' (1995) 23 *Federal Law Review* 149; Haward and Warden, *Australian Democrat*; Richard Ely (ed.), *A Living Force: Andrew Inglis Clark and the Ideal of Commonwealth* (Hobart: Centre for Tasmanian Historical Studies, University of Tasmania 2001).

[20] Clark, 'Australian Federation', 1.

secure the independence of the provincial governments'. Finally, he explained, the draft constitution presumed a continuance of cabinet government and dependency on the empire, and the Canadian model provided appropriate guidance in these respects.[21]

While Clark considered that the 'dependency' of the Australian colonies on the imperial Crown posed an obstacle to adopting a fully republican system in Australia, he also wondered whether 'the united intelligence of the [forthcoming] Convention [might] be able to suggest some method of meeting the difficulty'.[22] Clark in fact expressed severe reservations about responsible government. In this connection, he favourably discussed the American system, but particularly suggested that the Swiss system of a federal executive council was 'an example which might be followed', quoting Edward Freeman to the effect that the 'negative wisdom' of the Swiss government might be preferable to both the British and American systems.[23]

Clark's draft constitution was in the form of a bill to be passed by the imperial Parliament. The British North America Act therefore presented the most obvious statutory precedent for Clark's draft, but the United States Constitution, as well as the Swiss, provided most of the substantial guidance.[24] Thus, following the Canadian model, the draft bill was expressed to be premised on the 'desire [of the colonies] to be federally united into one Dominion', but in most other respects the draft tended to follow the American example. Limited powers were 'delegated' to the federal government, with all powers not delegated remaining with the provincial parliaments. The Senate consisted of six senators for each 'province', chosen by the provincial parliaments, and the House of Representatives was composed of members 'chosen . . . by the people of the several Provinces, on the basis of their respective populations'. The draft also provided for amendment of the Constitution by the Federal Parliament with the concurrence of two-thirds of the provinces.[25]

As will be seen in subsequent chapters, Clark's draft constitution was used as an essential starting point for the drafting of the Commonwealth Bill that later emerged from the federal convention of 1891, and that this bill in turn had a significant influence upon the drafting of the

---

[21] *Ibid.*, 2–6.    [22] *Ibid.*, 6.    [23] *Ibid.*, 5–7.    [24] *Ibid.*, 1–5.

[25] Andrew Inglis Clark, *A Bill for the Federation of the Australasian Colonies* (1891), (cited as Clark's draft constitution), cls. 18, 29, 93.

Constitution that was eventually approved by the convention of 1897–8 and ultimately given statutory sanction by the imperial Parliament. In his later book, *Australian Constitutional Law* (1901), Clark looked back on the Constitution that had come into being as a result of this process. In this work, Clark elaborated extensively on the nature of federalism and the features of the newly formed Australian Constitution. Dicey had written that in essence 'federalism means legalism and the supremacy of the Judiciary in the Constitution', and Clark seemed to agree. Federalism, Clark wrote, is a system where several 'separately organised communities are embraced in one comprehensive community'. Consequently there is, following Dicey, an elaborate 'division' of legislative and executive power between the comprehensive and component communities.[26] Unlike Dicey, however, Clark did not refer to a division of the 'original powers of sovereignty'. The central question of federalism, Clark asserted, was how to unite a number of separate political societies into a composite society in a manner that preserved the 'collective and corporate life of each State'. The American and Australian solution was to define the boundaries of the two sets of political communities, to create a dual citizenship and, most importantly, to give a majority of the component communities and the majority of the composite community 'concurrent powers of veto' over proposed legislation and proposed constitutional amendments. In Clark's view, therefore, the formative concern to preserve the constituent states led not only to a 'division of powers' between state and federal governments, but also to a system of state and national representation within the federal legislature and a method of constitutional amendment that recognised the constitutive status of the peoples of the component states.[27]

This vision of a 'federal republic' defined by its formative basis, representative institutions, configuration of power and amending processes would decisively shape Clark's direct contribution to the federal convention of 1891 as well as his indirect influence upon the deliberations of

---

[26] Clark, *Australian Constitutional Law*, 3. Clark also here emphasised the judgments of John Marshall, Chief Justice of the US Supreme Court, 1801–35.

[27] Clark, *Australian Constitutional Law*, 4–13, 359, 369–70. The argument was not dissimilar to the compactualist arguments of John C. Calhoun, briefly discussed in ch. 1. Clark even argued that ordinary Commonwealth laws should be passed only with a majority of senators in a majority of states: see Michael Roe, 'The Federation Divide Among Australia's Liberal Idealists: Contexts for Clark' in Haward and Warden, *Australian Democrat*, 95.

the convention of 1897–8. Clark's understanding of federalism would, in this sense, be of critical importance to the Constitution which emerged from that debate.

## Richard Baker

Accompanying Just's *Leading Facts* and Clark's draft constitution was Richard Chaffey Baker's *Manual of Reference*, specifically written for the 1891 convention, later followed by Baker's *Federation* and *The Executive in a Federation*, both written for the 1897–8 convention.[28] Baker was a conservative member of the Legislative Council of South Australia and an important delegate at both federal conventions; he would also be the first president of the Australian Senate.

Baker's stated objective in the *Manual of Reference* was to seek guidance 'from the study of existing Federal Constitutions and their working', by undertaking a comparison of the American, Canadian, Swiss and South African constitutions. The *Manual* accordingly included schedules containing the Quebec Resolutions, the Canadian Constitution, the American Constitution and the South African Union Act 1877. Baker's schedule of books cited indicates the sources upon which he drew and to which he directed his fellow delegates. They included many of the now familiar names, such as Adams and Cunningham, Bagehot, Bluntschli, Bourinot, Bryce, Dicey, Freeman, Smith, Hamilton, Madison, Jay, Kent, Montesquieu, Story, Tocqueville and Webster.[29]

Although the *Manual* was professedly intended only to provide information and reference to relevant authorities, its choice of references and its organisation provide an insight into the structure of Baker's reasoning about federalism. In particular, it is noticeable that he began with the 'mode of formation' of the four constitutions; he next considered the organisation of the executive and legislature, then the allocation of powers, and finally the ratification of the constitution and the use of referendums. The similarity to Madison's analytical scheme and the

---

[28] See La Nauze, *Making of the Constitution*, 23; Mark McKenna, 'Sir Richard Chaffey Baker – the Senate's First Republican', *The Constitution Makers, Papers on Parliament* no. 30 (Canberra: Department of the Senate, 1997); R. van den Hoorn, 'Richard Chaffey Baker: A South Australian Conservative and the Federal Conventions of 1891 and 1897–8' (1980) 7 *Journal of the Historical Society of South Australia* 24.

[29] Baker, *Manual of Reference*, 7–8.

structure of the American Constitution, as well as to Thomas Just's *Leading Facts*, is notable. This structure apparently shaped Baker's ultimate conclusions, although he expressed a number of views in the *Manual* that he would later modify.

Baker rejected John C. Calhoun's theory that the United States Constitution was 'a compact to which the States were parties in their sovereign capacities', and appeared rather to favour Daniel Webster's argument that the Constitution derived from 'the people of the United States'.[30] However, Baker also recounted the ratification of the American, Swiss and Canadian constitutions in a way that showed that their endorsement had been secured on a 'state-by-state' basis, contrary to Webster's contention and more in accord with Madison's analysis.[31] Baker also rejected Walter Bagehot's arguments against co-equal houses in a federal legislature, citing James Kent to the effect that the American Senate involved the recognition of the 'separate and independent existence' of the states.[32] At this early stage, Baker also favoured responsible government,[33] but he would soon conclude that the consolidating tendencies of responsible government were inconsistent with equality of representation of the states in a powerful Senate.[34]

Baker's overriding objective was that the 'powers of self-government' enjoyed by 'the Australian people' be 'increased', and that the exercise of those powers 'be delegated partly to a National or Federal Government and partly to the present Provincial Governments'.[35] As such, local self-government, state independence and state equality – expressed in the formative basis, representative structures and amending formula of the constitutions under discussion – emerged as key principles in Baker's argument. The representation of the people of the nation in the House of Representatives and the equal representation of the people 'as citizens of the States' in a Senate of 'at least co-equal power' were, he said, of 'the very essence' of federation.[36]

Baker also demonstrated knowledge of German *Staatslehre* (state theory) as it related to federalism. It is most significant in this respect that Baker adopted Johann Bluntschli's distinction between federation and

[30] *Ibid.*, 26; cf. Baker, *Federation*, 12.    [31] Baker, *Manual of Reference*, ch. 17.
[32] *Ibid.*, 59–66, citing Kent, *Commentaries*, I, 234.    [33] *Ibid.*, 43–6.
[34] *Ibid.*, preface of 1 May 1891 (entitled 'First Preface', apparently incorrectly).
[35] *Ibid.*, 33; Baker, *Federation*, 3.    [36] Baker, *Federation*, 3–5, 10, 19.

confederation on the basis that in the former there is direct central executive authority over individuals, and not on the basis of whether sovereignty is located within the nation or the states, as Georg Jellinek had done.[37] This enabled Baker to avoid the problem of identifying an ultimate locus of 'sovereignty' within the proposed Australian federation, and therefore to avoid ascribing sovereignty to either the nation or the states. Griffith, as will be seen, adopted a similar course. Griffith, Baker and Clark, despite their differences on a number of points of detail, were largely of one mind on this issue.

If Clark had asked whether there might be some way of adapting the conciliar federal executive of Switzerland to Australian circumstances, Baker's *Executive in a Federation* sought to provide an answer to this question. In this work, written during the convention of 1897–8, Baker explained why he now favoured a federalised executive council on the Swiss model and sought to show how it might be adopted in Australia.[38] The 'true line of federation', he argued, is an 'equilibrium' between 'centralisation and decentralisation'. This equilibrium was maintained, he said, in the United States and Switzerland, but was distorted by a 'strong national force' in Canada and by a 'strong local force' in Germany.[39] Baker was therefore critical of the draft constitution that had emerged from the convention of 1891 and again seemed to be materialising in 1897–8 because, while it maintained an appropriate 'equilibrium' as regards the federal legislature, the notion of executive responsibility to only the House of Representatives was a 'radical defect'.

Following James Bryce and Alpheus Todd, Baker was critical of responsible government for its consolidating tendencies as well as the American separation of powers for its tendency to disintegrate government and thus weaken governmental responsibility. Baker argued, on the contrary, that an executive chosen by both houses of the legislature would embody the strengths and avoid the weaknesses of the American and the

---

[37] Baker, *Manual of Reference*, 31, citing Bluntschli, *Theory of the State*. Griffith, *Notes on Australian Federation*, 5, also adopted Bluntschli's approach.

[38] Baker, *Executive in a Federation*, 3, 11. Adams and Cunningham, *Swiss Confederation*, 273–4, had praised the Swiss executive system. See also Baker, *Federation*, 19.

[39] Baker, *Executive in a Federation*, 5–8. In the late nineteenth century the formally centralist features of the Canadian Constitution seemed to outweigh the inherently pluralistic nature of Canadian society and the emergent interpretations of the Privy Council that were enhancing the independence and powers of the Canadian provinces *vis-à-vis* the Dominion.

British systems respectively.[40] In this connection, he also favoured election of the Senate in the manner decided by each state legislature in order to place some constraint on the gradual accretion of federal power that would be likely under a system of direct election, but he accepted that the direct election of senators by the people of each state would be 'consistent' with 'true Federation'.[41]

As will be seen, while Baker was not ultimately successful on this point,[42] his forceful arguments ensured that the more extreme nationalist views of other delegates did not prevail either. While in principle the convention finally came down on the side of responsible government, the hesitations of a substantial minority of the framers produced the compromise over the powers of the Senate contained in section 53 of the Constitution.[43]

## Samuel Griffith

The important role of Samuel Walker Griffith in the drafting of the Australian Constitution is well known. A former premier of Queensland and later Chief Justice of that state, Griffith was a principal member of the Constitutional Committee at the federal convention of 1891 and led a drafting committee which included Clark, Kingston and later Barton.[44] Under Griffith's leadership, the drafting committee prepared the bill that was ultimately debated, amended and approved by the convention.[45] While his position as Chief Justice in Queensland, as well as the fact that Queensland was not represented at all at the federal convention of 1897–8, precluded a direct part in the latter convention, he played a highly significant and influential role as an adviser and commentator, particularly

[40] *Ibid.*, 12, 17–19, citing Bryce, *American Commonwealth*, I, 155–60 and Alpheus Todd, *Parliamentary Government in the British Colonies* (London: Longmans, Green and Co., 1880).

[41] Baker, *Federation*, 17–18.

[42] *Convention Debates, Sydney* (1891), 439–40, 465–6; *Convention Debates, Adelaide* (1897), 28–31.

[43] See *Convention Debates, Adelaide* (1897), 66, 146–8, 184–5, 193–5, 211, 213–14, 247, 307, 315, 324, 330, 334, 345.

[44] *Convention Debates, Sydney* (1891), 509–10; La Nauze, *Making of the Constitution*, 337, n. 21.

[45] See Samuel Walker Griffith, *Successive Stages of the Constitution of the Commonwealth of Australia* [1891] (Griffith Papers, MS Q198, CY 221); Roger B. Joyce, *Samuel Walker Griffith* (Brisbane: University of Queensland Press, 1984), ch. 8; La Nauze, *Making of the Constitution*, 45–70. On the importance of the bill and the merits of those who drafted it, see Geoffrey Sawer, *Australian Federalism in the Courts* (Melbourne: Melbourne University Press, 1967), 10–12. On the role of Clark's draft constitution, see Reynolds, 'Clark's American Sympathies'.

in relation to the Constitution Bill of 1898.[46] Griffith's standing as one of the leading constitutional lawyers in Australia at federation led to his appointment as the first Chief Justice of the High Court of Australia upon its establishment in 1903.

Griffith's intellectual influence was particularly mediated, first, through his role in the federation conference in Melbourne in 1890, second, through his leadership in the federal convention of 1891, and third, through four important later publications, *Some Conditions of Australian Federation* (1896), *Notes on Australian Federation* (1896), *Notes on the Draft Federal Constitution* (1897) and *Australian Federation and the Draft Commonwealth Bill* (1899). These later writings particularly help to show how Griffith drew upon existing ideas about federalism and adapted them for his own purposes in the context of the debate over Australian federation.

At the federation conference in Melbourne in 1890,[47] Griffith observed that the Australian colonies had been 'accustomed for so long to self-government that we have become practically almost sovereign states, a great deal more sovereign states, though not in name, than the separate states of America'.[48] This remarkable statement lay at the heart of Griffith's vision of Australian federalism. It was a proposition pregnant with a variety of implications. On the one hand, it implied a practical, institutional constraint on Australian federation: the individual colonies would seek to preserve the constitutional status to which they had become 'accustomed'. But, on the other hand, the proposition also suggested a normative presupposition: that the Australian colonies were entitled to 'self-government', to 'sovereignty' and to 'separateness'. As Griffith continued:

> We have been allowed absolute freedom to manage our own affairs; and I know that there are many people who, although they are favourable to the idea of federation in the abstract, would yet hesitate to give up any of those rights which we have been in the habit of exercising.[49]

The difficulties that Griffith foresaw in the way of Australian federation were in the first place therefore practical ones; and they were difficulties

---

[46] See Joyce, *Samuel Walker Griffith*, 204–15; Reynolds, 'Clark's American Sympathies', 66; La Nauze, *Making of the Constitution*, 130–1, 168–70, 248, 267–8.
[47] See ch. 5.    [48] *Conference Debates, Melbourne* (1890), 10.    [49] *Ibid.*, 10.

that would emerge when the delegates returned to their respective parliaments. As Griffith put it:

> Some members of the Conference believe that a perfect Federation is possible now, others that it is not practicable, and they may feel it their duty to point out the difficulties. And those difficulties will have to be met. We cannot shut our eyes to them, and they will be the real difficulties that will meet us when we go to our respective Parliaments . . .[50]

The colonial legislatures were the representative institutions through which the colonies exercised powers of local self-government. Local politicians would have to be convinced to give up some of their powers, and their constituents could be expected to prefer to be ruled by governments 'in sight of the people'. As Griffith pointed out, Australian federation would ultimately turn, not on the opinions of the delegates, but on 'public opinion in the different colonies at the present time'. The question, therefore, was whether the different colonies would 'through their legislatures, permit such a federation as we may deem desirable'. As he further pointed out, 'it is no use for us to pass abstract resolutions here, or any resolutions, unless effect will be given to them by our respective legislatures'.[51] The practical task, therefore, was:

> to exchange ideas, and to consider, as practical men, how far we can go with any hope of success in asking the legislatures from which we come to entrust powers to a convention to frame a Federal Constitution.[52]

Notwithstanding this realism, Griffith still had his ideals. What he wanted was a 'complete Federal Government': what he called a 'complete Federal Parliament and Federal Executive, one Dominion with no rivalries', including a separate federal treasury, raised by 'the direct representatives of the people'.[53] For Griffith, this meant 'federation', as distinct from 'confederation'. According to him, a 'confederation' is a 'political association of several States, with a central Government and Legislature', but one in which 'the central authorities have to do with the constituent States only, having no direct relations with, or authority over, the people as individual citizens'. On the other hand, he said, a 'federation' is:

---

[50] *Ibid.*, vi.    [51] *Ibid.*, 8.    [52] *Ibid.*, 8.    [53] *Ibid.*, 8–9.

a political union of several States, which, for certain purposes, and within certain limits, is complete, so that the several States form one larger State with a common Government acting directly upon the individual citizens as to all matters within its jurisdiction, while, beyond those limits, and for all other purposes, the separate States retain complete autonomy.[54]

In thus adopting Bluntschli's definition of federation, Griffith, like Baker, avoided the assumption that the people of the federation as a whole must be 'sovereign'. This in turn left room for the patent fact that an Australian federation would be a union of several separate and autonomous states,[55] a feature common to both federations and confederations. On Griffith's view, what distinguished confederations and federations was whether the (people of) the constituent states agreed to create a federal government having direct executive power over individuals. Apart from this feature, on this approach there is no reason why the people of the states should not seek to have separate representation in the Federal Parliament and a separate voice on questions of constitutional amendment.[56] Moreover, since the origin of the federation lies with the separate states, on this view, the 'distribution' of powers between the states and the federation is likely to be expressed as a 'delegation', 'transfer' or 'surrender' of limited powers to the federal government, rather than as a 'division' of powers between the state and federal governments.[57]

Like Baker and Clark, therefore, the central political value in Griffith's vision of Australian federalism was one of local self-government, by which Griffith meant the self-government of each Australian colony as a separate body politic, and the self-government of the Australian colonies collectively.[58] Since federal power involved 'a corresponding diminution in the powers of the separate Governments and Legislatures', the guiding principle must be to surrender only those powers 'which may be exercised by the Federal Government with greater advantage than the separate

---

[54] Griffith, *Notes on Australian Federation*, 5. That Griffith intended to adopt Bluntschli's approach in this passage was made clear when Griffith later explained that the defining feature of a federation is that it is a 'political union of several autonomous States . . . [that] form a larger state with a common government acting directly on its individual citizens': Samuel Walker Griffith, *Australian Federation and the Draft Commonwealth Bill: A Paper Read before the Members of the Queensland Federation League* (Brisbane: Government Printer, 1899), 8.
[55] Griffith, *Notes on Australian Federation*, 6.    [56] *Ibid.*, 10.    [57] *Ibid.*, 6–7.
[58] See Griffith, *Draft Commonwealth Bill*, 5.

Governments'.[59] Again like Baker and Clark, Griffith 'called attention to the difficulties attendant upon an attempt to impose the present phase of responsible government, which may prove a passing one, upon a federation'. He pointed out that responsible government, at least at a federal level, was still an experiment: if it proves to work well 'it will last, and if it is not good it ought to be modified'. It should not be 'prescribed for all time'. By contrast, equality of representation in a powerful Senate was a federal imperative which must, he thought, be entrenched. Responsible government might be allowed to operate at the federal level, but the guiding principle must be federalism.[60]

Griffith's contribution to the federal conventions of 1891 and 1897–8 reflected these basic commitments, particularly in relation to the formative process itself, the representative structures to be adopted under the federal Constitution, the relationship between the federal executive and the Parliament, the powers of the Senate and the method of amendment of the Constitution.[61] For Griffith the essentials of federation were that the separate states were originally autonomous, that they would agree to surrender only so much of their powers as is necessary,[62] and that they would be equally represented in a Senate having virtually equal power with the House of Representatives.[63] And it was for the legislatures of the several colonies, he said, to determine the precise manner in which the Constitution would be submitted for ratification.[64] Indeed, Griffith argued that the fact that representatives in the convention of 1897–8 were directly elected need not determine the manner in which senators must be elected to the Federal Parliament. Griffith considered that conditions in the various colonies were different – some might call for direct election, but others, such as those in Queensland, might not – so it would be better to leave the issue to the determination of each state parliament. Such issues were 'a matter especially of State concern', he said, and 'true democracy' did not require direct election of senators.[65]

[59] *Conference Debates, Melbourne* (1890), 10.
[60] Samuel Griffith, *Notes on the Draft Federal Constitution Framed by the Adelaide Convention of 1897 (Australian Federal Convention Papers* (1897–8)), 4–5.
[61] See, in particular, *Convention Debates, Sydney* (1891), 31–2.
[62] *Convention Debates, Sydney* (1891), 31–2; cf. Griffith, *Notes on Australian Federation*, 6–7, 10.
[63] *Convention Debates, Sydney* (1891), 31–2.
[64] See Griffith, *Notes on Australian Federation*, 27. Griffith personally favoured 'State conventions', following the American precedent: La Nauze, *Making of the Constitution*, 88.
[65] Griffith, *Notes on the Draft Constitution*, 2; see Griffith, *Notes on Australian Federation*, 9–10.

## John Quick and Robert Garran

John Quick and Robert Garran are best known for their magisterial
*Annotated Constitution of the Australian Commonwealth*, published in
1901. As a commentary on the Constitution, the work was in its day
virtually unrivalled; as a work of scholarship, its influence on subsequent
interpretation has been unparalleled.[66] Part of the reason for the success
of the book is the fact that Quick and Garran were intimate participants
in the debates over the Constitution, particularly in the federal convention of 1897–8. In preparation for that convention, John Quick prepared
a *Digest of Federal Constitutions* in 1896, and in 1897 his younger col-
league, Robert Garran, published *The Coming Commonwealth*.[67] In Quick
and Garran's writings we encounter another vitally important Australian
adaptation of contemporary federal theory to Australian conditions and
aspirations.

Quick's *Digest* and Garran's *Coming Commonwealth* both commence
with an unequivocally Diceyan definition of federalism. According to
both writers, following Dicey, federalism aims to reconcile 'national
unity' with 'state rights', in order to bind 'a group of States into a Nation
without destroying their individuality as States'. This objective is
achieved, they continued (again echoing Dicey), by dividing 'the functions of government and the attributes of sovereignty between a central
national government and a group of local state governments', thus creating a 'two–fold sovereignty . . . within the limits of the same territory'.[68]
As Garran put it, the 'essential characteristics' of federal government are:

> (1) The supremacy of the Federal Constitution. (2) The distribution,
> by the Constitution, of the powers of the Nation and the States
> respectively. (3) The existence of some judicial or other body
> empowered to act as 'guardian' or 'interpreter' of the Constitution.'[69]

---

[66] The *Annotated Constitution* was, it is true, supplemented by Professor W. Harrison Moore's
*The Constitution of the Commonwealth of Australia* (2nd edn, Melbourne: Maxwell, 1910) and
has been matched in more recent years by *The Constitution of the Commonwealth of Australia
Annotated*, first edition by Kevin W. Ryan and R. D. Lumb (Sydney: Butterworths, 1974), as
well as Patrick H. Lane, *Lane's Commentary on the Australian Constitution* (Sydney: Law Book
Co., 1986).

[67] See also John Quick, *Legislative Powers of the Commonwealth and the States of Australia with
Proposed Amendments* (Melbourne: Maxwell, 1919); Garran, *Prosper the Commonwealth*.

[68] Garran, *Coming Commonwealth*, 15–16; cf. Quick, *Digest of Federal Constitutions*, 10–14.

[69] Garran, *Coming Commonwealth*, 23–4.

A system of judicial review is accordingly necessary, Garran thought, against the 'continental' tendency to treat such matters as merely 'administrative'. In the absence of judicial review, 'the superior sanctity of the Constitution is ineffectually guarded' in Switzerland, he concluded.[70]

Quick and Garran's *Annotated Constitution*, while less explicitly Diceyan, continued to reflect the basic ingredients in Dicey's federal theory, including the formative basis of such systems in a federating pact, the theory of national sovereignty and the idea of a division of powers. Combining impressive erudition and a 'sufficiently detached view of the history and drafting' of the Constitution,[71] Quick and Garran authoritatively recounted the making of the Constitution, explaining its key concepts and commenting upon its specific provisions. When discussing topics such as 'The People', 'Federal Commonwealth', 'Commonwealth', 'Sovereignty', 'States' and 'The Constitution', they canvassed a variety of viewpoints, reproducing substantial excerpts from a wide range of learned writers, including Hobbes, Locke, Rousseau, Blackstone, Jefferson, Madison, Wilson, Marshall, Calhoun, Foster, Willoughby, Story, Burgess, Maine, Freeman, Bryce, Bentham, Austin and Dicey.[72] However, as active participants in the debates about the Constitution, their commitments affected their commentary. Thus, while Quick and Garran cited a range of authors, they usually favoured the nationalist interpretations of Dicey and Burgess, and it was only in the face of this bias that their historical account of the making of the Constitution accurately recounted what Madison would have identified as the genuinely 'federal' formative processes by which the Australian federation came into being. The *Annotated Constitution* as a consequence would neatly embody the tension between the strictly compactual and nationalist conceptions of federalism.

Quick and Garran placed the Australian Constitution into the context of the colonies and confederations of history, comparing the city-states of ancient Greece with the various *colonia* of imperial Rome. According to Quick and Garran, the Greek cities were 'autonomous political communities', 'free and sovereign commonwealths' enjoying 'unfettered right[s] of self-government'. And yet, while autonomous in principle, these states

---

[70] *Ibid.*, 80, cf. 15–16, 65–6, 75–6, relying on Dicey, *Law of the Constitution*.

[71] Geoffrey Sawer, 'Foreword', Quick and Garran, *Annotated Constitution*, v.

[72] See Quick and Garran, *Annotated Constitution*, 285–7, 292–4, 311–17, 324–8, 332–42, 368–72, 380–3.

occasionally formed leagues which resembled, they wrote, 'something like' federal unions.[73] Quick and Garran also discussed modern European colonisation. Here they contrasted the 'unspeakable outrages' and 'unutterable ruin' spread by Spanish, Portuguese and French colonisation, with the 'charters of freedom' and germs of 'representative self-government' carried by English colonists, particularly to North America.[74] And yet, consistent with the importance they attached to the sovereignty of the imperial Parliament, Quick and Garran's emphasis was on the charters granted to the colonies. They overlooked the autochthonous covenants by which the American colonists asserted a self-constituting capacity to form independent bodies politic and ecclesiastic.[75]

In one important sense, the underlying tension in Quick and Garran's thought lay between the principles of imperial sovereignty and autonomous self-government.[76] Quick had written that a 'political federation' was a 'permanent union' of 'political communities' that nevertheless preserved their 'local independence, local self-government and internal sovereignty'.[77] Yet, particularly when it came to technical legal analysis, Quick and Garran usually placed the emphasis on the authority of the imperial Parliament and interpreted the Constitution in that light. This was especially the case when they attempted to resolve the second underlying tension in their thought as between compactual and national conceptions of federalism. Quick and Garran's familiarity with the process by which the Australian federation had been formed drew them towards compactualism, while their theoretical commitments drew them towards nationalism. Scholars such as Bryce and Freeman, in their historical orientation, partially reinforced the former tendency, but Dicey and Burgess generally had the decisive influence on Quick and Garran. This is especially seen in their discussion of sovereignty and federalism; it is also reflected in their comments on a number of substantive provisions in the Constitution.

Explicitly following Austin, Dicey and Burgess, Quick and Garran held that a 'clear conception of the meaning of "sovereignty" [was] the key to

---

[73] Quick and Garran, *Annotated Constitution*, 1–5. Quick and Garran would almost certainly have been drawing here on Freeman, *Federal Government*.

[74] Quick and Garran, *Annotated Constitution*, 9–11.

[75] *Ibid.*, 11–18. On the latter, see Lutz, *Colonial Origins*.

[76] See Quick and Garran, *Annotated Constitution*, 300–3, 327–8.

[77] Quick, *Digest of Federal Constitutions*, 10.

all political science', and that 'true political science seem[ed] to point to the conclusion that sovereignty is incapable of legal limitation'. Sovereignty, they wrote, is the 'most essential attribute of a State – that is, of an independent political community'.[78] Burgess had claimed that sovereignty was that 'original, absolute, unlimited, universal power over the individual subject and over all associations of subjects', and Quick and Garran explained that the 'sovereign' in any political community was the 'person, or determinate body of persons' that possessed such power. Following Dicey and Austin, the 'supreme organic unity' or 'ultimate legislative organ' in the United Kingdom was the British Parliament; in the United States it was the body of electors 'organised under the Constitutional provision for the amendment of the Constitution'.[79]

Thus, when discussing the recital in the preamble to the Australian Constitution that the people of the colonies had agreed to unite, Quick and Garran noted that it was the Enabling Acts passed in several of the Australian colonies that in fact provided for the 'popular' process of the referendum held in each colony – features that Madison would have called 'federal' in character. At the same time, however, they traced the idea of the 'sovereignty' of the people to the nationalist interpretation of James Wilson, who had affirmed that 'there is, and of necessity must be, a supreme absolute and uncontrollable authority', and that it resides in 'the people'.[80] Quick and Garran thus elided the problem of harmonising the nationalist conception of sovereignty with the role of the colonial legislatures in setting up referendum processes in each colony.

The amendment process under section 128 of the Australian Constitution (as well as Article V of the US Constitution and Article 78 of the German imperial Constitution of 1871) posed a further problem for the nationalist interpretation. Under these schemes, the representation of a particular state within the federal legislature cannot be altered without that state's specific consent. Can Austinian or Diceyean sovereignty be identified in such a context? As has been seen, Austin engaged in extended verbal gymnastics to identify one, whereas Burgess and Willoughby

---

[78] Quick and Garran, *Annotated Constitution*, 325.

[79] Quick and Garran, *Annotated Constitution*, 324–8, citing Burgess, *Political Science*, I, 51–2; Willoughby, *Nature of the State*, 214; Dicey, *Law of the Constitution*, 66, 137; Henry Sidgwick, *Elements of Politics* (2nd edn, London: Macmillan, 1897), appendix: 'On Austin's Theory of Sovereignty'; John Austin, *Lectures on Jurisprudence* (4th edn, London: John Murray, 1879), I, 253.

[80] Quick and Garran, *Annotated Constitution*, 285–7, 290–2 (incorrectly calling him 'John Wilson').

simply held that any purported limitation on the power of the nation could be disregarded as inconsistent with its sovereignty – and Quick and Garran seemed to agree.[81] However, the tension in their thought was exposed when they then recognised that the 'legal organisation and structure' of a (putatively) sovereign institution may in practical terms restrain the exercise of its powers.[82] In this Quick and Garran differed from Burgess and Willoughby, for the latter rejected all such restraints. Perhaps Quick and Garran's intimate involvement in the drafting of s. 128, or alternatively their recognition of the ultimate sovereignty of the imperial Parliament, led them to recognise the effectiveness of the fifth paragraph of section 128.

How, then, did Quick and Garran's approach to sovereignty influence their understanding of federalism? In a critically important treatment of the idea of a 'federal commonwealth' in the *Annotated Constitution*,[83] Quick and Garran began by observing that the federal idea 'pervades and largely dominates the structure of the newly-created community, its parliamentary executive and judiciary departments'. But just what was this 'federal idea'? In the words 'shall be united' in section 3 of the Constitution's 'covering clauses',[84] they found an unambiguous indication that the Australian system was 'neither a loose confederacy nor a complete unification, but a union of the people considered as citizens of various communities whose individuality remain[ed] unimpaired'. The Commonwealth of Australia was therefore clearly a federation, a *Bundesstaat* or composite state, they contended.[85] On the 'indissolubility' of the Commonwealth as recounted in the preamble to the Constitution, Quick and Garran forcefully drew attention to the 'disastrous doctrines of nullification and secession' advanced by Jefferson, Hayne and Calhoun,

---

[81] *Ibid.*, 325, 993. See Burgess, *Political Science*, I, 90, 107, 142–5, 151–4; II, 49, 115; Austin, *Lectures on Jurisprudence*, I, 253; Willoughby, *Nature of the State*, 214.

[82] Quick and Garran, *Annotated Constitution*, 326. In this connection, Quick and Garran were aware that Dicey had not proposed a universal theory of sovereignty; they also noted that the 'historical school' of jurisprudence had pointed to 'communities in which no sovereign can be discovered': *ibid.*, 325.

[83] See also the preliminary exposition of Quick and Garran, *Annotated Constitution*, 292–4, 332–42, in the introduction.

[84] Commonwealth of Australia Constitution Act 1901 (UK), s. 3.

[85] Quick and Garran, *Annotated Constitution*, 332, 334, 371, citing Garran, *Coming Commonwealth*, 17–18.

on the 'fatal and insidious' basis that the American Union 'was merely a compact among the states'.[86] Against this, Quick and Garran understood federation to be based on a constitution, rather than a treaty, adopting Story's interpretation.[87] Did this mean that Quick and Garran fully adopted the nationalist position, that the federation was based on the consent of the people as a whole?

When discussing the idea of a federal commonwealth, Quick and Garran systematically used Madison's analysis in *Federalist* no. 39 to identify the national and federal features of the Australian Constitution, specifically in its formative, representative and amendment aspects. This much would suggest that they were likely to adopt an accurate and mediating view of Australian federalism and to avoid the extremes indicated by the compactual and national approaches. They were influenced by Burgess as well, however, and distinguished between a 'union of states' and a 'federal state'.[88] As to the former, they said:

> The primary and fundamental meaning of a federation (from the Latin *fœdus*, a league, a treaty, a compact; akin to *fides*, faith) is its capacity and intention to link together a number of co-equal societies or States, so as to form one common political system and to regulate and co-ordinate their relations to one another.[89]

But as to the 'federal state':

> the word 'federal' is applied to the composite state, or political community, formed by a federal union of States. It thus describes, not the bond of union between the federating States, but the new State resulting from that bond. It implies that the union has created a new State, without destroying the old States; that the duality is in the essence of the State itself that there is a divided sovereignty, and a double citizenship. This is the sense in which Freeman, Dicey and Bryce speak of a 'Federal State'; and it is the sense in which the phrase 'a Federal Commonwealth' is used in this section and in the preamble [of the Australian Constitution].[90]

---

[86] *Ibid.*, 292. Warden, *Formation of the Australian Constitution*, 105, argues that Quick and Garran incorrectly attributed the Virginia Resolutions to Jefferson so that Madison would not be associated with the compact theory.

[87] Quick and Garran, *Annotated Constitution*, 292–4, 300–1, 314–17, 380.   [88] *Ibid.*, 336–40.

[89] *Ibid.*, 333.   [90] *Ibid.*, 333.

Moreover, following Burgess:

> In recent years it has been argued that the word 'federal' is
> inappropriately and inexactly used when applied to a State or com-
> munity; that there is no such thing as a federal State; that if there is a
> state at all it must be a national State; that anything short of the
> principal attribute of statehood and nationhood, viz: sovereignty, is a
> mere Confederacy; and that 'federal' can only be legitimately used as
> descriptive of the partition and distribution of powers which is
> peculiar to a federal system. Federal, it is said, is properly applied to
> denote a dual but co-ordinate system of government, under one
> Constitution and subject to a common sovereignty.[91]

Quick and Garran were caught in the tension between these definitions in
their various compactual, nationalist and mediating emphases. Thus,
they accepted the standard distinction between federation and confederation in terms of Bluntschli's idea of coordinate federal and state
governments each having direct legislative and executive power over
individual citizens.[92] They also recognised, with Bryce, that 'America is a
Commonwealth of commonwealths', a state which is itself composed of
constituent states more essential to its existence than it is to theirs.[93] And
yet, on the other hand, Quick and Garran repeated Dicey's conception of
federalism as a 'contrivance intended to reconcile national unity and
power with the maintenance of State rights',[94] and ultimately aligned
themselves with Burgess's insistence that a 'federation is merely a dual
system of government under a common sovereignty'.[95]

While preferring Burgess's more 'recent' approach, Quick and Garran
had to recognise important compactual dimensions, since Madison's
analysis drew attention to the ratification by the people of the several states.
In particular, Quick and Garran's care in doing justice to institutional

---

[91]  *Ibid.*, 333–4 citing Burgess, *Political Science*, I, 79; II, 18, and mentioning *The Federalist*, Freeman,
     Dicey and Bryce, without specific reference. Quick and Garran also distinguished a fourth sense
     in which 'federal' was 'descriptive of the organs of the central and general government'.
[92]  *Ibid.*, 334.
[93]  Bryce, *American Commonwealth*, I, 12, 15, cited in Quick and Garran, *Annotated Constitution*,
     370.
[94]  Quick and Garran, *Annotated Constitution*, 371, summarising Dicey, *Law of the Constitution*.
     But see Robert Randolph Garran, 'The Federation Movement and the Founding of the
     Commonwealth', *Cambridge History of the British Empire* (Cambridge: Cambridge University
     Press, 1933), vol. VII, PT I, ch. 15, 459.
[95]  Quick and Garran, *Annotated Constitution*, 371, summarising Burgess, *Political Science*.

complexity is seen in the following description of the manner in which the Australian Constitution came into being:

> The combined operation of the federal and national principles of the Constitution is illustrated in the manner in which it was prepared, viz., by a Convention in which the people of each colony were equally represented; and in the method by which it was afterwards submitted to the people of each colony for ratification or rejection. The Federal Convention was not a body composed of delegates elected by the people of Australia, as individuals, forming one entire community . . . On the other hand, there is, in part, a recognition of the national principle, by the Constitution being founded on the will of the people, and not on the mandate of the provincial legislatures.[96]

Following Wilson, Quick and Garran believed that the 'will of the people' was 'suggestive of a consolidating and nationalising tendency'.[97] But, following Madison, they also noted the 'conspicuous' fact that the people voted as 'provincial voters, a majority being required in each colony to carry the Constitution in that colony'.[98] Quick and Garran were therefore conscious of the control over the process of drafting and ratification exercised by the colonial legislatures, noting that artificial statutory majorities had been required by some. The federation was therefore a union of states as 'corporate' entities; but it was also a union 'of people'.

These facts could not easily be accommodated to Burgess's radically nationalist definition of federalism. Thus, while Quick and Garran were otherwise exhaustive in their analysis of the federal and national features of the Constitution, the telling omission was that they did not attempt a nationalist explanation of the formative process; its very nature precluded it. In this way, the nationalist approach forcefully testified to its own inadequacy as an explanatory theory, particularly when it came to the foundation of the system.[99] None the less, following Madison, Quick and Garran also understood the representative structures of the Australian Commonwealth to be partly national and partly federal, and understood these federal aspects of the representative structure to be derived from the formative basis of the Constitution.[100] Having concluded that 'there was

---

[96] *Ibid.*, 335–6.    [97] *Ibid.*, 336.    [98] *Ibid.*, 336, citing Madison, *Federalist* no. 39.
[99] See *ibid.*, 339–40.
[100] See *ibid.*, 417, citing *Convention Debates, Adelaide* (1897), 21–3 (Barton). Quick and Garran also contrasted the 'partly federal, partly national' character of the Swiss and

an expression of popular suffrage and State sanction united in the method in which the adoption of the Constitution was secured', in relation to the representative structure they pointed out:

> The Commonwealth as a political society has been created by the union of the States and the people thereof. That the States are united is proved by the words in clause 6, which provide that the States are 'parts of the Commonwealth'; that they are welded into the very structure and essence of the Commonwealth ... This is a federal feature which peculiarly illustrates the original and primary meaning of the term, as importing a corporate union.
>
>   ... As the Commonwealth itself is partly federal and partly national in its structure, so also is its central legislative organ the Parliament. Each original State is equally represented in the Senate ... The Senate derives its power from the States, as political and co-ordinate societies, represented according to the rule of equality... In this manner the states become interwoven and inwrought into the very essence and substance of the Commonwealth, constituting the corporate units of the partnership.[101]

Yet despite these very important acknowledgements of the Madisonian analysis, Quick and Garran concluded – on balance, it seems – that the 'true ideal of federalism', or at least the 'drift of the development of the American Constitution', was as described by Burgess.[102] And yet, they did so not by invoking the supposed sovereignty of the people of Australia as a whole, but rather by invoking the overarching sovereignty of the Parliament at Westminster. Thus, in the last pages of their commentary, they observed that the imperial Parliament might choose to overrule the special guarantees of the territorial and representational integrity of the states in the fifth paragraph of section 128. Quick and Garran concluded:

> [M]any profound political thinkers are of opinion that federalism ... is but a transitory form of government, midway between the condition of confederacy and that of a single sovereignty over a combined population and territory.[103]

---

American federal executives with the more 'national' system of responsible government in Australia.

[101] *Ibid.*, 336–7.

[102] *Ibid.*, 335–42, citing Burgess, 'Ideal American Commonwealth'. See also *ibid.*, 988.

[103] *Ibid.*, 992, citing Burgess, *Political Science*.

Quick and Garran believed that the nationalist interpretation of federalism accorded with 'the more modern scope of the word'.[104] However, integrative federations, such as the United States, Switzerland and Australia, came into being through formative processes that were too complicated to be reduced to a mere exercise or assertion of national sovereignty. For Quick and Garran a solution had to be found, and they discovered it in the overarching sovereignty of the imperial Parliament.[105]

## Charles Kingston

In addition to the draft constitution prepared for the 1891 convention by Andrew Inglis Clark was another prepared by a leading South Australian delegate and later premier, Charles Cameron Kingston.[106] Less explicitly theoretical than others, Kingston represents another important Australian approach to the meaning of federation. Like Griffith, Kingston was strongly supportive of the maintenance of local self-government at a colonial level. Unlike Griffith, however, Kingston was a radical democrat; and for Kingston, this meant the initiation of far-reaching democratic reforms at both a colonial and federal level.

Kingston's liberal democratic convictions were particularly reflected in his draft constitution through provision for popular initiative and referendum as a means of vetoing federal legislation, through the referendum as an intrinsic aspect of the means by which the proposed constitution could be altered or amended in the future, and by making provision for the direct election of the colonial governors.[107] Kingston at the same time remained strongly supportive of the continuing status and powers of the constituent colonies, and this was particularly reflected in the proposal that the Federal Parliament consist of a Senate and a National Assembly, that the powers of the Parliament were to be specifically enumerated, and that the Senate should consist of six senators from each colony, chosen by the colonial legislatures.[108] The draft constitution also made implicit provision for a system of parliamentary responsible government, by stipulating that the executive government of

---

[104] *Ibid.*, 335, 341–2.    [105] *Ibid.*, 380, citing Burgess, *Political Science*. See also *ibid.*, 928.

[106] Charles Cameron Kingston, *A Bill for an Act for the Union of the Australian Colonies* (1891) (cited as 'Kingston's draft constitution)'. See, further, Crisp, *Federation Fathers*, ch. 5.

[107] Kingston's draft constitution, Pts IX, X, XVII.

[108] *Ibid.*, Pts V–VI, XII–XIII. See *Convention Debates, Sydney* (1891), 152–64.

the proposed union should be exercised on behalf of the Queen by a governor-general acting on the advice of an Australian Privy Council, the members of which must eventually become members of the Federal Parliament. However, significantly, the draft constitution further stipulated that the Privy Council must consist of 'not less than six nor more than twelve' members, and that there must always be at least one member of the Privy Council for each of the Australian colonies.[109]

Thus, while Kingston's draft clearly anticipated a system of responsible government, the structure of the proposed executive council was strikingly reminiscent of the Swiss federal executive council. La Nauze was somewhat unfair to Kingston when he characterised his draft constitution simply as a 're-arranged version of Clark's draft, with some interesting additions of Kingston's own'.[110] It is probably more accurate to observe that while Kingston's draft constitution reflected a more populist orientation than Clark's, the federative logic of the two documents was largely the same.

In *Democratic Element in Australian Federation*, first published in 1895, Kingston strongly supported colonial legislation (which he had helped draft) that provided that delegates to the federal convention of 1897–8 would be directly elected by the voters of each colony.[111] As will be seen, the 1891 convention had consisted of delegates chosen by the colonial legislatures, and in 1895 Kingston was sharply critical of both this and the provision in the Commonwealth Bill of 1891 for the selection of senators by the state legislatures – even though his draft constitution had proposed the same.[112] In 1895 Kingston was now supportive of a thoroughly democratic foundation both for the election of delegates to the federal convention, as well as for the election of senators in the Federal Parliament, on the basis of a universal franchise.[113]

Indeed, throughout the discussion Kingston shows that he had become acutely aware of the relationship between the formative process by which

---

[109] Kingston's draft constitution, Pt IV. The draft also provided for the initiation of financial bills in the lower house, but affirmed the capacity of the Senate to reject supply: *ibid.*, Pt VII.

[110] La Nauze, *Making of the Constitution*, 24–7, 295; although see Alex Castles, 'Two Colonial Democrats: Clark and Kingston and the Draft Constitution of 1891' in Haward and Warden, *Australian Democrat*, 226, n. 18.

[111] Charles Cameron Kingston, *The Democratic Element in Australian Federation* (Adelaide: J. L. Bonython and Co., 1897), 5–8.

[112] *Ibid.*, 16.      [113] *Ibid.*, 11–16.

the proposed constitution would be debated and drafted, and the specific terms and structure of the constitution that would emerge from that process. According to Kingston, a thoroughly democratic formative process, expressed through the direct election of delegates and the ratification of the Constitution by direct referendum, was, along with the direct election of both houses of the Federal Parliament, foremost among the 'democratic essentials of a Federal Constitution'.[114] At the same time, Kingston wished to see what he regarded as a genuinely federal system, which would be devised by a federal convention representing the people of each colony on an equal basis, and which would provide for the equal representation of the people of each state in the Senate. He also thought it important that a federation of the Australian colonies adopt the American (and not the Canadian) scheme, under which only specific powers would be conferred upon the Federal Parliament, with the 'residue of powers' being 'preserved' to the local legislatures.[115] Moreover, he remained strongly supportive of a popular, though state-structured, referendum for the amendment of the Constitution.

In this way, Kingston's vision was for a federal constitution that was both thoroughly democratic and thoroughly federal in the modes of its formative foundations, representative structures, configuration of powers and amendment processes.

## Isaac Isaacs and H. B. Higgins

If Kingston supported a liberal-democratic constitution which was at the same time thoroughly federalistic in foundation and structure, an exclusively liberal nationalist interpretation of 'true federalism'[116] found its most complete expression in the views of Isaac Isaacs[117] and Henry Bournes Higgins.[118] Higgins's theory of federalism began with an insistence that there must in every political community exist some particular

---

[114] *Ibid.*, 8–10.     [115] *Ibid.*, 9.

[116] See Crisp, *Federation Fathers*, 173, for a discussion of other radical nationalists, such as George Dibbs, A. B. Piddington, Tom Price and George Reid. See e.g. Albert Bathurst Piddington, *Popular Government and Federalism* (Sydney: Angus and Robertson, 1898).

[117] See Zelman Cowen, *Isaac Isaacs* (Brisbane: University of Queensland Press, 1993).

[118] See John Rickard, *H. B. Higgins: Rebel as Judge* (Sydney: Allen and Unwin, 1984). La Nauze, *Making of the Constitution*, 102, 120, described Higgins as 'an obstinate individualist radical', yet 'learned and courteous' and 'heard with attention while he argued a hopeless case'.

institution or body in which 'ultimate sovereignty' is located.[119] Sovereignty, for Higgins, meant the capacity to determine the nature and terms of the constitution. Thus, following Dicey, Higgins pointed out that in England the House of Commons was 'truly sovereign' because 'it [could] change the Constitution as it like[d]'.[120] However, while acknowledging what he called the 'theoretical sovereignty of the British Parliament' over the Australian colonies, Higgins maintained that 'practical sovereignty' in Australia 'ought to rest with the Australian people'.[121] Following Locke, Higgins further argued that popular sovereignty must mean majority rule[122] and made clear that this meant that a majority of the people of Australia should prevail both within the representative institutions of the federation as well as in any decision to amend the federal Constitution. He probably also would have preferred that the very ratification of the Constitution be determined by an overall majority of 'the Australian people as a whole'.[123]

The problem, however, was that the scheme of federation of the Australian colonies was based upon the consent of the people of each colony. Speaking in 1898 in relation to the Constitution Bill that had emerged from the convention of 1897–8, Higgins thus despaired of the fact that the several states were proposed to be equally represented in the Senate notwithstanding substantial differences in population,[124] that the Constitution could only be amended by a majority of voters in a majority of states,[125] and that the equal representation of the states in the Senate could not be altered without the consent of the people of each particular state affected by any such proposal alteration.[126] Equal representation of the states in the Senate was not, as its proponents argued, something that was 'essential' to a federation, but was, Higgins thought, actually nothing more than a 'concession'.[127] It was also, following Burgess, an invitation to 'revolution' in that it undermined the essential sovereignty of the people of the entire nation-state.[128] Federation, for Higgins, was a 'grand ideal' which involved, essentially, the recognition that Australians were 'one people' with 'one destiny'. His objection to the Constitution Bill was not

---

[119] Higgins, *Essays and Addresses*, 9.
[120] *Ibid.*, 13, apparently relying upon Dicey, *Law of the Constitution* (4th edn, London: Macmillan, 1893), 135.
[121] *Ibid.*, 9.     [122] *Ibid.*, 13, 72, apparently relying upon Locke, *Two Treatises*, §96.
[123] *Ibid.*, 11.     [124] *Ibid.*, 12.
[125] *Ibid.*, 6–8; see also 52, 85, 104, 111, 115, citing Burgess, Ford and Goldwin Smith.
[126] *Ibid.*, 8.     [127] *Ibid.*, 15; cf. 109, 123, citing Bagehot, Dicey and Freeman.     [128] *Ibid.*, 73.

because it was 'federal' (as Higgins defined it) but because it was too 'provincial'.[129] For Higgins, the defining feature of a federal state was a division of powers between federal and state governments.[130]

The similarities between the views of Higgins, Dicey and especially Burgess are quite evident, but Higgins seems to have been hesitant to rely explicitly on these authors, possibly on account of their relatively conservative views.[131] By contrast, Isaacs was very ready to rely on Dicey and Burgess when their views accorded with his own. Following Burgess and Dicey, he held that the essential principle of federalism was the division of powers, not equality of representation.[132] On the question of constitutional amendment, he also followed Burgess, arguing for a relatively easy, national-majoritarian means of constitutional alteration in order to avoid an eventual 'stagnation'.[133]

As justices of the High Court of Australia, Higgins and Isaacs would eventually have the opportunity in a series of celebrated cases to state clearly their nationalist interpretations of the Australian Constitution. In the famous *Engineers Case*, one of Justice Isaacs's central premises was that the Constitution was 'the political compact of the whole of the people of Australia, enacted into binding law by the Imperial Parliament' – specifically rejecting the more compactual approaches adopted by Griffith CJ and Barton and O'Connor JJ in previous decisions.[134] In *Australian Democracy and Our Constitutional System* (1939), Isaacs repeated his national majoritarian interpretation of the Australian Constitution and called for an expansion of Commonwealth legislative powers.[135]

In the 1890s, however, the question was whether nationalist views such as these would prevail against the replies of those like Clark, who insisted that 'each State is a separately organised community which has a distinct collective and corporate life and distinct interests', requiring separate representation of the people thereof in the Federal Parliament and a

---

[129] *Ibid.*, 10.     [130] *Ibid.*, 100, 128.     [131] Although see *ibid.*, 73.

[132] *Convention Debates, Adelaide* (1897), 171–8, 660; *Convention Debates, Sydney* (1897), 303–13. Compare Isaac Isaacs, *Australian Democracy and our Constitutional System* (Melbourne: Horticultural Press, 1939), 33–4.

[133] *Official Record of the National Australasian Convention Debates, Third Session: Melbourne* (Melbourne: Government Printer, 1898), 716, 718–22 (Isaacs), 735 (Reid). Isaacs relied on Burgess, *Political Science*, I, 137, among others: see *Convention Debates, Melbourne* (1898), 722.

[134] *Amalgamated Society of Engineers* v. *Adelaide Steamship Co. Ltd* (1920) 28 CLR 129, 142. Compare *D'Emden* v. *Pedder* (1904) 1 CLR 91.

[135] Isaacs, *Australian Democracy*; see Crisp, *Federation Fathers*, ch. 4.

distinct say in the amendment procedure.[136] Madison's analysis of the American Constitution suggested that at the foundation of a federal system was a 'federating' process whereby, as the preamble to the Australian Constitution would declare, the peoples of several independent colonies separately agreed to unite in a federal commonwealth. This origin of the federation was, contrary to Burgess's abstract, nationalist conception, premised on the capacity of the representatives of the colonies to negotiate and agree on the terms of a federal union. As will be seen, a majority of their representatives understandably used that capacity to create a federation that was, like Madison's own, a composition of both federal and national elements.

---

[136] See Andrew Inglis Clark, 'Federal Government: The Commonwealth of Australia, No. 2' in Scott Bennett (ed.), *The Making of the Commonwealth* (Melbourne: Cassell, 1971), 101.

# 5

## Constitutional foundations

> These colonies cannot legislate for each other; the only authority which can legislate for all the colonies is the British Parliament. We have been granted powers of local self-government; let us exercise these powers to the fullest extent by constituting an Australian authority which, so far as regards this and other matters of a similar nature, can deal with Australia as a whole.
>
> Richard Baker (1897)

At least two persistent themes emerge from the movement to federation in Australia as it progressed during the last decades of the nineteenth century. First, despite the fact that the Australian colonies were united by a common law and the common overarching authority of the imperial Parliament,[1] the colonies insisted on exercising an autonomous capacity to decide whether to join an Australian federation and, if so, on what basis. While the Colonial Office at times sought to encourage federation, it recognised – especially in the light of its experience with the American colonies – that it would be best, in the final analysis, to allow the Australians to have the final say over their constitutional futures. The arrival of local self-government in the mid part of the century meant, therefore, that the prospects of federation would depend upon the cooperation and agreement of the parliaments and governments of each colony.

The second theme in the movement towards federation was a growing realisation among its proponents in Australia that voters in the several colonies would not support federation unless they were given a substantial sense of participation in the process. To similar effect, there was a realisation that many of the politicians of the time would only move from

---

[1] *R* v. *Kidman* (1915) 20 CLR 425, 435–6. Compare Henry Parkes's famous aphorism: 'The crimson thread of kinship runs through us all', announced at the conference of 1890: La Nauze, *Making of the Constitution*, 11; Quick and Garran, *Annotated Constitution*, 119.

rhetoric to action if compelled to do so by public opinion. In consequence of these two basic forces, the federation movement is said to have 'stalled' until the 'Corowa plan', devised in 1893, was adopted by the colonial premiers in 1895. The plan enabled the electors in the colonies and the colonial legislatures to have a vital part to play in the formation of the federal Constitution.

At a constitutive level therefore, and putting aside for the moment the role of the imperial Parliament, it could be said that the principles underlying the formation of the Australian Commonwealth were both 'federal' and 'democratic'. But precisely how were these principles embodied in that process? As between the two principles, did one dominate over the other, or was it possible to construct a formative process that gave due regard to both principles? These questions, and others, lie at the core of this and the following chapter. In order to understand the Australian Constitution, particularly in regard to its structures of representation, configurations of power and amendment procedures, it is necessary to appreciate the constitutional foundations upon which it was constructed as well as the formative processes by which it came into being.

## The formative preconditions of Australian federation

The 'settlement'[2] of Australia in the late eighteenth century was marked by three features important to the story of federation being developed here. First, the British Crown annexed the eastern coast of Australia in 1770 by dint of discovery, proclamation and occupation that has long been understood to be unquestionable in Australian courts.[3] By Order in Council of 6 December 1786, His Majesty's territory of New South Wales was declared to be a place for the reception of 'felons and other prisoners' pursuant to the Transportation Act 1784 (UK).[4] Second, by Letters Patent and Commission dated 2 April 1787, Captain Arthur Phillip was appointed governor and vice-admiral of the territory, and granted wide

---

[2] *Cooper* v. *Stuart* (1889) 14 App. Cas. 286, 291–4.

[3] *Coe* v. *Commonwealth (No. 1)* (1978–9) 24 ALR 118, 128–9; *Mabo* v. *Queensland (No. 2)* (1992) 175 CLR 1, 69; *Coe* v. *Commonwealth (No. 2)* (1993) 118 ALR 193, 198–9; *Walker* v. *New South Wales* (1994) 182 CLR 45, 47–50; *Wik Peoples* v. *Queensland* (1996) 187 CLR 1, 214. See Alex C. Castles, *An Australian Legal History* (Sydney: Law Book Co., 1982), ch. 2; John M. Bennett and Alex C. Castles (eds.), *A Source Book of Australian Legal History* (Sydney: Law Book Co., 1979), 255–8.

[4] For a discussion, see David Neal, *The Rule of Law in a Penal Colony: Law and Power in Early New South Wales* (Cambridge: Cambridge University Press, 1991), ch. 2.

powers of government.[5] For several decades thereafter, each succeeding governor had, or at least exercised, autocratic and arbitrary powers, moderated only by his personal humanitarian qualities or the defiance of his officers.[6] Moreover, although there was doubt concerning the authority that could lawfully be delegated to and exercised by the governor,[7] what authority existed derived from imperial sources. A Legislative Council for New South Wales, appointed by the King, was instituted in 1823[8] and reconstituted in an expanded form in 1828,[9] but did not include locally elected representatives until 1842.[10] Third, the authority of the governor extended territorially over the entirety of New South Wales, which as late as 1825 included more than half of the Australian continent, together with other 'islands adjacent in the Pacific', and until 1825 included Van Diemen's Land.[11] Accordingly, the settlements at Hobart (1803/4), Moreton Bay (1824), Port Phillip Bay (1835/6) and New Zealand at one time or another formed part of or were subject to the government of New South Wales.[12] The territory of South Australia, also originally part of New South Wales, was settled as a distinct colony in 1836;[13] Western Australia was settled separately from 1829.[14]

---

[5]  Castles, *Australian Legal History*, 34–5. See also the earlier Letters Patent of 12 October 1786 establishing the office of governor of New South Wales.

[6]  Compare Quick and Garran, *Annotated Constitution*, 36; Herbert Vere Evatt, 'The Legal Foundations of New South Wales' (1938) 11 *Australian Law Journal* 409, 421; Melbourne, *Early Constitutional Development*, 6–28; Castles, *Australian Legal History*, 38–45; McMinn, *Constitutional History*, ch. 1; Lumb, *Constitutions of the Australian States*, ch. 1; Alistair Davidson, *The Invisible State: The Formation of the Australian State 1788–1901* (Cambridge: Cambridge University Press, 1991), chs. 1–2.

[7]  In particular, there was doubt about the governor's practice of issuing general orders, these being legislative in character: Melbourne, *Early Constitutional Development*, 29–36, 74–87; Castles, *Australian Legal History*, 35–7, 80; Quick and Garran, *Annotated Constitution*, 35.

[8]  New South Wales Act 1823 (UK).

[9]  Australian Courts Act 1828 (UK). Compare Western Australia Act 1829 (UK), establishing a similar Council for Western Australia.

[10]  Australian Constitutions Act (No. 1) 1842 (UK), under which twelve members of the Legislative Council were appointed by the Queen and twenty-four were elected by the inhabitants of the colony.

[11]  Melbourne, *Early Constitutional Development*, 107; Castles, *Australian Legal History*, 25; Quick and Garran, *Annotated Constitution*, 35–6, 79.

[12]  From 1842/3 New South Wales was divided into electoral districts that included Sydney, Port Phillip Bay and, later, Moreton Bay, each returning its own members to a central legislature, the Legislative Council of New South Wales: Australian Constitutions Act (No. 1) 1842 (UK).

[13]  Under the South Australia Act 1934 (UK).

[14]  Possession of Western Australia was taken by Captain James Stirling in 1829 and a local Legislative Council was soon thereafter established pursuant to the Government in Western Australia Act 1829 (UK). See *Western Australia* v. *Commonwealth* (1995) 183 CLR 373, 424–5.

In sum, the beginnings of British settlement in Australia were marked by imperial sovereignty and an autocratic and unitary form of government exercised, at least in theory, over much of the continent. However, these autocratic and unitary features were gradually attenuated during the course of the nineteenth century. Between 1825 and 1859 the several settlements emerged as separate colonies,[15] and early in the second half of the century all but one of them became fully self-governing (Western Australia had to wait until almost the century's end for responsible government).[16]

These latter developments were marked by an aspiration for 'local self-government', expressed in several distinct ways. First, in response to the unitary characteristics of early colonial government centred in Sydney, the various settlements engaged in a 'struggle for separation' from New South Wales.[17] Primarily, this involved agitation on the part of those regions that would become self-governing colonies, such as Victoria and Queensland. But it also involved campaigns for local self-government and separation on the part of other areas, such as the Riverina and New England districts of New South Wales, and the north and central regions of Queensland.[18] Indeed, various imperial enactments, beginning with the Australian Constitutions Act (No. 1) 1842 (UK), provided for the possible separation of regions such as these, as well as for the formation of local, municipal governments.[19] But municipal governments were generally slow to develop and calls for further regional separation were not successful.[20] Second, in response to the autocratic and imperial features mentioned above, Australian colonists, like many of their counterparts elsewhere, progressively obtained representative legislatures,[21]

---

[15] Van Diemen's Land/Tasmania in 1825; Western Australia in 1829; South Australia in 1836; Port Phillip Bay/Victoria in 1851; Moreton Bay/Queensland in 1859.

[16] See Western Australia Constitution Act 1890 (UK), giving effect to the Constitution Act 1889 (WA).

[17] McMinn, *Constitutional History*, 35.

[18] A. J. Brown, 'One Continent, Two Federalisms: Rediscovering the Original Meanings of Australian Federal Ideas' (2004) 39(3) *Australian Journal of Political Science* 485.

[19] Australian Constitutions Act (No. 1) 1842 (UK), ss. 41, 51; Australian Constitutions Act (No. 2) 1850 (UK), ss. 20, 34; New South Wales Constitution Statute 1855 (UK), ss. 5–7; Western Australia Constitution Act 1890 (UK), s. 6. See also City of Sydney Incorporation Act 1842 (NSW) and Municipalities Act 1858 (NSW).

[20] See Melbourne, *Early Constitutional Development*, ch. 6; Frederick A. Larcombe, *The Development of Local Government in New South Wales* (Melbourne: Cheshire, 1961).

[21] Australian Constitutions Act (No. 1) 1842 (UK), s. 1; Australian Constitutions Act (No. 2) 1850 (UK), ss. 2, 7, 9, 35; Victoria Electoral Act 1851 (NSW); Constitution Act 1855–56 (SA), ss. 5, 14; Constitution Act 1889 (WA), ss. 11, 45. See also Quick and Garran, *Annotated*

responsible government[22] and a local capacity to alter their constitutions.[23] None the less, imperial sovereignty remained a part of the law in Australia up to and beyond federation in 1901; it was only in the twentieth century that the power of the Parliament of the United Kingdom to legislate with paramount force for Australia was at first qualified, and finally abdicated.[24] In this context, the movement towards self-government and federation depended, for its effectiveness, upon local initiative. In contrast to the imperialism, autocracy and unitary form of government that had characterised the initial stages of British settlement, constitutional initiatives in Australia were thereafter generally marked by calls for self-determination, representative government and local self-government – or, at least, this is how leading federationists, such as Quick and Garran, saw it.

The efforts of Henry George Grey, Third Earl Grey and Secretary of State for War and the Colonies (1846–52) are a case in point.[25] In a famous despatch of 31 July 1847, Grey stated:

> The principle of local self-government (like every other political principle) must, when reduced to practice, be qualified by many other principles which must operate simultaneously with it. To regulate such affairs with reference to any one isolated rule or maxim would, of course, be an idle and ineffectual attempt. For example, it is necessary that, while providing for the local management of local interests, we should not omit to provide for central management of all such interests as are not local. Thus, questions co-extensive in their bearing with the interest of the Empire at large are the appropriate province of Parliament.

*Constitution*, 38–44; McMinn, *Constitutional History*, chs. 2–3; Lumb, *Constitutions of the Australian States*, chs. 1–2.

[22] Constitution Act 1855 (NSW), s. 37; Constitution Act 1855 (Vic.), s. 37; Constitution Act 1855–56 (SA), s. 32; Constitution Act 1867 (Qld), s. 14; Constitution Act 1889 (WA), s. 74. See *Toy v. Musgrove* (1888) 14 VLR 349, 396–7. See also Quick and Garran, *Annotated Constitution*, 44–7; Melbourne, *Early Constitutional Development*, Pt V, ch. 6 and 443–5; Lumb, *Constitutions of the Australian States*, ch. 4.

[23] Australian Constitutions Act (No. 2) 1850 (UK), s. 32; New South Wales Constitution Statute 1855 (UK), s. 4; Victoria Constitution Statute 1855 (UK), s. 4; Order in Council (Qld), 5 June 1859, art. 22; Colonial Laws Validity Act 1865 (UK), s. 5; Western Australia Constitution Act 1890 (UK), s. 5. See Lumb, 'Bicentenary', 8–9; Geoffrey Sawer, *The Australian Constitution* (Canberra: Australian Government Publishing Service, 1975), 13–15.

[24] Statute of Westminster 1931 (UK); Statute of Westminster Adoption Act 1942 (Cth); Australia Acts 1986 (UK) and (Cth).

[25] See John M. Ward, *Earl Grey and the Australian Colonies: 1846–1857* (Melbourne: Melbourne University Press, 1958).

But there are questions which, though local as it respects the British possessions in Australia collectively, are not merely local as it respects any one of those possessions. Considered as members of the same Empire, those colonies have many common interests, the regulation of which, in some uniform manner and by some single authority, may be essential to the welfare of them all. Yet in some cases such interests may be more promptly, effectively, and satisfactorily decided by some authority within Australia itself than by the more remote, the less accessible, and in truth the less competent authority of Parliament.[26]

Grey's despatch distinguished between matters that were of special interest to the individual settlements, those that were of interest to the empire as a whole, and those falling into an intermediate category, being matters of collective concern to the Australian colonies as a group. The immediate cause of the despatch was, as it happened, to acknowledge in principle the demands of the settlement at Port Phillip for separation from New South Wales, in terms of Grey's first category of interests. However, another aspect of the despatch concerned Grey's intermediate category, and it was to meet this set of interests that Grey also proposed an Australian legislature consisting of two houses to be elected by district councils or municipal bodies established throughout the Australian colonies.

The Australian response to the latter proposal was to regard it as at best premature, and at worst misconceived, even mischievous.[27] In particular, the proposal of electing the House of Assembly indirectly on the basis of districts or municipalities was strongly opposed by colonial politicians for its tendency to undermine the emergent authority of the various colonial governments.[28] This opposition forced Grey to abandon the concept of an Australian legislature founded upon regional councils in his so-called 'Golden Despatch', issued a year later. In this document, Grey accepted the need for separate representative councils in Victoria, South Australia and Van Diemen's Land, and in this respect the despatch was warmly received. He continued, however, to adhere to the larger idea of an Australian legislature, this time composed of representatives of the several colonies.[29]

---

[26] As quoted in Quick and Garran, *Annotated Constitution*, 81.

[27] See Peter Cochrane, *Colonial Ambition: Foundations of Australian Democracy* (Melbourne: Melbourne University Press, 2006), chs. 9, 11.

[28] See e.g. McMinn, *Constitutional History*, 40–45; W. G. McMinn, *Nationalism and Federalism in Australia* (Melbourne: Oxford University Press, 1994), ch. 4; Ward, *Earl Grey*, chs. 3, 7.

[29] Quick and Garran, *Annotated Constitution*, 82–6; Ward, *Earl Grey*, ch. 4.

On the advice of the recently retired Under-Secretary of the Colonial Office, James Stephen, Grey moved the Privy Council Committee for Trade and Plantations in 1849 to propose that each of the colonies should be granted partly representative councils. The committee noted that the district councils provided for in the Australian Constitutions Act (No. 1) 1842 (UK) were practically extinct, and recommended that the Act be amended so as to place the initiative with the inhabitants of each district, who would be at liberty to petition the governor to issue charters incorporating municipal corporations to administer local affairs. The Committee also proposed that a General Assembly of Australia be established, having power to make laws with respect to a wide range of stipulated matters and any other matter unanimously requested by the colonial legislatures. The projected Assembly would this time consist of a governor-general and a House of Delegates composed of two members for each colony, together with an additional member for every 15,000 of the population of each colony.[30]

Grey arranged for a bill along these lines to be introduced into the Parliament at Westminster later that year. However, the 'federal' aspects were again forcefully opposed in Australia, this time particularly by the smaller colonies, because, as Quick and Garran put it, 'the overwhelming preponderance that the larger colonies would have in the Assembly would be greatly injurious to the lesser'.[31] An amended Bill in 1850 acknowledged this concern by providing that the General Assembly would only bind those colonies that convoked it, and that in the assembly each colony would be entitled to four members and an additional member for every 20,000 of population. None the less opposition remained, not least because the colonies had not requested the measure in the first place. As eventually enacted, the Australian Constitutions Act (No. 2) 1850 (UK) widened the franchise, separated Victoria from New South Wales, granted South Australia and Van Diemen's Land their own (partly) elected legislatures, but it did not grant responsible government and the federal aspects of the proposed scheme were for the time being abandoned.[32]

---

[30] Edward Sweetman, *Australian Constitutional Development* (Melbourne: Macmillan and Co., 1925), Appendix A, 365–81.

[31] Quick and Garran, *Annotated Constitution*, 86. New South Wales would have been entitled to twelve members, compared with Victoria's four members, Van Diemen's Land's five members and South Australia's four members.

[32] Australian Constitutions Act (No. 2) 1850 (UK). See Quick and Garran, *Annotated Constitution*, 83–8; McMinn, *Constitutional History*, 466–8; Cochrane, *Colonial Ambition*,

Grey's despatches, and the predominantly negative response that they engendered, anticipated recurrent themes in the movement toward federation. First, the rejection of Grey's proposal that the Australian legislature be indirectly elected portended the failure of the Commonwealth Bill of 1891, drafted by a convention that was nominated by the colonial legislatures. It also anticipated the eventual recognition that a successful bill would need to be produced by a directly elected convention. Second, Grey recognised that an Australian legislative congress represented a relative centralisation of authority 'as it respects any one' of the individual colonies. From an imperial perspective, he understood this as having to do with matters that were 'local as ... respects the British possessions'. The formation of a federal congress would substitute 'the more remote, the less accessible, and in truth the less competent authority of Parliament' with a system of government local to Australia, albeit continental in scope. This idea – that federation was essentially a means of achieving local self-governance – would re-emerge at critical points in the debate about the drafting of the federal constitution. As Quick and Garran observed, a central reason for the failure of Grey's federal initiatives was that each colony was intent 'on securing absolute power to manage its own affairs, and the importance of union was rather future than present'. Moreover, the 'intense localism' of the separate colonies, they said, meant that 'a satisfactory scheme of Australian union must be worked out in Australia, not in England'.[33] This did not mean that federation was necessarily opposed by Australians, but rather that any scheme likely to succeed would have to be an Australian initiative.

In fact, opinions in favour of federation, in one form or another, existed within the colonies. In 1850, John Dunmore Lang, James Wiltshire and Henry Parkes formed the Australian League with the union of the colonies into a federal republic as one of its objectives.[34] On the other side of

---

ch. 15. Grey persisted with the idea of an Australian governor-general, in 1851 commissioning Sir Charles Fitzroy as captain-general and governor-general of all Her Majesty's Australian possessions, with separate commissions as governor of New South Wales, Van Diemen's Land, South Australia and Victoria, and with lieutenant-governors in the latter three colonies. The scheme was abandoned at the end of Fitzroy's term: Quick and Garran, *Annotated Constitution*, 41, 89–90.

[33] Quick and Garran, *Annotated Constitution*, 89. See also Ward, *Earl Grey*, 4; La Nauze, *Making of the Constitution*, 4; McMinn, *Nationalism and Federalism*, chs. 3–4.

[34] Stephen G. Foster, Susan Marsden and Roslyn Russell (eds.), *Federation: The Guide to Records* (Australian Archives, Commonwealth of Australia, 1998), 3.

politics, William Charles Wentworth in 1853 initiated a Select Committee of the Legislative Council of New South Wales which, in addition to calling for responsible government (or at least a degree of it),[35] recommended that a General Assembly be created with power to make laws in relation to inter-colonial issues.[36] And yet, while Australian initiative was practically necessary, it was not sufficient. The immediate aim of the Select Committee was a new constitution for New South Wales. As far as wider ambitions were concerned, the committee was not concerned at this stage to create anything much more than a general legislative assembly – yet even this foundered on the rock of equal representation.[37] Thus, even though there were proponents of federation in the other colonies (for example, Charles Gavan Duffy in Victoria and Sir Adye Douglas and Rev. John West in Tasmania), Wentworth's proposal was not accepted by the other parliaments.[38]

Similar considerations appear to have influenced the attitude subsequently adopted by Henry Labouchere, Secretary of State for the Colonies (1855–8), to a 'Memorial showing need for Australian federation' produced by the General Association for the Australian Colonies held in London in 1857, again at Wentworth's initiative. A draft bill was appended to the memorial which empowered the colonial legislatures to form a convention, at which they would be equally represented, in order to create a Federal Assembly. Labouchere's response was to refer the initiative back to the colonies.[39] As Quick and Garran observed, 'the colonies had, by dint of much remonstrance, obtained recognition of the right to frame their own constitutions'.[40]

In 1857 the need for local initiative, equal representation of the colonies and the reference of powers to a Federal Assembly was likewise asserted by parliamentary committees in Victoria, New South Wales and South Australia. The Victorian committee, while divided on some of the details and timing, agreed that some form of federal union was necessary,

---

[35] Cochrane, *Colonial Ambition*, ch. 21.    [36] Quick and Garran, *Annotated Constitution*, 90.

[37] Irving, *Constitute a Nation*, 2; Foster, *Guide to Records*, 3; Duffy, *My Life*, 145–7. Wentworth, following Calhoun, rejected representation by population, and was withering in his criticisms of Lang. See, further, Cochrane, *Colonial Ambition*, chs. 13–14, 21.

[38] Foster, *Guide to Records*, 3, 18.

[39] *Ibid.*, 3–4; Quick and Garran, *Annotated Constitution*, 92–5; see McMinn, *Constitutional History*, 95.

[40] Quick and Garran, *Annotated Constitution*, 92.

and that each of the self-governing colonies should send three delegates to a conference empowered to 'frame a plan of federation' which would be submitted to the colonial legislatures, the people of the colonies or both. The committee thus recognised the idea that any 'plan of union' would have to be 'submitted to the people'. It was also cognisant of the different forms which such union might take. The alternatives included:

> merely a Consultative Council, authorized to frame propositions for the sanction of the State Legislatures, or a Federal Executive and Assembly, with supreme power on national and inter-colonial questions; or some compromise between these extremes.

Should such an Assembly be formed, further questions included:

> Is the Legislature to consist of one or two branches? Must an absolute majority of its members, or the representatives of a certain number of States concur, to make its decisions law? Are its laws to take effect directly on the entire population of Australia, or only after the assent of their respective States?

In the light of such far-reaching questions, the committee concluded that the 'negotiation demanding so much caution and forbearance, so much foresight and experience, must originate in the mutual action of the colonies and cannot safely be relegated even to the Imperial Legislature'.[41]

The New South Wales committee for its part endorsed the Victorian suggestion of a colonial conference, and further proposed that the colonies be represented by four members in a Federal Assembly and that the Assembly should have power to legislate on all matters referred to it by two or more colonies. While the committee accepted the need for imperial legislation, it also affirmed that any proposal must be 'initiated and recommended by the colonies themselves'.[42] In South Australia, the Victorian idea of a conference was also affirmed and delegates were appointed in anticipation. However, it was emphasised that any such conference must not bind the colonial legislatures. The Tasmanian House

---

[41] *Report from the Select Committee upon the Federal Union of the Australia Colonies*, in Clark, *Select Documents*, 445–8; cf. Duffy, *My Life*, 163–4; Childers to Duffy, 3 March 1857, Duffy Papers. The recommendations were unenthusiastically adopted: McMinn, *Constitutional History*, 96.

[42] Quick and Garran, *Annotated Constitution*, 96–8.

of Assembly subsequently resolved to send delegates and the Victorians resolved likewise.[43]

Despite broad support, however, these proposals ultimately failed. Changes of government in New South Wales, suspicions of a rapidly growing Victoria, and the decidedly guarded response elicited from a newly independent Queensland served to derail the proposed conference. According to Quick and Garran, Queensland 'was enjoying her new isolation, and looked on federation as a kind of re-annexation. "Complete independence" was her ideal for the moment.'[44] Even had a conference been held, moreover, there was no general enthusiasm for federation, and so there was doubt as to whether any conference would have produced practical results. Rather:

> Local politics, and the development of local institutions, engrossed the attention of the people; and probably no colony would have been prepared to accept the compromises and the partial sacrifice of local independence which a federal union would have involved.[45]

Irving has suggested that the basic reason for the failure of these proposals was that:

> While ... almost everyone agreed in principle that some sort of union was a good idea ... each successive proposal failed. British schemes invariably came up against Australian protests over failure to consult; proposals from New South Wales ... irritated the other colonies because New South Wales always seemed to allocate itself the pre-eminent place in its scheme. Victorian schemes were rejected by New South Wales because these did not sufficiently recognise that colony's pre-eminence. And so it went on.[46]

According to La Nauze, between 1860 and 1880 the colonies were busy enjoying 'the delights of parliamentary self-government' and developing their independent identities; and, given continuing inter-colonial rivalries, they were too busy to be overly serious about federation for the time being.[47] In sum, federation – if it came at all – would have to be a local initiative, without any 'meddlesome interference' from England, as one

---

[43] *Ibid.*, 98–9; McMinn, *Constitutional History*, 96; Duffy, *My Life*, 163–4.
[44] Quick and Garran, *Annotated Constitution*, 99.
[45] *Ibid.*, 99–100.    [46] Irving, *Constitute a Nation*, 3.
[47] La Nauze, *Making of the Constitution*, 2; cf. Foster, *Guide to Records*, 4.

premier of Queensland put it.[48] Moreover, each separate 'community' would have to join as an 'equal contracting partner', and therefore be represented equally in any federal conference or convention.[49]

Quick and Garran considered that the felt need for union primarily consisted in a desire to overcome 'the evils arising from conflicting tariffs and inter-colonial duties'.[50] Inter-colonial conferences were accordingly held to resolve these questions and to secure joint action on various topics, but with mixed success. At a conference held in 1871, delegates from five colonies insisted, as against the then Secretary of State for the Colonies, Lord Kimberley, that they had the right to enter into reciprocal arrangements for the establishment of free trade, notwithstanding imperial treaties and constitutional limitations on the powers of the colonies.[51] Lord Kimberley eventually acquiesced and the constitutional fetters were removed,[52] but the colonies were not able to agree on the terms of a customs union.

The only other definite step towards federation at this time was a Royal Commission in Victoria chaired by Charles Duffy in 1870. Like so many before, the commission unanimously affirmed the need for federal union, but was again divided on the form that such a union might take, some members supporting the recently formed Canadian model, others being content with a Federal Council.[53] Duffy's initiative was met with support from South Australia and Tasmania, but with less positive responses from New South Wales and Queensland.[54] Significantly, there was at this time explicit reflection on the formative basis of federation and the grounds of amendment or secession, John Davies considering that 'a partnership requiring mutual consent for its formation should require mutual assent' for its termination.[55]

---

[48] Lilley to Duffy, 7 November 1870, Duffy Papers, noted in Foster, *Guide to Records*, 18.

[49] Lang to Duffy, 21 May 1860; Martin to Duffy, 5 December 1870; Meredith to Duffy, 16 December 1870, Duffy Papers. An imperial Enabling Act would 'leave the various colonies at liberty to form a Federal Union, when they might consider it advantageous' and was 'the fairest mode to the lesser colonies': Palmer to Duffy, 23 November 1870; Boucant to Duffy, 19 December 1870, Duffy Papers.

[50] Quick and Garran, *Annotated Constitution*, 100–9.

[51] See Australian Constitutions Act (No. 2) 1850 (UK), s. 31.

[52] Australian Colonies Duties Act 1873 (UK).

[53] Quick and Garran, *Annotated Constitution*, 100–7; Foster, *Guide to Records*, 4–5.

[54] McAlister to Duffy, 29 November 1870, Duffy Papers, discussed in Foster, *Guide to Records*, 5.

[55] Davies to Duffy, 29 November 1870, Duffy Papers.

Further steps were taken by a conference held in 1880 and 1881 which passed resolutions proposed by Henry Parkes supporting creation of a Federal Council with equal representation for each colony. At the second sitting of the conference, at which the six Australian colonies and New Zealand were represented, Parkes submitted a draft bill with a memorandum which recited that 'the time is come' to create a Federal Council in order to 'pave the way to a complete federal organization'. Notably, Parkes emphasized that '[c]are has been taken throughout to give effective power to the proposed Federal Council, within prescribed limits, without impairing the authority of the colonies represented in that body'.[56] Nevertheless, the conference divided evenly on the bill and the idea lapsed. As Harrison Moore pointed out, such conferences had no corporate legal status, but depended on unanimity as between the several colonies; and such unanimity on the details of any proposal was consistently lacking.[57]

Accordingly, no more definite step in the direction of federation occurred until 1883, when external affairs, defence and other concerns prompted premiers Sir Thomas McIlwraith of Queensland and James Service of Victoria to propose an inter-colonial convention.[58] The convention, at which New Zealand, Fiji and the six Australian colonies were represented, adopted a bill drafted by Samuel Griffith providing for the establishment of a Federal Council of Australasia.[59] Addresses to the Crown supporting the bill were subsequently passed by all of the colonies except New South Wales and New Zealand. In New South Wales, Parkes particularly objected that the Council would be an inadequately constituted body, possessing no 'inherent power'. Nevertheless, the bill was eventually passed in modified form by the imperial Parliament in 1885.[60]

---

[56] *Minutes of Proceedings of the Intercolonial Conference, Sydney* (1881), in Clark, *Select Documents*, 451–2.

[57] Moore, *Constitution of the Commonwealth*, 35–6; see also Quick and Garran, *Annotated Constitution*, 110.

[58] See Geoffrey Searle, 'The Victorian Government's Campaign for Federation, 1883–1889' in A. W. Martin (ed.), *Essays in Australian Federation* (Melbourne: Melbourne University Press, 1969). Service considered that the convention 'should be thoroughly representative of the parliaments chosen from all parties': Foster, *Guide to Records*, 21.

[59] *Report of Proceedings of the Intercolonial Convention, Sydney* (1883), in Clark, *Select Documents*, 452–3.

[60] Federal Council of Australasia Act 1885 (UK). See Rae Else-Mitchell, 'The Establishment in 1885 of the Federal Council of Australasia' (1985) 59 *Australian Law Journal* 666; Alfred Deakin, 'Federal Council of Australasia' (February 1895) *Review of Reviews* 154.

The preamble to the Federal Council of Australasia Act recited that the Council was intended to deal with:

> such matters of common Australasian interest, in respect to which united action is desirable, as can be dealt with without unduly interfering with the management of the internal affairs of the several colonies by their respective legislatures.

By section 5 of the Act the Council was to consist of two representatives from each of the self-governing colonies (which included New Zealand), and one representative from the two Crown colonies (Western Australia and Fiji). Section 6 provided that each colony would determine how its representatives were to be appointed. Section 13 provided for a quorum consisting of 'a majority of the whole number of members of the Council for the time being, representing a majority of the [participating] colonies', and further provided that Council decisions would be taken by majority vote. The Council's legislative powers set out in section 15 included a specific list, as well as matters referred to it by the Queen on the 'request of the legislatures of the colonies'. Section 15 also contained a further detailed list of matters which could be 'referred' to the Council by 'any two or more colonies' and 'any other matter of general Australasian interest with respect to which the legislatures of the several colonies can legislate within their own limits, and as to which it is deemed desirable that there should be a law of general application'.[61] Section 22 in turn provided for the supremacy of any law passed by the Council which might be repugnant or inconsistent with a colonial law. By section 29, Council expenditure was to be met initially by the colony wherein the expenditure was incurred and ultimately by contributions paid by the colonies in proportion to their respective populations. Notably, two significant amendments were introduced at Westminster, modifying the original proposal. One of them gave each colony the right to secede from the Council – an adjustment calculated to induce New South Wales to participate. Thus, pursuant to sections 30 and 31, participation was voluntary and a colony could withdraw from the Council at will. The second amendment empowered the Queen, at the request of the colonies, to increase the number of members in the Council.

---

[61] See the discussion in Quick and Garran, *Annotated Constitution*, 109–15. Under s. 15 such laws would, however, only apply to such colonies as had referred the power to the Council.

Thus, the scheme as enacted was overwhelmingly 'confederal' rather than 'federal' in nature: each self-governing colony was equally represented and could secede at will. It is true that decisions were made by majority vote, rather than unanimously, which committed each participating colony to the destiny of the whole. Participation, however, was completely voluntary – South Australia participated only from 1888 to 1890 and New South Wales did not participate at all. With no federal executive or independent source of revenue, moreover, the Council was, with the passage of time, overshadowed by premiers' conferences and other forms of inter-colonial cooperation, notwithstanding the necessity of the agreement of all colonies for full cooperation to occur.[62] While the Council provided a regular forum at which colonial leaders could discuss and on occasion act on matters of collective concern, premiers' conferences, and not the Council, would in fact facilitate the Australasian federation conventions of 1891 and 1897–8 which ultimately drafted the Australian Constitution.

In 1889 Sir James Bevan Edwards, a major-general in the British army, delivered a report commissioned by the British government on the state of the Australian colonial defences.[63] Taking the opportunity afforded by the report, on 24 October 1889, Henry Parkes, once again premier of New South Wales, delivered his famous Tenterfield Oration, urging the creation of 'a great national Government for all Australia'. Parkes's scheme was that the colonial legislatures appoint delegates to attend a convention that would devise a constitution in order to create 'a Federal Government with a Federal Parliament for the conduct of national business.'[64] Parkes subsequently proposed to Premier Duncan Gillies of Victoria and the other premiers that at the convention 'the number from each colony should be the same', and be drawn from all sides in politics. He suggested that six members from each colony be chosen, four from

---

[62] R. D. Lumb and Gabriel A. Moens, *The Constitution of the Commonwealth of Australia Annotated* (5th edn, Sydney: Butterworths, 1995), 3; La Nauze, *Making of the Constitution*, 3.

[63] For the Edwards Report, see Clark, *Select Documents*, 463–7; Bennett, *Making of the Commonwealth*, 38–42.

[64] Clark, *Select Documents*, 467–70. See, generally, Henry Parkes, *Fifty Years in the Making of Australian History* (London: Longmans, Green and Co., 1892), 268–74, 337–58; Quick and Garran, *Annotated Constitution*, 115–18; Wise, *Making of the Commonwealth*, 1–9; Deakin, *Federal Story*, 15–16; La Nauze, *Making of the Constitution*, 9; McMinn, *Constitutional History*, 103; A. W. Martin, 'Parkes and the 1890 Conference', *Papers on Parliament* No. 9 (Canberra: Department of the Senate, 1990).

the legislative assemblies and two from the Councils. He also argued that the Federal Council was not up to the task of coordinating the defence of the Australian colonies and that, although the imperial Parliament could, 'on the application of the colonies', pass an Act constituting a federal army under one command, 'the colonies could never consent to the Imperial Executive interfering in the direction of its movements'. Hence, 'the imperative necessity for a Federal Government'.[65] Gillies, however, was more inclined to use the existing Federal Council and he suggested a meeting of the Federal Council together with representatives from New South Wales. The ultimate result was the Australasian Federation Conference held in Melbourne in 1890, in which two representatives from each colony, including New Zealand, participated.[66]

## The conference of 1890

The formative preconditions of federation outlined so far decisively shaped the formative and representative structures adopted in the conference of 1890, as well as the conventions of 1891 and 1897–8. These preconditions lay essentially in the principle that federation would be initiated, debated and concluded by the several colonies on the basis of equality of representation and unanimous consent. Each self-governing colony was in fact equally represented both at the conference and at the two conventions and, although decisions in those forums were taken by majority vote,[67] ultimate ratification of the Constitution would depend on the consent of the voters in each colony. In this respect, the formative preconditions of federation already had implications for the representative structure adopted within the conference and conventions.[68] In turn, these formative structures would influence the actual system of representation and modes of alteration adopted under the Commonwealth Bills of 1891 and 1898.

---

[65] Parkes to Gillies, 30 October 1889, in Clark, *Select Documents*, 470–2.
[66] See La Nauze, *Making of the Constitution*, ch. 2; Quick and Garran, *Annotated Constitution*, 117–19; cf. McMinn, *Nationalism and Federalism*, ch. 8.
[67] A significant deviation from the state-by-state voting at the Philadelphia Convention in 1787.
[68] As the premier of New South Wales, George Reid, lamented in his famous 'Yes-No Speech' delivered at the Sydney Town Hall, 28 March 1898. A report of the speech was published in the *Sydney Morning Herald*, 29 March 1898, and is reproduced in Scott Bennett (ed.), *Federation* (Melbourne: Cassell, 1975), 173–86.

Delegates to the conference of 1890 understood the proceedings to be provisional on a wider and more representative gathering. The immediate objective was not to draft a constitution, but to frame a set of resolutions testing the question 'whether it was worth taking pains to have one framed'.[69] Most of the debate concerned a motion by Henry Parkes anticipating an 'early union under the Crown', predicated on the 'developed national life of Australia . . . in self-governing capacity to an extent which justifies the higher act . . . of the union of the colonies, under one legislative and executive government, on principles just to the several colonies'.[70] The terms of Parkes's resolution were largely garnered from a Victorian resolution that had itself borrowed from the report of the Quebec Conference of 1864.[71] As the proposed Australian federation was to be 'under the Crown', Parkes expressed the opinion that Canada was the appropriate model for Australia.[72]

However, while Parkes's resolution was unanimously approved, the delegates had very mixed views of the Canadian model. The representatives of the smaller colonies in particular expressed a decided preference, as Clark put it, for 'true federation' along the lines of the United States, rather than the 'amalgamation' of the Dominion of Canada.[73] Drawing on a rapidly growing knowledge of the American system in all of its workings,[74] Clark insisted on two canons of federation. The first was the 'principle of the local legislatures being sovereign within their own spheres'; the second was the American scheme of a bicameral legislature in which the states were equally represented in one house and the people of the entire federation were represented in the other.[75] Bernhard Ringrose Wise later remarked that the resemblance between the Australian and American Constitutions was very largely due to the influence of Clark and

[69] La Nauze, *Making of the Constitution*, 15.    [70] *Conference Debates, Melbourne* (1890), x.
[71] La Nauze, *Making of the Constitution*, 14.
[72] Quick and Garran, *Annotated Constitution*, 118–19; La Nauze, *Making of the Constitution*, 17.
[73] *Conference Debates, Melbourne* (1890), 106. See Wise, *Making of the Commonwealth*, 74–5. Even the young Alfred Deakin of Victoria expressed a preference for the American system: Brian Galligan and Cliff Walsh, 'Federalism – Yes or No?' in Craven, *Australian Federation*, 195.
[74] La Nauze, *Making of the Constitution*, 13, 17, 234; Reynolds, 'Clark's American Sympathies'; Neasey, 'Clark and Australian Federation', 2; Williams, 'Clark and our Republican Tradition'; Alex C. Castles, 'Andrew Inglis Clark and the American Constitutional System'; but see Thomson, 'Clark and Australian Constitutional Law', 61–2.
[75] *Conference Debates, Melbourne* (1890), 108, 110. Compare the Australian Natives' Association Resolution of 1890: Quick and Garran, *Annotated Constitution*, 151.

that this speech in 1890 contained 'the germ of the ideas which dominated the Convention of 1891'.[76]

John Alexander Cockburn of South Australia likewise argued for a 'union of strong colonies', rather than a 'coercive', 'homogeneous National Union'. Demonstrating a familiarity with both American and Canadian developments, Cockburn supported the American 'compromise' between 'pure federation' and 'national union'. Avoiding the criterion of 'sovereignty', he understood the distinguishing feature between confederation and federation to be the direct relation between the central government and the individual. Following Madison, he thought that Americans had devised an appropriate reconciliation between 'pure federation' and 'pure national union': a combination of both.[77]

The significance of these early statements of principle should be noted. As Michael Zuckert has argued, the apparent compromise on representation within the American Senate and House of Representatives had been supported as a principled position by Dickinson from an early point in the Philadelphia Convention.[78] But whether a compromise or a principle in the United States, as will be seen, most of the Australians understood a dual system of representation to be a fundamental principle of federation.[79] As La Nauze observed, 'the voices of the colonies ... would be heard loud and clear when the powers and form of a federal legislature came to be defined'.[80]

It is apparent from the terms of debate in 1890 that a Diceyan analysis fails to capture the understanding of federalism of Clark, Cockburn and many others. In the minds of these delegates, Canada was not an appropriate model of federation because the Canadian provinces had not federated as 'sovereign' bodies politic on the basis of absolute equality. As a consequence, the Canadian Senate inadequately represented the provinces; the Dominion was given 'general' power to legislate, subject to an elaborate 'division' of responsibilities between the Dominion and the provinces (i.e. legislative power was not 'delegated' by the provinces to the Dominion); provincial legislation could be disallowed; and the

---

[76] Wise, *Making of the Commonwealth*, 75; cf. Deakin, *Federal Story*, 30; Neasey, 'Clark and Australian Federation', 2.

[77] *Conference Debates, Melbourne* (1890), 133–8. Playford and Lee Steere expressed views similar to Clark and Cockburn; Deakin, Macrossan and Gillies in some respects agreed.

[78] Zuckert, 'Federalism and the Founding'; see also Rakove, *Original Meanings*, 170.

[79] See chs. 7 and 8 below.   [80] La Nauze, *Making of the Constitution*, 17.

provincial governments were apparently subordinated through central-ised powers of vice-regal appointment. The very use of the term 'pro-vince' reinforced the perception that each region was but an administrative subdivision of the centre. While a commentator as emi-nent as Goldwin Smith may have suggested that Canada was a kind of 'federal republic' along the lines of the United States, Australians such as John Quick begged to differ, drawing attention to features such as these, which distinguished the Canadian from the American systems.[81]

Indeed, as Griffith at the time put it, the Australians had been 'accustomed for so long to self-government' that they regarded them-selves as having become 'practically almost sovereign states', indeed 'a great deal more sovereign states, though not in name, than the separate states of America'.[82] While absolute sovereignty could not be claimed, the use of the term 'state' by the Australians – following the United States example – reinforced in their minds the idea that each region was an equal, constituent member of the federation. Each state party would therefore insist on retaining its independent executive government and legislature; there would be a general demand for equality of representa-tion in the Senate; and only limited legislative power would be delegated to the federation.

This is not to suggest that the delegates agreed on all the details or that there was no dissent from the generally prevailing view. For instance, while Alfred Deakin echoed Cockburn's view that federation differed from confederation in the direct relation between the federal government and the individual, he understood the federal government to represent what he called a 'Sovereign state acting directly, without any intermediary, upon the citizens from which it springs'.[83] Likewise, as far as the federal executive was concerned, John Murtagh Macrossan of Queensland favoured the direct election of the governor-general together with a free veto over legislation, while Parkes supported the British tradition of parliamentary responsible government – a proposition that would, in due course, have to confront the federalist idea of the equal representation of the states in a powerful Senate.[84]

---

[81] Quick, *Digest of Federal Constitutions*, 59–60.
[82] *Conference Debates, Melbourne* (1890), 10.
[83] *Ibid.*, 26. Cf. Deakin, *Federal Story*, 41, 77, claiming that Cockburn actually wanted confederation.
[84] *Ibid.*, 73 (Macrossan), 91 (Gillies, summarising Parkes).

Such differences, however, did not prevent the conference from unanimously approving Parkes's resolution. Of greater immediate significance were Deakin's further resolutions concerning the steps to be taken in organising a future convention.[85] These resolutions, as agreed to by the conference, provided that the delegates should take such steps as may be necessary to induce their legislatures 'to appoint . . . delegates to a National Australasian Convention, empowered to consider and report upon an adequate scheme for a Federal Constitution'. No more than seven delegates from each self-governing colony and four delegates from each Crown colony were to be appointed.[86]

It was also of strategic significance that Griffith subsequently, but unsuccessfully, proposed that delegates to the convention should vote 'as colonies' on 'great matters'.[87] If put into effect, this would significantly have altered the voting patterns of the convention. Individual rather than block voting in the event would considerably weaken the sense in which the colonies participated as corporate units in the conventions of 1891 and 1897–8. None the less, the ratification process ultimately adopted would still require majorities in each colony, and this appreciably qualified the effect of the individual vote. The delegates to the conventions of 1891 and 1897–8 would be acutely aware that they had to draft a constitution that could garner the support of every colony, as Griffith pointed out in 1890.[88] Further, when the colonial legislatures proceeded to nominate their delegates, the delegates 'tended to deprecate specific instructions' from the colonial legislatures, for 'the hands of the delegates', it was said, 'should not be tied'.[89] This decision would also have an effect on the debate and voting patterns at the conventions of the 1890s.

While delegates of the same colony often shared very similar views, there were sometimes significant differences. As Quick and Garran observed in another connection, 'it seldom happened that any delegation voted solid'.[90] A requirement that delegates must vote 'in colonies' might

---

[85] See La Nauze, *Making of the Constitution*, 16; Quick and Garran, *Annotated Constitution*, 121–2.

[86] *Conference Debates, Melbourne* (1890), 261. Western Australia obtained full self-governing status later in the year.

[87] *Ibid.*, 261.  [88] *Ibid.*, 8.

[89] La Nauze, *Making of the Constitution*, 20. The issue of 'fettering' the discretion of delegates by 'special instructions' had been raised as early as 1857: Thomson to Duffy, 7 November 1857, Duffy Papers.

[90] Quick and Garran, *Annotated Constitution*, 186. See Wise, *Making of the Commonwealth*, 234–6.

have produced less diversity of opinion, but a requirement that they vote on instructions from their legislatures would most probably have prolonged and perhaps hindered deliberations within the federal conventions of 1891 and 1897–8. The rejection of block voting and voting on instructions weakened the sense in which the colonial governments could be conceived of as corporate constituent parties to a federal compact. When the delegates came to debate representation within the Federal Parliament and, in particular, the Senate, the fact that they debated and voted as independent representatives precluded any serious suggestion that senators be required to vote in blocs or on instructions – notwithstanding the fact that the 1891 convention adopted a system by which senators were elected by the state legislatures. How could senators be required to vote in blocs if delegates nominated to the convention – before any federation existed – had not been so required?[91] Already a decisive step towards federation had been taken.

Further decisive steps in this direction would be taken at the convention of 1897–8 when it was decided that the Senate should be directly elected by the people of the colonies. To this degree, it might be concluded that Richard Baker's losing battle to establish a Swiss-style federal executive, representative of the states *qua* states,[92] began in Melbourne in 1890 when the proposal that delegates to the convention vote 'as colonies' was rejected. But it would be premature to assume that this was the entire matter. As noted, the fate of Australian federation still remained with the colonial legislatures and, in the event, the peoples of the colonies, voting as colonies. The delegates certainly had no capacity to bind the legislatures that had nominated them, or the people who elected those legislatures. Thus, the formative structure of the conventions of the 1890s contained kernels of what would continue to be fundamental to the workings of the Australian Constitution in its representative and amendment provisions.

In any case, the necessary resolutions for the 1891 convention were in due course passed in the various colonies. New South Wales chose to nominate four delegates from its Legislative Assembly and three from its Legislative Council; in Tasmania, four delegates were nominated from the

---

[91] Notably, Bryce had likewise noted that American senators voted as individuals: Bryce, *American Commonwealth*, I, 97.

[92] See the discussion in chs. 4 and 6.

Assembly, two from the Council, and a further delegate was nominated by both houses; in the other colonies, the nominations were five from the Assembly and two from the Council. On Quick and Garran's account, the nominations were bipartisan: premiers, leaders of the opposition and former premiers were chosen. All in all, nine delegates were former premiers, and all were members of the colonial parliaments.[93] Nearly the full range of current political opinion was represented, with the notable exception of radical labour.[94] As Garran pointed out almost forty years later:

> During the course of the sessions of the Conventions there were cross-currents and divisions of every kind. Sometimes the divisions would be between free-traders and protectionists; sometimes between conservatives and liberals; sometimes large States against small States. Any two members might find themselves one day in agreement, and the next day in opposition.[95]

For example, on issues which related to federal structure and representation, a conservative Baker and a liberal Cockburn would agree on maintaining a powerful Senate in which the states were equally represented, but were opposed by a liberal Isaacs and, to a degree, a conservative William McMillan.[96] As Sawer pointed out:

> to an important degree an overwhelming majority of the delegates at all stages were State-righters. It was federation they aimed at, and furthermore a federation in which there was a strong emphasis on preserving the structure and powers of the States so far as consistent with union for specific and limited purposes.[97]

Such a perspective was reinforced, it can now be seen, by two factors. First, an overwhelming majority of the framers professed that it was right, as a matter of positive political morality and federal principle, that a

---

[93] Parkes, *Fifty Years*, 275–6; Quick and Garran, *Annotated Constitution*, 122–4; La Nauze, *Making of the Constitution*, 22; Crisp, *Australian National Government*, 11.

[94] For radical labour criticisms of the Commonwealth Bill of 1898, see Hugh Anderson (ed.), *Tocsin: Contesting the Constitution 1897–1900* (Melbourne: Red Rooster Press, 2000).

[95] Evidence of Robert Garran, Senate Select Committee on Standing Committees (1927–30), quoted in Crisp, *Australian National Government*, 13. See also La Nauze, *Making of the Constitution*, 47–8.

[96] See chs. 7 and 8. See also Parkes, *Fifty Years*, 295–308, contrasting himself and Dibbs.

[97] Sawer, *Australian Constitution*, 23.

federation of the colonies must proceed on the basis of inter-colonial agreement. Second, as a matter of *Realpolitik*, delegates to the federal conventions, as members of the ruling elite in each colony, were not about to abandon the prerogatives and powers of local self-government that they had secured and now controlled. The conventions of 1891 and 1897–8, as well as the Commonwealth Bills that emerged from those conventions, would be profoundly shaped by these factors.

On the eve of the convention of 1891, however, one last event of significance – all too often overlooked in accounts of Australian federation[98] – was to occur. The desire for independent local self-government for the northern and central regions of Queensland has been noted. In November 1890 the premier of Queensland, Sir Samuel Griffith, introduced a resolution into the Queensland Legislative Assembly which proposed, not the separation of the north and centre, but the transformation of the colony into a kind of federation of 'united provinces' consisting of the northern, central and southern districts, each possessing its own legislature and executive government.[99] Under the scheme, the existing colonial parliament and government would continue to exercise authority over the entire colony in certain explicitly defined matters, but this would be complemented by a generously defined set of powers and responsibilities to be exercised by the newly formed provinces. In this respect, the scheme followed the Canadian model of federation, as did the proposal that the executive power of each province be vested in a lieutenant-governor, appointed by the governor of the entire colony. Such an approach was to be expected, given that the 'federation' was, legally speaking, to be initiated by the colony as a whole – that is, a form of devolutionary, rather than integrative, federalism. What is most remarkable, however, is that not only did Griffith's scheme, following the American model, propose that the two houses of the legislature of the united provinces be chosen by the legislatures of the provinces and by the electors of the provinces respectively, but it was envisaged that once a federation of all the colonies of Australia was achieved, the governmental powers and functions of the United Provinces of Queensland would pass to the federation as a whole. Griffith's

---

[98] E.g. Quick and Garran, *Annotated Constitution*, 123; Brown, 'One Continent, Two Federalisms'. For useful background, compare Katherine McConnel, ' "Separation is from the Devil while Federation is from Heaven": The Separation Question and Federation in Queensland' (1999) 4 *The New Federalist* 14.

[99] See Queensland, *Legislative Assembly Debates* (1890), vol. LXII, 1330–1.

proposal was, alas, rejected by the Legislative Council. But if it had been passed as Griffith envisaged, the negotiating parties at the federal convention of 1891 might have been the independent provinces of the north, centre and south, and not the colony of Queensland as a whole.

Given Griffith's central role in the debate over federation, this shows that, for one outstanding figure at least, what was decisive in the discussion was not simply a desire to conserve and protect the existing powers and entrenched interests of colonial politicians, but also a willingness to acknowledge – and perhaps even a fervent belief in – the principles of local self-government and constitutional self-determination as essential to the idea of Australian federation.

# Formative institutions

[W]e must recognise this fact, that there is a feeling, and a natural feeling, though, perhaps, it may not be capable of the most logical justification, on the part of the parliaments and peoples of the different states, that they will require safeguards to be provided for the preservation of state interests before they will have anything to do with the adoption of a constitution providing for a federal government.

Charles Kingston (1891)

The hard realities of colonial politics, in conjunction with idealistic beliefs about the true nature of federalism, conspired to ensure that a federation of the Australian colonies would only occur on the basis of an intercolonial agreement negotiated by politicians and ratified by the voters of the constituent colonies. The two federal conventions held in 1891 and 1897–8 and a series of colonial referendums held between 1898 and 1900 were the primary decision-making mechanisms through which this was accomplished. A full account of the making of the Australian Constitution must necessarily grapple with the deliberations that occurred within the conventions and ratification debates of the 1890s. But before turning to the particularities of the debate, it is finally necessary to understand the procedures and processes that were adopted within the conventions in order to facilitate and shape that debate. It is therefore the objective of this chapter to explain the formative institutions through which the Australian Constitution was debated, drafted and ratified, before addressing in later chapters the precise terms of the debate and of the constitutional text that emerged from the entire formative process.

## The convention of 1891

The first federal convention, formally called the National Australasian Convention, was convened in Sydney on 2 March 1891 and ended its deliberations on 9 April 1891. The delegates were elected by their respective parliaments, all six Australian colonies as well as New Zealand being represented.

The first day of sitting was taken up with a number of formalities, including the appointment of Sir Henry Parkes as president and Sir Samuel Griffith as vice-president of the Convention.[1] Early on, the convention resolved to follow ordinary parliamentary rules of procedure, to admit the press to its proceedings and that an official record of its proceedings would be made public.[2] While each Australian colony was equally represented, and while delegates from each colony often held broadly similar views, each delegate had an individual vote. The convention spent a little more than half of its time debating, amending and approving a series of resolutions, moved by Parkes, which set out the basic principles to be embodied in a proposed federation of the Australian colonies.[3]

The convention then formed constitutional, finance and judiciary committees with a view to framing a bill for the establishment of a federation on the basis of those principles.[4] Each colony was again equally represented on each committee. The Constitutional Committee consisted of several leading delegates. Samuel Griffith was elected chair, and he was joined in particular by Henry Parkes and Edmund Barton of New South Wales, Duncan Gillies and Alfred Deakin of Victoria, John Downer of South Australia, Andrew Inglis Clark of Tasmania, Sir John Forrest of Western Australia and Sir George Grey of New Zealand. The Finance Committee was in turn chaired by James Munro of Victoria and included William McMillan of New South Wales, Sir Thomas McIlwraith of Queensland and Sir John Bray of South Australia, among others. The Judiciary Committee was chaired by Clark, and included Charles Kingston of South Australia, George Dibbs of New South Wales, Henry Wrixon of Victoria and John Hackett of Western Australia.[5]

As has been noted, Clark had come to the convention with a draft constitution which he distributed privately, but widely, among the delegates.[6] The second draft produced by Kingston was also distributed. These drafts, particularly Clark's, became the basis of the draft Commonwealth

---

[1] *Convention Debates, Sydney* (1891), 3–6.  [2] *Ibid.*, 9–10, 12–22; see also 937–8.
[3] *Ibid.*, 23, 499–500.  [4] *Ibid.*, 500–9.
[5] *Ibid.*, 509–10. See La Nauze, *Making of the Constitution*, 337, n. 21.
[6] See La Nauze, *Making of the Constitution*, 24. See also the discussion in ch. 4.

Bill famously prepared by a drafting committee led by Griffith, together with Clark, Kingston and later Barton, when aboard the Queensland government steamship *Lucinda* while cruising the Hawkesbury River.[7] The draft bill was then submitted to the convention sitting as a committee of the whole and, under Griffith's guidance, debated seriatim, amended and ultimately approved.[8]

On Griffith's motion, the convention then resolved to recommend that the colonial parliaments provide for the bill to be submitted to the people of the colonies for approval and that upon ratification by three colonies the bill should be presented to the imperial Parliament for enactment.[9] During general debate on the question of ratification, however, Sir George Grey of New Zealand proposed that the Commonwealth Bill should be approved in a plebiscite of the entire people of Australia, on the basis of the principle of 'one man one vote'.[10] Cockburn, a prominent delegate from South Australia, supported the general thrust of Grey's proposal, but argued that it should be resolved by a majority of voters in a majority of colonies, as well as a majority of the people of Australia as a whole.[11]

Griffith objected to both ideas, first on the ground that the entire formative process had been predicated upon the voluntary agreement of each colony, and second that the manner of ratification should ultimately be determined by the colonial legislatures. Griffith's own preference, he explained, was for ratification by specially elected conventions in each colony, as this would help to secure what he called the 'deliberate opinion' of the people. Griffith none the less considered it prudent to leave the matter to each parliament.[12] Munro for his part added that to do otherwise was to exceed the mandate that the convention had been given, limited as it was to the preparation of a draft constitution.[13] As Quick and Garran later put it, to do otherwise was contrary to the 'idea of a voluntary acceptance by each individual colony'.[14] Thus, while a number of delegates, like Thynne, Dibbs and Deakin, supported popular participation, they accepted that the mode of ratification would have to

---

[7] See La Nauze, *Making of the Constitution*, 23–8, 49–70.

[8] *Convention Debates, Sydney* (1891), 521, 905–27. For the text of the draft Commonwealth of Australia Bill, see *ibid.*, 943–64 (appendix).

[9] *Ibid.*, 927–37.    [10] *Ibid.*, 900–5, 937.    [11] *Ibid.*, 900.

[12] *Ibid.*, 900–1, 927–8. See also Griffith, *Notes on Australian Federation*, 27.

[13] *Convention Debates, Sydney* (1891), 902.    [14] Quick and Garran, *Annotated Constitution*, 142.

be determined, ultimately, by the colonial legislatures.[15] Griffith in this connection insisted that the convention could not dictate the manner in which the colonies would accept the constitution, and that each colony must be free to make its own decision whether to federate or not, and the convention ultimately agreed.[16]

There was also debate about whether the ratifying process ought to involve a detailed reconsideration of the proposed constitution or only a decision whether to accept or reject the bill as a whole. Understandably, most delegates were averse to re-opening debate over a document which represented so many weeks of laborious negotiation. Sir John Bray suggested that the draft constitution should only be submitted to the people of the colonies for their 'consideration' and that, if necessary, a second convention be convened to complete the process.[17] Griffith and Baker argued, on the contrary, that to do so would undermine the elaborate system of compromises that had been meticulously negotiated and carefully incorporated in the draft bill.[18] The convention agreed, ultimately resolving that the constitution be submitted to the colonies for approval, and that upon ratification by at least three colonies, the bill should be presented to Her Majesty's government for enactment.[19]

## The Commonwealth Bill of 1891

When the debate about the means of ratification of the Commonwealth Bill of 1891 is compared to the more regulated and widely consultative process adopted for the convention of 1897–8 and the referendums of 1898–1900, the fate of the 1891 bill is not surprising. While widely circulated and debated, the Commonwealth Bill of 1891 seemed destined not to prosper. It was criticised, variously, as overly liberal, too conservative, excessively republican, too centralist and as not democratic enough.[20] Despite the wishes of a majority of its framers, the bill was certainly not considered to be final or complete, by either the people or the legislatures.[21]

---

[15] See e.g. *Convention Debates, Sydney* (1891), 340, 903.   [16] *Ibid.*, 927–8, 937.
[17] *Ibid.*, 929–31.   [18] *Ibid.*, 932.   [19] *Ibid.*, 937.
[20] La Nauze, *Making of the Constitution*, 79–81, 90.
[21] Quick and Garran, *Annotated Constitution*, 143–4; cf. McMinn, *Constitutional History*, 105, noting a tendency to avoid the hard issues raised by the proposed bill.

There had been no labour delegate at the convention, and labour criticisms were accordingly severe; they were also diverse, and at times fanciful,[22] but uniform in seeking a more democratic constitution.[23] Hank Morgan, for example, saw that the constitutive basis of the convention would affect the kind of constitution produced, arguing that the convention must:

> voice the opinions, fairly and equally expressed, of the great masses of the people, and not have the results of their labours distorted and biased by the class feelings and ambitions of those elected by the plural votes of Conservative property holders.
>
> Therefore, until every Australian Province grants to its inhabitants exactly equal elective power, commonly termed 'one man one vote', which is only simple justice, the people should decline to have anything to do with Federation . . .
>
> Of one thing we may be perfectly sure, that if all the Australian Provinces do not secure Electoral Reform *before* Federation, they will stand a poor chance of getting it afterwards.[24]

Morgan also thought that the federation must be fully voluntary, which meant that there ought to be a right to secede unilaterally, grounded in the idea of an uncoerced union of independent states:

> Give every State the absolute right of secession on a certain proportion, say three-fourths of the adult inhabitants desiring it and agreeing to discharge all joint obligations. Voluntary Union is the only Union worth having, and if any State has the right to refuse to join, it should have the same right to refuse to remain.[25]

Indeed, the voluntary foundations of the proposed constitution implied that federal laws, although they ought to be enacted by a unicameral Federal Parliament elected solely on a population basis, should only apply to those states whose parliaments had formally approved of the law.[26]

The Commonwealth Bill fared little better in the colonial legislatures. It was delayed and severely criticised in the New South Wales Parliament (despite Parkes's efforts) and it suffered a similar fate in the other

---

[22] Quick and Garran, *Annotated Constitution*, 144.

[23] Clark, *Select Documents*, 494; La Nauze, *Making of the Constitution*, 95; Bennett, *Federation*, 9–13, 43–7.

[24] Morgan, *The Hummer* (Wagga) 19 March 1892, in Clark, *Select Documents*, 494–6.

[25] *Ibid.*   [26] *Ibid.*

colonies. In the New South Wales Legislative Assembly, George Reid was particularly critical of the extensive powers of the proposed Senate and the omission of responsible government 'as a necessary part of the Constitution'.[27] In Victoria, the Legislative Assembly spent some eight days in general debate and another week in committee. The leading critic was Sir Bryan O'Loghlen, who criticised the powers of the Senate, particularly the power to amend supply bills, and insisted on the principle of 'one man, one vote'.[28] The South Australian Legislative Assembly spent six nights debating the bill, but spread these over a period of almost three months. Notably, it amended the bill so that senators would be directly elected by the people of the state and constitutional amendments approved by referendums in each colony.[29] In Tasmania, Clark proposed that the two houses consider the draft bill and then remit it for consideration by a colonial convention elected by the voters, thereby following the way in which the US Constitution had itself been ratified.[30]

Generally, the smaller states looked to New South Wales to advance the matter. Edmund Barton in the Assembly and Richard O'Connor in the Council sought to progress the bill but were met by resistance on the part of both free traders and labour. In this context, Barton's programme became one of having the bill debated and amendments proposed by the parliament, then laid before a second convention, subsequently resubmitted to each parliament, and finally presented to the people for final approval.[31] Even so, progress was difficult, and Parkes eventually concluded that the legislatures were not suited to the work of considering and approving a federal constitution. In his view, the problem lay with the fact that members were elected to represent local districts and to address local issues, and so the parliaments made local issues their first priority. Given that the legislatures were not elected 'upon this exceptionally large question', he proposed that the voters of the colonies elect a convention specifically for the purpose of revising the draft constitution and designing a new one if necessary.[32]

---

[27] Quick and Garran, *Annotated Constitution*, 145; cf. Parkes, *Fifty Years*, 370–80; McMinn, *Constitutional History*, 106–8.

[28] Quick and Garran, *Annotated Constitution*, 146; see also 148–9.

[29] *Ibid.*, 147.    [30] *Ibid.*    [31] *Ibid.*, 148–9. Compare the process of 1897–8.

[32] New South Wales, *Parliamentary Debates* (1892), Legislative Assembly, vol. LVII, 5878, in Clark, *Select Documents*, 492–4; and see Irving, *Constitute a Nation*, 140; Quick and Garran, *Annotated Constitution*, 148–9; *The New Federation Movement*, in Clark, *Select Documents*, 498–500.

However, little further progress was made. As Quick and Garran observed: 'the Parliamentary process of dealing with the Commonwealth Bill had broken down hopelessly'.[33]

## The parliaments and the peoples

The initiative for the time being thus fell to extra-parliamentary activities. At a famous meeting of the Australasian Federation League at Corowa in 1893, Dr John Quick proposed his celebrated resolution:

> That in the opinion of this Conference the Legislature of each Australasian colony should pass an Act providing for the election of representatives to attend a statutory convention or congress to consider and adopt a bill to establish a federal constitution for Australia, and upon the adoption of such bill or measure it be submitted by some process of referendum to the verdict of each colony.[34]

The proposal is widely regarded as significant.[35] Quick and Garran, both as participants and chroniclers, considered that earlier efforts had failed on two accounts: members of the colonial legislatures wanted a say on matters of detail and the people of the colonies wanted popular participation.[36] Irving identifies the significance of the Corowa plan in the legitimacy it gave to the federal movement – an appeal to 'the people'.[37] This was certainly Quick and Garran's perspective: the failure of the 1891 bill showed, against the 'adherents of the Parliamentary system', that public confidence in the process was 'more important even than the *personnel* of the Convention'.[38] Less enthusiastically, Macintyre has characterised the Corowa proposal as a remarkable act of political ventriloquism, in which the 'people' were called upon to confer legitimacy on a programme initiated by politicians.[39] The novelty of Quick's proposal did not lie in

---

[33] Quick and Garran, *Annotated Constitution*, 150.

[34] *Official Report of the Federation Conference Held in the Court-House, Corowa, on Monday 31st July, and Tuesday, 1ˢᵗ August, 1893* (Corowa: James C. Leslie, 1893), 27. On the possible role of Henry D'Esterre Taylor in first suggesting this course of action, see Deakin, *Federal Story*, 57–9.

[35] Wise, *Making of the Commonwealth*, 193; La Nauze, *Making of the Constitution*, 90, 161–2; Clark, *Select Documents*, 497; Crisp, *Australian National Government*, 8; Hirst, *Sentimental Nation*, 123.

[36] Quick and Garran, *Annotated Constitution*, 154, 160.

[37] Irving, *Constitute a Nation*, 137.    [38] Quick and Garran, *Annotated Constitution*, 154.

[39] Stuart Macintyre, 'Corowa and the Voice of the People', *The People's Conventions: Corowa (1893) and Bathurst (1896), Papers on Parliament* no. 32 (Canberra: Department of the Senate, 1998), 11.

the calling of a second convention or in the referendum, however, or in the idea of a directly elected convention *per se*. Its novelty, and its importance, lay in bringing these elements together into a process 'pre-ordained by Enabling Acts in all the colonies'.[40] Soon after Corowa, Quick drafted an Australian Federal Congress Bill along the lines of the proposal. The Australasian Federation League supported the general idea, but, under Barton's leadership, proposed popular conventions in each colony to formulate schemes to be presented for consideration by a subsequent federal convention elected by the colonial legislatures.[41]

These schemes were not the only possibilities under consideration. Some favoured development of the Federal Council of Australasia.[42] On the other side of the ledger, leaders of the Labor Electoral League were promoting the formation of a unitary 'democratic republic' of Australia, governed by a unicameral Parliament possessing plenary legislative powers and elected on the basis of 'one man one vote' throughout the nation.[43] In similar terms, the premier of New South Wales, Sir George Dibbs, proposed a scheme of 'unification' for New South Wales and Victoria. The two colonies would form a 'complete' union under one governor and one parliament having 'supreme control', with local governments confined to local, subordinate powers.[44] While Dibbs's scheme had its supporters, it met with a cool response from the Victorian premier, Sir James Patterson. As Quick and Garran would later point out, federation was more appropriate to Australian conditions than amalgamation, especially given the vast areas, unique conditions and local patriotisms of the different colonies.[45] As they also observed, the Dibbs proposal 'really meant little more than undoing the work of separation and the re-establishing the earlier complete unity'.[46] The colonies had only just been established as self-governing communities and were not about to submit to being subordinate parts of a unitary system. Dibbs's supporting argument – that the other colonies would be attracted 'within the sphere of [its] extended influence' and 'accept the terms dictated, or

---

[40] Quick and Garran, *Annotated Constitution*, 154; Hirst, *Sentimental Nation*, 123.
[41] *Australian Federation League Report* (28 February 1894), Baker Papers; Quick and Garran, *Annotated Constitution*, 155; Irving, *Constitute a Nation*, 138; Hirst, *Sentimental Nation*, 127–8.
[42] Irving, *Constitute a Nation*, 139–40.    [43] Macintyre, 'Voice of the People', 8–9.
[44] Quick and Garran, *Annotated Constitution*, 155–7; Crisp, *Federation Fathers*, ch. 2.
[45] Quick and Garran, *Annotated Constitution*, 157.    [46] *Ibid.*, 156.

stay outside'[47] – only served to reinforce the suspicions of the smaller colonies of an overweening New South Wales collaborating with a similarly powerful Victoria.

Shortly thereafter, Reid, now premier of New South Wales, proposed a premiers' conference to discuss the problem. He was impressed by (but not committed to) the Quick scheme and seemed to accept Quick's diagnosis of the bill of 1891: it 'never quite came home to the hearts of the masses of the people'.[48] At the same time, Reid wished to ensure that only leading politicians would be elected, and so he maintained that the colonies must vote as one electorate.[49] In the upshot, on Reid's initiative and by a majority of four to two, the premiers' conference of 1895 eventually agreed on a three-step process. First, a convention 'consisting of ten representatives from each colony' and 'directly chosen by the electors' would be 'charged with the duty of framing a Federal Constitution'. Second, the constitution framed by the convention would be 'submitted to the electors for acceptance or rejection by a direct vote'. Third, the constitution, 'if accepted by the electors of three or more colonies', would be 'transmitted to the Queen by an Address from the Parliaments of those colonies praying for the necessary legislative enactment'.[50]

While he ultimately agreed with the resolution, Charles Kingston of South Australia said that he preferred that an imperial Enabling Act empower the colonies to adopt a constitution without further imperial involvement. Hugh Nelson, then premier of Queensland, went so far as to dissent from the resolution, insisting that the approval of each colony be 'obtained in such manner as each colony may prescribe'.[51] Sir John Forrest, premier of Western Australia, also dissented, maintaining that the 1891 bill should first be considered by the colonial parliaments, that any suggested amendments be referred to a second convention appointed by the parliaments after a general election, and that the bill produced by the second convention be submitted for imperial enactment without a referendum.[52]

---

[47] *Ibid.*, 155.   [48] *Argus*, 24 January 1895, quoted in Irving, *Constitute a Nation*, 139.
[49] Hirst, *Sentimental Nation*, 128–9.
[50] *The Resolutions of the Premiers' Conference* (Hobart, 1895), in Clark, *Select Documents*, 501–2.
[51] Quoted in Quick and Garran, *Annotated Constitution*, 159.
[52] *Ibid.* Frank Crowley, *Big John Forrest 1847–1918: A Founding Father of the Commonwealth of Australia*, 2 vols. (Perth: University of Western Australia Press, 2000), 176, observes that Forrest understood the constitution to be a kind of inter-colonial 'treaty'.

A draft bill prepared by Kingston and George Turner of Victoria was subsequently accepted by a majority of premiers, Nelson again expressing reservations and Forrest absent from the meeting and uncommitted. The important modification of Quick's idea to be noted was that the convention would frame a draft constitution and then adjourn, allowing time for amendments to be made by the legislatures for the consideration of the convention when it resumed. Moreover, the means of appointment of delegates was left to the determination of each colony.[53]

## The Enabling Acts

The essential step was thus taken.[54] Predictably, the premiers' bill became the model for the Enabling Acts that were subsequently passed by the colonial legislatures. Pursuant to these Acts, the convention of 1897–8 would consist of three separate sessions, giving the legislatures and the general public an opportunity to debate and comment on the process. As Quick and Garran observed, the new scheme:

> secured popular interest, by providing that the members of the Convention should be elected by the people themselves, and that the Constitution should be submitted to the people themselves for acceptance. It conciliated the Parliaments by giving them a voice in initiating the process, a voice in criticizing the Constitution before its completion, and a voice in requesting the enactment of the Constitution after acceptance.[55]

These were the key features of the formative basis of the Australian Constitution, as it would be drafted, ratified and enacted into law over the course of the next five years – but subject to three important qualifications. The first was that the imperial Parliament ultimately enacted the Constitution Act after insisting on certain amendments, particularly where British interests were at stake. Secondly, the 'popular interest' was secured, not by a nationwide plebiscite, but by referendums held in each of the colonies. And, thirdly, the colonial parliaments were not merely 'conciliated': notwithstanding the role which was given to the voters,

---

[53] Quick and Garran, *Annotated Constitution*, 159; cf. Kingston, *Democratic Element*, 5–6.

[54] See Brian K. de Garis, 'How Popular was the Popular Federation Movement?', *Papers on Parliament* no. 21 (Canberra: Department of the Senate, 1993).

[55] Quick and Garran, *Annotated Constitution*, 160; see also Irving, *Constitute a Nation*, 140.

their Enabling Acts determined the entire process. Thus the Western Australian Parliament could insist upon nominating its delegates to the convention and Queensland could choose not to participate at all. Moreover, special majority requirements for the referendum were prescribed in New South Wales (a minimum of 50,000 'yes' votes, later amended to require 80,000 votes),[56] Victoria (50,000 votes) and Tasmania (6,000 votes).[57] The New South Wales minimum would mean the failure of the referendum in 1898, although supported by a narrow majority of persons casting a vote.[58]

In New South Wales other amendments to the premiers' bill were also proposed, but to no avail. Amendments requiring consideration of the 1891 bill and providing for parliamentary rather than popular election of the convention were lost, the latter by a vote of 62 to 5. A. B. Piddington unsuccessfully proposed that representatives be selected by a college of federal electors.[59] Others proposed that the colonies be represented in the convention more or less according to population (with a maximum of ten and a minimum of five for each colony), rather than equally.[60] In support of this, it was argued that the convention could not represent the people of Australia unless on a population basis, but the counter-argument was that the convention must represent the people of the colonies on equal terms. Noting that New South Wales more than any other colony stood to benefit by the motion, it is remarkable that it failed by 45 votes to 26. Labour leaders were aware that the constitutive basis of the convention would influence the representative structures which would be adopted. They could be pleased that parliamentary nomination of convention delegates, together with the parliamentary election of senators

---

[56] Enabling Act 1895 (NSW), s. 35; Enabling Act Amendment Act 1897 (NSW), s. 2. In New South Wales there were approximately 300,000 enrolled voters in June 1898: Helen Irving, 'New South Wales', in Helen Irving (ed.), *The Centenary Companion to Australian Federation* (Cambridge: Cambridge University Press, 1999), 78. See also Wise, *Making of the Commonwealth*, 282; Crisp, *Australian National Government*, 12; Quick and Garran, *Annotated Constitution*, 160–2, 193–4. On Reid's arguments in favour of the minimum, yet his 'personal reasons' for opposing it, being one reason for earning him the nickname 'Yes–No Reid', see Clark, *Select Documents*, 510.

[57] Quick and Garran, *Annotated Constitution*, 160–2; e.g. Enabling Act 1896 (Vic.), s. 36; Enabling Act 1895 (SA), s. 36.

[58] See e.g. Irving, *Constitute a Nation*, 152. Another qualification was that following the failure of the New South Wales referendum further amendments were introduced at the premiers' conference of 1899.

[59] Crisp, *Federation Fathers*, 130–1.    [60] Irving, *Constitute a Nation*, 147.

which it implied, had lost favour.[61] However, the insistence on equal representation even within the parliament of the most populous of the colonies meant that the democratic credentials of the Constitution would still have to be adapted to federalism.

Queensland was not represented in the convention because the north and central divisions of the colony were seeking subdivision into independent, self-governing colonies, and the parliament was not able to agree on the terms of an Enabling Act. According to Quick and Garran, representatives of the northern and central regions saw federation as a step towards separation and local self-governance, and they wished to have separate representation in the convention. Premier Nelson therefore, and despite remonstrances from other premiers, introduced a bill in which representatives would be elected by the Legislative Assembly, grouped into the three districts, and under which the government would be under no obligation to submit any constitution to a referendum for approval. The bill was passed by the Legislative Assembly, but the Legislative Council insisted on an amendment providing for election by both houses. The Assembly, however, refused to concede the point on the basis that the Council was nominated and unrepresentative, and the bill failed.[62] Having no representation in the second convention, the Central Queensland Territorial Separation League resorted to petitioning the convention. Its memorial of 1897 noted Griffith's proposed 'federative division of the colony into three provinces with separate Governments and Legislatures'. The League argued that the central and northern regions had a legitimate interest in self-government, pointing out that Nelson had intended that they be separately represented at the convention. It also argued that the federal constitution should not contain any provision preventing a state from being subdivided without the sanction of the state parliament.[63]

---

[61] La Nauze, *Making of the Constitution*, 94–5, observed that popular ratification and the rise of the Labor Party motivated conservatives to be more liberal, and liberals to be more consistently so.

[62] Quick and Garran, *Annotated Constitution*, 162; Irving, *Constitute a Nation*, 141. As it turned out, s. 7 of the Constitution would allow for the division of Queensland into districts, a recognition of regional differences within that colony.

[63] 'Separation League to President of the Australian Federal Convention' (2 April 1897), *Australian Federal Convention Papers* (1897–8), no. 1, Series 1/8, doc. 51, enclosing a *Memorial From the Central Queensland Territorial Separation League* (1897), *Australian Federal Convention Papers* (1897–8), no. 2, series 4/1, item 51.

Western Australia was also experiencing regional separatism: a significant proportion of people in the eastern goldfields sought both separation and federation.[64] Resisting this push for self-government, the Western Australian Enabling Act provided for the appointment of representatives by both houses of Parliament and that the proposed constitution would only be referred to referendum following approval by the parliament.[65] As a result, while the vast majority of delegates to the convention of 1897–8 would be directly elected, the West Australians were nominated.

It is worth noting in this connection that a 'People's Federal Convention' was held in Bathurst late in 1896. The popular basis of the convention may be doubted, but as Irving points out, the popular designation was probably adopted to distinguish it from the 'statutory convention' that would be convened under parliamentary authority. Bathurst, it was thought, would give voice to organisations lying outside the colonial political arena.[66] And, indeed, the rhetoric of 'representation' and of 'the people' abounded at Bathurst, a rhetoric most notably expressed by colonial politicians. Reid said that the official convention would be representative of 'the people themselves', and thus distinct from the failed convention of 1891. William Lyne said that it would be representative of 'all shades of political belief'. Barton also spoke of federation as the 'transfer' of 'certain things from the people acting in one capacity to the people, acting in another'. In this spirit, the people's convention produced a manifesto which recorded what would prove to be non-negotiable for the vast majority of delegates to the statutory convention: a 'worthy and powerful Federation' consisting of 'states perfectly autonomous as regards their own affairs'. The convention's motto, *Foedere Fato Aequamur*, suggested that only through federation would the Australian colonies realise their destiny.[67]

---

[64] See John Kirwan, *My Life's Adventure* (London: Eyre and Spottiswoode, 1936), ch. 7.

[65] Quick and Garran, *Annotated Constitution*, 162–3; Irving, *Constitute a Nation*, 142; Crisp, *Australian National Government*, 9. In fact, Western Australia appointed different delegates to the Adelaide and Sydney sessions of the 1897–8 convention.

[66] Irving, *Constitute a Nation*, 144–5.

[67] *Proceedings of the People's Federal Convention at Bathurst* (Sydney: Gordon and Gotch, 1897), 90, 93–4, 101–2, 189–91. See Garran, *Prosper the Commonwealth*, 108–9; Quick and Garran, *Annotated Constitution*, 163; Irving, *Constitute a Nation*, 146–7; Hirst, *Sentimental Nation*, 139.

Declarations of this kind no doubt helped to promote the cause of federation, but the real business remained to be transacted through the process prescribed by the Enabling Acts. Thus, while an elected convention and ratification by referendum conferred upon the federative process a certain degree of democratic legitimacy, it was the Enabling Acts established by the colonial legislatures which provided the necessary legal foundation for the entire process. Colonial constitutive powers did not extend, however, to the formation of a federal government: hence the need for imperial enactment. Accordingly, just as the legal basis of the Australian Constitution lay with the imperial Parliament, so the legal basis for the formative political process lay, in a sense, with the colonial legislatures. Each element in the formative process would have an impact on the terms and structure of the Constitution that eventually emerged. The essential role of the imperial Parliament meant that the Australian Constitution would be contained within an imperial statute. The facilitative role of the colonial parliaments, acting in concert, meant that in crucial respects the cooperative action of the state parliaments would still be required under the Constitution. Likewise, the direct election of representatives at the federal convention of 1897–8 and the ratification of the Constitution by popular referendums held in each colony profoundly shaped the structure of representation and mode of alteration adopted in the Constitution.[68] In particular, direct election of the convention made direct election of the Senate unassailable, and constitutional alteration by referendum virtually assured.[69] However, the logic of direct popular involvement was not to prevail with respect to the resolution of deadlocks between the houses, and the amendment provision required parliamentary, rather than popular, initiative before proposed changes could be referred to referendum.[70]

---

[68] Irving, *Constitute a Nation*, ch. 8, draws attention to the parallels between the formative, representative and amending provisions of the Constitution. However, she interprets these almost solely in terms of the principle that 'the people' were the 'legitimating force' behind the Constitution – as diverse and 'federally organised' as this 'concept of the people' might be: see 152, 154–5.

[69] See Kingston, *Democratic Element*, 16; Irving, *Constitute a Nation*, 148–50. But query the degree to which the mode of election affected the profile of convention representatives. See Quick and Garran, *Annotated Constitution*, 123–4 and 163–5.

[70] Compare Irving, *Constitute a Nation*, 154–5.

## The convention of 1897–8

Elections for the federal convention were held in 1897 in New South Wales, Victoria, South Australia and Tasmania, while delegates for Western Australia were nominated by the colony's two houses of parliament around the same time. Queensland, for reasons already explained, was not represented. In South Australia, women voted and Catherine Helen Spence stood, unsuccessfully, as a candidate.[71] For the most part, the elected representatives, as well as the nominated ones, were colonial politicians, divided fairly evenly between conservatives and liberals, free traders and protectionists, small colonies and large colonies. Only a few representatives were elected who might be expected to represent the interests of labour. All were men.[72]

The first session of the convention was held in Adelaide between 22 March and 23 April 1897, the second in Sydney between 2 and 24 September, and the third and final session in Melbourne from 20 January to 17 March 1898. Reflecting the statutory foundation of the entire process, the first task of the convention was to recite the convening proclamations made by the colonial governors under the Enabling Acts of the several colonies.[73] Among procedural matters of consequence, it was agreed to publish the proceedings of the convention and to admit the public, the convention once again being anxious to bring the people 'into confidence' and avoid all appearance of 'subterfuge'.[74] Kingston was elected president of the convention and fellow South Australian Richard Baker as acting president and chairman of committees.[75] Also of importance, it was resolved to commence with resolutions to be drafted by the leader of the convention, Edmund Barton, rather than to begin with the bill of 1891, even though the bill would 'by common consent [be] taken as the foundation of the work of the Convention'.[76]

---

[71] See Catherine Helen Spence, 'Federal Convention Elections and Effective Voting' (Eildon, St Peters, 16 March 1897).

[72] See, generally, Helen Irving, 'Fair Federalists and Founding Mothers', in *A Woman's Constitution? Gender and History in the Australian Commonwealth* (Sydney: Hale and Iremonger, 1996).

[73] *Convention Debates, Adelaide* (1897), 1.      [74] *Ibid.*, 7–8 (Holder), 13–16 (Carruthers, Barton).

[75] *Ibid.*, 2–3.

[76] *Ibid.*, 10–17; Moore, *Constitution of the Commonwealth*, 47; Quick and Garran, *Annotated Constitution*, 165.

Barton's resolutions were duly debated between 23 and 31 March 1897 and ultimately approved *en bloc*.[77] Constitutional, finance and judiciary committees were then formed, comprised of equal numbers of members from each colony, as nominated by each colonial delegation, with the premiers *ex officio* members of every committee. The Constitutional Committee included several leading representatives, including Edmund Barton, Richard O'Connor, Richard Baker, John Cockburn, John Downer, John Gordon, Alfred Deakin, Isaac Isaacs, John Quick and John Hackett.[78] A drafting committee of Barton, O'Connor and Downer then produced a draft bill which was debated between 12 and 23 April and, with amendments, provisionally approved.[79]

The absence of Queensland, combined with the fact that the Western Australian delegates were not able to participate in the convention for the entire period due to a general election in that colony, clearly affected the small colony–large colony balance in the convention. Indeed, the Western Australian delegates asked during the Adelaide session that the convention discuss the controversial financial clauses as a first priority so that they would be present to defend their interests and strengthen the vote of the smaller colonies.[80] During the debate on the financial clauses, Forrest often, and 'cheerfully',[81] declared that the smaller colonies had a majority on the crucial question of the Senate's power over financial bills. While conceding that equal representation of the colonies in the convention was a 'necessary principle in an assemblage of contracting states', Quick and Garran subsequently argued that the smaller colonies were forced to recognise that majorities in the convention would have to 'defer to the wishes of majorities outside', meaning the larger colonies, and that this engendered a spirit of compromise.[82] Just as plainly, however, the necessity for ratification of the proposed constitution by majorities in each of the colonies meant that large colony delegates had to recognise

---

[77] *Convention Debates, Adelaide* (1897), 17–27, 395.

[78] *Minutes and Records of the Constitutional Committee, Australian Federal Convention Papers* (1897–8), no. 2, series 8/13.

[79] *Convention Debates, Adelaide* (1897), 431–2.

[80] *Ibid.*, 411–28, 459–65.

[81] Quick and Garran, *Annotated Constitution*, 172.

[82] *Ibid.*; cf. Wise, *Making of the Commonwealth*, 234–6. Specifically, Quick and Garran referred to the gradual concession by representatives of the smaller states of Reid's amendment which specifically denied to the Senate a power to amend financial bills.

the claims of the smaller colonies, so that the need for compromise cut both ways.

After the passage of Barton's draft Constitution Bill at the Adelaide session, the convention adjourned, effectively until 2 September 1897.[83] During the interval, the colonial legislatures as well as the general public had an opportunity to examine the draft and express their views. They took full advantage of the opportunity. The New South Wales Legislative Assembly strongly attacked equal representation of the states in the Senate and proposed that deadlocks between the houses be referred to a 'mass referendum'. It also proposed that the Constitution be amended by a mass, national referendum. The Council likewise opposed equal representation in the Senate, but went further: it substituted 'Dominion' for 'Commonwealth' and removed the term 'federal' throughout the text. Reflecting its own status as an upper house, however, the Council maintained the capacity of the Senate to suggest amendments to money bills and was silent on deadlocks.[84] This lower house–upper house dichotomy was even more evident in Victoria. The Victorian Assembly denied the Senate a power to suggest amendments, removed the prohibition on tacking extraneous bills to financial bills, proposed a series of deadlock-breaking mechanisms, suggested that constitutional amendments be referred to a referendum by either house and removed the protection of state representation from the amending formula. The Council, by contrast, affirmed a power to amend money bills and left the deadlock provision unchanged.[85]

On the other hand, at this time, Baker published his appeal for a Swiss-style federal executive council and convinced the South Australian Legislative Council to propose that the federal executive should consist of three members chosen by the House of Representatives and three by the Senate.[86] The Assembly, however, did not agree, but proposed on the contrary that the Federal Parliament be elected on a 'one adult, one vote' basis and that deadlocks be resolved by dissolution or referendum. Both houses affirmed the Senate's power to amend money bills and the Council proposed that the High Court consist of a Supreme Court judge

---

[83] There was a very brief sitting in Adelaide on 6 May 1897.

[84] Quick and Garran, *Annotated Constitution*, 182–4. These provisions are explained in chs. 7 and 8.

[85] *Ibid.*, 184–5.

[86] Baker, *Executive in a Federation*, discussed in ch. 4. See also Leslie Zines, 'The Commonwealth' in Craven, *Australian Federation*, 98.

from each state. In Tasmania both houses similarly affirmed a Senate power to amend money bills and rejected a deadlock-breaking scheme, although the Assembly made a provisional suggestion for avoiding deadlocks should the convention insist. Clark unsuccessfully proposed the election of senators by the state parliaments, but was successful in having the Tasmanians propose that the question of responsible government be left open, as in 1891. In Queensland, Griffith also cast doubts on responsible government. The Western Australian houses similarly affirmed a power to amend money bills in the Senate. As Quick and Garran concluded, the two larger colonies favoured 'the absolute supremacy of the majority, independent of State boundaries', while the other colonies preferred 'some degree of control by a majority of states.' At the same time, the lower and upper houses of the several colonies revealed a conservative–liberal cleavage.[87]

The draft bill was also referred to the Colonial Office. While this anticipated the necessity of imperial legislation, the Colonial Office remained discreet in relation to those matters which did not affect imperial interests. As the lessons of earlier decades had counselled, federation was something to be worked out between the colonies.[88] And yet this did not prevent the imperial officers from attempting to shape the Constitution through various indirect means, principally by engaging Reid to make arguments on their behalf.[89]

The convention resumed in Sydney to address the 286 amendments proposed by the colonial legislatures.[90] Apart from the financial settlement, the key issues concerned the question of federal representation: the composition and powers of the Senate and the resolution of deadlocks between the houses.[91] After the Sydney sitting, attempts were made within the Queensland Parliament to have Queensland join the convention, but the divisions within that colony continued to stand in the

---

[87] 'Schedules of Amendments of the South Australian Legislative Assembly and Council', Baker Papers; Quick and Garran, *Annotated Constitution*, 185–6; La Nauze, *Making of the Constitution*, 161–6; Griffith, *Notes on the Draft Constitution*.

[88] For a discussion, see La Nauze, *Making of the Constitution*, 170–6 and Brian K. de Garis, 'The Colonial Office and the Commonwealth Constitution Bill' in Martin, *Essays in Australian Federation*, 94–108.

[89] La Nauze, *Making of the Constitution*, 85–6, 170–6, 183–6.

[90] See Patrick H. Lane, *An Introduction to the Australian Constitution* (4th edn, Sydney: Law Book Co., 1987), 216.

[91] Quick and Garran, *Annotated Constitution*, 189–93. See chs. 7 and 8 below.

way. Opposition to federation was also evident in New South Wales, where an amendment to the Enabling Act raised the minimum affirmative vote required from 50,000 to 80,000.[92]

When the convention resumed in Melbourne in early 1898, the bill underwent a thorough revision by the drafting committee and was meticulously reviewed in committee of the whole before being finally adopted. Quick and Garran considered that the key issues in Melbourne concerned finance, railways and control over river navigation, but consideration was also given to matters relating more directly to the representative scheme, particularly the deadlock provision.[93]

### Ratification and enactment

In accordance with the Enabling Acts, the Constitution Bill was then submitted to the electors in New South Wales, Victoria, South Australia and Tasmania. In New South Wales, powerful objections to the bill were made by radical and labour politicians, particularly against equal representation in the Senate, the powers of the Senate over money bills and the absence of a referendum for the resolution of deadlocks.[94] There was also opposition to the financial clauses and especially the so-called 'Braddon blot',[95] Premier Reid famously stating that while he would personally vote for the bill, he could not recommend it to the voters.[96] In Victoria, support for the bill was strong; even the labour representative at the convention, William Arthur Trenwith, supported the bill.[97] However, H. B. Higgins forcefully opposed ratification on the ground that the 'out and out provincialism' of equal representation of the states in the Senate was yet another form of 'rotten borough' which even infected the House of Representatives, and that this 'ridiculous' and 'pernicious' system could not be removed from the Constitution without the consent of the

---

[92] *Ibid.*, 193–4.    [93] *Ibid.*, 194, 202–4.    [94] See Bennett, *Federation*, 9–13, 43–7.

[95] Under which three-quarters of Commonwealth net revenue from customs and excise duties would be redistributed to the states. See *Convention Debates, Melbourne* (1898), 2378–9; Higgins, *Essays and Addresses*, 89–90; Quick and Garran, *Annotated Constitution*, 197–9, 824–9; *Bathurst Times*, 12 June 1899, *Wagga Wagga Advertiser*, 13 May 1899, in Bennett, *Federation*, 21–4.

[96] George Reid, 'Speech at Sydney Town Hall', 28 March 1898, in Bennett, *Federation*, 173–86.

[97] See the replies by Trenwith, in Higgins, *Essays and Addresses*, 37–55.

states involved.[98] In Tasmania, Clark also refused to support the bill, but for very different reasons, insisting that senators ought to be elected by the state parliaments and that ministers ought not to be required to sit in Parliament.[99]

Higgins's forceful criticisms and Clark's ambivalence did not prevent decisive majorities in Victoria and Tasmania from ratifying the bill during the referendums held in 1898. A strong majority in South Australia also affirmed the bill. Queensland and Western Australia, however, remained slow to move and in New South Wales a close numerical majority in favour actually fell short of the 80,000 votes required by the Enabling Act. The failure of the New South Wales referendum was significant for it brought to an end the participatory processes initiated and sustained by the several colonial Enabling Acts. Quick and Garran later observed that this suspension of the movement to federation underscored the fact that federation rested on the 'federal' principle that the consent of the people of each of the constituent colonies would be required. If the constitution had rested on the principle of a national majority vote, the referendums of 1898 would have been a complete success, since an overall majority of eligible Australian voters had approved the constitution.[100]

In New South Wales, however, Reid continued to object to particular provisions in the bill, including the three-fifths majority in the joint sitting, in the context of equal representation in the Senate.[101] In the forthcoming general election, Reid's Liberal Federal Party insisted on seven specific amendments, whilst Barton's National Federal Party conceded the need for three of these, including the removal of the three-fifths majority. Both sides affirmed their support for federation.[102] After the election, the Legislative Assembly resolved, among other things, that a national, not a dual, referendum be adopted for constitutional amendment, but the Legislative Council rejected the proposal.[103]

---

[98] Higgins, *Essays and Addresses*, 8–16; Quick and Garran, *Annotated Constitution*, 211. See also Crisp, *Federation Fathers*, ch. 3. It was called by its opponents a 'fatuous Federation' and an 'Australian Fetteration': *Tocsin*, 29 June 1899 and *Clipper*, 16 April 1898, in Bennett, *Federation*, 43–5; Anderson, *Tocsin*, 40.

[99] La Nauze, *Making of the Constitution*, 192, 230; Bennett, *Federation*, 105, 118.

[100] Quick and Garran, *Annotated Constitution*, 336.

[101] *Ibid.*, 214, 216–17. On the manoeuvrings of Reid and Barton, see Hirst, *Sentimental Nation*, 186–200.

[102] See Quick and Garran, *Annotated Constitution*, 216.     [103] *Ibid.*, 217–18.

Despite setbacks in New South Wales, slow movement in Western Australia and division in Queensland, a premiers' conference held in January 1899 was able to exert a new impetus towards federation. All of the colonies were represented (including Queensland), and each premier spoke with an equal voice. The conference, this time unanimously, affirmed a series of alterations of the Constitution Bill. In particular, the premiers approved an amendment which enabled Queensland to be divided into electorates for the purpose of elections to the Senate in order to placate regional sentiment within Queensland. They also agreed that the Braddon clause would have a mandatory operation for only ten years after the establishment of the Commonwealth. The premiers finally arranged for the duly amended Constitution Bill to be submitted to the voters in New South Wales and, consequent on its approval in that colony, submitted in the other colonies. And a simple majority of voters in each colony, it was agreed, would be sufficient for the acceptance or rejection of the bill.[104]

The premiers now had to convince their legislatures to adopt this course. In New South Wales there was opposition in the Legislative Council and some delay, but an Enabling Act requiring a simple majority was eventually passed. At the ensuing referendum a majority approved the bill. In due course strong majorities also approved the bill in Victoria, South Australia and Tasmania.[105] In Queensland an Enabling Act was also passed and, despite pressure for amendments to be made, the Constitution Bill as approved at the premiers' conference was appended, unchanged, as a schedule to the Act. The northern and central regions of Queensland tended to favour federation, believing that their goal of separation from Queensland would be better served in that way. There was nevertheless concern that section 124 of the bill required the approval of the Queensland Parliament before they could separate – a majority in the Parliament would thus be able to prevent regional majorities from separating.[106] Separatists in Rockhampton and antifederal sentiment in Brisbane did not, however, prevent an overall majority in Queensland from eventually approving the bill in late 1899.

---

[104] *Minutes of the Conference of Premiers on the Commonwealth Bill*, Melbourne, *Argus*, 3 February 1899, in Clark, *Select Documents*, 510–16; Quick and Garran, *Annotated Constitution*, 218. See Irving, *Constitute a Nation*, 142.

[105] Quick and Garran, *Annotated Constitution*, 221–3.     [106] *Ibid.*, 224.

Similar obstacles stood in the way of approval in Western Australia. Voters in the eastern goldfield region strongly favoured federation, but the western (coastal) parts of the colony were more ambivalent.[107] A select committee of the Legislative Assembly recommended that four amendments to the Constitution Bill be required, and a bill to submit it to the electors was blocked in the Council. Premier John Forrest subsequently travelled to the eastern colonies in an effort to obtain concessions but, as Quick and Garran pointed out, it was impolitic to amend further a bill that had been approved by the people of the other colonies.[108]

It is worth emphasising again the critical role played throughout this process by the elected governments and legislatures of the colonies, while at the same time noticing the prevailing principle that the Constitution be approved directly by the voters in each colony. The premiers were ultimately able to insist on certain amendments to the Constitution Bill and the colonial legislatures passed the requisite Enabling Acts to give legal force to the referendums that would give 'legitimacy' to the process. The formative conditions of federation meant that the colonies were insistent on being treated as equal contracting partners. The way in which the colonies gave expression, legally and politically, to their agreement to federate involved both elected representatives and direct mandates, yet with variations in the detail. These variations eloquently testified to the fact that federation could not be forced on any of the colonies and that the manner in which each colony gave expression to its agreement to federate was under its own control.

Prior to the final submission of the proposed Constitution to the voters of Western Australia, a further premiers' conference agreed to send a delegation to be present at the introduction of the Constitution Bill into the imperial Parliament. However, as Western Australia had not yet approved the bill, the colony was not referred to in the preamble to the bill that was presented to the imperial Parliament – again suggesting that there was no intention to force a colony into federation against its will. But while Western Australia was omitted from the preamble, special provision was made in covering clause 3. This clause authorised the Queen by proclamation to unite the people of the several colonies into one federal commonwealth, and it specifically affirmed that Her Majesty

[107] Kirwan, *My Life's Adventure*, ch. 7.   [108] *Ibid.*, 226–8.

might declare that the people of Western Australia were included, provided that she was satisfied that they had 'agreed thereto'.

When the Commonwealth Bill was forwarded to the imperial authorities, each colony, including Western Australia, was represented in the Australian delegation, and it was intended that the delegation would unitedly support the passage of the bill without further amendment. The imperial Crown Law Officers objected, however, to the restriction of appeals to the Privy Council effected by section 74 of the Constitution, and various amendments to the covering clauses were proposed. As Lumb pointed out, the Australian delegates argued that it was just as inappropriate for changes to be made to the covering clauses as to the Constitution itself, for both had the sanction of the colonial Enabling Acts.[109] In fact, with the important exception of section 74, there were only insubstantial amendments the bill passed early in July 1900. In late July, a referendum in Western Australia approved federation and on 17 September 1900 the Queen proclaimed that the Constitution would come into force on 1 January 1901.

## Conclusion

On the results of the referendums, Quick and Garran exulted that the figures were:

> striking proof of the extent and sincerity of the national sentiment throughout the whole of Eastern Australia; and they are also a unique testimony to the high political capacity of the Australian people. Never before have a group of self-governing, practically independent communities, without external pressure or foreign complications of any kind, deliberately chosen of their own free will to put aside their provincial jealousies and come together as one people, from a simple intellectual and sentimental conviction of the folly of disunion and the advantages of nationhood.[110]

Crisp contended, by contrast, that the referendum results actually showed that the supposed 'popular movement' for federation was, 'in reality, an

---

[109] Lumb, 'Bicentenary of Australian Constitutionalism', 14; Quick and Garran, *Annotated Constitution*, 228–50; La Nauze, *Making of the Constitution*, 239–69; de Garis, 'Colonial Office', 118–21; Peter Howell, 'Joseph Chamberlain and the Amendment of the Australian Constitution Bill' (2001) 7 *The New Federalist* 16.

[110] Quick and Garran, *Annotated Constitution*, 225.

unofficial movement of *élites* and pressure groups to stir up popular pressure upon the anti-federalists'.[111]

Certainly, the popular basis of the federation can be exaggerated. According to McMinn, 'the vision of a nation for a continent had seized the imaginations of no more than about a quarter of the people of New South Wales and South Australia, and less than 40 per cent of those even of Victoria'.[112] Voting was voluntary and the franchise was limited. Voter participation in the election of convention delegates and the referendums of 1898 and 1899 varied between 30 per cent and 67 per cent, and was on the whole lower than participation in colonial general elections during the same time period.[113] It seems difficult, therefore, to sustain the proposition that the Constitution was founded on popular approval.[114]

Irving has tellingly argued, however, that 'to claim that Federation was a popular movement is not the same as to claim that it was a mass movement'.[115] She has pointed out that the legal mechanisms for the adoption of the Constitution required popular involvement and successive drafts increasingly embodied 'democratic' structures and mechanisms. Certainly, there were paradoxes and ambiguities about the kind of citizen who participated in these popular processes: a property qualification still existed in some quarters, Aborigines did not vote, and women voted only in South Australia and Western Australia.[116] Yet the lower house franchise was used for the referendums, and the first national labour government in the world was soon formed under the Constitution.[117] Thus the Constitution enabled a more participatory system to develop in the future, indeed, rather rapidly. When assessed in the context of its time, and especially when compared to the processes in the United States in the 1780s and Canada in the 1860s, the process in Australia was remarkably open to popular scrutiny, public debate and voter approval.[118]

The formative processes by which the Australian federation came into being can therefore be summarised as follows. First, Enabling Acts were

---

[111] Crisp, *Australian National Government*, 8. Compare Macintyre, 'Voice of the People'.

[112] McMinn, *Nationalism and Federalism*, 180, 190.

[113] Crisp, *Australian National Government*, 12.

[114] Compare *Theophanous* v. *Herald & Weekly Times Ltd* (1994) 182 CLR 104, 171.

[115] Irving, *Constitute a Nation*, 153.

[116] See *ibid.*, chs. 6, 7, 9 and 10; Quick and Garran, *Annotated Constitution*, 249.

[117] E.g. *Enabling Act 1896* (Vic.), s. 33; Irving, *Constitute a Nation*, 143, 192–5.

[118] Compare Hirst, *Sentimental Nation*, 248–71.

passed by each of the colonial legislatures – providing the legal basis for the entire process of federating so far as the colonies were concerned. Second, Commonwealth Bills were drafted and debated in conventions at which each colony was entitled to be equally represented.[119] Third, while the delegates to the convention of 1891 were nominated by the colonial legislatures, the representatives at the convention of 1897–8 of all but one of the colonies were directly elected by the voters of the respective colonies (pursuant, again, to the Enabling Acts).[120] Fourth, debate and voting at the conventions was by majority; delegates were not required to vote on instructions from their respective colonial legislatures, and delegates for each colony were not required to vote *en bloc*.[121] Fifth, each colonial legislature reserved to itself the capacity to criticise the draft bills; indeed, the process in 1897–8 expressly allowed for such criticisms and suggestions to come before the convention in a subsequent session.[122] Sixth, overarching supervision exercised by the colonial premiers was reflected in their capacity to agree, unanimously, to further amendments to the bill. Seventh, the Constitution Bill of 1898 was ratified by referendums held in each of the colonies, again pursuant to the Enabling Acts.[123] Eighth, no colony was forced to federate; entry into the federation was on the basis of unanimous agreement. Under the Enabling Acts, the Constitution Bill would be forwarded to the Queen for enactment if three or more colonies accepted it; but the Act would not apply to any colonies which did not accept the bill.[124] Ninth, each colony sent a delegate to the United Kingdom, to submit the bill for enactment and to defend its integrity. And finally, the Constitution Bill was ultimately enacted into law by the imperial Parliament in terms substantially identical to those agreed to by the six colonies.

It is thus of great importance to note that throughout, federation proceeded on the basis of the consent of each colony. No colony was compelled to participate in any aspect of the process of negotiating

---

[119] See e.g. Enabling Act 1896 (Vic.), s. 6.

[120] Excepting the legislative nomination of Western Australian delegates to the second convention.

[121] E.g. Enabling Act 1896 (Vic.), s. 18, enabled the convention to adopt its own standing orders, but s. 25 dictated that voting in the convention would be by an ordinary majority of members present.

[122] E.g. Enabling Act 1896 (Vic.), ss. 26–7.

[123] Reference of the bill to the voters was automatic: e.g. Enabling Act 1896 (Vic.), s. 33.

[124] E.g. Enabling Act 1896 (Vic.), s. 37.

federation (witness New Zealand's decision to remain aloof and Western Australia's reticence to join the federation until the last moment). As was seen in earlier chapters, this insistence on unanimity as the fundamental decision-making rule for the formation of integrative federal systems is an important respect in which such federations are difficult to distinguish from confederations, alliances and mere treaties. All such forms of federal union are in the nature of a compact in respect of this principle of unanimity and its corollary, equality of representation.[125]

In Australia, unanimity in decision-making was predicated on the equal status of each colony, and thus the equality of representation for each colony throughout the formative process. Each colony enjoyed an equality of representation and an equal vote, initially in the Federal Council of Australasia, next in the various premiers' conferences, also in the conference of 1890, likewise throughout the conventions of 1891 and 1897–8, and, eventually, in terms of the ratifying referendums held in each colony.

Further, the colonial governments and legislatures (under conditions of parliamentary responsible government) retained control of the entire formative process. As has been seen, treaties, confederations and federations are commonly distinguished on the basis of the decision-making institution or process by which the union is formed, whether by executive agreement, legislative enactment or popular ratification through elected conventions or referendums.[126] But while the formation of the Australian federation derived much of its legitimacy from its ratification in popular referendums, the process was legally overseen and controlled by the several colonial legislatures. In this respect, again, the process exhibited qualities supposedly characteristic of confederations, not federations.

The formative process certainly exhibited several important features which gave it a more federal and consolidated appearance. In particular, most of the representatives in the convention of 1897–8 were directly elected, and voting in the conventions was by simple majority of the whole – rather than by unanimity (or even special majority) or by bloc voting. This prevented the views of each colony from solidifying into a cartel, a position from which each colony might threaten to boycott federation as a bargaining chip in the drafting process. This concession to consolidation must be balanced, however, by the fact that the colonial

---

[125] See ch. 2.    [126] See ch. 2.

legislatures retained the authority to criticise the draft produced by the convention and that the ultimate fate of the Constitution Bill continued to lie with the legislature and government of each colony.

The formative preconditions of Australian federation were decidedly compactual in so far as they embodied principles of unanimity, equality of representation and legislative control. And yet these principles were significantly qualified by majority voting within the conventions and popular ratification through the referendums. As will be seen, all of these formative features had a marked impact – both as a matter of professed principle and pragmatic negotiation – on the representative structures, configuration of power and amending processes actually embodied in the Australian Constitution.

# PART III

Australian federation

# Principles of representation

[W]ho are the people whose views we are going to take? The voice of the people must rule, of course, but we want to be sure about what we mean when we talk about the voice of the people.

John Cockburn (1897)

Within the philosophical and institutional context outlined in previous chapters, delegates to the conventions of 1891 and 1897–8 drafted Commonwealth Bills for the formation of an Australian federation. The Commonwealth Bills contained representative structures deeply influenced by those formative conditions.

The bills grew progressively out of Andrew Inglis Clark's draft, modified under the leadership of Samuel Griffith in 1891 and Edmund Barton in 1897–8. While important changes were made, Clark's structural framework was largely preserved, particularly the relationship between the formative basis of the proposed federation and the representative institutions, configuration of power and amendment provisions to be adopted. In particular, Clark's scheme for the composition of the Federal Parliament and the structure of the Constitution's text remained largely intact.[1] While later changes moved the Constitution in relatively more nationalist directions, the formative processes through which Constitution came into being constrained that movement significantly.

While these practical constraints limited what was arguable and feasible within the federal conventions of 1891 and 1897–8, there was significant debate about the details, and philosophical factors were

---

[1] See Neasey, 'Clark and Australian Federation'. La Nauze, *Making of the Constitution*, 278, observed: 'After Clark and Griffith had done their work any discussion of a federal constitution for Australia . . . would proceed by way of variation from their blue-print. No one else could again play their roles of 1891.' For Griffith's own comparison between the bill of 1891 and the draft bill of 1897, see Griffith, *Notes on the Draft Constitution*.

prominent. Broadly speaking, there were three main lines of division.[2] The first of these was a division between liberals and conservatives. The basic principle of the liberals was the idea of popular and progressive government. On the liberal view, the people should rule, and this meant a broad franchise and majority rule. By contrast, the conservative objective was to preserve the status quo, and therefore to restrain, through various checks and balances, the capacity of governments to introduce radical change.

Arguments between liberals and conservatives, however, proved to be less important than the contest between nationalists and proponents of states' rights. This was not simply a division between liberals and conservatives. While many of the nationalists were also liberals, a significant number of avowed liberals were, on the contrary, states' righters, and much of the argument about states' rights was couched in liberal rather than conservative terms. Nationalists, as liberals, were concerned to promote popular government, but unlike states' righters they believed that 'the people' should be understood in national rather than regional terms, so that a national majority should have ultimate control over government in Australia. Following writers such as James Wilson, John Burgess and A. V. Dicey, Australian nationalists like H. B. Higgins and Isaac Isaacs accepted that the Australian people might decide to institute a 'dual' system of government, but they wanted to insist that the national government represent an overall majority of Australian voters and that the Constitution should ultimately rest on the Australian people as a whole.

On the other hand, the states' righters, while not Calhounian compactualists, were concerned to promote the values of local autonomy and self-government. As liberals, John Cockburn and Clark, for example, strongly favoured progressive, democratic government and a broad franchise. They had learned much from their local experiences of colonial self-government, and they found such lessons to be confirmed in the works of James Bryce, E. A. Freeman and James Madison. In Cockburn's phrase, 'local government, self government, and government by the

---

[2] See Wise, *Making of the Commonwealth*; Deakin, *Federal Story*; G. W. McDonald, 'The Eighty Founding Fathers' (1968) 1 *Queensland Historical Review* 38; Peter Loveday, 'The Federal Convention, an Analysis of the Voting' (1972) 18(2) *Australian Journal of Politics and History* 169. The division between free traders and protectionists did not affect structural issues significantly.

people are analogous terms' and 'there can be no government by the people if the Government is far distant from the people'.[3] Accordingly, states' righters wished to protect the local autonomy of the states and to ensure that they were adequately represented in the Federal Parliament.

The nationalist–states' rights division was the most important line of cleavage. A closely related third division was also manifest: between those who favoured responsible government at a national level, and those who opposed it. Many of those favouring responsibility to the popular house were strong nationalists in the sense described above. A greater proportion of the supporters of responsible government are, however, best described as 'moderates', since they also favoured equal representation of the states in a relatively powerful Senate.

Those in favour of responsible government were opposed by a significant number of framers who, as radical states' righters, preferred what they considered to be a genuinely 'federal' executive, rather than the 'national' executive implied by responsible government. On this side, Richard Baker proposed a Swiss-style executive, derived from and responsible to both houses of the federal legislature, and prominent delegates like Griffith and Clark tended in virtually the same direction. That this approach was a radical one is demonstrated, ironically, by the classically conservative arguments put in favour of traditional responsible government by nationalist liberals such as Alfred Deakin and Higgins, as will be seen below.

In the end, a majority upheld the received conception of responsible government, whether for conservative or liberal-nationalist reasons. But while the moderates among them ultimately accepted responsible government, they also insisted on equal representation of the states in a relatively powerful Senate. For Barton, for example, this mediating position was the most effective way to meet two desiderata of Australian self-government that had been discerned since the days of Wentworth. The separation of the several colonies from New South Wales had been necessary, he thought, because a centralised government could not effectively govern such a large territory, but a 'federal' government was needed to deal with matters that

---

[3] *Convention Debates, Adelaide* (1897), 338–9. As Cockburn later observed: 'My struggles for the Senate have simply been struggles for autonomy, for home rule, for local government': *Convention Debates, Sydney* (1897), 679.

required collective effort.[4] In coming to this conclusion, Barton adopted the 'partly national, partly federal' reasoning of James Madison and Joseph Story as reflecting a 'reasonable compromise' and 'just mean' between the two extremes of compactual confederation and nationalist consolidation.[5] The moderate stance was a mediating, covenantal one.

Within this institutional and philosophical context, the framers settled the details of the Federal Constitution. The procedure adopted at both conventions was to debate a series of broad resolutions which defined the general features of the proposed constitution, and then to debate the details of a text produced by a drafting committee. At the second convention the further innovation was that after a preliminary bill had been settled, the draft was distributed to the legislatures for discussion and proposed changes. The convention then reassembled to debate the proposals and to settle a final bill to be submitted to the people of the colonies for approval at referendums. If approved, the bill would then be transmitted to the imperial Parliament for enactment.

This chapter will trace the debate about the representative structures adopted in the Constitution. The general approaches and specific platforms of nationalists and states' righters will first be examined. It will then be possible to consider the way in which these approaches, within the formative context of the convention, interacted in the debate. As will be seen, the matters raised by the debate were manifold. A fundamental question concerned the composition of the two houses of the Federal Parliament. Would the House of Representatives represent the people of the entire nation in proportion to population? Would the Senate represent the states? Or would these principles need to be compromised in one direction or another? Further, would local electorates be used for Senate and House of Representative elections? And would such matters be entrenched in the Constitution or left to the discretion of either the federal or state parliaments?

A second series of fundamental questions concerned responsible government. Would ministers be required to hold seats in Parliament? Would the powers of the Senate be moderated to enable the lower house to control government finance? Would provision be made for the resolution of deadlocks between the houses? If so, would deadlocks be

---

[4] *Convention Debates, Sydney* (1897), 626 (Barton, Trenwith).    [5] *Ibid.*, 340.

resolved by referendum, dissolution or joint sitting? And what would be the numerical size of the two houses?.

## Parkes's resolutions – consensus and division

The nature of federation and the structure of representation were questions of vital importance to the delegates to the federal conventions of the 1890s. Sir Henry Parkes's famous resolutions debated by the first convention held in Sydney in 1891 and Barton's comparable resolutions debated at the second convention in 1897 set out the basic features of the proposed Constitution.[6]

Even at an early stage in the convention of 1891, the broad outlines of the Constitution were reasonably identifiable, at least so far as the views of a majority of the delegates were concerned.[7] According to Parkes's resolutions, matters of federal principle were of foremost importance: the whole purpose of the convention was 'to establish and secure an enduring foundation for the structure of a federal government'.[8] Clearly, the only viable union would be a federal one. Indeed, the Enabling Acts had stipulated that the conventions were limited to the establishment of a 'federation', and this injunction was urged against any suggestion of 'unification'.[9] Moreover, in Parkes's resolutions, the proposed Federal Parliament was 'to consist of a Senate and a House of Representatives, the former consisting of an equal number of members from each province' elected through a rotational system so as to give it a 'perpetual existence', the latter 'to be elected by districts formed on a population basis'.[10] Two different conceptions of representation were thus embraced. The Senate was to represent the states as equal partners in federation; the House was to represent local districts formed on 'a thoroughly popular basis'.[11] And if the Senate was to represent the states as equal partners, differences in state population would be irrelevant to its composition.

It is of significance, however, that Parkes's first draft of the resolutions, framed prior to the convention, did not contain what would become the

---

[6] *Convention Debates, Sydney* (1891), 23, 499–500; *Convention Debates, Adelaide* (1987), 17, 395.
[7] La Nauze, *Making of the Constitution*, 40.
[8] *Convention Debates, Sydney* (1891), 23. For the resolutions as finally approved, see *ibid.,* 499–500.
[9] E.g. *Convention Debates, Sydney* (1897), 590 (Symon).
[10] *Convention Debates, Sydney* (1891), 23.     [11] *Ibid.,* 26 (Parkes).

first 'principle' in the resolutions as eventually moved by Parkes and adopted by the convention:

> That the powers and privileges and territorial rights of the several existing colonies shall remain intact, except in respect to such surrenders as may be agreed upon as necessary and incidental to the power and authority of the National Federal Government.[12]

It seems that Parkes altered his first draft after discussions with a smaller group including four other premiers (Griffith, Munro, Fysh and Playford) as well as Clark, Gillies and Kingston.[13] As La Nauze pointed out, Clark and Kingston were probably included in this select group because they had already produced draft constitutions,[14] and the additional resolution may have been formed because these drafts already embodied the principle of the reservation of the powers, privileges and territorial rights of the colonies.

So far, the resolutions reflected the consensus view. Parkes's description of the executive, however, reflected a faith in responsible government which was not so widely shared. As introduced by Parkes, the relevant resolution provided that the House of Representatives was 'to possess the sole power of originating and amending all bills appropriating revenue or imposing taxation' and that advisers to the governor-general were to be 'persons sitting in Parliament and whose term of office shall depend upon their possessing the confidence of the House of Representatives, expressed by the support of the majority'.[15] After eleven days of debate, however, the contentious aspects of this proposed resolution were left open; the resolution as ultimately settled was silent on whether the ministry must sit in or be responsible to either house of Parliament.[16]

Similarly, the resolutions originally moved by Parkes did not include a guarantee of the ongoing territorial integrity of the states. But as ultimately adopted, the resolutions stated that:

---

[12]  *Ibid.*, 23.

[13]  Griffith, *Successive Stages*; Parkes, *Fifty Years*, 359–60, 366–70; Quick and Garran, *Annotated Constitution*, 125–6; Wise, *Making of the Commonwealth*, 118–19.

[14]  La Nauze, *Making of the Constitution*, 36.

[15]  Parkes's earlier draft did not provide that the advisers should sit in Parliament. La Nauze, *Making of the Constitution*, 36, considered that Griffith and Clark would have tried to convince Parkes to adopt Griffith's preferred wording: that they be '*eligible* to sit in either House of Parliament'.

[16]  *Convention Debates, Sydney* (1891), 499–500; Quick and Garran, *Annotated Constitution*, 128.

> No new State shall be formed by separation from another State, nor
> shall any State be formed by the junction of two or more States or
> parts of States, without the consent of the Legislatures of the States
> concerned, as well as of the Federal Parliament.[17]

Thus, while marginally nationalist as originally proposed, Parkes's resolutions were modified in a more compactual direction. As one might
expect, the debate that led to these conclusions sheds a great deal of light
on the federal ideas of many of the framers.

The critical debate in 1891 concerned responsible government and the
Senate's powers. Most of the framers intended that the Senate would
embody the rights and interests of the states and many held that it must
have powers equal to those of the House of Representatives in order to do
so. Those who objected to a powerful Senate feared that it would stymie
the workings of responsible government, meaning responsibility to the
lower house, and would allow representatives of a minority of Australians
to veto the views of representatives of a majority. In this context, equal
representation and substantial power for the Senate were effectively
unchallenged. Nationalists focused their attention, rather, on the maintenance of responsible government as a democratic principle, and the
crucial point here was the control of government finance in the form of
appropriation, taxation and loan bills. The majoritarian strategy was to
seek to qualify the powers of the Senate over financial measures, particularly in regard to their initiation, amendment and rejection.

At the heart of the debate about Parkes's resolutions, therefore, were
contending views of representation, federalism and democracy. An
examination of the arguments canvassed reflects the relative depth of the
delegates' comprehension of federal and democratic theory and practice,
especially as it related to the issue of representation.

## The presuppositions of federalism – autonomy and equality

For Griffith, the 'essential' and 'preliminary' condition of federation was
that:

> the separate states are to continue as autonomous bodies, surren-
> dering only so much of their powers as is necessary to the

---

[17] *Convention Debates*, Sydney (1891), 499–500.

establishment of a general government to do for them collectively what they cannot do individually for themselves, and which they cannot do as a collective body for themselves.[18]

As has been seen, according to Griffith a federation is a 'political union of several autonomous States . . . [which] form a larger State with a common government acting directly on its individual citizens'.[19] The original 'autonomy' of the states and the voluntary 'surrender' of powers were for Griffith essential. Drawing on the formative process by which the American federation came into being, Griffith believed that these presuppositions unavoidably implied a second, similarly 'essential', condition: the equal representation of the states in the Senate and the representation of the people in the House of Representatives. And this, in turn, he said, had implications for the 'relationship of the executive to the Parliament'. Responsible government assumes a 'preponderating influence' of one of the Houses of Parliament. But, he argued:

> if you recognise the principle – and I think we must if we are to get federation of the Australian colonies – that the states must also concur by a majority in every proposal, then one house cannot have that preponderating influence. There must be on all important matters a deliberate and not a coerced concurrence of the two branches of the legislature.[20]

To give the lower house 'sole power' over financial bills would thus be 'quite inconsistent with the independent existence of the senate as representing the separate states'.[21]

For Griffith the essentials of federation were that the separate states were originally autonomous, that they would agree to surrender only so much of their powers as was necessary, and that they ought to be equally represented in a Senate having equal power with the House of Representatives. Subject to the question of equal power, this was the mainstream view.[22] Such a perspective contrasted, however, with the

---

[18] *Ibid.*, 31–2; cf. Griffith, *Notes on Australian Federation*, 6–7, 10.

[19] Griffith, *Draft Commonwealth Bill*, 8.    [20] *Convention Debates, Sydney* (1891), 31–2.

[21] *Ibid.*

[22] For a similar and typical view, contrasting the 'division of power' in Canada, see George B. Barton, *The Draft Bill to Constitute the Commonwealth of Australia as Adopted by the Convention of 1891* (1891), 35: 'the Bill adopts the principle established in the United States, where the federal powers . . . are strictly delegated powers; the result being that as to matters

views of a minority like Isaacs, who steadfastly opposed equality of representation in the Senate and, following Dicey, envisaged a 'division' of powers between the federal and state parliaments, rather than a 'surrender' of particular powers by the states. As it turned out, while nationalists like Isaacs were not able to overturn equality of representation, they were able in some degree to qualify the powers of the Senate in order to make at least some room for 'responsible government'.

Griffith's basic concern was that the Senate should 'represent the States', and it was sufficient that senators be chosen by the state legislatures. Alfred Deakin disagreed, arguing that the people of each state would be better represented by direct election. He stated:

> I cannot conceive of an entity called the state apart from the people whose interests it embodies; nor can I conceive anything within the state which can claim an equal authority with the final verdict, after solemn consideration, of the majority of its citizens. If the hon. Gentleman [Griffith] has any metaphysical entity in his mind which can be placed above this, I shall be glad to learn its nature.[23]

Griffith did not attempt to describe any such entity, but rather fell back on the idea that the states were to be understood as 'aggregations of their own people' and that 'the majorities of the separate States might be of a different opinion from the majority of the people of Australia, taken as one'.[24] Barton developed the idea by pointing out that it would be 'possible for the representative principle to be preserved and instituted from its very foundation in two chambers just as well as in one', and that the Senate could be 'part of the organ by which the will of the people is expressed'. One chamber 'called *par excellence* the House of Representatives' would represent the people organised in localities, and the other would represent the people as states.[25] As Kingston later put it, 'while the electors are the same, the electorates are different'.[26]

Despite the arguments of Deakin and Isaacs, a consistent theme of 1891 was the prevalence of state-oriented points of view over national ones. Equality of representation of the states in a perpetually existing Senate was almost universally accepted. Even Deakin, a key exponent of

---

not specified as being within the exclusive jurisdiction of Congress, the States retain all the powers vested in them by their respective Constitutions.'

[23] *Convention Debates, Sydney* (1891), 74–5.    [24] *Ibid.*, 78.
[25] *Ibid.*, 91. Also see *ibid.*, 63 (McIlwraith).    [26] *Ibid.*, 159. Also see *ibid.*, 111 (Baker).

the nationalist perspective, levelled his attack on the powers and not the composition of the Senate.[27] In conceding equal representation, the more 'democratically' inclined were forced to admit a significant qualification of the national majoritarian principle.[28]

For some delegates a rationale for equal representation was that the Senate would be the guardian of states' rights. Deakin countered by challenging them to define these 'rights' and, having defined them, to show how in the exercise of limited federal legislative power those rights could be infringed. Behind this was the view that states' rights were the residual legislative powers of the states, which would be protected by the division of powers in the Constitution, and enforced by the courts.[29] To this argument Barton's response was that what were actually at stake were states' interests.[30] Baker likewise argued that equal representation in the Senate would enable the people of the states to have a say on federal policy within federal areas of legislative competence.[31] As Baker later put it, 'the division of power between the central and the local Governments is not, and cannot be, strictly defined'; there must be an 'overlapping' or 'concurrent jurisdiction'; and there will inevitably be a 'disputed border line' between the two – a boundary that will necessarily evolve over time.[32]

While Deakin's democratic nationalist position was forceful and consistent in terms of its premises, it contained the important concession of equality of representation.[33] Six years later, an even more radical nationalist like Higgins was not prepared to concede this without argument and a division. But the concession of equal representation in the Senate was a prerequisite to the consent of the smaller colonies, reflecting the equality they enjoyed in the federal convention itself, and would enjoy in the ratification of the Commonwealth Bill. Indeed, in the hands of the

---

[27] *Ibid.*, 68–88. For similiar reasons, Higgins was later forced to withdraw his proposal to reduce the term of the Senate from six to four years: *Convention Debates, Adelaide* (1897), 676–7.

[28] E.g. *Convention Debates, Sydney* (1891), 215 (Wrixon).

[29] Although Deakin spoke not of a 'division', but of 'limited' federal powers: *ibid.*, 79, 82.

[30] *Ibid.*, 89–90.

[31] *Ibid.*, 111, 113. See also Moore, *Constitution of the Commonwealth* (1st edn, London: John Murray, 1902), 123.

[32] Richard Baker, 'Sir Richard Baker at Norwood', *The Register*, 1 March 1901 (Baker Papers, series 1, vol. 7 ('Election Speeches')). Clark likewise thought that the states must be able to protect themselves through the Senate rather than rely only on a division of powers enforced by the courts: *Convention Debates, Sydney* (1891), 111, 252.

[33] The speeches on this point collected in Clark, *Select Documents*, 487–92, are not representative of the debate.

South Australians the need for negotiation was elevated into a principle of federalism. Baker maintained that federation was in essence a 'compact made between the constituent states'.[34] Cockburn added that federation was 'a compromise and essentially a bargain' and for that reason a compromise between separation and union.[35] Underlining its contractual character, John Gordon thought that the constitution would be 'a mere commercial treaty', for '[w]e are not here to raise a national standard, but to enter into a bargain, colony with colony, on terms which we think advantageous to each'.[36] Kingston reminded the convention:

> we are dealing with autonomous States, who have long enjoyed the blessing of self-government, and who should not be asked – and who, if asked, would not be likely to accede to the request – to sacrifice any of their existing powers other than those which it is absolutely necessary should be surrendered in the national interest.[37]

Thus, for many the issue was more than simply one of protecting state interests or rights. Equal representation was something to which the peoples of the states were entitled as a matter of 'right', an extension of their entitlement to self-government, a means by which they would participate in the government of the entire federation.[38] The Senate and the House represented a principled compromise between unification and confederation in the composition of the federal organs of government.[39] For some, it was a cardinal principle of federation; for others merely a compromise, but always an unavoidable one, against which all of the arguments of Deakin, Isaacs and Higgins could not prevail.[40]

John Macrossan's perception that the party system would provide the motive force in federal politics, so that senators would vote along party lines, seemed to fall on deaf ears for the moment.[41] Bryce had emphasised the operation of the party system in the United States, and taught that the Senate did not protect the small states.[42] Predictably, Deakin and others

---

[34] *Convention Debates, Sydney* (1891), 111.   [35] *Ibid.*, 197, 199.   [36] *Ibid.*, 451.

[37] *Ibid.*, 153.   [38] E.g. *ibid.*, 40 (Griffith), 62 (McIlwraith), 91–3 (Barton).

[39] E.g. *ibid.*, 278 (Hackett), 445 (Parkes).

[40] Deakin wrote to Pearson, 25 March 1891: 'the Bill represents a compromise but considering that we are 7 against 38 in the Convention & 4 against 10 in the Committee I hope you will not be disappointed with the result': MS7319, box 439/5(a), Pearson Papers.

[41] *Convention Debates, Sydney* (1891), 434 (Macrossan). See also *Convention Debates, Sydney* (1897), 584 (Deakin).

[42] See Bryce, *American Commonwealth*, II, *passim*.

urged this against the proponents of states' rights.[43] Bryce had, however, also praised the Senate, and those in favour of coordinate powers were not reticent in citing Bryce to this effect, even if it meant acknowledging that the small state–large state question had become a non-issue in the United States.[44]

This easy dismissal of Deakin and Macrossan's argument is comprehensible when it is recalled that a number of the framers recognised the close relationship between responsible government and strict party discipline, and were opposed to both.[45] If the convention were to reject responsible government – as they hoped – party discipline would be likely to be relatively weaker. While the Senate might not always protect small states against large states, weaker party discipline would make representatives in both houses relatively more independent. In this context, Macrossan may have accurately predicted the role of party politics in the Senate. But in 1891, many of the framers were quite unsure about responsible government, and the belief that the Senate could operate as a states' house was not completely unreasonable in the circumstances.

Eventually, however, provision was clearly (if elliptically) made in 1897–8 for responsible government, and a further answer to Deakin's argument was necessary.[46] Sir John Downer sought to do so when he pointed out that so long as the Senate was founded 'fairly', with equal representation of the states:

> state rights will come very little into these matters, and the results will be highly satisfactory, because we shall know that we really have become so much one people that these smaller considerations never occur to anybody at all.[47]

John Winthrop Hackett's observation in 1891 had been similar:

> [T]he main function of the Senate . . . [is] to cement these isolated communities together, to make a dismembered Australia into a single nation . . . to convert the popular will into the federal will . . . to give

---

[43]  Convention Debates, Sydney (1891), 335–7 (Deakin).

[44]  Bryce, American Commonwealth, I, 93–120; Convention Debates, Sydney (1891), 147–8 (Rutledge).

[45]  See e.g. Convention Debates, Sydney (1897), 185 (Dobson), 584, 677–8 (Cockburn). Compare Willoughby, Australian Federation, 64, 74.

[46]  See Convention Debates, Sydney (1897), 585 (Deakin).

[47]  Ibid., 269; and cf. Convention Debates, Adelaide (1897), 539, 646, 665 (Glynn).

full voice to the wishes of the populace, but, at the same time, to take
care before that voice issues forth as the voice of Australia that it shall
be clothed with all the rights and duties of the federal will.[48]

Downer and Hackett seemed to suggest that a successful Senate would be
marked by a sense of unity and national purpose. Senators from particular states need not always or even usually vote in blocs. They would,
instead, be involved individually in national policy debate, and might
even be aligned with political parties. Downer might also have been
arguing, as Hackett seemed to suggest, that equality of representation
would ensure that the people of each state would be properly represented
as 'a people'. This security would free them to engage in national debate
in a non-sectarian manner, knowing that they were entitled to that equal
share of representation which befits an independent body politic, and
could make use of this if their sectional interests were ever seriously or
unambiguously in jeopardy. In this sense, equal representation in the
Senate would serve to unify rather than divide the nation.

A final line of argument against the Senate was to characterise it as a
conservative upper house, with the implication that it lacked democratic
credentials and that it should therefore be subordinate to the more
popular lower house.[49] The response, however, was that the Senate was to
be properly understood as the states' house, and this view prevailed.
Sir Thomas McIlwraith, for example, contested outright the assumption
that the Senate would represent the monied class.[50] Baker pointed
out that the Senate would not be a nominated body or elected by a
property-owning constituency.[51] He and Cockburn therefore supported
the Senate as a 'council of states', provided that it was directly elected,
anticipating 1897.[52] A few, however, embraced the suggestion that the
Senate would function as an upper house. Nicholas Fitzgerald accepted
that the Senate would be a 'conservative' institution and a check on the
impetuosity of the popular will.[53] Parkes likewise thought that the Senate

---

[48] *Convention Debates, Sydney* (1891), 280.
[49] Compare Crisp, *Australian National Government*, 14–21.
[50] *Convention Debates, Sydney* (1891), 63.     [51] *Ibid.*, 111.
[52] *Ibid.*, 111, 200. Crisp, *Australian National Government*, 15, 18, argued that conservatives saw a
    Senate appointed by the state parliaments as a check on democratic social legislation, since the
    state upper houses retained a property franchise. But this does not entirely explain the
    attitudes of a conservative Baker and a liberal Cockburn.
[53] *Convention Debates, Sydney* (1891), 171.

would be, like the House of Lords, a vehicle of a 'moral and just conservatism', but he insisted that it would embody 'the only conservatism possible in a democracy – the conservatism of service, of length of experience, and weight of character'.[54]

Thus, the attack on equal representation did not succeed in 1891, even on the basis of election by the state legislatures. Writing soon after the convention, Edmund Barton's elder brother, George Burnett Barton, commented that the framers of the 1891 bill were 'virtually constrained' to adopt the American 'principle' that the Senate would be composed of an equal number of senators from each state. He pointed out that 'the reasons which prevailed with the American statesmen' applied 'as forcibly to the circumstances' of the Australian colonies. 'The States require to be represented as States', he said, 'and that can only be effected by placing the election of their representatives in the hands of the State Legislatures.' Each state would be able to 'enforce its policy on State questions' in the Senate through the election of representatives having the 'confidence' of each state parliament.[55]

In this way, argued Barton, comparable formative conditions produced similar representative structures in the United States and Australia. In 1897, direct election would be substituted for election by the state legislatures, reflecting a change in the composition of the second convention. But the convention was still premised on state equality and unanimity, and Deakin's concession that he would allow wide powers for the Senate if its composition was elective meant that Higgins's attack on equal representation in a directly elected Senate was doomed to failure.[56]

## Responsible government and the powers of the Senate

If the impregnability of equality of representation was a victory of federal principles over those of majoritarian democracy, the nationalist response was, as has been noted, to seek to limit the powers of the Senate in the

---

[54] *Ibid.*, 319.

[55] Barton, *Draft Bill*, 23–4; cf. 28. See also Quick and Garran, *Annotated Constitution*, 305–8, 313.

[56] See *Convention Debates, Sydney* (1891), 74; *Convention Debates, Adelaide* (1897), 650–1 (Deakin), 641–9 (Higgins). Deakin's latter comments explain why he did not contest equal representation in 1891: he saw the necessity for compromise. In 1891 he stressed logic; in 1897 he stressed conciliation. On this point, even Isaacs 'deserted' Higgins for reasons of political necessity: *Convention Debates, Adelaide* (1897), 660.

name of responsible government. Now the Senate's powers might be limited in one of two ways. The first, and most important, was to limit its power over financial bills. The second was to institute a deadlock-breaking mechanism to reduce the long-term capacity of the Senate to resist the will of the House. But in 1891 as well as in 1897–8, there was a definite limit to the extent to which nationalists could compromise the powers of the Senate.

Inclusion of a deadlock-breaking mechanism seemed to enjoy a significant level of support in 1891, even though the final bill did not contain such a provision. James Munro argued that if the Senate could amend money bills then deadlocks would be very likely and the views of a section of the people would prevail; a minority would govern the majority. Andrew Thynne, with Deakin's support, therefore proposed that deadlocks between the two houses be settled 'on sound democratic lines' by a dual, popular referendum – the people as a whole, together with the people of the states, would resolve the impasse.[57] Argument about the use of the Swiss referendum for the breaking of deadlocks and the amendment of the Constitution would re-emerge at crucial points in the debate, particularly in 1897–8. But in 1891, Thynne's proposal was met by the considerable authority of Griffith who thought that a really serious deadlock between the Houses would amount to 'revolution'. He observed:

> Every constitutional government consists of two or more parts, each one of which can put the machine out of gear. That is the essence of constitutional government. The only means of avoiding collision is to have autocracy.[58]

Baker took the argument one step further by applying it to the composition of the executive government itself and proposing a definite alternative to a system of government responsibility to the lower house. He warned that responsible government, though democratic, tends to centralisation of power, whereas federalism diversifies it. Federalism, meaning the equal representation of the states in a powerful Senate, is inconsistent with traditional responsible government, he said. A form of federal executive consistent with federalism was thus necessary. He

---

[57] *Convention Debates, Sydney* (1891), 441. For Thynne's support for popular ratification, see *ibid.*, 340.

[58] *Ibid.*, 429–31. Compare *ibid.*, 106 (Thynne); *Convention Debates, Melbourne* (1898), 2192 (Wise): 'Dead-locks are the price we pay for constitutional liberty.'

therefore proposed a Swiss-style executive council consisting of six ministers, three appointed by each house – and preferably one minister from each state.[59]

A number of delegates, many of them South Australian, explicitly supported the proposal.[60] Cockburn's argument in support was that federalism was inconsistent with parliamentary sovereignty. Following Dicey, he pointed out that neither the federal and state governments were 'sovereign' in a federal system, but were subject to the 'supreme' authority of a rigid constitution, authoritatively adjudicated by the courts. Responsible government, Cockburn added, had only emerged under parliamentary sovereignty, and for reasons which he did not clearly articulate, it was doubtful whether it would survive in a federation. It would be better therefore to adopt the Swiss system, he concluded.[61]

On the other hand, nationalist democrats promoted responsible government and lower house control of money bills. Henry Wrixon pointed out that '[f]inance is government, and government is finance, and under the English system of government one or other house must appoint the executive'. For governments to be based on national majorities, he said, finance must be under the final control of the lower house. If the Senate were to control money bills, 'the real effect' would be 'to give the determining power of government into the hands of, it may be, a small minority of the people'.[62]

However, against this argument Hackett's famous aphorism prevailed, at least in 1891. '[T]here will be one of two alternatives', he said, 'either responsible government will kill federation, or federation in the form in which we shall, I hope, be prepared to accept it, will kill responsible government'.[63] While federalism did not kill responsible government at the convention of 1891, it did prolong its hesitating conception until the second convention in 1897–8. At the first convention, Griffith asked whether a Senate composed of equal representatives of the several states and possessing powers equal to the lower house could be compatible with

---

[59] *Convention Debates, Sydney* (1891), 439–40, 465–6; *Minutes of the Constitutional Committee* (7 April 1897), *Australian Federal Convention Papers* (1897–8), no. 2, series 8/13, items 91, 96–7.

[60] See e.g. *Convention Debates, Sydney* (1891), 102 (Downer), 122 (Bird), 135 (Smith), 162 (Kingston), 277–80 (Hackett); *Convention Debates, Adelaide* (1897), 193 (Dobson), 211–14 (Downer).

[61] *Convention Debates, Sydney* (1891), 198. Contrast Deakin, *Federal Story*, 35–6, treating Baker's proposal as inherently conservative.

[62] *Convention Debates, Sydney* (1891), 214–15.    [63] *Ibid.*, 280.

responsible government. Since responsible government was a recent and evolving institution, he suggested that the delegates should leave the Constitution 'elastic', so as to 'allow of any necessary development that may take place'.[64] Accordingly, the 1891 bill provided in ch. II, cl. 4 that ministers of state would be 'capable' of being chosen as members of either house. Griffith's intention was 'to frame the Constitution that responsible government may – not that it must – find a place in it'.[65]

The vital, closely related question of the powers of the Senate over financial bills was similarly resolved, despite the range of views initially expressed on the issue. Munro, for example, thought that the House of Representatives 'ought to be supreme in questions of finance'. Deakin similarly denied the Senate an absolute veto power, although he conceded greater powers if it should act 'under the control, and only by the authority of the people'. Barton likewise maintained that the Senate should have equal powers with respect to financial and taxation bills, provided that it was directly elected. Baker, on the other hand, sought full power over financial bills, while Kingston, a dissentient among the South Australians, only tentatively supported a power of amendment. Griffith, however, pointed out that the distinction between veto and amendment was insignificant, since the power of rejection was the really important power, the power to bring down a government. Fitzgerald supported the veto in detail exercised by a 'conservative' Senate acting as a 'check on the people's will'.[66]

On this point, Clark considered that the strongest argument against amendment was that it would amount to control of the majority by the minority. However, the answer to this, he said, was that British responsible government was not, in any case, 'founded on the principle of an absolute rule of the majority' since:

> single and equal electoral districts have never yet been adopted in England, and have not been adopted, so far as I know, in any of the

---

[64] *Ibid.*, 35–8, 40–1; cf. *ibid.*, 244 (Clark), 259 (Bray); Wise, *Making of the Commonwealth*, 123, 128–9; Griffith, *Conditions of Australian Federation*, 5–7; Griffith, *Notes on Australian Federation*, 17–19. The Australians were aware that American federalism and the separation of powers had developed prior to the development of responsible government in the United Kingdom: *Convention Debates, Sydney* (1891), 279.

[65] *Convention Debates, Sydney* (1891), 955; Quick and Garran, *Annotated Constitution*, 132, 139. Wrixon unsuccessfully proposed the words 'responsible Ministers of the Crown': *Convention Debates, Sydney* (1891), 527.

[66] For references, see *ibid.*, 53 (Munro), 78 (Deakin), 91–3 (Barton), 113 (Baker), 163 (Kingston), 35–8, 40–1, 427–9 (Griffith), 171–2 (Fitzgerald).

> Australian colonies. The electoral districts remain at the present time ... very unequal in numbers and as to the amount of representation assigned to them; and the consequence is that many important measures are decided ... by a majority in [the] legislature who were returned by, and who represent, an absolute minority of electors.[67]

For Clark, the remedy for inadequate representation lay in the Hare system of proportional representation; it did not lie in limiting the powers of the Senate on what were speciously democratic grounds. Representative government, for Clark, did not require equality of voting power but a genuine attempt to 'get the intelligence and judgment of the community'. In all electoral systems, even with equal electoral districts, a minority could prevent a majority from getting its way, he said. The important thing was that a minority have the opportunity to be represented, put their case, and ultimately become a majority. But those who opposed equal representation of the states and equal powers for the Senate, Clark pointed out, did not take their principle of majoritarianism to its logical conclusion and adopt the French system under which the majority was given an absolutely dominant voice.[68]

It will be recalled that Parkes's resolution originally provided that the House would 'possess the sole power of originating and amending all bills appropriating revenue or imposing taxation'. Downer sought to amend the resolution by deleting the reference to amendment, and later moved that the Senate should have a power of veto in detail.[69] The first amendment was successful but Wrixon countered by proposing a further amendment limiting the Senate's power to one of rejection, not amendment, directed against Downer's second proposal.[70] At this point, positions were stated and a crisis reached, with veiled threats of a 'packing

---

[67] *Ibid.*, 247.

[68] *Ibid.*, 247–51. On the Hare system, see Thomas Hare, *A Treatise on the Election of Representatives, Parliamentary and Municipal* (new edn, London: Longman, Brown, Green, Longmans and Roberts, 1861); John Stuart Mill, *Considerations on Representative Government* (1861), ch. 7, in *Utilitarianism, On Liberty and Considerations on Representative Government*, H. B. Acton (ed.) (London: Dent, 1983), 261–75.

[69] *Convention Debates, Sydney* (1891), 375–6, 380. Downer preferred a government responsible to both houses, in accord with Baker's call for an adoption of the Swiss system: *ibid.*, 102. Warden, *Formation of the Australian Constitution*, 125, overlooks this when critiquing Downer's reliance on the American model.

[70] *Convention Debates, Sydney* (1891), 381.

up of portmanteaux' and a failure of federation.[71] Others sought com-promise or reference to a committee.[72] In the end, however, Griffith convinced Downer that the power of veto in whole was the significant power – an important point.[73] In this way, a compromise was reached. Downer and Wrixon withdrew their amendments, so that the resolution as agreed to was silent on the question of veto, in whole or in part.[74]

In this context, a significant number of delegates saw federalism, a strong Senate and independent state government as more progressive and genuinely representative than national majoritarianism. Ironically, it was Deakin who appealed to classically conservative arguments in favour of responsible government and the dominance of the lower house – as 'institutions which have the sanction of long experience'[75] – whereas it was Macrossan who promoted federalism as progressive and democratic, observing that Switzerland was the most democratic country in the world, yet one of the most federal also.[76] Clark likewise at this point appropriated Freeman's view that federalism was 'the most finished and the most artificial production of political ingenuity'.[77] Cockburn agreed: federalism was 'the highest form of Government of which human nature is capable'.[78] Indeed, Cockburn saw the independence of the South Australian people to determine local policy as an important facilitator of social pro-gress. The progressive resolution of collective problems could best be solved at a local level, he thought, rather than through uniform laws promulgated by a distant, national Parliament.[79] At this, Lieutenant-Colonel William Smith was surprised that Cockburn, whose 'instincts were liberal . . . almost democratic and socialistic', should support a powerful Senate since it would actually represent wealth. Cockburn responded that the opposite would be the case.[80]

All in all, the debate on Parkes's resolutions revealed the fundamental issues at stake over the formation of the federation and the representative structures to be adopted thereunder. The House of Representatives would be a 'national' and 'popular' house, but it would also be the house of 'locality'. The Senate would for some be a 'conservative' check on the

[71] *Ibid.*, 417 (Barton), 389 (Munro), 396 (McIlwraith), 397–8 (Smith), 403 (Kingston).

[72] *Ibid.*, 414, 418 (Barton), 459 (Bray).     [73] *Ibid.*, 442–4.     [74] *Ibid.*, 463.

[75] *Ibid.*, 84. See also *ibid.*, 144 (Rutledge).     [76] *Ibid.*, 433.     [77] *Ibid.*, 243.

[78] *Convention Debates, Adelaide* (1897), 346.

[79] *Convention Debates, Sydney* (1891), 201. See also *ibid.*, 451 (Gordon, who thought likewise).

[80] *Ibid.*, 399.

popular house, but for almost all, it would be a 'Council of States', composed of representatives chosen by the state parliaments. Responsible government sat uneasily with such a Senate, and efforts were made to modify its powers, but largely to no avail. The prevailing assumption was that the colonies were entering the federation as equal and autonomous parties, and their delegates were in a position to insist that the representative structures must reflect this – both as a matter of principle and pragmatic politics.

## Barton's resolutions – conceptions of democracy and federalism

The debate on Barton's resolutions highlights what was distinctive about the second convention of 1897–8.[81] First of all, the discussion was more sophisticated. The issues of 1891 were well aired during the ensuing six years, and in 1897 the representatives of the five colonies built on the earlier discussion and demonstrated deeper knowledge of the theory, history and available forms of federalism. Secondly, all of the delegations except the Western Australians were directly elected by the people of the colonies. Liberals were hopeful that this would secure a more national-democratic outcome.

The convention began by debating fresh resolutions instead of building directly on the 1891 bill. The resolutions were not, however, appreciably different from those of 1891, indicating that the general outlines were, again, largely agreed. Moreover, the representatives at the 1897 convention were influenced by the manner of their own election, and demonstrated a marked preference for direct election, particularly when debating the representative structures and amending formula.[82] The Constitution produced in 1898 was in a number of respects more democratic and nationalistic than the bill of 1891.[83] Even so, how far

---

[81] See Quick and Garran, *Annotated Constitution*, 167. The Victorian Crown Law Office in 1897 published an illuminating comparison of the Federal Constitution framed in 1891 with the Commonwealth Bill adopted in Adelaide in 1897. See 'Draft of Federal Constitution 1897', *Australian Federal Convention Papers* (1897–8), no. 1, series 1/20, item 2.

[82] A connection noted (and lamented) by Griffith, *Notes on the Draft Constitution*, 2.

[83] Kingston, *Democratic Element*, 7, 16; Quick and Garran, *Annotated Constitution*, 135; La Nauze, *Making of the Constitution*, 72, 79–80, 94–5, 124, 128, 137, 152. However, Griffith, *Draft Commonwealth Bill*, 6–7, thought that there were no changes in 'essential details'.

the nationalist and the democratic perspectives would prevail was an open question. As La Nauze put it, 'the formal requirements of democracy would at some point be confronted with those of federalism'.[84]

One aspect was strikingly democratic. Barton's resolutions recited that 'in order to enlarge the powers of self-government of the people of Australia, it is desirable to create a Federal Government which shall exercise authority throughout the Federated Colonies'.[85] A justice of the High Court has interpreted this to mean that the Constitution was ultimately concerned with the self-government of the Australian people through a system of representative democracy.[86] Bernhard Wise certainly exalted in the recital as a declaration that the Constitution 'emanates from the people, and that it is for the benefit of the people as a whole'. The declaration indicated where the 'seat of sovereignty' lay, he said, just like the words 'We, the people of the United States'.[87] However, the comments of other representatives suggest that the prevailing understanding was that the recital was about local self-government, not national sovereignty.[88] Henry Dobson, certainly not a democrat, did 'not care whether the Bill [was] on an ultra-democratic, a democratic, a liberal, or a conservative basis. It [would] enable the people of Australasia to acquire a larger measure of self-government.'[89] Cockburn, emphatically a democrat and a states' righter, thought that the enlargement of the powers of self-government had to do with the ability of the several colonies to 'manage [their] own affairs'. Federation would secure their 'autonomy', he said, by 'safeguarding [them] against all possible aggression'. It was therefore imperative that there be safeguards to protect local self-government from 'being unduly encroached upon by the federal or central authority' – against the 'vortex that continually tends to draw everything to the centre, and to increase the centralizing powers'. As Cockburn explained, 'local government, self government, and government by the people are analogous terms . . . [C]entralization is opposed to all three, and there can be no

---

[84] La Nauze, *Making of the Constitution*, 95, cf. 125; and see Irving, *Constitute a Nation*, 155 and ch. 11.

[85] *Convention Debates*, Adelaide (1897), 17. The reference was later changed to 'Australasia': *ibid.*, 395.

[86] *Australian Capital Television Pty Ltd* v. *Commonwealth of Australia* (1992) 177 CLR 106, 228 (McHugh J).

[87] *Convention Debates*, Adelaide (1897), 115.

[88] La Nauze, *Making of the Constitution*, 112–13. Cf. Griffith, *Draft Commonwealth Bill*, 5.

[89] *Convention Debates*, Adelaide (1897), 191.

government by the people if the Government is far distant from the people.'[90]

Nevertheless, there were important democratic elements introduced in 1897, and the change in orientation was apparent from the beginning of the convention. Of greatest significance was the movement towards a directly elected Senate. Barton's resolutions left the matter open, but in his introductory speech, when noting that some representatives approved direct election, Barton was met by a resounding 'hear, hear' from the convention – while the alternative view brought forth no response. When he turned to the House of Representatives, which was to be elected on a population basis, he was again met by a resounding 'hear, hear', for on this (he said) 'there can perhaps be no denial' – and again, the response was a resounding 'hear, hear'.[91]

For some members of the convention, direct election was necessary because the upper houses in some of the colonial legislatures were nominated or elected on a limited franchise, and this would prejudice the choice which the state legislatures would make.[92] Others pointed to failures in the American system and demands for reform.[93] Following Deakin's lead in 1891, a significant number felt that the powers of the Senate would turn on its composition and were explicit about their change of mind since 1891.[94] Deakin, who had seconded Barton's resolutions, was delighted to observe the shift in viewpoint. With the 'general sense' and 'common influence' of the convention in this direction, he could now be in the majority on certain points.[95]

The shift to direct election for the Senate unavoidably raised the question of whether or not the States would be divided into electorates, and who would decide this question. At this early stage, Barton staked out his preference for the states to vote as single electorates, in order to express the principle that each state as a whole is represented. This

---

[90] *Ibid.*, 338–9. He also said: 'Of course majorities must rule, for there would be no possible good government without majorities ruling, but I do not think the majority in South Australia should be governed by the majority in Victoria, or in New South Wales': *ibid.*, 340. See also *ibid.*, 127 (Symon: federation will not 'curtail the liberties of the people').

[91] *Ibid.*, 22.      [92] *Ibid.*, 39 (Turner).      [93] *Ibid.*, 176 (Isaacs).

[94] *Ibid.*, 189 (Quick), 209–10 (Downer).

[95] *Ibid.*, 285 (Deakin). Despite the 'great change of opinion', some maintained a preference for the state legislatures choosing their senators e.g. *ibid.*, 248 (Forrest). It is no coincidence that Premier Forrest had also insisted that Western Australian delegates be nominated by the colonial parliament.

coincided with the way in which the representatives had been elected to the convention, he pointed out, and it would make the composition of the House of Representatives and the Senate sufficiently different.[96]

Another related, important and relatively new issue in 1897 concerned the question of the franchise, for the 1891 bill had left the franchise to the determination of the states and did not prohibit plural voting, meaning a right to cast more than one vote.[97] On the whole, the viewpoints were liberal for the time. A recurring aphorism was 'one man, one vote', a phrase often associated with the idea of equality of voting power. However, the representatives at the convention did not mean equality of voting power when they used this expression.[98] The representatives were rather more concerned to proscribe plural voting – a different (though related) matter.[99] That 'one man, one vote' did not mean 'one vote, one value' appears explicitly from almost every representative who spoke to the matter.[100] For instance, Sir George Turner supported 'one man, one vote' while treating it quite separately from the number of electors who would be represented by each member of the House.[101] William Trenwith, an opponent of equal representation in the Senate and

---

[96] *Ibid.*, 26 (Barton), 270 (Reid).

[97] Barton and Cockburn had respectively argued for federal control and a more liberal franchise, but without success: *Convention Debates, Sydney* (1891), 91, 200, 628, 636. In 1897, Holder proposed an adult franchise: *Convention Debates, Adelaide* (1897), 149; Downer a liberal one: *ibid.*, 212; Lyne a franchise at age 25 or 30 for the Senate: *ibid.*, 161. Dobson sought one vote per person plus one vote for thrift: *ibid.*, 192, but was criticised by Fysh: *ibid.*, 242. Forrest wanted to leave the matter to the states: *ibid.*, 246, 250. Holder's proposal failed, but he alternatively proposed that 'no elector now possessing the right to vote shall be deprived of that right'. As Quick and Garran, *Annotated Constitution*, 173–4, later pointed out, this would have required a uniform franchise, enfranchising women. As a compromise, the present s. 41 of the Constitution was carried by a vote of 18 to 15, ensuring that those who had the vote in 1901 could not be subsequently denied it when the Commonwealth passed a uniform franchise law.

[98] This is not to deny that outside the convention the expression was used in that sense or, at least, associated with ideas of equality of voting power, particularly by labour representatives. See, for example, Higgins, *Essays and Addresses*, 15; Parkes, *Fifty Years*, 298, 306; but contrast Deakin, *Federal Story*, 33. George Barton used the expression in this sense, but rejected the proposal. To 'prescribe a uniform system of qualifications', he said, would violate the 'fundamental principle' of the Constitution that 'the internal affairs of the States were not to be interfered with where interference could safely be avoided'. The separate colonies regarded control over their electoral systems as one of their 'rights': Barton, *Draft Bill*, 28.

[99] Contrast *Attorney-General (Cth); Ex rel McKinlay* v. *Commonwealth* (1975) 135 CLR 1, 72.

[100] E.g. *Convention Debates, Adelaide* (1897), 79 (Fraser), and 437 (Isaacs). But see *Convention Debates, Sydney* (1897), 271 (Carruthers).

[101] *Convention Debates, Adelaide* (1897), 41 and cf. 250 (Forrest).

a proponent of equality of voting power, also supported 'one man, one vote', but he saw these as different issues.[102] Perhaps the clearest expression of this distinction came from John Quick. He supported a liberal franchise to be fixed in the Constitution, but the words he used were very clear: 'no person ... shall vote more than once at any federal election'. And he distinguished this from the determination of House of Representative electorates, which he regarded as 'a mere matter of detail', to be left to the state parliaments, subject to federal supervision as it 'should see fit'.[103] It is true that Barton's resolutions also referred to 'districts formed on a population basis', and there was a discussion of how the proportion of members to voters should be worked out. But Turner emphatically denied any implication of equality of electorates:

> I should like it to be distinctly understood that, as far as I am con-
> cerned, I do not intend that we shall take 40,000 people wherever we
> can find them and say, 'You shall have one member,' as in many of
> the colonies, and particularly in Victoria, if we did so we would do a
> grave injury to the country and confer a benefit on the towns.
> I understand we are to allow each colony to fix what may be considered
> fair constituencies and allot the colonies one member for every 40,000
> of their population.[104]

Responsible government also fared better at Adelaide, coinciding with the more nationalist tone of 1897.[105] A system of government responsible to the lower house of Parliament alone was supported by liberals such as Higgins once again making conservative arguments favouring Anglo-Saxon institutions over continental ones, experience over theory, and the familiar over 'unfound novelties'.[106] Baker, however, repeated his objection to responsible government on federal grounds, arguing from the examples of Switzerland, Germany and the United States, and distinguishing Canada.[107] He again urged the convention to adopt a federal executive on the lines of the Swiss system, and was directly supported in this by Gordon and Cockburn,[108] with Holder, Braddon, Dobson,

---

[102] *Ibid.*, 330–2.    [103] *Ibid.*, 187.    [104] *Ibid.*, 41.

[105] For example, see *ibid.*, 72 (Glynn), 106–7 (Wise's change of mind).

[106] *Ibid.*, 96–7. See, likewise, the arguments of A. B. Piddington in the New South Wales Legislative Assembly, 24 May 1897, recorded in Crisp, *Federation Fathers*, 132–3.

[107] *Ibid.*, 28–31; see Baker, *Executive in a Federation*; La Nauze, *Making of the Constitution*, 129, 138; Hunt, *American Precedents*, 22.

[108] *Convention Debates, Adelaide* (1897), 324, 345.

Downer, Forrest, Walker, and even Quick and Trenwith, expressing varying degrees of support or interest.[109] From Queensland, Griffith similarly 'called attention to the difficulties attendant upon an attempt to impose the present phase of responsible government, which may prove a passing one, upon a federation'. He again pointed out that responsible government, at least at a federal level, was still an experiment: if it proves to work well 'it will last, and if it is not good it ought to be modified'. It should not be 'prescribed for all time'. By contrast, Griffith insisted, equality of representation in a powerful Senate was a federal imperative that must be entrenched. Responsible government might be allowed to operate at the federal level, but the guiding principle ought to be federalism.[110]

Baker's proposal met a formidable array of opposition, however, including the leader of the convention, Barton, as well as Turner, O'Connor, Glynn, Higgins, Wise, Symon, Lyne, Isaacs, McMillan, Reid, Deakin and Trenwith.[111] Higgins saw clearly that Baker's reasoning was to argue from the formative basis of the federation to an appropriate system of representation. On the premise that the Constitution would be formed on the consent of both the states and the people, Baker maintained that there should be equal representation in the Senate and popular representation in the House of Representatives, and that the executive should be responsible to both houses.

Notably, Higgins was 'convinced' by Baker's 'logic', and had to respond by 'deny[ing] the premise'. Higgins held that the formative basis of the federation should be the consent of the entire people of the nation, and that the people alone should be represented in the Federal Parliament.[112] Wise, however, pointed out the difficulty for Higgins's radical nationalism: Australian federation very plainly required the unanimous consent of the several colonies. In response, Higgins was forced to concede the point, but then shifted ground from the formative basis of the Constitution to the representative structures to be adopted thereunder. 'The consent of the states is necessary when you are going into a league', he said, 'but as soon as you are in a league the consent of the people is sufficient.'[113]

---

[109] *Ibid.*, 66, 146–8, 184–5, 193–5, 211, 213–14, 247, 307, 315, 330, 334.

[110] Griffith, *Notes on the Draft Constitution*, 4–5.

[111] *Convention Debates, Adelaide* (1897), 24, 44, 51–2, 72, 96–7, 106–7, 118, 133–4, 167–9, 222, 244, 255, 274, 286–8, 380.

[112] *Convention Debates, Sydney* (1897), 259–60.  [113] *Ibid.*, 260.

Higgins's initial argument against Baker had thus been premised on a nationalist account of the formative process. But this approach could not account for the patently compactual origin of the federation, and he had to concede Wise's observation. His revised strategy was to disjoin formation and representation, and to focus on the latter.[114]

The debate over the relationship between the executive and parliament also involved an important confrontation between two kinds of liberal democrats. For his part, Cockburn supported the Baker scheme on the basis of an opposition between self-government and centralised government, which he characterised as distant and potentially tyrannical. In Cockburn's words: 'I would do my utmost to prevent [centralisation].' The Senate would be a safeguard against centralisation, he thought, and for the same reason, he favoured an executive which was drawn from the several states and responsible to both houses.[115] On the other hand, nationalist liberals like Higgins and Isaacs insisted on majority rule in a strong national government. Higgins warned those whom he called the 'small state radicals' that 'the stiffest Tories are leaning all their hopes upon equal representation in the Senate', since the experience of America showed that the small states with equal representation were but 'pocket borough[s] for the silver kings'.[116] Isaacs further argued that far from representing an essential principle of federation, equal representation was actually a compromise achieved at Philadelphia between the two logically coherent positions of confederation and national union, and that the Senate was originally intended to be a conservative upper house.[117] However, Gordon's response was to insist that the 'genius ... of South Australian politics' had been 'local government', to which he contrasted 'a huge system of centralisation'.[118] Likewise, Cockburn thought that 'State rights and provincial rights are the strongest bulwarks against despotism. In a Federation, diversity is freedom, uniformity is bondage', he said.[119]

Charting a middle course typical of many others from New South Wales, Wise pointed out that the same nationalist majoritarian arguments

---

[114] Compare the exchange between Higgins and Barton, discussed in the next chapter.

[115] *Convention Debates, Adelaide* (1897), 343–5. This seemed to mean that he dissented only from the Swiss practice of electing the executive council for a fixed period of three years. Cf. Griffith, *Conditions of Australian Federation*, 10; Griffith, *Notes on Australian Federation*, 19.

[116] *Convention Debates, Adelaide* (1897), 101–2.    [117] *Ibid.*, 171–3.    [118] *Ibid.*, 318.

[119] *Ibid.*, 339.

had been put at Philadelphia in 1787, but had to succumb to the practical need for a federal pact to which the delegates of all the states would agree. As with the celebrated Connecticut 'compromise' in the United States, Australian federation would necessarily rest on a compromise over equal representation, despite the complications of responsible government, financial control and deadlocks.[120] The instincts of moderate delegates like Wise, Barton and others were not very far removed from the mediating views that had motivated Dickinson and other moderates during the Philadelphia Convention. In the final outcome, a majority of the convention would come down in favour of both responsible government and the equal representation of the states in a substantially powerful Senate, and the provision for the resolution of deadlocks between the houses would follow similar suit.

After a week of debate on his resolutions, in his address in reply Barton would trade scholarship with Isaacs in one of their typical confrontations, this time over the referendum and its relationship to parliamentary government.[121] Edward Freeman had made the extraordinary claim that the English system of representative government had grown out of a federalist union of constituent political units, and Barton cited him to this effect.[122] As has been seen, Freeman had argued that within the traditional communal assemblies of the older Swiss cantons the ancient 'Teutonic' institutions had been best preserved. He further maintained that these institutions underlay contemporary English institutions, so that the English system had evolved federalistically, from *mark* to *hundred* to *shire*. This suggested, remarkably enough, that the English Parliament had been constituted more like the Swiss Federal Assembly than the majoritarian legislature of France.[123] Even England now began to look like Althusius' federative commonwealth. In the immediate context, Barton used Freeman in an argument over the utility of the referendum *vis-à-vis* parliamentary representation. But in drawing attention to the federative origin of the English Parliament, Barton was plainly influenced by Freeman's idea that political societies are properly formed through the

---

[120] *Convention Debates, Adelaide* (1897), 105–10.

[121] See La Nauze, *Making of the Constitution*, 121; *Convention Debates, Adelaide* (1897), 180, 392, 394.

[122] For a discussion of the passage in the context of Freeman's thought, see the discussion in ch. 3.

[123] *Convention Debates, Adelaide* (1897), 388, citing Freeman, *English Constitution*, 9–10.

federation of constituent societies and that the structure of parliamentary representation should reflect that fact.

In ways such as this, the Australian framers were partly conscious, partly unconscious heirs to a rich tradition of federal thought derived from the American, Swiss and English experience. This tradition of thought underscored the idea that the formative basis of a federal system in the free agreement of constituent states had very definite implications for the representative institutions that ought to be established thereunder. The framers of the Australian Constitution often reasoned in these terms, even when it came down to determining the fine details of the representative institutions that would be adopted under the Constitution. It remains in the next chapter to show exactly how this was the case.

# Representative institutions

There is no constitution which I know of in existence in Australia, or in any other British community, which provides within its four corners, with the definiteness which is proposed by this resolution, that there shall be responsible government – that there shall be an executive, whose existence must depend on the goodwill and support of the popular house. It appears to me that there is no such constitution in existence; and as has been pointed out by the hon. member, Sir Samuel Griffith, in the absence of such a provision responsible government in its ordinary sense can hardly be deemed an essential of any Australian constitution.

Charles Kingston (1891)

A majority of the framers accepted that the autonomy and equality of the colonies was an unavoidable presupposition of Australian federation. Some, like Alfred Deakin and John Quick, saw it as a necessary concession, others as a normative principle, but they agreed that it meant that the states must be equally represented in one house of the Federal Parliament.[1] It was only a minority of rigorous nationalists, such as H. B. Higgins, who started from the premise that the federation must be founded upon the 'sovereign people' of the entire nation and concluded that representation in both houses should be in proportion to population.[2]

These basic perspectives led to diverging conclusions when it came to defining the structure of the federal government in more precise terms. As has been seen, if nationalists could not compromise the principle of equal representation in the Senate, they sought to qualify its powers – as a dictate of both national democracy and responsible government. The power of the Senate over financial bills must be qualified, they said, by

---

[1] E.g. *Convention Debates, Adelaide* (1897), 303 (Clarke), 650 (Deakin), 656 (Quick).
[2] *Ibid.*, 98.

limiting its power over money bills, and the Senate's capacity to resist the will of the House of Representatives generally must be curtailed by some deadlock-breaking mechanism, preferably one which would allow the will of a national majority to prevail. By contrast, states' righters wished to maintain the powers of the Senate, and many of them doubted the compatibility of responsible government and federalism. This meant that the Senate should have full power over money bills and should not in any sense be subordinated to the House of Representatives through a dead-lock-breaking mechanism that would allow the will of the House ultimately to prevail.

Because a majority in 1897–8 concluded that responsible government was desirable, the debate centred on whether the Senate would have a power to amend financial measures. A majority in 1897–8 also considered that a deadlock-breaking mechanism was necessary, and the debate concerned the precise form that this would take. On this last question, the basic choices were between dissolution, referendum and joint sitting, and each of these could be arranged and weighted in different ways. The weight of voting in a joint sitting, for instance, would be affected by the relative size of the two houses.

Connected to these issues were questions relating to the precise composition of the two houses. Would the Senate be chosen by the state legislatures or directly elected, as the liberal democrats preferred? If elected, would the people of each state vote as one electorate or be divided into a number of electorates? And would this be entrenched in the Constitution, or would the federal or state legislatures decide such matters? Different conceptions of democracy and federalism informed the delegates' views on questions such as these.

Such conceptions also influenced their views on the precise composition of the House of Representatives. How would the House of Representatives be conceived? Would it represent the nation or local electorates? If it represented the entire nation, would the people be represented strictly in proportion to population, or would each state be entitled to a minimum of representation, even in the lower house? Further, if the House was to be 'popular', would an equality in the size of electorates be guaranteed by the Constitution, or would the representation of local electorates be left to the discretion of the federal or state parliaments? And if the House was to be 'local', would it be elected by districts formed on a population basis, or would it be tied to the size of the Senate?

## The composition of the Senate

The discussion of the precise terms of what became section 7 of the Constitution absorbed a substantial proportion of the debates as a whole in both 1891 and 1897–8. The attention given to this reflects the significance that the delegates accorded to the issue of federal representation.

In 1891, following the precedent of the United States Constitution as it then stood, Clark's draft provided that senators would be chosen by the state parliaments.[3] This reflected the mode of representation in the Federal Council of Australasia; it also reflected the manner in which the delegates were elected to the convention of 1891.[4] The Commonwealth Bill of 1891 followed this scheme, despite arguments to the contrary by Deakin and Charles Kingston. Kingston unsuccessfully proposed that each state have the power to decide how its representatives in the Senate be chosen, himself favouring direct popular election.[5]

While Kingston failed in 1891, from the first session of the second convention held in Adelaide in 1897 it was apparent that the consensus had shifted to the direct election of senators by the people of each state.[6] Samuel Griffith, responding to the Adelaide draft, maintained that direct election of representatives in the convention need not determine the manner of election of senators. He argued that conditions in the various colonies were different – some might call for direct election, but others, such as those in Queensland, might not – so it would be better to leave the matter to the determination of each state parliament. Such issues were 'a matter especially of State concern', he said, and 'true democracy' did not require direct election of senators.[7] Griffith was on this point unsuccessful; the direct election of representatives to the convention strongly implied the direct election of senators under the Constitution.

None the less, the draft Bill produced at Adelaide in 1897 retained a federalist focus in two important respects. First, it retained equality of

---

[3] Clark's draft constitution, ch. IV, cl. 18. Kingston's draft constitution was in the same terms: La Nauze, *Making of the Constitution*, 24–6, 295–6. It was not until the 17th Amendment in 1913 that US senators became directly elected.

[4] La Nauze, *Making of the Constitution*, 2.

[5] *Convention Debates, Sydney* (1891), 158. See Quick and Garran, *Annotated Constitution*, 136–7.

[6] *Convention Debates, Adelaide* (1897), 641, 1190, 1210, 1223.

[7] Griffith, *Notes on the Draft Constitution*, 2; cf. Griffith, *Conditions of Australian Federation*, 9–10. Baker agreed: 'Suggestions by Sir Richard Chaffey Baker of proposed amendments', *Australian Federal Convention Papers* (1897–8), no. 1, series 1/20, item 8.

representation for the states and, second, the choice was to be made 'by the people of the State *as one electorate*'.[8] At Sydney concerted attempts were made to qualify these principles. Higgins, supported by proposals of the New South Wales Parliament, sought to democratise the Senate by removing equality of representation, subject to a guarantee of at least three senators for each state.[9] William McMillan similarly sought to qualify the principle that the people of each state should vote as one electorate.[10] McMillan was partly successful. By contrast, Higgins's attempt to compromise equality of representation of the states in the Senate was a resounding failure.

## *Equal representation*

Higgins's argument against equal representation was premised on the view that the proper end of all government, including federal government, is the benefit of the people – regarded as individuals, incorporated into an undifferentiated whole, without any 'arbitrary' institutions, such as states or local governments, intervening. The purpose of federation, therefore, was to enlarge the powers of self-government of the people as a whole, not a 'minority' of them. Higgins opposed the idea that the Senate should be a house of 'confederacy'. It was absurd that 'a man in New South Wales is to be treated as equal only to one-eighth of a man in Tasmania', he said.[11]

Higgins's conception of 'true' federation required a central legislature that was fully national, with 'unification on the subjects which are federal, and a severance of the subjects which are not federal' – which is to say, he interpreted federalism according to the Diceyan 'division of powers'. On subjects of general concern, he said, a majority of the whole people should decide. Both houses should be popularly elected in order to reflect the national consensus, the 'mass of the people'. The Senate, Higgins argued, amounted to an 'ingenious device' to thwart 'the will of the people, as a mass', and to prevent 'liberal and radical legislation'. The

---

[8] *Convention Debates, Sydney* (1897), 388 (Holder).

[9] Quick and Garran, *Annotated Constitution*, 183; *Convention Debates, Sydney* (1897), 358.

[10] *Convention Debates, Adelaide* (1897), 641, 670; *Convention Debates, Sydney* (1897), 259–62, 355, 368–71, 390–1.

[11] For Higgins's arguments, see *Convention Debates, Adelaide* (1897), 641–9; *Convention Debates, Sydney* (1897), 259–65, 345–51.

'best' of the Philadelphia Convention voted against equal representation and the same should occur in Australia in 1897, Higgins concluded. Joseph Carruthers, who voted with Higgins, similarly argued that equal representation was analogous to the South Australian Legislative Council being composed of one member for Adelaide and another from 'some paltry, petty municipality'. Rather, 'there should be ultimate rule by the people, not by broad acres, or arbitrary boundaries, or other accidental occurrences in our Australian civilisation'.[12]

However, Higgins fell far short of prevailing, even though he was prepared to allow some weighting to the smaller states.[13] Significantly, he did not even have the vote of Deakin or Isaacs. For his part, Deakin recognised that the 'compactual' origins of the federation must influence its representative structures:

> [It is] not merely a question as to which form can be most logically deduced from certain premises which may or may not be generally accepted; it is a question between equal contracting parties, as to the terms and conditions on which they will enter the Federation.[14]

Pushing Higgins to the logical conclusion of his premises, Deakin pointed out that pure majority rule would require a single chamber and, indeed, the referendum instead of a legislature. The problem, therefore, lay with Higgins's premises. While Deakin expected that the party system would undermine the representation of the states in the Senate,[15] he also saw that the parties would adapt themselves to the electors in the states in proportion to their voting power, thus recognising the 'dignity' of each of these 'communities'.[16]

Isaac Isaacs also voted with the inevitable majority, but not without first pronouncing a very full argument against equal representation in principle. He argued that equality of representation had been a compromise in the United States, not a principle. Following Burgess and Dicey, he held that the essential principle of federalism was the division of powers, not

---

[12] *Convention Debates, Adelaide* (1897), 540–1.

[13] The vote was 32 to 5 in Adelaide and 41 to 5 in Sydney: *ibid.*, 668; *Convention Debates, Sydney* (1897), 355.

[14] *Convention Debates, Adelaide* (1897), 650.

[15] *Ibid.*, 287–8; *Convention Debates, Sydney* (1897), 584–5; and see Crisp, *Australian National Government*, 20–1; Michael Crommelin, 'The Federal Model' in Craven, *Australian Federation*, 44.

[16] *Convention Debates, Adelaide* (1897), 650–1; *Convention Debates, Sydney* (1897), 331–6 (Deakin), cf. 267 (Downer), 276 (Glynn).

equality of representation.[17] But despite these arguments, most of the framers continued to hold that both federal representation and an allocation of powers were necessary for 'true federation'. Like Josiah Symon, they wished to have both 'federal government' (equal representation in the Senate and popular representation in the House) and a 'federal system' (limited powers 'given' to the Commonwealth).[18]

Two exchanges between Higgins and Barton illustrate how arguments about federal representation were related to the formative basis of the federation. One of Higgins's arguments had been that there was no equality of representation in the Canadian Senate or the German *Bundesrat*. But when Barton interjected that Prussia's strength was 'engendered more by domination than by consent', Higgins responded: 'We are dealing with what exists. The genesis of the German system has nothing to do with the question.'[19] In this exchange, it is instructive that Barton connected the representative structure of the federation to its formative basis, whereas Higgins was concerned only with the outcome, 'the system as it exists'.

In a second exchange, Barton had argued that '[e]qual contracting parties ought to have equal representation'. Higgins's response was: 'If several men . . . form a partnership agreement, they stand equal until it is formed; but when it is formed they have a clause which provides for the majority of partners ruling.'[20] Unlike the argument he had earlier mounted against Richard Baker,[21] Higgins now accepted that equal representation was appropriate during the formative process, and was on strong ground in identifying a tendency to shift from equality and unanimity in the formative process to majority rule under the representative structures. But Higgins did not make clear who the 'partners' were in

---

[17] *Convention Debates, Adelaide* (1897), 171–8, 660; *Convention Debates, Sydney* (1897), 303–13. Compare Isaacs (1939), 33–4.

[18] *Convention Debates, Sydney* (1897), 296.

[19] *Convention Debates, Adelaide* (1897), 99–100 (Barton, Higgins). See, likewise, *Convention Debates, Sydney* (1897), 262–3, 266 (Higgins), 279–82 (Glynn), 298 (Symon); *Convention Debates, Melbourne* (1898), 1993 (Barton). Prussia dominated the German imperial federation by virtue of its overwhelming size and military power. Under the imperial Constitution of 1871, the king of Prussia was designated German emperor and president of the confederation (Art. 11), the chancellor was appointed by the emperor (Art. 15), Prussia was strongly represented in the Bundesrat (Art. 6), and the Constitution could not be amended without the support of Prussia's representatives in the *Bundesrat* (Art. 78).

[20] *Convention Debates, Adelaide* (1897), 665.    [21] See ch. 7.

this analogy. If they were individuals, it followed that 'partnership' decisions would be decided by majority vote among those individuals. On the
other hand, if the parties were the states, partnership decisions would be
decided by a majority of states. The analogy did not resolve this question,
and it was this question that lay at the heart of the controversy.

Higgins's difficulty was that the vast majority of framers accepted the
patently compactual nature of the formative process: that the peoples of
the states, not the mass individuals of the entire continent, were the
parties to the federal compact. Barton's was a mediating perspective
which recognised the compactual characteristics of the formative process
and the consolidating characteristics of the representative structures and
amending process adopted thereunder. And, on this, he clearly represented the majority position. Even Quick – someone deeply influenced
by Burgess – maintained that the Connecticut 'compromise' was in an
important sense a vital political principle, based on the fact that the
states were 'sovereign entities' and 'equal contracting parties'.[22] Bernhard
Wise similarly cited Joseph Story's moderate nationalist adaptation of
Madison's 'partly federal and partly national' idea, 'grounded' in the
original existence of the states. Story, he pointed out, had considered the
compromise over the Senate to be 'well founded' in 'reason and justice'
and to be 'fully vindicated upon the highest principles of political wisdom
and the true nature of the government'.[23]

Also following Story, Barton explicitly affirmed the 'partly federal,
partly national' character of 'federal government'. The 'extreme federalist',
Barton argued, 'goes so far in one direction as to make the constitution
entirely of the type one would call a confederation', demanding 'equal
representation in both houses'. The 'extreme nationalist', on the other
hand, seeks to 'subordinate every federal interest to a national interest', and
'demands proportionate representation in both houses'. 'These being the
extremes', Barton reasoned, 'what is the just mean, what is that reasonable
compromise at which to arrive in order to give due force to the federal
principle, and also to see that the national government of affairs proceeds
without undue interruption?' Barton's solution was to seek an appropriate

---

[22] *Convention Debates, Adelaide* (1897), 656.
[23] *Convention Debates, Sydney* (1897), 325–6; also quoted by Quick and Garran, *Annotated
Constitution*, 415.

mean: 'proportionate representation in the one chamber' and 'equal representation in the other'.[24]

Other moderates took the same approach. Patrick Glynn, for example, relied on James Madison's explanation in *Federalist* no. 62 that in a 'compound government' of national and confederal elements, the Senate reflected the federal principle through equal representation of the states.[25] In this connection, Glynn and Symon also cited Edward Freeman's study of the ancient Greek federations of city-states to support the same principle.[26] In these and many other ways, the framers of the Australian Constitution drew on the available scholarly literature on the question of federalism, marshalling this learning at decisive stages in the debate. Australian federation was to this extent a matter of both negotiated agreement and political principle, derived from the results of then state-of-the-art inquiries and investigations.

### Representing the states

A number of views were also expressed in relation to the structure and conduct of Senate elections. Some wished to see each state as a single electorate; others preferred multiple intra-state electorates. And as between these views, some considered that either the federal or the state parliaments should have discretion to determine Senate districting, while others sought to have the matter entrenched in the Constitution.

William Lyne, for example, favoured the division of the states into electorates so that 'each person standing for election can go through the whole of his electorate and make himself known to the whole of his constituents'.[27] Those, however, who wished to see each state represented as 'one corporate body' supported the 'one electorate' provision, with or without a Commonwealth override.[28] According to Barton, for example,

---

[24] *Convention Debates, Sydney* (1897), 340.

[25] *Convention Debates, Adelaide* (1897), 664–5; *Convention Debates, Sydney* (1897), 276–82. Glynn incorrectly referred to no. 72 and attributed it to Hamilton rather than Madison, but later corrected the error: Hunt, *American Precedents*, 108.

[26] *Convention Debates, Adelaide* (1897), 664; *Convention Debates, Sydney* (1897), 291–6, 348 (*contra* Higgins).

[27] *Convention Debates, Sydney* (1897), 366.

[28] E.g. Barton, Holder, O'Connor, Glynn, Reid, Downer, Kingston, Quick: see *ibid.*, 360, 366, 371–3, 374, 377, 388, 380, 382, 387; *Convention Debates, Melbourne* (1898), 1923–4. See also Griffith, *Notes on Australian Federation*, 13.

the federal principle dictated that just as the House should represent locality, the Senate should represent each state as a whole.[29] If the Senate were to be chosen by intra-state electorates, the representation of the state as an entire body of people would be compromised. Other delegates, along with the parliaments of South Australia, Tasmania and Western Australia, shared this concern, but thought that this could be best achieved by allowing each state to determine its representation in the Senate.[30] John Cockburn supported this approach since 'the greater diversity we allow the greater our freedom from bondage will be'.[31] But he was opposed by other delegates on the ground that this could lead to inconsistency and gerrymandering.[32] Federal control was thus urged, notwithstanding Sir Edward Braddon's concern that this might enable federal interference 'in local and state elections'.[33]

Across this welter of views, thought was given to whether intra-state electorates for the Senate should be equal in population. On this, Lyne had expressed concern that if the states voted as single electorates, the cities would 'obliterate' the country towns.[34] Isaacs much later proposed that the state parliaments be given a voice, subject to the superintendence of the Commonwealth, with a default provision of 'one electorate'. McMillan, however, asked whether there would be 'any provision about having an equal number of electors in each district'. 'Would the State Parliament', he inquired, 'have the right to divide the State as it likes?' Isaacs replied that the state parliaments would have power to determine electoral divisions as they pleased, and could thereby 'protect' the country against the towns.[35] McMillan's point was not taken up by the other speakers who addressed Isaacs's proposal, which was defeated by 27 to 16.

In the outcome, the Federal Parliament was given power to divide the states into multiple electorates, but in the absence of legislation to that

---

[29] *Convention Debates, Adelaide* (1897), 669; *Convention Debates, Sydney* (1897), 360–1, 377; *Convention Debates, Melbourne* (1898), 1923–5.

[30] E.g. Symon, Brown and Clarke: see *Convention Debates, Sydney* (1897), 294, 364, 367, 384.

[31] *Convention Debates, Sydney* (1897), 379.

[32] E.g. McMillan, Higgins, Downer: see *ibid.*, 369–72.   [33] *Ibid.*, 383.

[34] *Ibid.*, 364–6, 369, 385–6; *Convention Debates, Adelaide* (1897), 668–9; cf. *Convention Debates, Sydney* (1897), 381 (Howe).

[35] *Convention Debates, Melbourne* (1898), 1923. Forrest was also concerned about the 'preponderating influence' of the 'larger centres of population': *Convention Debates, Melbourne* (1898), 1927.

effect, each state would vote as one electorate.[36] In this connection, the delegates expressly considered the possibility of entrenching a require-ment that electoral divisions be proportionate to population, but the suggestion was discarded, even by Isaacs. As will shortly be seen, the debate about the composition of the House of Representatives, as ultimately provided for in section 24, gave further opportunity to con-sider the possibility of entrenching equality of electorate sizes. What was clear about section 7, however, was the significant 'infringements of simple majority rule' that it embodied.[37]

## The composition of the House of Representatives

If the Senate embodied a considerable infringement of national majority rule precisely because it was the states' house, most of the framers accepted that the House of Representatives would be the 'popular' house. The question of precisely who or what would be represented in the House was, however, a contested issue. At least four different views emerged. The House could represent the Australian people as a whole, the majority of the people as a whole, the people grouped in localities, or the people as individuals. McMillan, for example, saw the House of Representatives as the 'great popular house' in which the entire people would be repre-sented.[38] Barton, by contrast, thought that the House should represent localities.[39] Synthesising both views, George Reid argued that the House must be both 'national', as well as the chamber in which 'locality . . . is deliberately considered by the arrangement of the electorates'.[40] Deakin, for his part, saw the House as representing individual electors, not localities, but promoted the Hare system as a means of representing every sector of the population – city, town and country, including both agri-cultural and pastoral interests within the country.[41] Others wished to see the states have a minimum representation in the House.[42]

---

[36] See Commonwealth Constitution, s. 7, but note the exceptional provision made for the state of Queensland in para. 2 of s. 7.

[37] La Nauze, *Making of the Constitution*, 166.     [38] *Convention Debates, Sydney* (1897), 437.

[39] *Convention Debates, Melbourne* (1898), 1925.     [40] *Convention Debates, Sydney* (1897), 445.

[41] *Convention Debates, Melbourne* (1898), 1925–7; cf. Quick and Garran, *Annotated Constitution*, 447–8.

[42] E.g. *Convention Debates, Sydney* (1891), 208 (Brown), 215 (Wrixon); *Convention Debates, Adelaide* (1897), 309 (Walker).

Views concerning the precise representative character of the House of Representatives affected many issues. How would electoral districts be defined? Should the federal or state parliaments decide such matters, or should they be entrenched in the Constitution? If entrenched, should an equality in the size of electorates be guaranteed, and thus an equality in voting power for each locality and for the voters therein? If representation in the House was proportional to population, would it be tied to the size of each electorate, or to each state? And would there be a minimum representation for the states in the House? Specific proposals for determining the size of electorates would have an effect on the size of the House of Representatives, and the relative size between the two houses. And this question of relative size implicated the relative dignity and strength of the two houses, especially if a joint sitting were adopted for the resolution of deadlocks.

### Representing the nation, localities or individuals?

As adopted in the Commonwealth Bill of 1891, chapter I, clause 24 provided:

> The House of Representatives shall be composed of Members chosen every three years by the people of the several States, according to their respective numbers; and until the Parliament of the Commonwealth otherwise provides, each State shall have one Representative for every thirty thousand of its people.
>
> Provided that in the case of any of the existing Colonies . . . until the number of the people is such as to entitle the state to four Representatives it shall have four Representatives.[43]

In contrast to the Senate, the House would thus represent 'the people', and representation would be in proportion to population: 'one Representative for every thirty thousand'. However, the clause also contained significant qualifications of the nationalist principles that this seemed to embody: 'the people of the several States' were represented, and it was the 'states' that would enjoy the benefit of representation in proportion to population. Moreover, the states were guaranteed a minimum of four representatives in the House, an important federalising change to Clark's draft, which had not guaranteed a minimum representation. In these

---

[43] *Convention Debates, Sydney* (1891), 947.

respects, the 1891 bill followed the American precedent in regarding the states as constitutive members of the federal body politic and carrying this through into the structure and composition of the House of Representatives.[44] Moreover, the clause did not explicitly adopt Parkes's idea, encountered in the previous chapter, that the House would be 'elected by districts formed on a population basis'.[45] Certainly, the 30,000:1 ratio came close to this; however, strictly speaking, it was open for electorates within a state to contain any number of people so long as there was the appropriate ratio between the total population of the state and the total number of its representatives. In other words, the 'peoples of the States' were the beneficiaries – not individuals, localities or the people of the nation as a whole.

In 1897–8, there were several important changes, however. Richard O'Connor successfully proposed the substitution of 'people of the commonwealth' for 'people of the several states' – rendering section 24 in this respect even more nationalist than its counterpart in the US Constitution.[46] When considered in conjunction with the provision for responsible government and a deadlock-breaking mechanism, this was an important nationalising amendment. But this change was matched by three important federalising developments. The first of these was that the minimum representation of the states in the House was raised from four to five. Second, there was a change in the way in which proportionality to population was expressed in the successive drafts. Barton's initial wording, 'there shall be one member for each quota of the people of the State', seemed to have particular local electorates in view and could arguably have implied an equality of population for each district.[47] This reverted at Melbourne into language more like its final form, i.e. 'the number of members to which each state is entitled', 'the number of members to be chosen in each state' and, finally, 'the number of members chosen in the several States'.[48] The provision as finally drafted thus focused entirely on

[44] See ibid., 290 (Cuthbert), and compare US Constitution, Art. I, s. 2, cls. 1 and 3.
[45] Convention Debates, Sydney (1891), 23, 499–500. Barton's resolutions provided likewise: Convention Debates, Adelaide (1897), 17.
[46] Convention Debates, Melbourne (1898), 1827–8. The US Constitution, Art. I, s. 2, stipulates that the House of Representatives is to be composed of members 'chosen . . . by the People of the several States'.
[47] The words were introduced by Barton: Convention Debates, Adelaide (1897), 683, 1191, 1225.
[48] Convention Debates, Melbourne (1898), 1827–8, 1838, 2435.

the states. Moreover, this shift from the representation of equal electorates towards the proportionate representation of the states was confirmed by a third development: the replacement of the 30,000 quota by a 2:1 nexus between the size of the House and the size of the Senate. The number of members of the House would henceforth be 'as nearly as practicable, twice the number of senators'. It could have been argued that a fixed quota suggested the idea of equal electorates, but now the quota was completely supplanted by the nexus.[49]

### Quota or nexus?

The argument between those supporting a fixed quota and those supporting the 2:1 nexus sheds light on the delegates' visions of federal and national democracy and the degree to which the Australian Constitution embodies these principles.[50]

It is significant that the 2:1 nexus appears to have been an idea first proposed by Richard Baker within the Constitutional Committee.[51] But as acting president and chair of committees, he did not speak to the issue in the convention. When introducing the idea to the convention, Barton noted that members of the House would still 'be chosen by the people of each State, according to the number of its population', but that a 2:1 nexus would protect the integrity of the States Assembly (as the Senate was called in Barton's draft).[52] He pointed out that the nexus effectively produced a quota of 50,000, but with the minimum representation for each state, it would be difficult to effect a 2:1 ratio precisely, so the bill would require a 2:1 nexus 'as nearly as practicably'.[53] O'Connor further explained that the fixed quota had been abandoned in order to avoid the problem that, without parliamentary amendment, a quota would

---

[49] These factors were not emphasised by Quick and Garran, *Annotated Constitution*, 450, 466; cf. 455, 447–50.

[50] Its importance was noted in *McGinty v. Western Australia* (1996) 186 CLR 140, 276–7 (Gummow J).

[51] *Minutes of the Constitutional Committee* (8 April 1897), *Australian Federal Convention Papers* (1897–8), no. 2, series 8/13, items 104, 110–11; La Nauze, *Making of the Constitution*, 138. See Deakin, *Federal Story*, 81; Higgins, *Essays and Addresses*, 17, 62, 80.

[52] Its name later reverted to the 'Senate' by a vote of 27 to 21: *Convention Debates, Adelaide* (1897), 482.

[53] *Ibid.*, 435–7.

produce an alarmingly oversized lower house as the population of Australia grew, according to available forecasts.[54]

There was a subsequent debate about the meaning and effect of the clause, with Higgins and George Turner concluding that the nexus was introduced with the 'Norwegian' joint sitting as a means of resolving deadlocks in mind – something that they opposed, preferring the referendum.[55] Higgins argued that representation in the House should be population based, not state based. Since 'the people ought to rule', the clause should revert to a fixed quota, and let Parliament adjust it as population increases required.[56] Turner likewise insisted that the House must increase with population, since it was to be, by definition, the popular house. There had to be a fixed quota of 50,000, he said, in order that the people might be 'represented as individuals'.[57] Isaacs also objected to the nexus, principally because it would weaken the representation of states with lower growth rates, as was expected to be the case in Victoria and South Australia. Victorians would reject the idea, he said, because under a fixed nexus their proportion of the fixed number of seats in the House would steadily decrease.[58] He argued that the nexus was undemocratic and illiberal, even though the voting power of the people of each state would remain proportional. While proportionality to population was democratic, he argued, the nexus would have a 'conservative' impact on the size of constituencies. A gradual increase in the quota, on the other hand, would control the size of the House yet maintain a fixed ratio to population. As a result, there would be a gradual increase in representation for all growing states, despite disparities in the rate of growth.[59]

Barton, often a successful architect of compromise with those holding more extreme views than himself, in this case actively promoted the

---

[54] *Ibid.*, 683–6. O'Connor had drafted the clause: *ibid.*, 436, 682–3.

[55] *Ibid.*, 687–8, 692. Under the Constitution of Norway (1814), Art. 76 provides for the resolution of deadlocks between the *Odelsting* and *Lagting* by a plenary session of the *Storting*. This amounts to a joint sitting, as members of the *Odelsting* and *Lagting* are chosen from the *Storting* (see Art. 73).

[56] *Convention Debates, Adelaide* (1897), 692; cf. 269 (Reid, suggesting a 60,000 quota). See also Higgins, *Essays and Addresses*, 43–4, who considered that the 1891 bill was 'more liberal' than the 1898 bill with the nexus provision.

[57] *Convention Debates, Adelaide* (1897), 686, 701.

[58] This occurred in Victoria in the 1906, 1911 and 1921 redistributions: P. A. Patterson, 'Federal Electorates and Proportionate Distribution' (1968) 42 *Australian Law Journal* 127, 129.

[59] *Convention Debates, Adelaide* (1897), 694–8.

nexus.[60] He maintained that those from the larger states 'ought to be prepared to concede what are the principles of Federation' by ensuring a relative numerical strength between the two houses. While the United States did not maintain a fixed nexus between the two houses, the Senate was strengthened by virtue of its executive powers in relation to major appointments and the ratification of treaties. But since this would not be the case in Australia, a 2:1 nexus was, he thought, an 'essential of Federation'.[61] Indeed, this time it was Deakin who sought out a middle way, arguing that while a nexus might be appropriate for the time being, it should not be entrenched beyond ten or twenty years:

> But as it is, this provision may last in the Constitution for fifty, 100 or 150 years. And which of us can foresee, or dare attempt to decree an iron condition which is to bind these colonies under circumstances to exist a hundred years hence[?].[62]

Turner alternatively proposed to alleviate the rigidity of the nexus by giving Parliament power to legislate to the contrary. But his amendment was defeated by a vote of 26 to 9 and the convention approved the 2:1 nexus.[63]

The same ground was covered in Sydney when proposals of the New South Wales and Victorian Legislative Assemblies to re-introduce the 30,000 quota were considered. Turner again supported the proposals, restating the view that the House was to 'represent the people in the various states as individuals'.[64] Barton replied that the states as original parties to the federal pact would require equal representation in a Senate having a substantial level of power and standing, and this required a 2:1 nexus to keep the two houses in proper balance.[65] Frederick Holder agreed, noting that the nexus effectively imposed a quota of 1/72 of the national population for lower house electorates, rather than a fixed quota of 30,000 or 50,000. Like some delegates, he spoke almost as if intra-state electoral divisions should reflect the quota, so that 'there should be one

---

[60] The 2:1 ratio was in this sense a compromise: it gave the House a predominance in numbers, but it meant that while the national population would increase the nexus would remain.

[61] Ibid., 703–7.

[62] Ibid., 702–3. Trenwith similarly argued that 'it is unwise . . . to tie the hands of people that are not yet born': ibid., 708.

[63] Ibid., 709–10.  [64] Convention Debates, Sydney (1897), 420–1.  [65] Ibid., 423.

member to every seventy-second part of the population'.[66] McMillan, however, objected to the nexus, distinguishing sharply between the 'characteristics of representation' of the two houses. The Senate would represent each state 'in its corporate capacity', whereas in the House the method of representation should be calculated to 'ascertain the actual opinion of the people of the country' through the various 'constituencies' of 50,000, 70,000 or 100,000 people, so as to represent 'all interests combined' in 'that great popular house'. There could therefore be 'no analogy between the representation of the senate and the representation of the house of assembly', he concluded.[67]

Overall, the delegates who stressed the population basis for representation in the House generally rejected the 2:1 nexus and supported the fixed quota (for example, Isaacs, Higgins, Kingston, Quick, Reid, Turner, McMillan and Peacock). Isaacs argued that just as the small states claimed equal representation in the Senate:

> when we come to deal with the House of Representatives, it is our turn to claim . . . that we shall have representation in that house on the basis of population, uninterfered with by the number of people in the states, and absolutely independent of the constitution of the Senate.[68]

But the nationalists did not prevail even when it came to the popular house. In the matter of the 2:1 nexus, the O'Connor/Barton position was upheld in Sydney by a vote of 26 to 17.[69]

At Melbourne in 1898, Turner decided to test 'the feeling of the convention' just once more, proposing a 50,000 quota, subject to parliamentary adjustment. Isaacs again rehearsed the argument that the compromise on the Senate as a states' house called for a corresponding compromise to make the House of Representatives a truly popular house. Again, he criticised the 2:1 nexus as 'conservative' and 'anti-popular'. Apparently threatening to campaign against the bill, Isaacs argued that the nexus would turn the Constitution from 'a free and democratic constitution', a 'liberal constitution' with a wide franchise, into a Constitution more conservative than any colonial one, and even more conservative

---

[66] *Ibid.*, 424. The 1:72 proportion was calculated by reference to the total number of members of the House, i.e. twice the number of senators, assuming six senators for each of six states.
[67] *Ibid.*, 436–7.    [68] *Ibid.*, 425.    [69] *Ibid.*, 452.

than the British.[70] Nevertheless, Barton carried the day with a vote of 25 to 15,[71] arguing that the 50,000 quota was 'aimed, whether directly or not, at the subversion of every principle of federal government'. In response to an interjection by Isaacs, Barton alleged that Isaacs was seeking indirectly but intentionally to undermine the Senate as representing the states in their corporate capacities. For 'we are dealing with a Federal Constitution, and we do presume to preserve some equilibrium of power as respects the two Houses', he concluded.[72]

## Minimum representation

The minimum representation of the states in the House of Representatives, though a highly significant qualification of the national democratic credentials of the House, can be dealt with briefly. The American Constitution guaranteed each state at least one representative.[73] Nicholas Brown of Tasmania went far beyond this in 1891 when he suggested a minimum of twelve.[74] While such an extraordinary proposal was rejected, the bill of 1891 guaranteed each state a minimum representation of four members in the House.[75]

Barton's draft bill of 1897, as well as introducing the 2:1 nexus, increased the minimum representation to five for each state.[76] Two amendments were subsequently proposed. While both were unsuccessful, they shed further light on the general views of the convention. Vaiben Louis Solomon of South Australia protested that the two large states would still dominate Parliament. The Senate, he thought, no longer had any substantial power over money bills, and New South Wales and Victoria with a total of 50 members would control the House of Representatives – there would only be 26 members from the remaining four states. Objecting that 'representation purely on a population basis is not fair or equitable in any way', he proposed a sliding scale in which each state would be entitled to six members for the first 100,000 of its population, three for

---

[70] *Convention Debates, Melbourne* (1898), 1831–4.

[71] Quick and Garran, *Annotated Constitution*, 447, said the vote was 25 to 10, but see *Convention Debates, Melbourne* (1898), 1837. Here, as elsewhere, Quick and Garran's summaries of the debate cannot always be relied upon.

[72] *Ibid.*, 1835.    [73] US Constitution, Art. I, s. 2, cl. 3.

[74] Supported by Wrixon, but opposed by Macrossan: *Convention Debates, Sydney* (1891), 208, 215, 436.

[75] *Ibid.*, 947.    [76] *Convention Debates, Adelaide* (1897), 683.

the next 100,000, two for the next 100,000 and one for every additional 100,000 thereafter. His proposal was negatived amid numerous caustic interjections.[77]

On the other side, Reid proposed, but under pressure later withdrew, an amendment that the minimum representation for a state be reduced from five to four, as in the 1891 bill.[78] The convention thus settled on a minimum of five members for each states as a balance appropriate to a federal union of what was hoped would be as many as six colonies – as compared to the thirteen colonies of which the United States was originally composed, which by the time of the Australian convention of 1897–8 had increased to forty-five in total.

### Equal electoral divisions and equality of voting power

Equality of voting power entails the idea that the legislature should represent individual citizens equally. On this view, representation in a genuinely popular house will be proportionate to the national population, unaffected by 'artificial' state and local boundaries. A majority in the chamber will represent a majority of citizens of the entire nation.

If Parkes's idea of 'districts formed on a population basis' were to be applied to the drawing of electoral boundaries, each electorate would need to be tolerably equal in population.[79] Indeed, it has been argued that the requirement in section 24 that the House consists of members 'directly chosen by the people of the Commonwealth' implies that representation in the House must be proportionate to population.[80] The three specific features of section 24 of the Constitution just discussed contradict any such implication, however. The 30,000 quota was replaced by the 2:1 nexus, weakening the idea that each local electorate must have a population of 30,000. The rule concerning proportionality to population

---

[77] Ibid., 710–13. Quick and Garran, Annotated Constitution, 447, indicated that his proposal 'was not taken seriously and was negatived without division'.

[78] Convention Debates, Adelaide (1897), 714–15.

[79] Parkes may have intended this: see Parkes, Fifty Years, 298, supporting (and equating) 'one man one vote' and electorates having equal numbers of electors in New South Wales. Compare the original version of his resolutions, which referred to 'districts possessing severally an equality of representation': ibid., 360; La Nauze, Making of the Constitution, 35–8. See also Cochrane, Colonial Ambition, 256–66.

[80] Attorney-General (Cth); Ex rel McKinlay v. Commonwealth (1975) 135 CLR 1; McGinty v. Western Australia (1996) 186 CLR 140; cf. Wesberry v. Sanders 376 US 1 (1963).

only applied to states, not localities. And the minimum representation of each state plainly qualifies any absolute principle of equality of individual voting power. In these respects, the idea that the House would represent individuals equally was profoundly negatived.

Two further observations reinforce this conclusion. First, during the debate on sections 7 and 24, the framers explicitly considered the entrenchment of a requirement that electorates be of equal size. Many delegates, both conservative and liberal, nationalist and federalist, considered the question and unambiguously rejected it. Second, in section 29 of the Constitution the matter of electoral districting was specifically addressed and the determination of electoral boundaries was deliberately left to the state and federal parliaments. Section 29 does not prescribe the basis upon which electoral districts must be defined and at the time elicited only cursory consideration, indicating that the matter was not considered to be of great importance.[81] Moreover, the discussion which did occur suggests that the state and federal legislatures would be entirely free to exercise their discretion in districting decisions.

Section 29 went through three important stages, resulting in a provision having an effect very much like its American counterpart.[82] But unlike the American provision, from Clark's draft onwards the Australian provision was explicit about the power of the federal and state parliaments to determine electoral districting. Chapter I, clause 31 of the 1891 bill provided that:

> The electoral divisions of the several States for the purpose of returning members of the House of Representatives shall be determined from time to time by the Parliaments of the several States.[83]

Consistent with the general tendency of the second convention, however, at Sydney in 1897 the clause was approved in the following form:

> Until the [Commonwealth] Parliament otherwise provides, the electoral divisions of the several States for the purpose of returning members of the House of Representatives, and the number of members to be chosen for each electoral division, shall be determined from time to time by the Parliaments of the several States. Until division each state shall be one electorate.[84]

[81] *Convention Debates, Adelaide* (1897), 715; *Convention Debates, Sydney* (1897), 454–5; *Convention Debates, Melbourne* (1898), 1840, 2528.
[82] US Constitution, Art. I, s. 4, cl. 1.    [83] *Convention Debates, Sydney* (1891), 948.
[84] *Convention Debates, Adelaide* (1897), 715; *Convention Debates, Sydney* (1897), 454–5.

In the event, the default provision was that each state would be one
electorate, the state legislatures would have primary responsibility for
districting, and the Commonwealth Parliament would have a supervisory role. The only qualification on parliamentary control was that in
Melbourne Barton moved the convention to insert the words, 'No electoral
district shall be formed out of parts of different States', in order to forestall
a contrary implication from the reference to the 'the people of the Commonwealth' in section 24.[85] This had the effect of again reinforcing the
sense in which the people of each state were to be represented in the House.

State control was thus qualified by Commonwealth supervision.
Barton explained that the change was to prevent 'gerrymandering'. While
districting decisions were 'properly left in the hands of the Parliaments
of the several states':

> a reserve power [was] given to the Parliament of the federation, not
> to be exercised in any ordinary case but in case there should happen
> to be some such state of things as once occurred in the United States.
> It is a reserve power left to the Parliament of the federation to see that
> the House, which is the most important of the federal legislature
> should not have its efficiency impaired or its representation made,
> I would not say, corrupt but ineffective or improper by any course
> that might be taken by a state.[86]

When subsequently seeking to explain the provision, Quick and Garran
would refer to the possibility of both gerrymanders and malapportion-
ment, noting that American courts had intervened where state laws were
clearly in contravention of state constitution equality requirements. Quick
and Garran thus reflected a more centralist orientation than Barton, stating
that in section 29:

> State Parliaments are, for the time being, exercising a delegated
> authority; they are acting merely as legislative agents of the Federal
> Parliament, which may, at any time, interpose and undertake the
> work. This ultimate control over electoral divisions is another illus-
> tration of the national principles on which the House of Represen-
> tatives is founded.[87]

---

[85] *Convention Debates, Melbourne* (1898), 1840; Quick and Garran, *Annotated Constitution*, 465–6.
[86] *Convention Debates, Sydney* (1897), 454. This followed the approach of the US Constitution:
*Wesberry* v. *Sanders* 376 US 1 (1964), 30–40 per Harlan J (dissenting).
[87] Quick and Garran, *Annotated Constitution*, 466.

While this reflects the legal meaning of the words 'until the Parliament of the Commonwealth otherwise provides', it is also an important example of the way in which a literal reading of the Constitution has often led to an expansion of Commonwealth legislative power, against the apparent intention of the framers of the Constitution. Barton clearly saw parliamentary override in section 29 as a 'reserve power', 'not to be exercised in any ordinary case'. Further, the requirement that no division shall be 'formed out of parts of different States' is capable of a more state-oriented nuance: that it preserves the integrity of the House as representative of the states on a state-wide proportionate basis.[88]

None the less Barton understood the provision 'until the Parliament of the Commonwealth otherwise provides' to be a method by which constitutional change could be secured without resort to formal constitutional amendment. While certain parts of the Constitution were entrenched and the basic law could not be changed except by referendum, at significant points Barton's bill left the 'amendment' of the Constitution to Parliament. The Constitution thus made specific provision on the issue, but left it open to Parliament to make changes if it saw fit. 'Parliament should have power from time to time to legislate', Barton explained, 'without the form of referendum being gone through.'[89] This reflected Barton's basic antipathy to the referendum. Following Freeman, he saw Parliament as embodying the constituent elements of the body politic, and resisted recourse to the more 'primitive' referendum.[90] Barton believed that the 'irresistible implication' to be drawn was that Parliament would on incidental matters such as these possess a power to 'amend' the Constitution – so far from his intention was it that provisions of this nature would allow far-ranging implied limitations on legislative power. Parliament, not the High Court, was to guard against the gerrymander.[91]

That Barton reflected the consensus of the convention is suggested by the lack of discussion on section 29. That no implication of equality of voting power was intended is made abundantly clear from the explicit consideration that was given to the question. Certainly, Parkes's and Barton's resolutions referred to 'districts formed on a population basis'. And, indeed, some delegates spoke of the lower house being 'thoroughly

---

[88] *Convention Debates, Melbourne* (1898), 1840.
[89] *Convention Debates, Adelaide* (1897), 455.    [90] *Ibid.*, 388.
[91] Quick and Garran, *Annotated Constitution*, 466.

popular', and representing 'every unit in each of the States equally'.[92]
Baker even stated that the House was to be elected 'by the people grouped
in electoral constituencies containing probably an equal number of
voters'.[93] But when the issue was specifically raised, the delegates were
very clear that they did not wish to entrench a requirement of equality.

Turner, it has been seen, was very clear that while each state should
enjoy proportionate representation in the House, it was not necessary for
each electorate to have the same population.[94] Deakin agreed. At one
point he stated that the key principle of federation must be 'the rule of the
majority', for 'our whole history is the history of a struggle to give more
and more effect to that principle'. Wise interjected that 'if that principle
were in full force in Victoria, Melbourne and the suburbs would return
nearly half the members'. Deakin responded that this was 'another branch
of the subject' concerned with differences in the numerical size of electoral
divisions based on 'the sacrifices imposed upon the respective voters. It is
scarcely a qualification, and practically the principle of the rule of the
majority is not departed from.'[95] Along similar lines, Glynn stated:

> You do not, even under the constitution, carry out the ratio of
> population with the strictest accuracy. You find . . . for instance in
> South Australia – that in some electorates 2,000 people return two
> members, while in others 15,000 people return only the same number
> of members. Under federation or pure consolidation you cannot carry
> out any absolute strictness of principle in regard to representation.[96]

Indeed, the point was so widely accepted that Wise could safely use it as a
premise in his argument about equal representation in the Senate. He
argued: 'where you have different districts and separate local interests,
those districts should be represented irrespective of the fact that they
contain a minority of population'. Therefore, '[i]t is not one vote, one
value, and it ought not to be, and no one wishes that it should be in local
politics. Why, then, do we ask for it in federal politics?'[97] Wise clearly saw
an analogy between the representation of localities in lower houses and
the representation of states in the Senate. Both groupings were entitled to

---

[92] E.g. *Convention Debates, Sydney* (1891), 26 (Parkes); *Convention Debates, Adelaide* (1897), 331
(Trenwith).

[93] *Convention Debates, Sydney* (1891), 111.

[94] *Convention Debates, Adelaide* (1897), 41, discussed in ch. 7.

[95] *Ibid.*, 289–90.     [96] *Convention Debates, Sydney* (1897), 446–7.     [97] *Ibid.*, 317.

representation, despite differences in population. Even Higgins supported this when he interjected: 'it can be all met in fixing the districts!'[98]

Thus, the debate on sections 7, 24 and 29 clearly reveals that the
delegates chose not to entrench a requirement of equal-sized electorates.
The tone and pattern of the discussion makes it difficult to conclude that
equality of voting power or electorates of equal size was an intended
implication of the language of section 24. Certainly, the words 'chosen by
the people of the Commonwealth' are an index of the national character
of the House. However, delegates as often considered that the House
would represent localities as they considered it would represent the
aggregate of individuals throughout the entire nation. This even led some
observers to conclude that the Senate would turn out to be 'more
"national" than the national chamber itself'.[99] The result in sections 24
and 29 was accordingly a balance between local, federal and democratic
principles. In this way, section 24 embodied the principle of federalism as
much as the principle of national democracy.

## The relative powers of the two houses

The composition of the two houses represented negotiated compromises
in which federal principles decisively qualified the national majoritarian
ones. As has been seen, the nationalist response to this was to seek to
limit the powers of the Senate, particularly over money bills, and to
provide for a deadlock-breaking mechanism. The debate on these two
issues culminated in sections 53 and 57 of the Constitution.[100]

### The Senate, money bills and responsible government

The debate about the Senate's powers regarding money bills lay at the
heart of the 1891 convention, and behind this was a debate between
federalism and responsible government. In 1891 the prevailing view was
that responsible government was an evolving institution and that it was

---

[98]  *Ibid.* But compare Higgins, *Essays and Addresses*, 15.

[99]  E.g. Moore, *Constitution of the Commonwealth*, 98.

[100]  Winterton, *Parliament, Executive and Governor-General*, 1–17, 71–85; Brian Galligan and
James Warden, 'The Design of the Senate' in Craven, *Convention Debates*; James Warden,
'Federalism and the Design of the Australian Constitution' (1992) 27 *Australian Journal of
Political Science* 143.

best to leave the Constitution 'elastic' as regards the question whether ministers must sit in Parliament.[101] This led to the conclusion that the Senate should have equal power with the House, except that it would not originate or amend taxation and appropriation bills, although it could suggest amendments and reject such bills outright.[102] As Edmund Barton's brother, George Barton, argued soon after the 1891 convention, this represented a compromise between the British and American approaches, following the position in South Australia and Western Australia. Unlike the House of Lords, the proposed Senate would have the right to suggest amendments; unlike the American Senate, the Australian Senate would not be able to make amendments on its own initiative.[103]

By 1897 the consensus had definitely shifted towards responsible government, although very little was changed in the bill as a consequence. The provision that was to become section 64 was amended to prohibit a minister of state from holding office for more than three months unless he became a member of Parliament.[104] This did not, however, resolve the question of whether the executive would be responsible to the House of Representatives alone or to both houses. This would turn on the relative powers of the two houses, particularly over money bills.[105] Quick and Garran observed that the debate on the money bill clauses was 'certainly the most momentous in the Convention's whole history', for it ushered in the true 'federal spirit of compromise'.[106]

Barton's draft of 1897 departed from the compromise of 1891. It limited the Senate's powers in respect of the origination and amendment of annual appropriation bills and the origination of taxation bills,

---

[101] *Convention Debates, Sydney* (1891), 35–8, 40–1.

[102] *Ibid.,* 706, 762, 953–4; Quick and Garran, *Annotated Constitution,* 131–2. The Senate was also protected by the provision that taxation bills could 'deal with the imposition of taxation only' and 'one subject of taxation only' and that no extraordinary appropriations could be added to the ordinary Appropriation Bill: ch. I, cl. 55.

[103] Barton, *Draft Bill,* 39–40.

[104] *Convention Debates, Adelaide* (1897), 1233, *Convention Debates, Melbourne* (1898), 2534; Quick and Garran, *Annotated Constitution,* 169. See also ss. 81 and 83 of the Constitution. The House of Representative's sole power of initiation of money bills meant that a government would certainly need the confidence of the House.

[105] *Convention Debates, Adelaide* (1897), 443–4 (Barton). See *Northern Suburbs General Cemetery Reserve Trust v. Commonwealth* (1993) 176 CLR 555, 578.

[106] Quick and Garran, *Annotated Constitution,* 172. They saw this as a recognition by the smaller colonies that, although they had a majority in the Convention, federation would fail if not accepted by the two larger colonies.

although it enabled the Senate to amend taxation bills.[107] Later, at Reid's initiative, taxation bills were included in the prohibition by a vote of 25 to 23, thus returning to the compromise of 1891.[108] This position was essentially carried through the Sydney and Melbourne sessions, although drafting changes ultimately created the Delphic form of the present section 53, which denies a power of amendment but is silent on rejection.[109]

The delegates persistently drew a distinction between amendment and rejection, so that the decision to limit the powers of the Senate only in respect of amendment in this context strongly suggested that a power of rejection was intended.[110] Higgins thus foresaw the significance of the Senate's power: it could 'keep on requesting' amendments, he said, and thus delay supply bills; it could threaten to and actually reject supply bills; it could therefore 'keep Ministers on tenterhooks' and, indeed, force them to 'yield'.[111] However, as has been seen, Baker positively wanted the ministry to be responsible to both houses, and even Barton came close to affirming that the executive government would be responsible to the Senate as well as the House.[112] Thus, while many delegates thought that the government should only be responsible to the lower house, a significant number disagreed; and the federal conventions, in giving the Senate the legal power to reject supply, left the issue open. Although the resistance to the Constitution Bill in New South Wales elicited some changes to the bill at the premiers' conference of 1899, Reid was forced to acknowledge that the power of rejection was 'a real living power'.[113] This would lead in turn to his legendary 'Yes-No' speech of 1898 in which he said he felt personally bound to vote for the bill himself but could not recommend that the voters of New South Wales do likewise.[114]

---

[107] *Convention Debates, Adelaide* (1897), 441–2, 469, 480.    [108] *Ibid.*, 484, 574–5.

[109] *Ibid.*, 1232; *Convention Debates, Sydney* (1897), 467, 481, 537; *Convention Debates, Melbourne* (1898), 2532–3. Baker sought to minimise the adoption of responsible government by enhancing the power of the Senate over money bills: *Australian Federal Convention Papers* (1897–8), no. 2, series 8/13, items 76–7, 82.

[110] On the exercise of this power in 1975, see the brief discussion in chapter 12.

[111] Higgins, *Essays and Addresses*, 16–17.

[112] See *Convention Debates, Sydney* (1897), 620, 622–3.

[113] See also Quick and Garran, *Annotated Constitution*, 214, 216–17, 673; Piddington, *Popular Government*, 6–8. Despite the failure of the 1898 referendum in New South Wales, Reid merely affirmed the position that the Senate must not amend money bills.

[114] See Reid's criticisms of the equal power of the two houses in Reid, 'Speech at Sydney Town Hall', in Bennett, *Federation*, 173–86.

## Deadlocks

The associated means of containing the power of the Senate was a provision for the resolution of deadlocks between the two houses, as ultimately contained in section 57 of the Constitution. While on Griffith's authority the idea had been rejected in 1891,[115] in 1897 a majority accepted that a 'safety valve' would be needed where, in Deakin's words, the 'irresistible force' of the House and the 'immovable object' of the Senate were 'brought into contact'.[116] Resistance to the proposal was offered by those, like John Forrest, who argued that under the pressure of public opinion the deliberative processes of the houses would resolve any serious deadlock.[117] During the Sydney sitting in 1897, however, a majority of delegates in principle approved of a deadlock procedure in a test vote of 30 to 15.[118] And yet the problem remained to identify which particular mechanism or combination of mechanisms should be used.

The possibilities concerned various combinations of dissolutions of the houses, joint sittings and direct, popular referendums. At Adelaide in 1897, Wise had suggested a dissolution of the House of Representatives, Higgins a double dissolution and Isaacs a dual referendum, but all of these proposals were negatived.[119] During the adjournment between the Adelaide and Sydney sittings, the New South Wales Legislative Assembly proposed that deadlocks be resolved by a 'mass' or 'national' referendum at which a simple majority would decide the matter,[120] and much of the debate at Sydney in 1897 would centre on attempts to amend this proposal in one direction or another.[121] Many representatives of the smaller colonies predictably preferred a dual referendum which would look to the peoples of the states as well as the people of the nation as a whole, but they were met by a significant number from the more populous colonies who argued that this would merely transfer the dispute from the two houses of Parliament to the peoples of the states and the Commonwealth, and would be unlikely to resolve the deadlock.

---

[115] *Convention Debates, Sydney* (1891), 759–62.     [116] *Convention Debates, Sydney* (1897), 582.
[117] *Ibid.*, 609.     [118] *Ibid.*, 708–9, 980–1; *Convention Debates, Melbourne* (1898), 2249.
[119] *Convention Debates, Adelaide* (1897), 1150–73. See Quick and Garran, *Annotated Constitution*, 181–2.
[120] *Convention Debates, Sydney* (1897), 541, 709.     [121] See *ibid.*, 541–778, 807–980.

Reid proposed a compromise that would limit the referendum to those matters in which the states were particularly interested.[122] This suggestion was countered by the argument that virtually all subjects of legislation could involve matters of concern to the states – this being one of the considerations that had led to equality of representation in the first place.[123] Alternatively, then, Symon proposed a simple dissolution of the House of Representatives followed, if necessary, by a dissolution of the Senate.[124] Lyne, Turner and Wise next proposed amendments which in different forms would have added a national referendum following the dissolution of the two houses,[125] but these suggestions were, again, negatived.[126] A way forward was finally secured when Carruthers proposed that a simultaneous dissolution of the Senate and the House that would be followed, if necessary, by a joint sitting of both chambers at which a majority of three-fifths would be necessary to pass the measure.[127] Amendments to this proposal by James Howe that would have increased the required majority to two-thirds and by Kingston that would have adopted a dual referendum instead were both negatived, and Carruthers's amendment was affirmed.[128]

The Sydney sitting had settled, more or less, upon simultaneous dissolutions, followed by a joint sitting and essentially this scheme would be adopted at Melbourne in 1898 and enacted into law by the imperial Parliament. Thus, while Symon's scheme of successive House and then Senate dissolutions was initially upheld at Melbourne, it was soon struck out in favour of a double dissolution and joint sitting with a special majority.[129] Again, a proposal by Isaacs for a dual referendum (he personally favoured a national referendum) was rejected by 30 to 15, and a proposal by Higgins that the special majority at the joint sitting be replaced by a simple majority was lost in a vote of 27 to 10.[130] A Constitution Bill containing the three-fifths majority was accordingly presented to the electors in 1898. However, following the failure of

---

[122] *Ibid.*, 648–59; compare *ibid.*, 699–700 (Kingston) and see Quick and Garran, *Annotated Constitution*, 190.

[123] E.g. *ibid.* 659–72 (Isaacs), 672–80 (Cockburn).     [124] *Ibid.*, 709, 725, 738.

[125] *Ibid.*, 739 (Lyne), 743 (Turner), 758, 923–4 (Wise), 926 (Lyne), 928 (Turner).

[126] *Ibid.*, 928, 930.     [127] *Ibid.*, 930.

[128] *Ibid.*, 931 (Howe), 967 (Kingston), 974, 980 (Carruthers' proposal affirmed).

[129] *Convention Debates, Melbourne* (1898), 2134, 2170, 2247, 2249. See Quick and Garran, *Annotated Constitution*, 202–3.

[130] *Ibid.*, 2221, 2226.

the first referendum in New South Wales, the premiers' conference of 1899 determined that the joint sitting would vote by absolute majority and it was in this form that the Constitution Bill was ultimately approved by the voters in the several colonies and enacted into law in 1900.[131]

The significance of this outcome is best understood in the light of the arguments for and against the various proposals. In general terms, supporters of the referendum opposed the joint sitting as less than fully democratic. The successive dissolution of the House followed by the Senate was in turn opposed by supporters of responsible government because the Senate would be able to put the House and the government to an election without immediate risk to itself. Supporters of a strong Senate for their part objected to a simultaneous or double dissolution as inconsistent with the principle that the Senate have a 'perpetual' existence through election of senators by way of successive, periodical ('half-Senate') elections.[132] Moreover, both the national and dual referendum alternatives were contested on the ground that they would weaken the deliberative processes of Parliament and diminish ministerial and parliamentary responsibility.

The multiplicity of proposals and the variety of points of view accordingly ensured a protracted and at times heated debate. The contest between successive and simultaneous dissolution of the two houses thus waylaid the discussion for a significant period of time even though an overall majority would eventually support the double dissolution option. Moreover, supporters of the referendum were split as to whether it should be national or dual, and many delegates from the smaller colonies voted against the referendum in either form. The result was that the national referendum was rejected by a vote of 36 to 10, and the dual referendum was rejected by 27 to 18.[133] Even Carruthers's joint sitting faced disagreement over the required majority, but in this case the

---

[131] *Minutes of the Conference of Premiers on the Commonwealth Bill*, Melbourne, *Argus*, 3 February 1899, in Clark, *Select Documents*, 510–16; *Agreement of the Premiers of New South Wales, Victoria, Queensland, South Australia, Tasmania and Western Australia* (3 February 1899), in 'Australian Federation: Various Papers', Baker Papers.

[132] On the rotation of senators, see Barton, *Draft Bill*, 25, discussing James Harrington, *The Commonwealth of Oceana* (1656) (Cambridge: Cambridge University Press, 1992).

[133] *Convention Debates, Sydney* (1897), 928, 930. Compare Quick and Garran, *Annotated Constitution*, 192.

split was not ultimately significant enough to scuttle the proposal altogether.[134]

Rejecting any deadlock provision in principle, Forrest argued that 'mutual good-will, conciliation, and common-sense', under the pressure of public opinion, would generally resolve matters satisfactorily.[135] Barton initially agreed, arguing that there was no 'absolute necessity, in the working of the constitution, to make any artificial provision against what are called deadlocks'. Nevertheless, recognising the weight of popular interest in such a provision, he favoured dissolution as an outworking of the principle of governmental responsibility, and a double dissolution because the principle of responsibility applied equally to both houses. Barton opposed the referendum as a 'sap' upon the principle of responsibility.[136]

On the other hand, Isaacs wished to require the Senate 'to give way' to the House, arguing that such a mechanism was necessary in order to obtain the agreement of the larger colonies. He opposed the dissolution since it would not necessarily alter the situation, and the deadlock would remain. He favoured the referendum as the most democratic way to resolve such differences, and was prepared to accept a dual referendum since the principle of equal representation in the Senate had already been fixed.[137] Similarly, Higgins insisted on the rigorous application of the principle that the 'wishes of the people' were not to be 'permanently thwarted'. He therefore opposed both the joint sitting and the dual referendum, and supported a national referendum.[138] Cockburn, also typically, agreed that 'the people' should rule, but responded that democracy meant autonomy, home rule and local self-government. A mass referendum was an attack on these principles, as it was an attack on the composition and powers of the Senate.[139]

In this context, Wise strongly supported the double dissolution as a method consistent with representative and parliamentary government.[140] Turner, agreeing with Barton, held that 'we have to regard the people as individuals, and as constituting each state'. Wishing to give due weight to the principles of federalism, representative government and popular rule, he thought it both 'just' and 'expedient' that the houses should be

---

[134] *Convention Debates, Sydney* (1897), 974, 980.   [135] *Ibid.*, 609–10.   [136] *Ibid.*, 619.

[137] *Ibid.*, 662–70.   [138] *Ibid.*, 684–7.   [139] *Ibid.*, 672–3, 676–9.

[140] *Ibid.*, 647–8; *Convention Debates, Melbourne* (1898), 2187–203, citing David Syme, *Representative Government in England: Its Faults and Failures* (London: Kegan Paul, Trench and Co., 1881), 123.

dissolved simultaneously, and if the deadlock continued, the question be resolved by a dual referendum.[141]

Higgins later criticised the deadlock-breaking mechanism adopted by the convention as insufficient to counteract the power of the Senate over money bills, with all of the implications for responsible government that this entailed. In particular, the mechanism would not be available to resolve urgent disputes over supply, so that the government might be forced to yield to the Senate.[142] Thus, while the existence of a deadlock-breaking mechanism was in a sense a nationalist victory, the actual mechanism embodied a compromise between federal and national majoritarian principles.

The nationalist response to equality of representation in the Senate was to seek to qualify the Senate's powers and to introduce a deadlock-breaking mechanism. However, there remained a limit to the extent that this could be achieved. In 1891, there was a compromise on the Senate's powers, and in 1897–8 nationalists were not able to make any further advance. While responsible government was recognised by section 64, the provision merely required that ministers hold seats in either house of Parliament and the Senate retained the power to reject money bills. Moreover, while provision was made for the breaking of deadlocks, the relative status of the Senate was largely preserved through the 2:1 quota, simultaneous dissolution and the joint sitting.[143] There was, thus, a definite limit in the extent to which 'federal principles' were compromised to make room for responsible government.

## Conclusion

It was with good reason that Australian framers spent a great deal of time arguing about representative institutions and processes. Here, the basic problem concerned the composition and powers of the two houses, a problem that was expressed in debate over equality of representation, the relative size of the houses, control over money bills and the resolution

---

[141] *Convention Debates, Sydney* (1897), 629–35.    [142] Higgins, *Essays and Addresses*, 18–19.

[143] Cf. 'Sir Richard Baker Praises the Bill' (undated press clipping), Baker Papers. Galligan and Walsh, 'Federalism – Yes or No?', 109, suggest that the deadlock provisions were 'very far from the position originally envisaged by the small States, and perhaps not so far from the preferred position of the majoritarians'. However, this does not take into account the outcome of the debate on the 2:1 nexus.

of deadlocks. Behind these arguments were differences as to the relative importance of responsible government and federalism, as well as differences about the nature of federalism itself. Throughout, the formative basis of the Constitution constrained the arguments and the voting. Most of the small-state representatives as well as a significant number of large-state representatives held that equality of representation was both a practical necessity and a matter of principle, even if that principle rested in the fact that federation would unavoidably be a kind of 'compromise', ultimately rooted in the idea of federation as a kind of 'compact' between mutually independent colonies.

Unavoidably, therefore, there had to be an accommodation of nationalist and provincialist perspectives. There was no room for a radical insistence on the sovereignty of either the states or the Commonwealth. Where constitutional provisions premised upon radical views such as these were proposed, they failed. Australian federation, like its American and Swiss predecessors, did not allow for a concentration of sovereignty in any particular institution. In an important sense, the result was an accommodation, a 'mediating' outcome, best understood in covenantal terms.

The bare existence of the House and the Senate represented the accommodation in the most obvious and simple terms, but in the debate about details of the composition, size and powers of the two houses, as well as the debate about the relations between them, the same basic accommodation had be found. While some debates ended in a relative success for nationalists, these were consistently matched by federalist counter-victories. In all of these, the formative conditions of Australian federation constrained the outcome – in both institutional and philosophical terms. The several colonies regarded themselves as independent self-governing bodies politic. The colonial legislatures prescribed the form in which the federal conventions and ratifying referendums would be held. Federation was thus premised on autonomy, equality and unanimity among the states. These fundamental ideas and formative circumstances defined the parameters and course of debate.

But if the representative institutions adopted by the federal conventions of 1891 and 1897–8 were a negotiated settlement between representatives of several separate and independent states, the terms upon which the Constitution itself could be altered in the future loomed as an equally vital question. Accordingly, how the framers understood the amending process, how they actually structured it, and how it was influenced by the formative

basis and representative provisions already agreed upon must be considered. And yet, before the amendment of the Constitution can be
addressed, another vital part of the picture must be taken into view,
namely the configuration of power between the states and the Commonwealth. For the way in which the powers of the Commonwealth and the
states were dealt with would similarly be shaped by the formative basis of
the Constitution, premised as it was upon the free agreement of the peoples
of the several colonies to unite in an indissoluble federal commonwealth.

# 9

# The states and the Commonwealth

[A federation is] a political union of several States, which, for certain purposes, and within certain limits, is complete, so that the several States form one larger State with a common Government acting directly upon the individual citizens as to all matters within its jurisdiction, while, beyond those limits, and for all other purposes, the separate States retain complete autonomy.

Samuel Griffith (1896)

## Statements of fundamental principle

### The convention of 1891

Australian federation was premised on the principle, expressed in the first resolution introduced by Henry Parkes in Sydney in 1891, that:

the powers and privileges and territorial rights of the several existing colonies shall remain intact, except in respect to such surrenders as may be agreed upon as necessary and incidental to the power and authority of the National Federal Government.[1]

In other words, Australian federation presupposed the existence of the several colonies as independent, self-governing bodies politic. Federation would involve establishment of a federal government, to which particular powers would be surrendered, but apart from those specific surrenders, the existing powers, privileges and territorial rights of the colonies would remain as they were prior to federation. Further, the objective would be to surrender those powers necessary and incidental to the establishment of a federal government, but the determination of precisely what was necessary and incidental would be a matter of agreement between the

---

[1] *Convention Debates, Sydney* (1891), 23.

colonies themselves. In this sense, Parkes's first resolution echoed the fundamental principle laid down a year earlier at the inter-colonial conference held in Melbourne, namely that the proposed union of the colonies 'under one legislative and executive government' would only occur 'on principles just to the several colonies', meaning principles that the colonies themselves agreed to be just.[2] The proposition that federation must be on terms just to all the parties was often repeated during the conventions of 1891 and 1897–8.[3]

But what did it mean to federate on terms just to the several colonies, and how well did this principle cohere with the notion that federation would be based upon a freely negotiated agreement between the parties? Parkes himself explained that the objective of the resolution was to satisfy the colonies that there was no intent in any way to impair either the 'security' of their territorial rights or the 'efficiency' of their legislative powers.[4] And, indeed, virtually all of the delegates who spoke to the resolution considered this principle to be absolutely foundational. Thomas McIlwraith, for example, understood it to be 'the germ and foundation of federal government'.[5] Charles Kingston, it will be recalled, spoke of the colonies as 'autonomous states', which 'should not be asked – and who, if asked, would not be likely to accede to the request – to sacrifice any of the existing powers other than those which it is absolutely necessary should be surrendered in the national interest'.[6]

Following Samuel Griffith's lead, most of the delegates considered that one of the most important protections of the rights and interests of the colonies would be the equal representation of the original states in the Senate.[7] Debate on Parkes's first resolution often, therefore, merged into a debate about the composition and powers of the Senate. And, as has been seen, two very different conceptions of federalism emerged at this point. On one hand there was the minority who considered the equal representation of the states in a powerful Senate to be unnecessary

---

[2] *Conference Debates, Melbourne* (1890), x, repeated at the very outset of the convention of 1891: *Convention Debates, Sydney* (1891), 2.

[3] E.g. *Convention Debates, Sydney* (1891), 100 (Downer), 104 (Thynne), 116–20 (Bird), 225 (Deakin), 227 (Gillies), 257 (Bray), 286 (Cuthbert), 305 (Suttor), 382 (Munro); *Convention Debates, Adelaide* (1897), 19, 395 (Barton's Resolutions), 662 (Trenwith), 814 (Downer), 1131 (Turner).

[4] *Convention Debates, Sydney* (1891), 24.     [5] *Ibid.*, 60.     [6] *Ibid.*, 153.

[7] *Ibid.*, 29 (Griffith); see e.g. 100 (Downer), 111 (Baker), 120 (Bird), 172 (Fitzgerald), 175 (Dibbs), 222 (Forrest), 243–52 (Clark), 279–80 (Hackett), 283–4 (Moore).

precisely because, as Alfred Deakin put it, 'the federal government is to have a strictly limited power', that is, 'strictly limited to certain definite subjects', and that the states 'are to retain almost all their present powers'.[8] On the other hand, there were those, like Richard Baker and Andrew Inglis Clark, who recognised even at this early stage that it would not be possible to define with absolute clarity the precise boundaries of the division of power between the federal and the state governments; that the jurisdiction of both would be largely concurrent; that the 'border line' between the two would be contested and would evolve with the passage of time; and that therefore the colonies could not rely simply upon a division of powers to be enforced by the courts, but would need the additional protection of a powerful Senate in which each state would be equally represented.[9]

As important as it was, this difference of opinion about the Senate did not mean that delegates like Baker and Clark took a more expansive view of the powers that were to be transferred to the Federal Parliament. All of the delegates who spoke to the issue seem, like Deakin, to have envisaged a federal government of strictly limited powers.[10] Indeed, some of them even understood Parkes's resolution to imply something similar to the explicit reservation of powers to the states expressed in the Tenth Amendment to the United States Constitution. According to James Munro, for example, there was a degree of ambiguity about the resolution, and he proposed a clarification not only that the powers of the federal government ought to be specifically set forth in the Constitution, but that the powers 'not delegated' to the federal government should be 'reserved to the colonies respectively or to the people'.[11] While not all were prepared to go quite so far, there was a definite consensus in favour of the American scheme of conferring on the federal government only limited powers, rather than the Canadian scheme of conferring general powers on the central government and allocating specific powers to the regional governments.[12] Indeed, there was a general insistence that the

---

[8] *Ibid.*, 79, 82 (Deakin); see also 230–1 (Gillies).   [9] *Ibid.*, 111, 113 (Baker), 252 (Clark).

[10] See *ibid.*, 153 (Kingston, who referred to a 'consensus' on this point). See also *ibid.*, 166 (Fitzgerald), 231 (Gillies), 280 (Hackett), 281–2 (Moore). While McMillan certainly favoured the creation of a strong central government possessing 'all the elements of sovereignty', he did not mean a government of plenary legislative competence, but a government possessing a fully independent power of taxation, for example: see *ibid.*, 267, 671–2, 691.

[11] *Ibid.*, 50–1 (Munro); compare 191 (Lee Steere).

[12] *Ibid.*, 153 (Kingston), 328 (Playford), 342 (Dibbs).

Australian colonies ought not to be referred to merely as 'provinces' (as in Canada), but by the more dignified designation of 'states' (as in the United States).[13] As John Cockburn put it, 'to define means to limit', and it was not intended that the powers retained by the states would be limited in any respect.[14] Griffith moreover pointed out that the colonial constitutions conferred upon the legislatures full power to make laws 'for the peace order and good government' of each colony, and that this amounted to virtual autonomy. The colonies would have to 'surrender' some of their 'absolute powers' to the federation, but they would otherwise remain in the condition of practically autonomous political communities.[15]

Edmund Barton also said that he understood Parkes's resolution to encompass the proposition that the territory of a state would not be altered or diminished without the consent of that state, a proposition on which there was very general agreement, some delegates noting the possible subdivision of Queensland into separate states and thus the possible need in the future to admit additional states to the federation, but only with the consent of the states concerned.[16] Indeed, Macrossan considered the resolution to be ambiguous on this point and proposed explicit words along these lines, and Barton later successfully proposed an additional resolution which made the point clear.[17] In its final form, this resolution stated:

> No new state shall be formed by separation from another state, nor shall any state be formed by the junction of two or more states or parts of states, without the consent of the legislatures of the states concerned, as well as of the federal parliament.[18]

If federation itself was to rest upon an agreement among the colonies, then it was essential that any change to the territorial boundaries of the states under the federation would also require the consent of the states concerned. But because federation also meant the creation of new body politic, the consent of the federal government was also required.

Parkes's original resolution, together with Barton's supplementary one, assumed not only the existence and territorial integrity of the colonies, but also the institutions and powers established under the colonial constitutions. Thus, John Macrossan expressed concern that the resolution

---

[13] *Ibid.*, 183 (Dibbs), 373 (Cockburn).    [14] *Ibid.*, 201.    [15] *Ibid.*, 338.

[16] *Ibid.*, 90 (Barton), 109 (Baker), 124–5 (Jennings), 153–4 (Kingston), 166 (Fitzgerald), 183–4 (Dibbs), 221–2 (Forrest), 229–30 (Gillies), 257 (Bray).

[17] *Ibid.*, 326 (Macrossan), 337, 344, 476–7 (Barton).    [18] *Ibid.*, 499.

ought to be amended so as to make clear that it did not preclude the future amendment of the state constitutions, particularly with a view to the reform of the state Legislative Councils along liberal lines.[19] Similarly, Sir George Grey proposed an additional resolution that provision should be made in the federal Constitution that the people of each colony be able to adopt their own constitution by majority vote.[20] In response, Duncan Gillies thought the additional resolution to be unnecessary, insisting most emphatically that no delegate in the convention wished to interfere in any way with the capacity of each colony to remain fully in control of its own constitution.[21] Thomas Playford confirmed this when he pointed out that the colonial constitutions would remain a matter for each state and that it was beyond the competence of the convention to interfere with the state constitutions in any way.[22] Otherwise, as Deakin pointed out, the convention would find itself having to determine an ideal constitution and electoral system to be imposed upon each state, a task that lay completely outside the convention's proper task.[23]

A substantial number of delegates, including Griffith, Barton and Parkes, agreed with Gillies, Playford and Deakin.[24] Others, however, including Cockburn and Bray, were sympathetic to Grey's proposal, essentially for its democratic tendencies.[25] At stake was the question of whether the delegates possessed an open-ended mandate to address all questions relating to the good government of the several colonies,[26] or whether their task was limited to the framing of a federal constitution which presupposed and did not presume to interfere with the colonial constitutions upon which federation would be based.[27] Even Cockburn, who was supportive of Grey's proposal, thought that it should be limited to the indication of very general principles, strongly rejecting the Canadian idea that the convention descend to a detailed specification of the state constitutions. And yet, because the state legislatures would be an integral part of the federation, he considered the constitutions of those legislatures to be very relevant to the debate about the nature of the federation to be created.[28]

---

[19] *Ibid.*, 325.     [20] *Ibid.*, 327–8, 330–2, 477–8.     [21] *Ibid.*, 327.
[22] *Ibid.*, 328–9.     [23] *Ibid.*, 335.
[24] *Ibid.*, 329 (Downer), 329–30 (Griffith), 330 (Jennings), 336 (Barton), 478 (Parkes).
[25] *Ibid.*, 334 (Cockburn), 340 (Thynne), 341 (Bray).     [26] *Ibid.*, 478–9 (Grey).
[27] *Ibid.*, 478 (Parkes), 480–1 (Gillies), 483–4 (Parkes).
[28] *Ibid.*, 479–80, 481–2 (Cockburn); see also 482 (Thynne).

To this, Gillies and Munro replied that Grey's resolution called for amendment of the state constitutions by referendum of the voters, which entailed a far-reaching modification of the constitutions as they then stood.[29] Kingston's rejoinder was that federation would mean a surrender of the legislative powers of the colonies, and such a surrender would involve an alteration to their constitutions, so why could not the federal convention address the state constitutions in relation to both the composition of the legislatures and the amendment of the constitutions in all of their details?[30]

In the event, the convention charted a middle course. Griffith pointed out that an adequate scheme of federation must insist that the constituent states could not entirely change their nature.[31] This did not mean imposing requirements upon the colonies, because the scheme of federation would be agreed to by the colonies themselves. But it did mean an agreement on certain characteristics of the state constitutions that would be considered fundamental.[32] Thus, when Grey subsequently proposed an amended resolution which merely affirmed the capacity of each state to 'make, vary or annul its constitution', even this was further amended so that it would apply only to those changes that might be 'necessary for the purposes of federation', and in this narrow form the resolution was carried.[33]

## The convention of 1897–8

While it is true, as has been seen, that the second convention was more sophisticated and more democratic than the first, some elements remained very definitely the same. Most important among these was the principle that federation would be the result of an agreement among the peoples of the colonies, negotiated and drafted by their elected representatives. Barton's resolutions proposed at the convention of 1897–8 thus repeated the principles of 1891, almost in identical terms. Thus, the first two of Barton's resolutions introduced in 1897 and carried without amendment, stated:

> I. That the powers, privileges, and territories of the several existing colonies shall remain intact, except in respect of such surrenders as may be agreed upon to secure uniformity of law and administration in matters of common concern.

---

[29] *Ibid.*, 481 (Gillies), 482 (Munro).    [30] *Ibid.*, 482–3.    [31] *Ibid.*, 485.
[32] *Ibid.*, 489–91.    [33] *Ibid.*, 486, 495.

II. That, after the establishment of the Federal Government, there shall be no alteration of the territorial possessions or boundaries of any colony without the consent of the colony or colonies concerned.[34]

The only difference between 1891 and 1897–8 – a difference of making explicit what was already implicit in 1891 – were the additional, introductory words proposed by Barton (but originally inspired by Bernhard Wise),[35] which emphatically stated that the guiding purpose of federation was to 'enlarge the powers of self-government of the people of Australia'.[36] As Barton explained, this was to make clear that although a 'surrender' of certain capacities would be necessary, this would give the Australian people the capacity to govern themselves on a 'national' scale, whereas previously they had had to rely upon piecemeal negotiation between their respective governments or else imperial intervention by the British government.[37] With this grand overarching objective in mind, the specific resolutions laid down the particular conditions upon which a federal government exercising authority throughout the federated colonies would be founded. And, as far as the powers, privileges and territories of the colonies were concerned, these would be absolutely preserved, subject only to such surrenders as would be freely agreed. As such, Barton's resolutions fully retained the fundamental principle that Australian federation would have to be based upon the free agreement of the constituent colonies.

If the fundamental principles remained the same, the discussion was certainly more sophisticated in 1897–8. Thus, during the debate over Barton's resolutions there was much more discussion of the basic principles that would determine the allocation of powers to the federation. Again, there remained an overwhelming consensus in favour of allocating only limited powers to the new federal government, with the remainder being retained by the states.[38] But attempts were now made to express the principle upon which particular powers would be transferred. Richard O'Connor, for example, insisted that the colonies should retain to themselves power over all matters they could handle themselves and that only those powers 'necessary' should be conferred upon the federation.[39]

---

[34] *Convention Debates, Adelaide* (1897), 17, 395.
[35] See *ibid.*, 115, 366; Quick and Garran, *Annotated Constitution*, 166.
[36] *Convention Debates, Adelaide* (1897), 17.    [37] *Ibid.*, 20.
[38] *Ibid.*, 29 (Baker), 41–2 (Turner), 175 (Isaacs), 245 (Fysh), 271 (Reid), 318 (Gordon), 338 (Cockburn), 377 (Barton).
[39] *Ibid.*, 50–1.

Necessity could mean many things, however. Frederick Holder said that the colonies should retain control of every matter that was 'local' or related to each state alone, whereas matters of 'national' or 'inter-state' character or importance should be conferred upon the federation. Moreover, powers should be transferred, he explained, only in cases where they could be exercised 'more wisely and well and effectively' by the federation.[40] Henry Dobson put the matter perhaps more clearly when he said that the constitution should reserve to the states 'those powers which they can better carry out for themselves', while conferring upon the federal government 'those powers of common or general concern which a united Government can manage much better for the good of the people than the individual States'.[41] William McMillan added that sufficient power ought to be given to the federal government to enable it to be a 'strong, stable national government...able to confront the whole outside world', while reserving to the states those powers necessary to enable them to manage their local affairs.[42]

Opinions inevitably varied as to precisely which powers fell into which category, and it would, as Carruthers pointed out, ultimately depend on the particularities and circumstances of each case.[43] However, there seemed to be a general consensus in support of the kind of criteria proposed by Holder and Dobson.[44] It was also generally expected that most of the powers conferred upon the federation would be concurrent, and that federal laws would prevail over state laws in cases of inconsistency.[45] Further, the Commonwealth Bill of 1891 loomed large in the debate, with its explicit list of federal powers, and thus specific heads of power were also proposed, including most prominently powers over taxation, customs, defence, inter-state trade and commerce, postage, telegraphs and railways.[46] Moreover, it was now very specifically envisaged that there would be a supreme federal court which would function as an arbiter of disputes concerning the rights and powers of the states and the federation, as well as, as Barton proposed, a general court of appeal.[47]

---

[40] *Ibid.*, 144.   [41] *Ibid.*, 191.   [42] *Ibid.*, 223.   [43] *Ibid.*, 87.

[44] See e.g. *ibid.*, 254 (Solomon), 328 (Trenwith), 370 (Barton).

[45] *Ibid.*, 115 (Wise), 293–4 (Deakin).

[46] See e.g. *ibid.*, 42 (Turner), 61–2 (O'Connor), 87–8 (Fraser), 111–14 (Wise), 223–4 (McMillan), 263–6 (Solomon), 371 (Barton).

[47] *Ibid.*, 24–5 (Barton), 115 (Wise), 129 (Symon), 272 (Reid), 336 (Trenwith), 369 (Barton).

The principles discussed during the debate over Parkes's and Barton's resolutions at the conventions of 1891 and 1897–8 proved to be fundamental to the way in which the Australian Constitution would ultimately deal with the constitutions and powers of both the states and the Commonwealth. And yet the devil was in the details. As to those details, the remainder of this chapter will address the treatment of the state constitutions. The next chapter will address the distribution of powers as between the Commonwealth and the states.

## The continuing states

A central presupposition of Australian federation was that the several constituent colonies would continue to exist as autonomous states, indeed as 'original states', within the federation.[48] Thus, while under section 7 of the federal Constitution the Senate would be 'chosen by the people of [each] State', only the original states were guaranteed an equality of representation in the Senate under section 7, as well as a minimum of representation in the House of Representatives under section 24.[49] This special treatment of the original states reflected their constituent status in the federation. The original states did not derive their existence as bodies politic from the federation; the federation was derived, at least in political terms, from them.

Accordingly, although the several colonies were in a sense transformed into states under the Constitution, they are not said to have been 'constituted' or 'established' thereunder, but rather the Constitution consistently refers to them as 'continuing'.[50] Thus, covering clauses 3, 4 and 6 of the Commonwealth of Australia Constitution Act 1900 (UK) noticeably provide for the 'establishment' of the Commonwealth pursuant to the Act, whereas covering clause 6 defines 'The States' in a way that recognises the prior existence of the several colonies without in any way suggesting that the colonies were in any sense established thereby. It is true that covering clause 6 refers to certain colonies or territories that

---

[48] See *Convention Debates, Sydney* (1891), 15–16 (Griffith); Griffith, *Notes on Australian Federation*, 6–7, 10.

[49] Original states are defined in covering cl. 6 of the Commonwealth of Australia Constitution Act 1900 (UK) as those states which are 'parts of the Commonwealth at its establishment'. As it happened, all six of the Australian colonies became original states.

[50] Commonwealth Constitution, ss. 106, 107.

might, in the future, be 'admitted into or established by the Common-wealth', but the reference to such colonies being established is certainly not a reference to any of the pre-existing colonies that would become original states.[51]

That the several states 'continued' within the federation had important implications for the existing state constitutions and the admission of new states, as well as for the configuration and allocation of powers between the states and the Commonwealth.

### The state constitutions

While the juridical existence of the colonies was taken for granted, the framers did not simply leave the continuing status of the states to the earlier imperial Acts that had created the several colonies. Rather, they made specific provision for the continuation – but not the establishment – of the constitutions, powers and laws of the states. In particular, sections 106–8 of the Constitution affirmed that each state constitution would, subject to the federal Constitution, 'continue . . . until altered in accord-ance with the Constitution of the State', that state legislative powers would 'continue', and that the laws of each colony would 'continue in force' until specifically altered or repealed.

These principles can be traced to Clark's draft constitution of 1891, although, in certain respects, Clark's draft was not always consistent. As has been noted, the draft was premised on the 'desire' of the colonies of Australasia to be 'federally united' into 'one Dominion', which Clark called the 'Federal Dominion of Australasia'. The draft accordingly pre-supposed the prior existence of the colonies and in large part carried through the idea that the provincial constitutions would continue to operate subject only to the specific provisions of the proposed federal constitution. Thus, it was provided that the executive authority in each province would 'continue' and that the legislative powers of the provincial Parliaments would 'remain vested', except for those powers specifically 'transferred or delegated' to the Federal Parliament.[52] Among the range of

---

[51] It is also true that special legislative powers were conferred upon the states specifically to enable them to legislate for federal elections (see e.g. covering cl. 4 and ss. 7–10, 12, 15, 29–31), but apart from this special exception, the powers of the states continued, as provided for in ss. 106 and 107.

[52] Clark's draft constitution, cls. 71, 74. Compare Kingston's draft constitution, Pt XIII.

powers conferred upon the Federal Parliament, moreover, Clark's draft gave power both to divide and amalgamate parts of the provinces, and to create new ones, subject to the consent of the relevant provincial legislatures.[53] While the power conferred was significant, the requirement of provincial consent secured to the provinces ultimate control over any such proposal. To an extent following the Canadian precedent, and yet proceeding in a proto-republican manner, Clark's draft also made specific provision for particular aspects of the provincial constitutions, such as providing that provincial governors would be chosen by the provincial parliaments, and granting each parliament full power to amend the provincial constitution.[54] Furthermore, Clark's draft gave the federal legislature power not only to establish and admit new provinces to the federation, but also to establish their constitutions.[55] While provisions of this kind within an imperial statute were not inconsistent with the colonial status of the provinces, they were arguably inconsistent with the idea that the federal constitution was fully premised on the prior existence of the colonies, and not vice versa.[56]

Compared to Clark's draft, the Commonwealth Bill of 1891 was more thoroughly consistent with the theory that the federation was founded upon the colonies, and not the other way around. Thus, at the outset, it was decided that the colonies would be referred to as 'states', a term thought more appropriate to their proper status within the proposed federation.[57] Indeed, following the language of Clark's draft, the draft bill prepared on board *Lucinda* in March 1891 had originally provided that the powers of the state parliaments would 'remain vested'.[58] However, in the form that it was later presented to and ultimately adopted by the convention of 1891, the Commonwealth Bill expressly added that those powers were 'reserved' to the states, thus adopting the idea of a reservation of powers from the American Constitution.[59] The fact that such powers were to be reserved to the 'Parliaments of the States', and not to 'the States respectively, or to the people' as in the American Tenth

[53] Clark's draft constitution, cls. 45 (xxiii), (xxiv), 47, 49.
[54] See Clark's draft constitution, cls. 67, 76.    [55] Clark's draft constitution, cl. 48.
[56] Thomson, 'Clark and Australian Constitutional Law', 68–9, argues that Clark's draft would most probably have made the provincial constitutions relatively more vulnerable to federal interference than the current s. 106 of the Constitution.
[57] *Convention Debates, Sydney* (1891), 523 (Griffith).
[58] Clark's draft constitution, cl. 74; draft Commonwealth Bill, 30 March 1891, ch. V, cl. 1.
[59] Draft Commonwealth Bill, 31 March 1891, ch. V, cl. 1; Commonwealth Bill 1891, ch. V, cl. 1; see *Convention Debates, Sydney* (1891), 530, 849–50, 960.

Amendment, suggested a strongly compactual perspective in which the legislatures were the parties to the federal agreement.[60]

This did not mean that the Commonwealth Bill of 1891 made no provision for the state constitutions at all. But in so far as this was the case, care was taken to ensure that such provision fully recognised the constitutional autonomy of the states. For example, the Commonwealth Bill of 1891 stipulated that there must be a governor in each state, but unlike Clark's draft constitution it did not stipulate how the governors would be chosen.[61] Indeed, as Griffith explained, there was good reason to take this course because it underscored the equality and sovereignty of the states – precluding any suggestion that some states might be governed merely by lieutenant-governors or administrators.[62] More remarkably, however, the bill of 1891 also provided that executive communications between the governor of a state and the Queen could not be made directly, but would have to be made through the governor-general.[63] The principal objection to this clause, as articulated by Wrixon, Gillies, Downer and Kingston, was that it posed an unnecessary interference with the states.[64] Griffith nevertheless defended the provision on the basis that in such matters Australia should speak 'with one voice', and other delegates who likewise strongly supported the rights of the states, such as Clark and Baker, saw no problem with the provision so long as the governor-general was only to function as 'channel of communication' and was precluded from interfering in any substantial way with communications between the states and the imperial government.[65] Deakin also supported the provision, but he understood it to involve a very substantial capacity of the governor-general to express the views of the Commonwealth government concerning any representation that a state might wish to make to the imperial authorities.[66] In 1897–8, such a provision would be thought both

---

[60] The equivalent provision was called the 'reservation clause' even as late as 1898: see *Convention Debates, Melbourne* (1898), 502 (Kingston, Barton).

[61] Clark's draft constitution, cl. 67; Commonwealth Bill 1891, ch. V, cl. 7.

[62] *Convention Debates, Sydney* (1891), 865–6.    [63] Commonwealth Bill 1891, ch. V, cl. 5.

[64] *Convention Debates, Sydney* (1891), 535–6 (Wrixon), 850 (Gillies), 851–2 (Downer), 861–2 (Kingston).

[65] *Ibid.*, 530–1 (Griffith), 547 (Clark), 850–1 (Griffith), 852–3 (Baker).

[66] *Ibid.*, 856 (Deakin), a position he would press as prime minister in 1906, notwithstanding the fact that the Commonwealth Constitution as finally enacted did not contain such a provision in explicit terms. See Anne Twomey, *The Constitution of New South Wales* (Sydney: Federation Press, 2004), 131.

unnecessary and dangerous,[67] but in 1891 the clause was approved by a close majority of 22 to 16 on the basis that it was only a formal provision.[68]

Apart from these two clauses, the convention of 1891 was very careful to keep interference with the state constitutions to a necessary minimum. The general principle was preserved that each state constitution would continue until amended by the state parliament in accordance with the state constitution, language traceable more to Kingston's draft than to Clark's.[69] Likewise, rather than stipulate the manner in which state governors would be appointed (as Kingston's and Clark's draft constitutions had done),[70] it was affirmed in the bill of 1891 that it would be entirely for the parliament of each state to determine matters relating to the office of governor, such as manner of appointment, term of office and removal from office – and even such a circumspect provision was carried by only the narrowest of margins, a vote of 20 to 19.[71] Arguing against the clause, Gillies expressed concern that it would enable the states to provide for the direct election of the governors, and that this would be inconsistent with responsible government.[72] McMillan added that the convention had been convened solely to formulate a federal constitution and should not interfere unnecessarily with the colonial constitutions – a point with which Baker very strenuously agreed.[73] Munro and Clark responded that the provision merely left the colonial constitutions in the hands of the people of each state, acting through their elected representatives.[74]

Significantly, Griffith added that one of the objectives of federation was to obviate the need for either the Commonwealth or the states to rely in the future upon the imperial Parliament for changes to their respective constitutions.[75] The convention of 1891 was premised on the

---

[67] *Convention Debates, Adelaide* (1897), 454 (Barton).

[68] *Convention Debates, Sydney* (1891), 864. The significance of the issue was made clear some years later, when the state of Western Australia sought, through communications directly with the Queen, to secede from the Commonwealth.

[69] Compare Kingston's draft constitution, Pt XI; Clark's draft constitution, cls. 71, 74; Commonwealth Bill 1891, ch. V, cl. 6; *Convention Debates, Sydney* (1891), 864–5.

[70] Kingston's draft constitution, Pt X, 'Provincial Constitutions. – Executive Power'; Clark's draft constitution, cls. 67–73.

[71] Commonwealth Bill 1891, ch. V, cl. 8; *Convention Debates, Sydney* (1891), 877.

[72] *Convention Debates, Sydney* (1891), 866–8.    [73] *Ibid.*, 870 (McMillan), 871 (Baker).

[74] *Ibid.*, 869–70 (Munro), 870–1 (Clark).    [75] *Ibid.*, 874–5.

semi-constitutive authority of the colonial parliaments, and the various provisions discussed so far clearly affirmed the ultimate authority of each state parliament to determine the content of its constitution. As Griffith put it, 'we do not want the parliament of the commonwealth to interfere with the states' constitutions, nor do we want the Parliament of Great Britain to interfere with them'. A provision affirming the power of the state parliaments to regulate the office of governor, he explained, would be the means by which the imperial Parliament would finally 'give us leave once and for all to manage for ourselves'.[76] As will be seen in chapter 11, Griffith would seek to follow these principles through to their logical conclusion in relation to formal amendment of the federal Constitution as well as the constitutions of the several states.

The convention of 1897–8 maintained essentially the same outlook, albeit with some important changes, some of them inserted at a late stage in the process. At Adelaide in 1897, the clauses that would become sections 107 and 108 of the Constitution – ensuring that the powers and laws of the colonies would be preserved under the federation – were carried without substantial debate.[77] It was not until the final weeks at the Melbourne sitting in 1898 that the clause which became section 107 shifted from providing for a 'reservation' of powers to affirming that the powers of the states would 'continue'.[78] Notably, the continuance of powers was a slightly weaker statement compared to reservation. Reservation envisages the states as parties to an agreement under which they actively reserve their powers. None the less, the provision in its final form clearly affirmed that state powers would continue; it certainly did not provide in any sense that they would be established by the federal Constitution. Continuation represented in this respect a middle ground between reservation and establishment. Just as the convention of 1891 was constituted in a way that reflected a relatively more 'compactual' approach to Australian federation, the convention of 1897–8 shifted the balance ever so slightly towards a more 'covenantal' stance.[79]

---

[76] Ibid., 874.    [77] Convention Debates, Adelaide (1897), 991.

[78] The official records do not actually recount any point at which this change was formally approved by the Convention. Compare draft Constitution Bill, 24 September 1898, cl. 99; draft Constitution Bill, 1 March 1898, cl. 99; Convention Debates, Melbourne (1898), 642–3, 1010, 1816, 2541; Quick and Garran, Annotated Constitution, 933.

[79] I refer here to the distinctions between compactual, covenantal and nationalist approaches to federalism discussed particularly in ch. 1.

What significance is to be drawn from such a subtle shift in language is highly debatable. The well-known 'reserved powers' doctrine developed by the High Court during its first seventeen years of operation rested very substantially on an interpretation of section 107 which read it as 'reserving' to the states an exclusive capacity to regulate certain matters deemed to fall within their 'domestic' affairs.[80] And, indeed, what is clear from Barton's discussion of the precursor of section 107 is that he very definitely understood the provision as carving out for the states a sphere of reserved power in fields not explicitly granted to the Commonwealth. Thus, during the debate concerning the power to be given to the Commonwealth to legislate with respect to interstate trade and commerce, Barton pointed out that the power by its terms clearly extended to the regulation of the navigation of rivers for the purposes of interstate trade, but he just as emphatically maintained that this did not extend to matters such as water conservation and irrigation, these being reserved to the states by the clause that would become section 107. Describing the provision as 'that powerful clause' which 'preserves every power' of the states, he argued that the Commonwealth's power to regulate Australian rivers for the purposes of maintaining freedom of interstate trade and commerce could 'not go a jot further' than allowed by that clause.[81]

Barton's argument was that because the expression 'water conservation and irrigation' finds no mention among the powers of the Commonwealth, the power must be one that is reserved to the states. The reserved powers doctrine, as later developed by the High Court, rested precisely in the proposition that what the Constitution does not say may be just as significant as what it says. As will be seen in the next chapter, the language in which legislative powers were conferred upon the Federal Parliament was deliberately circumscribed – the silences and omissions were deliberate – in order to preserve state competence to legislate in fields represented by those silences and omissions. Barton was no doubt a party to the alteration of the wording of section 107 from 'reservation' to

[80] *Attorney-General (NSW)* v. *Brewery Employees Union of NSW* (1908) 6 CLR 469.
[81] *Convention Debates, Melbourne* (1898), 502–4, 596–7, 600, 1008–10. Others expressed their general agreement with Barton's argument: e.g. *ibid.*, 504–5 (Symon). As explained in the next chapter, the specific issue would be finally resolved in the terms of ss. 98–100 which on one hand declare that the trade and commerce power extends to control of river navigation, but which also declare that it does not extend to giving any preference to a particular state or abridging the right of a state or its residents to the reasonable use of river water for conservation or irrigation.

'continuation'. In light of his arguments, however, as well as the stance he took when appointed to the High Court, it is difficult in the extreme to think that he meant thereby to reject the idea that certain powers would be reserved to the states.

The clause that became section 106 of the Constitution likewise provided that the state constitutions would 'continue', until altered 'in accordance with the provisions of their respective constitutions'.[82] At Adelaide in 1897 Cockburn expressed the hope that the federal Constitution might go further, by expressly dispensing with the existing requirement that states obtain imperial approval for the amendment of their constitutions. He argued:

> it is an inalienable principle in a Federation that the States within the Federation should be at liberty to decide themselves as to what form of Constitution they will live under. They should not require [sic] to go to any outside authority.[83]

Cockburn's suggestion was met with some astonishment by Isaacs and Deakin. In their view the provision as it stood sought to guarantee precisely that principle. Deakin rhetorically asked whether Cockburn wished to reduce the states to the same position as the Canadian provinces, referring to their lack of power to amend their constitutions.[84] Barton likewise pointed out that:

> there are a great many people who, reading a Federal Constitution, are apt to call out... 'They want to take from us our rights and liberties under our Constitution, and give us nothing back.' That is to say, there is a considerable demand for an express declamation on the face of the Federal Constitution that the states shall keep their Constitutions, and also have power to alter them if they want to do so.[85]

---

[82] See e.g. draft Constitution Bill, 12 April 1897, cl. 101.

[83] *Convention Debates, Adelaide* (1897), 991, although see *Convention Debates, Melbourne* (1898), 644–5.

[84] *Convention Debates, Adelaide* (1897), 992. In the draft Constitution Bill of 1897, cl. 102 provided that there should be a governor in each state. Barton and Griffith supported this provision in order to negative any implication that state governors should be in the same position as the Canadian lieutenant-governors. Others objected to dealing with this matter in the federal Constitution. Ultimately, the clause was struck out: see *Convention Debates, Sydney* (1891), 865–77; *Convention Debates, Adelaide* (1897), 992–1001.

[85] *Convention Debates, Melbourne* (1898), 645. A similar debate occurred in the Tasmanian House of Assembly in 1897, when Clark proposed that the Constitution Bill provide that the executive power of each state be vested in its governor and that each state have the power to

Despite their different interpretations of the effect of the words used in section 106, Cockburn, Barton and even Deakin accepted that the colonies were pre-existing, constitutionally independent bodies politic. While the colonies would be transformed into states, the Constitution would treat them as continuing entities, established independently of the federation. The common concern of all three was that the federal Constitution must not 'interfere' with the state constitutions except as necessary in order to confer particular powers on the Federal Parliament. As Henry Wrixon had put it in 1891, 'everything outside those powers is left...to the states'.[86]

Barton's draft bill of 1897, like the Commonwealth Bill of 1891, contained a further provision which stipulated that there must be a governor in each state, but did not contain any provision conferring or confirming state power in relation to the appointment, tenure and removal of governors.[87] Cockburn thought that such provision should be included, for fear that otherwise the appointment of state governors would be controlled by the governor-general acting on the advice of the federal government,[88] while in quite the other direction Charles Grant proposed that the state officials be called lieutenant-governors.[89] In support of the original clause, Barton cited the arguments that Griffith had raised in 1891, principally that the state governors were to be independent of, and not derive their authority from, the governor-general.[90] Apart from Grant's idiosyncratic proposal (which was not supported by any speaker), the overriding concern of the delegates was that the independence of the states must be preserved and that making the state governors in any way dependent upon the federal government was simply unacceptable.

Two further issues were involved. The first was whether the federal Constitution should be used to enable the states to alter the constitutional provisions concerning their governors without reference to the imperial government.[91] The second concerned the possibility (apparently favoured by some) that a state might use the power to provide that the

---

appoint and dismiss its governor in the manner which it thought fit. (His draft of 1891 had provided similarly.) However, this was rejected on the ground that the states must be kept independent and separate from the federation: Frank M. Neasey, 'Andrew Inglis Clark and Federation after 1891' in Haward and Warden, *Australian Democrat*, 40–1.

[86] *Convention Debates, Sydney* (1891), 534.
[87] Draft Constitution Bill, 12 April 1897, cl. 102; *Convention Debates, Adelaide* (1897), 992.
[88] *Convention Debates, Adelaide* (1897), 992–3.   [89] *Ibid.*, 993.   [90] *Ibid.*, 994–5.
[91] *Ibid.*, 993–4 (Wise), 996–7 (Kingston).

governor be directly elected by the people. Against this last possibility, however, it was urged that it would politicise the role of the governor and thereby undermine the system of responsible government.[92] Josiah Symon went even further: he objected to any provision in the federal Constitution stipulating the content of the state constitutions, even in the limited terms of Barton's clause. The states – their powers and their constitutions – were presuppositions of federation, he argued, and not vice versa.[93] On the other side, Wise objected to the retention of Barton's clause without any specific affirmation of state power to regulate the office of governor on the ground that it would positively entrench the office, placing it beyond the capacity of the states to alter.[94] The matter was finally resolved when Cockburn agreed to withdraw his amendment and Barton agreed to omit the clause altogether.[95]

The idea that each state should communicate with the Queen through the governor-general was similarly dealt with in 1897. Deakin proposed a return to the provision of 1891, but he was opposed by Dobson and Kingston, as well as by Isaacs, on the ground that a central objective of federation was to ensure that the states would continue to govern themselves as far as they could without interference by the federal government. Each colonial governor was fully and equally a representative of the Queen, and it was inconsistent with the continuing standing of the states for them to be obliged to communicate with the Queen through the governor-general.[96]

The issue pulled in various directions, as it raised not only the question of the independence of the states from the Commonwealth, but also the question of Australian independence from the British government.[97] It might be consistent with the general idea of federation that the Commonwealth should speak with one voice to the outside world, but the independent constitutional status of both the Commonwealth and the states still depended on their separate respective relationships with the imperial government. While that remained the case, a majority of delegates concluded that each state should continue to communicate with the Queen directly. Deakin's proposal was negatived.[98]

These issues were finally revisited at Melbourne in 1898, when Forrest again proposed that there should be lieutenant-governors in each state,

---

[92] *Ibid.*, 995–6 (Barton), 997–9 (O'Connor), 999 (McMillan).     [93] *Ibid.*, 999–1000.
[94] *Ibid.*, 1000–1001.     [95] *Ibid.*, 1001.     [96] *Ibid.*, 1178 (Douglas, Isaacs).
[97] *Ibid.*, 1179 (Cockburn).     [98] *Ibid.*, 1181.

appointed by the governor-general in council (as in Canada) and that communications with the imperial government should be channelled through the governor-general.[99] Forrest's suggestion was supported by Wise on what he called the 'practical' grounds of efficiency and cost.[100] Barton, however, objected to the proposal principally on the basis that it contradicted the fundamental idea of federation which, according to Edward Freeman, was that the Commonwealth and the states should remain 'sovereign' within their respective 'spheres' and that appointment by the governor-general would actually render the lieutenant-governors subject to the federal government.[101] Cockburn agreed, adding that appointment by the federal government would not only undermine the independence of the state governments but would serve to politicise the office.

Noting that one of the objectives of Forrest's proposal was to bring vice-regal appointments under Australian control, Cockburn proposed an amendment that would empower the states to make provision for the appointment, tenure and removal of the state governors.[102] Against this, though, both Reid and Symon objected that both Forrest's and Cockburn's proposals involved an improper interference with the state constitutions.[103] While in reply Forrest insisted on his position, he admitted the objection of Reid and Symon to be a weighty one.[104] In the event, Cockburn's amendment was lost by a vote of 24 to 12 and Forrest's by a vote of 26 to 10.[105] As a consequence, the only provision in the federal Constitution to deal with the office of state governor would be merely declarative.[106]

Three years later, in their *Annotated Constitution*, Quick and Garran drew attention to the overriding conception of the 'continuing' states, noting that the individual American states had been separately established, and comparing this to the 'establishment' and 'erection' of the several Australian colonies under various imperial Acts prior to federation. As a consequence, the Australian case was, they said, one of 'pre-existing

---

[99] *Convention Debates, Melbourne* (1898), 1702–6.
[100] *Ibid.*, 1709–11 (Wise); see also 1714 (Howe).
[101] *Ibid.*, 1706–8 (Barton); see also 1708–9 (Douglas), 1713–14 (Braddon).   [102] *Ibid.*, 1711–12.
[103] *Ibid.*, 1712–13 (Reid), 1715 (Symon).   [104] *Ibid.*, 1715–17 (Forrest).   [105] *Ibid.*, 1717.
[106] Section 110 of the Constitution provides that 'The provisions of this Constitution relating to the Governor of a State extend and apply to the Governor for the time being of the State, or other chief executive officer or administrator of the government of the State.' See *Convention Debates, Melbourne* (1898), 645–6 (Cockburn).

colonies, converted into States', whose constitutions were 'confirmed and continued by the Federal Constitution, not created thereby'. They further explained that, in the light of the 'supreme and absolute sovereignty of the Empire', the imperial Constitution Act 'partition[ed] or distribute[d]' the powers of '*quasi*-sovereignty' possessed by the 'people of the Commonwealth' between the federal government and the states. They even implausibly suggested that the state constitutions were 'incorporated into the new Constitution', with the implication – not stated – that the state constitutions might be amended in any particular through an amendment of the Commonwealth Constitution.[107] It is, however, very doubtful whether the framers would have regarded the notion of 'continuation' – as distinct from 'establishment' – of the state constitutions as implying that those constitutions were thereby directly subject to the general amending provision in section 128 of the federal Constitution.[108] Although federation meant a significant curtailment of the constitutional powers of the colonies, the vast majority of the framers of the Constitution were consistently concerned to maintain the independence not only of the governing institutions of the states, but also the independent identity of their respective state constitutions.

## The admission of new states

Notably, the 'continuing' status of the states provided for in sections 106–8 of the Constitution applies both to original states and to any states subsequently admitted to the federation. While only original states enjoy special rights to representation in the Federal Parliament under sections 7 and 24, the continuing status of the state constitutions, powers and laws under sections 106–8 applies to all states without discrimination. Subject, therefore, to the overriding principle that all states would have a continuing status, what special provision did the framers make for the admission and standing of 'new States'?

In the first place, provision was made in section 111 of the Constitution for the surrender of territory by a state to the Commonwealth,

---

[107] Quick and Garran, *Annotated Constitution*, 343–4, 927–30. Quick and Garran did not draw attention to statements by Barton and others which contradicted their views on s. 106. However, when the Convention consensus accorded with their own views, they cited the debates extensively: e.g. Quick and Garran, *Annotated Constitution*, 931–2.

[108] For a further discussion, see ch. 11.

together with section 122, under which the Commonwealth was empowered to make laws for the government of any territory surrendered to and accepted by the Commonwealth, including laws providing for the representation of such territory in the Federal Parliament.[109] The hope, expressed by a number of delegates, was that such territories might in the future develop into fully orbed states, and they were referred to as 'embryo states' for that reason.[110] For this reason also, provision was made in section 121 for the establishment or admission of new states upon 'such terms and conditions, including the extent of representation in either House of the Parliament, as [the Parliament] thinks fit'. Further, under section 124, a new state might be 'established' or 'formed' by separation from the territory of an existing state or through the union or amalgamation of two or more states, but only with the consent of the parliament or parliaments of the state or states concerned. In either case, the consent of the relevant parties would therefore be necessary.[111] An independent body politic lying outside the territory of the Common-wealth might thus be 'admitted', but the terms of such admission would first have to be negotiated between the Commonwealth and the new state.[112] In this way, the rules for the establishment and admission of new states continued the basic principle that Australian federation would rest on the consent of the constituent states. Moreover, it was made clear that the word 'establish' only meant establishment as a member of the federation, not establishment as a body politic in the first place.[113]

Such was the outcome of the debate during the conventions of 1891 and 1897–8 on the question of new states. During that debate, two issues received the most scrutiny. The first was whether the consent of the state parliament should be necessary before a state could be subdivided into separate states. The second concerned the kind of representation that would be appropriate to new states. It is convenient to address each of these in turn.

---

[109] See *Convention Debates, Adelaide* (1897), 1012–18; *Convention Debates, Melbourne* (1898), 698–9.

[110] E.g. *Convention Debates, Melbourne* (1898), 257 (Deakin).

[111] See *ibid.*, 695 (Barton), 697 (Kingston, Barton). See also s. 123 and s. 128, para. 5, which make any alteration to the limits of a state dependent upon the consent of the people of the state, as discussed in ch. 11.

[112] Contrast the proposal of Western Australia which sought to dispense with any role for the Commonwealth Parliament, a proposal that was negatived without debate: *ibid.*, 694.

[113] *Ibid.*, 696 (Higgins, Isaacs).

It has been suggested by one commentator that by the end of the nineteenth century the consolidated power of the existing colonies, exercised over vast tracts of territory, had come to dominate Australian conceptions of federalism. While there had been movements in the earlier part of the century towards regional devolution and separation, it has been argued that by the 1890s federalism was dictated by the entrenched powers and status of the six colonies.[114] That a distinction should be drawn in the Constitution between original states and new states subsequently to be admitted to the federation certainly reflected the constitutive status of the original colonies and the control that they exercised over the process of federation. Further, the course of debate about the way in which the federal Constitution would deal with the possible subdivision of states underscored the controlling influence of colonial parliaments in the whole question of federation. But was this the entire story?

In this last respect, the colony of Queensland presented a particularly difficult problem. Demands for separation were being made by the northern and central regions of the colony, and these had the knock-on effect, as has been noted, that Queensland was not represented at the convention of 1897–8.[115] It was claimed by separationists in the north and centre that under the relevant imperial legislation,[116] the Queen enjoyed the prerogative to subdivide the colony further simply upon request of the inhabitants thereof and without reference to the Queensland Parliament.[117] How, then, the question was asked, should the federal Constitution treat this matter? On the assumption that the Crown indeed enjoyed such a prerogative, Barton described the dilemma in the following way: if the federal Constitution were to provide explicitly for the prerogative to continue, it would risk alienating the majority of the population located in the south of the colony, whereas if the consent of the Parliament were constitutionally prescribed for any future subdivision it would alienate the residents of the north and central regions.[118]

Later during the Melbourne sitting, James Walker submitted to the convention a clause that took the former course.[119] He was greeted with a mixed response. Deakin argued that the power to subdivide colonies

---

[114] Brown, 'One Continent, Two Federalisms'.
[115] See *Convention Debates, Melbourne* (1898), 293–5.
[116] New South Wales Constitution Statute 1855 (UK), s. 7.
[117] *Convention Debates, Melbourne* (1898), 699–700 (Walker).    [118] *Ibid.*, 699–700 (Barton).
[119] *Ibid.*, 1690–2.

should not rest with the imperial authorities but with the Federal Parliament. Forrest insisted that the consent of the parliament of each state should be required. Isaacs questioned whether the royal prerogative to subdivide the colony further had not in any case been exhausted following the separation of Queensland from New South Wales in 1859.[120] In response to this last point, Barton acknowledged that there was at least some doubt about the legal position and proposed, as a 'middle course', that the matter be referred to the Queensland government for its opinion, a suggestion with which Walker agreed.[121] Nine days later, the Queensland government indicated that it did not support the inclusion of Walker's clause, while at the same time representatives of central Queensland sent a telegram to the convention asking that explicit provision be made for the admission of central and northern Queensland to the federation as separate states.[122] Doubts about the existence of the prerogative as well as the response of the Queensland government seem to have been decisive. When Walker again submitted the clause it was negatived without a division.[123]

Accordingly, while the Constitution that emerged from the convention of 1897–8 certainly envisaged the possible creation of new states either through the admission of external territories or the subdivision of existing states, and while special provision would be made in s. 7 for the representation of the three divisions of Queensland in the Senate, control over the process remained securely within the hands of the state and Commonwealth parliaments. In one sense, this meant that the aspirations for separation harboured by the inhabitants of a number of regions within the various colonies would remain subject to forces beyond their local control. None the less, it remained the case that many of the framers looked forward to the prospect of the future division of Australia into a larger number of states,[124] and they made explicit and extensive provision for it in the Constitution. And yet, the controlling interest that remained in the hands of the Commonwealth and state legislatures serves to illustrate yet another instance in which the Australian Constitution came to embody, at least to some degree, a 'compactual' conception of federalism.

[120] *Ibid.*, 1692–3 (Deakin), 1693 (Forrest), 1693–4 (Isaacs).
[121] *Ibid.*, 1695–7 (Barton), 1698, 1702 (Walker); see 1698–1700 (Solomon).    [122] *Ibid.*, 2171.
[123] *Ibid.*, 2398–400.    [124] See e.g. *Convention Debates, Adelaide* (1897), 786 (Wise).

The second point of contention which arose in relation to the admission of new states concerned the question of representation. In this connection, it will be recalled that while equality of representation of the states in the Senate was ultimately admitted as an essential feature of Australian federation, some regarded this as an unavoidable concession and compromise, while others considered it to be a matter of principle and right. When the Victorian Legislative Assembly proposed in the context of the convention of 1897–8 that new states should not be entitled to equality of representation, it made for an interesting test case.[125] On one hand, it provided an opportunity for those who held equal representation to be a right to show they were genuine in their adherence to the principle by insisting that it must apply to all states, even where the particular interests of their own states were not at stake. On the other hand, if equal representation was the result of a negotiated compromise, it would follow that the representation of new states should also be subject to negotiation. The question was not merely theoretical. It was quite conceivable that, rather than join the federation as an entire state, Queensland might actually be divided into three separate colonies, and these might seek admission as separate states, each claiming the right to equal representation in the Senate.

Cockburn, Symon and Gordon made very clear their view that equal representation was a 'cardinal principle' to which all states, including new states, must be entitled. Certainly, they accepted that the Commonwealth would have to agree to admit such states,[126] but they insisted on equal representation as a necessary term of admission.[127] On the other hand, Isaacs argued that equal representation was merely a concession, and that it was quite consistent with this that the representation of new states be left to negotiation. Barton agreed, arguing that equal representation was a compromise, essentially because federation was itself a compromise between the nationalist and compactual points of view.[128] Matthew

---

[125] See *Convention Debates, Sydney* (1897), 311–12 (Isaacs), 394 (Victorian Legislative Assembly proposal).

[126] Barton's draft Constitution Bill originally held open the opportunity for all of the existing Australian colonies to enter the federation after the Commonwealth had been formed upon the same terms as those enjoyed by original states. However, the convention of 1897–8 ultimately decided against this, placing all potential new states in the same position. See *Convention Debates, Adelaide* (1897), 1012–18.

[127] *Convention Debates, Sydney* (1897), 231 (Symon), 395 (Cockburn), 395–8 (Gordon); *Convention Debates, Melbourne* (1898), 696–7 (Cockburn).

[128] *Convention Debates, Sydney* (1897), 311–12 (Isaacs), 406–9 (Barton).

Clarke also agreed, but put the matter in terms of the formative basis of the federation: the original states were accorded equal representation as a condition of their entry into the federation as pre-existing, self-governing colonies.[129]

In the outcome, it may be of some significance that the Victorian proposal was narrowly upheld by a vote of 25 to 20, suggesting that for a majority of framers equal representation, if a principle, was one that applied only to the original states.[130] The most fundamental principle of Australian federalism was, it seems, that federation would rest upon an agreement among constituent states, so that the terms of federation would be matters ultimately for debate and negotiation between the parties and not simply matters of abstract and idealistic political philosophy.

---

[129] *Ibid.*, 411–12.

[130] *Ibid.*, 415; cf. *Convention Debates, Melbourne* (1898), 696–8 (South Australian House of Assembly proposal). However, see the position adopted by Lyne, who while opposed to equal representation of the states, thought that if the original states were to enjoy this right, then all new states ought to enjoy the same right: *Convention Debates, Melbourne* (1898), 697.

# 10

---

# Configurations of power

[U]nless we conserve to the states not a mockery of their rights, but an effective assertion of them . . . we shall soon find many who will regret their compact, and if it is a compact that they find indissoluble, then so much the worse for the union. So I take it that if you wish to preserve the goodwill of the states, and their adherence to the general constitution, not as a matter of compulsion, but as a matter of loyal good faith, you will do all that you can to secure, and not to reduce, the power to provide against any encroachment.

Edmund Barton (1891)

## Distributing competencies

### The convention of 1891

When introducing the draft Commonwealth Bill prepared for the consideration of the convention of 1891, Samuel Griffith explained that the drafting committee had taken much care to ensure that the legislative powers conferred upon the proposed Parliament were consistent with Parkes's first resolution relating to the surrender of powers by the colonies to the federation. This meant, for Griffith, that it was important not to propose to transfer any power which could be 'better exercised' by the states, or the exercise of which by the federation was 'not necessary for its good order and government'.[1] Griffith acknowledged that it would be for the convention as a whole, as well as the public, to judge whether the drafting committee had succeeded in fulfilling its task in accordance with these principles. He also noted that many of the specific powers proposed to be conferred upon the Federal Parliament were not particularly controversial and likely to be widely acknowledged as properly falling within

---

[1] *Convention Debates, Sydney* (1891), 523.

the province of the federation.[2] In this respect, Griffith drew particular attention to the powers concerning inter-state trade and commerce, customs, excise and bounties, taxation, borrowing, postal and telegraphic services, and defence, among a number of others.[3]

Griffith explained that most of the powers proposed to be conferred upon the Commonwealth would be exercised by the states and the Commonwealth concurrently, and that federal law would only prevail in the event of any inconsistency between state and federal law, except in the case of a minimal list of powers to be conferred exclusively upon the Commonwealth.[4] He also explained that the Canadian expedient of enumerating the powers of the states had not been adopted, not from want of a desire to preserve the powers of the states, but because such an enumeration was both 'unscientific' and 'impossible'.[5] The impossibility of enumeration was due to the indefinitely large range of matters reserved to the states. While Griffith did not say so explicitly, its unscientific character presumably derived from a conception of federation as involving a compact among pre-existing states under which they consent to confer specific powers on the federal government which they agree to form. But in order to address any fear of some sinister intention to 'deprive the state legislatures of their autonomy', it is noteworthy that he also thought it necessary to make plain that the scheme left the states entirely free to continue to regulate their own constitutions, as well as such matters as the borrowing of money, the complete control of the government of the state, property and civil rights, public lands and mines, registration of titles, education, criminal law, hospitals, local works and undertakings, municipal institutions, licensing, administration of civil and criminal justice, the establishment of courts and the disposal of state revenue.[6]

It was clearly the general intention of the delegates to establish a genuinely federal government that would possess the institutional infrastructure and governmental powers necessary to enable it to function as a sovereign nation within its sphere of authority. Indeed, Clark's draft constitution had deliberately refrained from referring to the legislative powers of the Federal Parliament as being for the 'peace, order and good government' of the Commonwealth for fear that this would imply a plenary power analogous to the power conferred upon the Canadian

[2] *Ibid.*, 523–4.    [3] *Ibid.*, 524.    [4] *Ibid.*, 524–5.    [5] *Ibid.*, 525.    [6] *Ibid.*, 525–6.

Parliament.[7] However, from the beginning Griffith's draft bill invariably used this technical expression of constitutional law to ensure that the powers of the Commonwealth Parliament would be read broadly, albeit always within the limited fields specifically allocated. It was accordingly recognised that the powers to be granted to the Commonwealth would have to be expressed in general terms, and that large powers over such matters as interstate trade and commerce, defence, taxation and borrowing would be necessary to enable the Commonwealth to function as a 'federal body' possessing the essential ingredients of 'sovereign power'.[8] In addition to the specific legislative, executive and judicial powers transferred to the Commonwealth, all powers 'incidental' to the carrying into execution of those powers would be explicitly conferred upon the Commonwealth.[9] As Deakin later put it, the Commonwealth was not intended simply to be 'a kind of glorified Federal Council', but rather 'the popular and central Government of the whole of Australia'.[10]

Compared with debate about other parts of the proposed Constitution, there was often general agreement concerning the specific powers and functions that ought to be exercised by the Commonwealth, and the debate tended to focus upon the likely interpretation of the words used and whether the words used were adequate to achieve what was intended. Remarkably, almost all of the federal powers proposed in Griffith's draft bill were approved without amendment, and many were not even discussed at all.[11] The outstanding exception that proved the rule was Kingston's proposal that the Commonwealth be given power to establish courts of conciliation and arbitration for the settlement of industrial disputes.[12] In response, Griffith objected that such a power would involve an interference with the states' jurisdiction over 'property and civil rights'.[13] Deakin's concern was that federal control would get in the way of the necessity for 'experimental legislation' in each of the states.[14] Kingston replied that the federal power would not displace the states'

---

[7] Clark's draft constitution, cl. 45; see *Convention Debates, Sydney* (1897), 1036–7 (Barton, citing a proposal of the Tasmanian Parliament initiated by Clark).

[8] *Convention Debates, Sydney* (1891), 663–4 (Clark), 671–2 (McMillan).

[9] Clark's draft constitution, cl. 45(xxx); Commonwealth Bill 1891, ch. I, cl. 52(32); Constitution Bill 1898, s. 51(xxxix); *Convention Debates, Sydney* (1897), 1190–1 (Isaacs); *Convention Debates, Melbourne* (1898), 226–7 (Barton).

[10] *Convention Debates, Melbourne* (1898), 202.

[11] *Convention Debates, Sydney* (1891), 662–704.    [12] *Ibid.*, 688–9, 780–1.    [13] *Ibid.*, 781.

[14] *Ibid.*, 781.

existing power to deal with such matters.[15] While this convinced Deakin, the proposal was rejected in 1891 by a vote of 25 to 12 (but was successfully revived, as will be seen, in 1897).[16]

But while wide and extensive powers were conferred, the consensus remained that the Commonwealth Parliament was to be a legislature of enumerated and limited powers. The prospect that the Commonwealth might manipulate the provisions of the Constitution in order to expand its powers beyond those intended was considered something to be guarded against. Recognising, for example, the possibility that the Commonwealth might use its financial powers to extend its influence into fields otherwise reserved to the states, Andrew Thynne proposed an additional subclause which specified that the Commonwealth would have power to make laws for 'the appropriation of any moneys raised by the commonwealth for any purpose authorised by the constitution'.[17] While the proposed subclause was contained in the general clause conferring legislative powers of the Commonwealth Parliament it is noticeable that Clark understood the proposal to be one of 'confin[ing] the federal parliament strictly to the powers conferred upon it by the constitution, and not to let it in any indirect way, by the appropriation of money, exercise a power which is not directly conferred upon it'. In other words, Clark thought that a positive grant of power expressed in limited terms implied a 'prohibition' and that the proposal was unnecessary because the courts would be sure to declare invalid any federal law that sought by indirect means to expand the powers of the Commonwealth in this way.[18] As he explained, a 'prohibition' upon the Commonwealth was clearly implied by 'the fact that only certain distinct powers are specifically delegated to the Federal Parliament, and that they cannot exercise any powers other than those which are specifically delegated to them'.[19]

Griffith shared Clark's doubt about whether the provision was necessary, but suggested that limiting the power of the Commonwealth to borrowing 'for the purposes of the commonwealth' might meet the case.[20] Deakin likewise argued against the provision, but for very different

---

[15] *Ibid.*, 782.    [16] *Ibid.*, 785; *Convention Debates, Melbourne* (1898), 180–215.

[17] *Convention Debates, Sydney* (1891), 698.    [18] *Ibid.*, 698.

[19] *Ibid.*, 699. As further explained in ch. 12, reasoning like this would form an integral part of the reserved powers doctrine as developed by the High Court between 1903 and 1919 under the leadership of Griffith CJ, Barton and O'Connor JJ.

[20] *Convention Debates, Sydney* (1891), 699–700.

reasons: that it would make the Constitution too rigid, lead to exaggerated scrutiny of federal appropriation bills and prevent the Commonwealth from responding to unforeseen emergencies.[21] Somewhat ironically, the suggestion that the Commonwealth ought to be free to spend money on any matter that it thought necessary convinced Clark of the necessity of an explicit prohibition,[22] but Griffith pointed out that a prohibition should not be included in a clause conferring powers on the Commonwealth, so Thynne ultimately withdrew the amendment.[23] Similarly, when Thynne proposed a similar clause be added to the chapter dealing with finances, Griffith again expressed his agreement with the objective, but thought an explicit provision to be unnecessary given that Chapter IV clause 1 required that all moneys received by the Commonwealth must form one consolidated revenue fund to be appropriated 'in the manner . . . provided for by this Constitution'.[24]

Essentially the same concerns shaped the treatment of the executive power of the Commonwealth. Griffith's draft bill limited the executive power to matters in respect of which the Commonwealth had power to make laws, but added an explicit prohibition in respect of matters 'within the legislative powers of a state' or in respect of which the state 'for the time being exercises such powers'. The drafting was clumsy, but the intention was clear. In order to simplify the drafting but maintain the same intent, Griffith himself proposed an amendment which limited the clause to a positive statement of the scope of the executive power, namely the 'execution of the provisions of this constitution, and the laws of the Commonwealth'.[25] The amendment was approved without discussion, and substantially the same words would be adopted in 1897–8.

Throughout the drafting process in connection with the Commonwealth Bill of 1891 there was a consistent intention that the Commonwealth's executive and legislative powers be limited to particular, prescribed topics, and that the limited conferral of power implied a prohibition on the Commonwealth and a reservation of powers to the states. Originally, a number of provisions expressed the negative prohibition and reservation

---

[21] *Ibid.*, 700.    [22] *Ibid.*, 701.    [23] *Ibid.*, 701.

[24] *Ibid.*, 789. It is illuminating to compare the tenor of the debate over these provisions during the convention debates with the position adopted by the High Court on Commonwealth appropriations in *Attorney-General (Vic.); Ex rel Dale* v. *Commonwealth* (1945) 71 CLR 237 and, more significantly, *Victoria* v. *Commonwealth and Hayden* (1975) 134 CLR 338.

[25] *Convention Debates, Sydney* (1891), 777–8.

explicitly, and some of these were redrafted into positive statements, but this, it appears, was done solely to simplify the drafting and not to negative the implied reservation that was intended.

## The convention of 1897–8

While the Constitution Bill of 1897–8 would include a longer list of federal legislative powers, the same basic conception of the relationship between the powers of the Commonwealth and the states remained. Moreover, once again there was general agreement concerning the powers to be conferred upon the Commonwealth, and the debate usually focused on minor amendments and points of interpretation. As in 1891, virtually all of the clauses proposed in Barton's draft bill were approved without amendment, and a substantial number, having been debated in and drafted by the Constitutional Committee, were not discussed in the convention at all.[26]

Hirst has suggested that one reason why there was relatively little debate over the powers to be conferred upon the Commonwealth was that, unlike the Canadians before them, the Australians already had a sense of nationhood. Federation was therefore more a matter of breaking down artificial barriers so that the underlying reality could be revealed, rather than one of constructing something new that did not already exist.[27] Thus the dismantling of trade barriers between the colonies played a far more significant role in the movement towards federation than arguments over what responsibilities would be transferred to the Commonwealth.[28]

None the less, on the occasions when the scope of specific powers to be conferred upon the Commonwealth was debated, a concern often expressed was that if too many responsibilities were conferred upon the federation, this would undermine the capacity of the people of each state

---

[26] *Convention Debates, Adelaide* (1897), 760–829; *Convention Debates, Sydney* (1897), 1035–85; *Convention Debates, Melbourne* (1898), *passim.*

[27] Hirst, *Sentimental Nation*, 165.

[28] The principle of inter-colonial free trade was prominent in both Parkes's and Barton's resolutions: *Convention Debates, Sydney* (1891), 23, 499–500; *Convention Debates, Adelaide* (1987), 17, 395. On the debate over the guarantee that became s. 92 of the Constitution, see J. A. La Nauze, 'A Little Bit of Lawyers' Language: The History of "Absolutely Free", 1890–1900' in Martin, *Essays in Australian Federation*.

to govern themselves.[29] It was hence often thought desirable that the Constitution leave room for 'varied local development', particularly on questions of moral or social policy.[30] Even when delegates disagreed about specific heads of power, the underlying principle was that what could best be administered locally ought not to be transferred to the Commonwealth; only matters of 'national concern' should be handed over to the federal government.[31] It was even urged that in some contexts, an efficient federal administration of a particular matter would necessarily involve a high degree of local administration under federal supervision.[32]

The distribution of power between the Commonwealth and the states raised issues that were different from those which attached to the composition of the Federal Parliament and, in particular, the equal representation of the states in the Senate. Delegates well known to favour 'states' rights' in relation to the Senate were often prepared to confer extensive legislative powers upon the Commonwealth, where it was thought that particular matters could be better administered on a national scale. At the same time, 'nationalists' as far as the constitution of the Federal Parliament were concerned sometimes drew attention to proposals which in their view conferred excessive powers upon the federation.

A good example of the former occurred when delegates from South Australia proposed a federal power over 'navigable streams and their tributaries'.[33] The South Australian delegates, while often especially concerned to protect the rights of the states to continue to operate as self-governing communities, none the less strongly supported federal control of navigable rivers with a view to protecting their interests in the waters of the Murray. They were principally met, however, by delegates from

---

[29] See e.g. *Convention Debates, Adelaide* (1897), 769 (Carruthers), 779 (Symon); *Convention Debates, Sydney* (1897), 1077 (O'Connor).

[30] *Convention Debates, Adelaide* (1897), 786 (Wise); *Convention Debates, Sydney* (1897), 1046 (Curruthers), 1078–9 (Wise); cf. *Convention Debates, Melbourne* (1898), 22 (Deakin).

[31] See e.g. *Convention Debates, Adelaide* (1897), 767 (Holder), 769 (Carruthers), 770 (Deakin), 772 (Cockburn), 774 (Reid), 776–7 (Carruthers), 788 (Symon), 792 (Braddon); *Convention Debates, Melbourne* (1898), 11 (McMillan), 24 (Trenwith), 28 (Downer), 213–14 (Barton).

[32] *Convention Debates, Adelaide* (1897), 775 (Braddon).

[33] *Ibid.*, 794; cf. *Convention Debates, Melbourne* (1898), 31–2. Another example was the proposal that the Commonwealth have unqualified power concerning lighthouses, lightships, beacons and buoys. See *Convention Debates, Sydney* (1897), 1069–71; *Convention Debates, Melbourne* (1898), 265; Quick and Garran, *Annotated Constitution*, 565.

New South Wales who wished to preserve state control over the tributaries of the Murray, such as the Murrumbidgee and the Darling, particularly for purposes of irrigation and conservation.[34] Debate about the issue was extraordinarily protracted and ended in something of a compromise, especially reflected in sections 98–100 of the Constitution, under which control of river navigation would be included within the Commonwealth's power to regulate interstate trade and commerce, but would not extend to giving any preference to a particular state or abridging the right of a state or its residents to the reasonable use of river water for conservation or irrigation.[35] During the debate, there were many appeals to principle and justice, but in this case at least the delegates from South Australia and New South Wales were very evidently driven by the distinct material and economic interests of their respective colonies.

Two particularly clear examples of 'nationalists' intervening to restrict the scope of federal power are also revealing, but for a different reason. The first occurred when Isaacs expressed concern that the transfer to the Commonwealth of power to legislate with respect to 'banking' would include a power to regulate 'state banking'.[36] While Isaacs was not immediately successful, it is notable that at Sydney in 1897 the provision was amended to make clear that federal power would not extend to the regulation of state banking.[37] The final wording of the banking power, like the insurance power,[38] owes in this respect a great deal to Higgins who pointed out in respect of the insurance power that a prohibition upon the Commonwealth would have to be expressed clearly by negative words. As has been seen in previous chapters, for both Isaacs and Higgins, 'states' rights' meant nothing more, but also nothing less, than the division of powers between the Commonwealth and states.[39] Higgins suggested, therefore, that the conferral of power upon the Federal Parliament be qualified by the words 'except State insurance', Kingston suggested the word 'excluding' and the convention eventually settled on 'other than'.[40]

---

[34] *Convention Debates, Adelaide* (1897), 794–820.

[35] See *ibid.*, 794–829; *Convention Debates, Melbourne* (1898), 31–150, 376–642, 1947–90, 2386–90. See, further, Quick and Garran, *Annotated Constitution*, 138, 170–5, 194–7, 872–80, 887–94.

[36] *Convention Debates, Adelaide* (1897), 778.     [37] *Convention Debates, Sydney* (1897), 1074–5.

[38] Constitution, s. 51(xiii) and (xiv).

[39] See e.g. *Convention Debates, Adelaide* (1897), 779 (Isaacs).

[40] *Ibid.*, 780 (Higgins, Kingston), 782 (Higgins); *Convention Debates, Sydney* (1897), 1074–5; *Convention Debates, Melbourne* (1898), 2531.

The second example of a nationalist seeking to ensure that states' rights would be protected arose when Isaacs pointed out that Barton's proposal to confer upon the Commonwealth a power to acquire property 'from any State or person' would necessarily include compulsory acquisition, and that care should be taken to ensure that the provision did not contradict the principle that a state would not be deprived of territory without its consent.[41] The acquisition of property is different from the acquisition of jurisdictional rights over territory,[42] but the broad underlying principle of protecting the rights of the states was the same. Barton, who had introduced the proposed clause, agreed to withdraw it pending further consideration, and when O'Connor reintroduced it there was added the qualification that, not only must the acquisition be for a purpose in respect of which the Commonwealth Parliament has power to make laws, but the acquisition must be 'on just terms'.[43] Again, a requirement of just terms is not as far-reaching as a requirement of state consent to an acquisition, and yet the revised clause was apparently accepted as sufficiently protective of the interests of the states.

As will be noted in the final chapter, the difference between the explicit prohibition contained in the banking and insurance powers, the qualified terms of the acquisition power and the merely limited positive words contained in other heads of Commonwealth legislative power has proved decisive in High Court interpretations of the scope of power conferred upon the Commonwealth and of the powers reserved to the states. As members of the High Court, Griffith, Barton and O'Connor would formulate the doctrine of 'state reserved powers' precisely on the basis of the limited positive words of the trade and commerce power,[44] whereas Higgins and Isaacs would later be members of a differently constituted court which would strike down the reserved powers doctrine on the

---

[41] *Convention Debates, Melbourne* (1898), 153.

[42] See, similarly, the debate concerning the Commonwealth's power over the seat of the Commonwealth government and federal territories (e.g. *ibid.* 256–62), during which Isaacs drew the distinction between the Commonwealth holding territory as a sovereign and holding land as a proprietor (*ibid.*, 257, 260–1).

[43] *Ibid.*, 1874.

[44] In this respect also to be noted is the discussion which surrounded the proposal to qualify the interstate trade and commerce power and the guarantee of freedom of interstate trade so as to reserve state power to regulate internal trade and commerce as well as liquor imported into each state. See *Convention Debates, Sydney* (1897), 1037–59; *Convention Debates, Melbourne* (1898), 1014–20.

ground that a prohibition reserving powers to the states could only be founded upon an explicit negative provision of the kind Higgins had proposed for the insurance power.[45] And yet, remarkably enough, the High Court has been willing to use the qualified terms in which the banking, insurance and acquisition powers are conferred to cut down the scope of other heads of power.[46]

Nationalists voting to restrict federal power and states' righters voting to expand it were exceptions, however, rather than the rule.[47] Generally, the overwhelming tendency of the delegates was to ensure that the powers conferred upon the Commonwealth were carefully drafted and defined. Thus, as in 1891, so in 1897–8, when particular heads of power were discussed, it was usually with a view to making careful distinctions between matters that would come within federal power and those that would remain outside it.[48] An especially good example of this occurred at Sydney in 1897 when Higgins proposed, with the support of Kingston, that the Commonwealth be given the power to regulate 'industrial disputes extending beyond the limits of any one state'.[49] On its face, Higgins's proposal was broader than Kingston's had been in 1891 because it was not limited to the establishment of conciliation and arbitration courts. Concerns were expressed, therefore, about the scope of the power, and Symon suggested that it be limited to the use of arbitration as a means of resolving disputes.[50] Kingston responded that power to establish courts of conciliation and arbitration was what Higgins had in mind, and agreed that the motion should be amended to make this clear.[51] Higgins did so, but the motion was initially lost by a vote of 22 to 12.[52] When, however, at Melbourne in 1898 Higgins proposed, again in limited terms, a power to legislate with respect to the 'conciliation and

---

[45] See *Amalgamated Society of Engineers* v. *Adelaide Steamship Co. Ltd* (1920) 28 CLR 129.

[46] See e.g. *W. H. Blakeley Co.* v. *Commonwealth* (1953) 87 CLR 501, 521; *Attorney-General (Cth)* v. *Schmidt* (1961) 105 CLR 361, 371–2; *Bourke* v. *State Bank of NSW* (1990) 170 CLR 276, 286–9.

[47] For another example, on the contentious question of railways, see *Convention Debates, Melbourne* (1898), 156 (Symon, Isaacs), 168 (Reid, Cockburn).

[48] In some cases, the distinctions, limitations and qualifications became very complex indeed. One of the most complex issues concerned the regulation and administration of railways. Debate on the issue arose on more occasions than can conveniently be documented. For the outcome of the debate, see ss. 18, 51(xxxii)–(xxxiv), 98, 102 and 104 of the Constitution.

[49] *Convention Debates, Adelaide* (1897), 782 (Higgins), 782–3 (Kingston).

[50] *Ibid.*, 790 (Symon).    [51] *Ibid.*, 790–91 (Kingston).    [52] *Ibid.*, 793.

arbitration for the prevention and settlement of industrial disputes extending beyond the limits of any one State', the proposal was adopted, after an extended debate, by a narrow vote of 22 to 19.[53]

A similarly deliberate restriction on the scope of a head of power concerned the power in respect of corporations. As initially proposed in Barton's draft bill, the power extended only to 'foreign corporations and trading corporations formed in any State or part of the Commonwealth'.[54] A critical distinction between municipal, trading and charitable corporations had been drawn by Griffith in 1891,[55] and Barton explained that the qualifying words had been used deliberately to exclude municipal corporations from the scope of the power, so that their regulation would remain a matter for the states.[56] On the other hand, in order that the power would definitely extend to banks and building societies, Abbott proposed the addition of the words 'financial corporations', and the clause was approved without further discussion.[57] A bare reference to 'corporations' was intentionally avoided so as to restrict the scope of the power and make its scope more precise.

## Configurations of power

A. V. Dicey influentially argued that a federal system of government consisted of three essential ingredients: a division of powers between national and state governments, a binding constitution in which these powers were reduced to writing and an independent judiciary by whom the terms of union were conclusively interpreted.[58] To a certain extent, Dicey's model of federalism was reproduced in Australia. At a number of points, however, there were significant divergences. Quite apart from the importance the framers accorded to the idea that a federation is formed through the free agreement of constituent states – and the impact that this had on the representative institutions and amending formula adopted thereunder – the framers of the Australian Constitution provided for the distribution of legislative, executive and judicial power in a way not fully concordant with Dicey's conception of 'coordinate'

---

[53] *Convention Debates, Melbourne* (1898), 180–215.
[54] *Convention Debates, Adelaide* (1897), 793.    [55] *Convention Debates, Sydney* (1891), 686.
[56] *Convention Debates, Adelaide* (1897), 793–4.    [57] *Ibid.*, 794.
[58] Dicey, *Law of the Constitution*, 130–55, 410–13.

federalism. The most apparent way in which this occurred was through the conferral upon the Commonwealth of mostly concurrent legislative powers and the reservation, as it were, of all powers not conferred to the constituent states. Moreover, there were attempts to shape the way in which the High Court of Australia would be constituted and exercise its powers that did not altogether conform to Dicey's account. In the remaining parts of this chapter, these points will be covered, beginning first with the issue of exclusive and concurrent powers, turning next to the related question of the supremacy of federal laws and concluding with the composition, powers and functions of the High Court.

## Concurrency, exclusivity and federal supremacy

Under the Constitution as enacted in 1900, the vast majority of powers conferred upon the Commonwealth are concurrent (section 51), enabling the states to continue to legislate in such fields so long as such legislation is not inconsistent with federal legislation: for in the event of inconsistency, Commonwealth law prevails over state law (section 109). The meaning and significance of this scheme, so far as the framers were concerned, is well illustrated by the debate about James Howe's ultimately successful proposal for a federal power over 'invalid and old-age pensions'.[59]

William Trenwith, the only labour delegate at the convention of 1897–8, remarkably opposed Howe's proposal on the ground that it would have a tendency to delay the implementation of social security measures by the states.[60] Cockburn, a radical liberal who was likewise supportive of social legislation of this kind, but who was also most emphatically a 'states' righter', supported the proposal, however, spe-cifically on the ground that the power was merely concurrent, so that the states would remain free to enact such laws, subject only to supervening federal legislation.[61] Confusion soon surfaced about the meaning of concurrency, exclusivity, supremacy and inconsistency when George Reid emphatically asserted that such powers would not be shared with the

---

[59] *Convention Debates, Sydney* (1897), 1082, 1085–8; *Convention Debates, Melbourne* (1898), 6–8, 1991–6. His argument appealed to the example of Germany: *Convention Debates, Sydney* (1897), 1086.

[60] *Convention Debates, Melbourne* (1898), 8–9; cf. Trenwith's similar attitude to the proposal that the race power be exclusive to the Commonwealth: *ibid.*, 235–8.

[61] *Ibid.*, 9–10.

states but would rather be 'absolutely and exclusively within the province of the Federal Parliament'.[62] Kingston naturally responded that the power was proposed to be concurrent, so that not only state laws, but also state power to legislate on the subject, would continue to exist, and that it would only be if and when the Commonwealth chose to legislate on the topic in a manner that was inconsistent with state law that any state law would cease to apply.[63]

All of the delegates were aware that it was not proposed that the power should fall within the category of explicitly exclusive powers which would in due course be contained in section 52 of the Constitution. The disagreement had to do with the circumstances in which federal and state laws would be inconsistent with each other. And the debate reveals that at this stage the delegates who spoke to the matter did not as yet clearly comprehend the different ways in which inconsistency might possibly arise.[64]

The most obvious form of inconsistency would occur when federal and state laws imposed inconsistent duties or where one law conferred a liberty and the other law imposed inconsistent duty.[65] However, laws granting entitlements to the payment of government pensions would not, in their application to the ordinary citizen, impose duties or liberties of this kind. The question of whether federal and state social security schemes were inconsistent would – to use the language that the High Court later developed on this topic – be more likely to involve the issue of whether the Commonwealth Parliament intended to 'cover the field', displacing state law within that field.[66] As might be expected, the delegates were not able to analyse the different kinds of inconsistency with the precision that later case law now allows, and this led to disagreement and confusion about the meaning of concurrency and exclusivity in the context of Howe's proposal.

Trenwith's attitude to Howe's proposal was significant in another respect. Although, as a labour delegate, he was very strongly supportive of social legislation of this kind, he specifically pointed to the capacity of the states to refer legislative powers to the Commonwealth as the way in which the issue might be federalised in future.[67] As will be seen in the next

---

[62] *Ibid.*, 10, 15–16.    [63] *Ibid.*, 12–13.    [64] Compare *ibid.*, 15 (Symon), 27 (Deakin).
[65] *Australian Boot Trade Employees Federation* v. *Whybrow & Co* (1910) 10 CLR 266; *R* v. *Licensing Court of Brisbane; Ex parte Daniell* (1920) 28 CLR 23; *Clyde Engineering Co. Ltd* v. *Cowburn* (1926) 37 CLR 466.
[66] *Ex parte McLean* (1930) 43 CLR 472.
[67] *Convention Debates, Melbourne* (1898), 8–9 (Trenwith), 21 (Deakin).

chapter, the framers understood the reference power to be a very significant way in which the allocation of powers as between the Commonwealth and the states might be adjusted in the future without recourse
to formal constitutional amendment. And Trenwith was not the only
delegate who, while supporting the general policy of introducing old-age
pensions, was concerned that if too many powers were conferred upon the
Commonwealth the debate about the ratification of the Constitution
Bill might be mired in unnecessary controversy. Alexander Peacock, with
some prescience, argued that if a power over pensions was transferred to
the Commonwealth it would be difficult to resist the logic that the
Commonwealth would also need to have power over other aspects of social
policy, such as hospitals and education.[68] Given, in addition, conservative
opposition to social legislation of this kind, Howe's proposal faced serious
obstacles at more than one level, and was initially rejected by a vote of
25 to 20, only to be later approved, remarkably enough, by a vote of
26 to 4.[69] As Higgins explained, his initial opposition to the power was in
the hope that the states would become the location for important social
experiments and that each state would learn from the experiences of the
others. But the conferral of concurrent power upon the Commonwealth to
legislate in the field would not automatically exclude the possibility of state
experimentation, and so he changed his mind.[70]

The second important aspect of the configuration of federal and state
power was that some of the powers of the Commonwealth were indeed
intended to be exclusive, thus displacing state legislative power over those
topics.[71] And, as Quick and Garran would later explain, the powers
conferred upon the Commonwealth could be exclusive for two very different reasons.[72] First, some subject matters had simply not fallen within

---

[68] *Ibid.*, 14.    [69] *Ibid.*, 29, 1996.    [70] *Ibid.*, 1993–4.

[71] Perhaps the most significant withdrawal of power from the states was the conferral of exclusive
power on the Commonwealth to impose customs and excise duties under s. 90 of the
Constitution. While the need for federal control over customs was generally acknowledged, the
impact on state finances was significant. Indeed, it was said that the 'hardest nut to crack' was
the settlement of the financial clauses. See e.g. *Convention Debates, Sydney* (1891), 789–801;
*Convention Debates, Adelaide* (1897), 835–6; *Convention Debates, Sydney* (1897), 9; *Convention
Debates, Melbourne* (1898), 263–5, 909–10, 936–8, 940–64, 990–8. For a discussion, compare
Galligan, *Federal Republic*, ch. 9 and Cheryl Saunders, 'The Hardest Nut to Crack: The Financial
Settlement in the Commonwealth Constitution', in Craven, *Convention Debates*, VI, 89–112.

[72] Quick and Garran, *Annotated Constitution*, 509, 656, 933–4, 938.

the original jurisdiction of the colonies, and conferring a positive power on the Commonwealth on such topics did not alter that pre-existing state of affairs. Second, other heads of power were deliberately and explicitly conferred in exclusive terms. However, the debate over the proposed exclusive powers of the Commonwealth reveals a subtlety in the scheme that is not always appreciated.

In Griffith's draft Commonwealth Bill of 1891, the so-called 'race' power was proposed to be an exclusive power of the Commonwealth. This remained the case in the bill until the final session at Melbourne in 1898, when it was converted into a concurrent power.[73] The principal objection to the exclusivity of the power as first raised by Deakin, and later by Isaacs, was that while a power of this sort should be conferred upon the Commonwealth, the states should not be debarred from legislating on the topic.[74] Because the debate about the race power thus progressed in terms of the question of whether the states should or would, under the clause, continue to have power to legislate, the debate sheds light, not only on the meaning of the race power, but also on the meaning of exclusivity.

Griffith's initial intention appears to have been that an exclusive race power would absolutely prevent the states from legislating on the topic, whether or not the Commonwealth had chosen to so legislate.[75] Clark insightfully pointed out that the power only operated in relation to a race in respect of which it was 'deemed necessary to make laws', and this identification of a particular race or races to which the power applied could only occur once the Commonwealth actually legislated on the topic. Until then, not only would state laws continue to operate, but the states would continue to have power to legislate with respect to the people of particular races.[76]

---

[73] *Convention Debates, Sydney* (1891), 701–4; *Convention Debates, Adelaide* (1897), 830–2; *Convention Debates, Melbourne* (1898), 227–56. The reason for exclusivity, it appears, was to place the Commonwealth under an urgent necessity to legislate on the topic: see e.g. *Convention Debates, Melbourne* (1898), 254 (Downer).

[74] *Convention Debates, Sydney* (1891), 702–3 (Deakin); *Convention Debates, Melbourne* (1898), 227–8 (Isaacs), 230–2 (Deakin).

[75] Griffith's draft bill, ch. I, Pt. V, cl. 53; ch. V, cl. 1(2); *Convention Debates, Sydney* (1891), 702–3 (Griffith).

[76] A proposition with which Griffith appeared to agree. See *Convention Debates, Sydney* (1891), 703–4 (Clark), 704 (Griffith, Deakin); see, likewise, *Convention Debates, Melbourne* (1898), 248 (Kingston), 253 (Downer).

While some failed to appreciate it at the time, Clark's point was ultimately well taken and was one of the reasons the race power was eventually converted into a concurrent one. And yet the use of the expression 'deemed necessary to make laws' made the race power a special case. What if one were dealing with some other topic over which the Commonwealth was given exclusive power, such as the power to legislate with respect to a place acquired by the Commonwealth?[77] Clearly, the policy was that once the Commonwealth in fact legislated, state laws would be inoperative. But what if the Commonwealth had acquired such a place, but had not yet legislated in respect of that place? What would be the effect of state laws operating in respect of that place at that time? And would the states continue to have the capacity to repeal or amend such laws until the Commonwealth should legislate?

Questions such as these went to the general nature of the exclusive powers of the Commonwealth, rather than the unique characteristics of the race power in particular. Because, however, most of the substantive debate in the federal conventions about the meaning of exclusivity happened in the context of the race power and not the other proposed heads of exclusive power, the two sets of issues were often confused. Thus, it was often said that the states would (or should) continue to be able to legislate until the Commonwealth did so. But were such comments directed to Clark's and Deakin's point that until a particular race was 'deemed' by the Commonwealth to warrant special laws, exclusivity was not yet triggered in relation to that race, or were they directed to the nature of exclusivity in general, suggesting that exclusivity would not be triggered until the Commonwealth in fact legislated?

Questions such as these are not of any direct relevance to current legal debate simply because the Commonwealth some time ago legislated in a way that clarified the status of state laws in respect of areas of exclusive Commonwealth power, such as places acquired by the Commonwealth.[78] However, the convention delegates' discussion of these issues sheds significant light on how they understood the relationship between the legislative powers of the Commonwealth and the states and, in particular,

---

[77] See Griffith's draft bill, 30 March 1891, cl. 52(2); Commonwealth bill 1891, cl. 53(2); Commonwealth Bill 1898, s. 52(1).

[78] E.g. Commonwealth Places (Application of Laws) Act 1970 (Cth).

how they understood the exclusivity and the supremacy of Commonwealth laws.

The general effect of exclusivity did not depend simply on the terms in
which each head of exclusive power was vested in the Commonwealth,
but more generally upon the provisions dealing with the continuing
powers and laws of the states.[79] The bedrock principle was that the
powers of the states would continue subject to the powers exclusively
vested in the Commonwealth or otherwise withdrawn from the states,
and on this point there was no doubt and no dissent.[80] Griffith's draft bill
accordingly appeared to prevent the states from legislating within the
scope of exclusive Commonwealth powers entirely.[81] In the Commonwealth Bill of 1891 the relevant provision (which would eventually
become section 108 of the Constitution) was amended to make clear that
until the Commonwealth should exercise its legislative powers, the states
would remain able to legislate.[82] Read literally, as well as taken within the
context of the debate of 1891, the change appears to have applied to the
fields over which the Commonwealth was granted not only concurrent,
but also exclusive, powers. But the clause did not make this absolutely
clear because it referred simply to the '[L]egislative powers of the Parliament of the Commonwealth' without explicitly indicating whether
concurrent or exclusive powers (or both) were in view; and nor did
section 108 in its final form.[83] It could therefore be argued, as Quick and
Garran later did, that the preservation of state legislative power could
not, by definition, apply to fields of exclusive Commonwealth power.[84]
Quick and Garran had to acknowledge that Commonwealth exclusivity
was not entirely absolute because it was at least clear from the first half of
section 108 that pre-existing state laws on topics within the exclusive

---

[79] See *Convention Debates, Melbourne* (1898), 231 (Deakin).

[80] See Griffith's draft bill, ch. V, cl. 1(1); Commonwealth Bill 1891, ch. V, cl. 1; Constitution Bill
1898, s. 107.

[81] Griffith's draft bill, ch. I, pt V, cl. 53; ch. V, cl. 1(2).

[82] Commonwealth Bill 1891, ch. V, cl. 2.

[83] Section 108 provides: 'Every law in force in a Colony which has become or becomes a State,
and relating to any matter within the powers of the Parliament of the Commonwealth, shall,
subject to this Constitution, continue in force in the State; and, until provision is made in that
behalf by the Parliament of the Commonwealth, the Parliament of the State shall have such
powers of alteration and of repeal in respect of any such law as the Parliament of the Colony
had until the Colony became a State.'

[84] Quick and Garran, *Annotated Constitution*, 657–8, 938.

powers of the Commonwealth would continue to operate. But if this was so, the argument from the very nature of exclusivity was contradicted in its very premise: if the first half of section 108 preserved pre-existing state laws notwithstanding exclusivity, why would not the second half of section 108 preserve the power of the states to repeal or amend those laws notwithstanding exclusivity – so long as the Commonwealth had not legislated within that field?

During the debate about the exclusivity of the race power, while the delegates clearly recognised that pre-existing state laws would continue within fields exclusive to the Commonwealth until the Commonwealth chose to legislate, they certainly did not envisage the states having a general continuing capacity to legislate in such fields.[85] But what did they mean, then, by providing in section 108 that, until the Commonwealth should legislate on the topic, pre-existing state laws could be 'repealed or altered' by the state parliaments?[86] Did they mean to refer to state laws on topics falling only within the Commonwealth's concurrent powers, or did they also mean to include the Commonwealth's exclusive heads of power? On this point, there was confusion.[87] Barton, for example, on one hand initially referred to federal legislation on an exclusive topic as displacing state law, but that the power would not become exclusive until the Commonwealth legislated – leaving open the possibility that the states could still legislate in such fields, until the Commonwealth did so.[88] But very soon thereafter he seemed to suggest that while existing state laws would continue to operate, once the Commonwealth's exclusive power to legislate came into force, the states would no longer have the capacity to make new laws.[89] George Turner similarly said on one hand that state laws would lapse from the time when the Commonwealth legislated, but also said that the exclusivity of the power would prevent the states from legislating altogether.[90] For his part, O'Connor pointed out that the clause which became section 108 would continue state laws in operation

---

[85] See e.g. *Convention Debates, Melbourne* (1898), 231 (Kingston, Deakin), 232 (Barton), 233–4 (Turner), 234 (O'Connor), 239–40 (Isaacs), 254–5 (Glynn, Barton), 255 (Reid).

[86] Constitution Bill 1897 (Adelaide), ch. V, cl. 100.

[87] Even Isaacs, when trying to clarify the issues to a perplexed Wise, seemed to confuse the matter. See *Convention Debates, Melbourne* (1898), 239–40 (Wise, Isaacs). As noted earlier, it is difficult to be sure whether the confusion was due to the way in which the race power was defined (viz., 'deemed necessary to make laws') or about the nature of exclusivity itself.

[88] *Ibid.*, 228.     [89] *Ibid.*, 232.     [90] *Ibid.*, 233–4.

until the Commonwealth legislated, but also seemed to think that exclusivity would prevent the states from enacting any new legislation.[91]

The disagreement came to a head when Trenwith argued that exclusivity meant that from the time the Constitution was adopted the states would have absolutely no power to legislate on the topic, only to be countered by Dobson that the precursor of section 108 specifically preserved states' power to alter or repeal their existing laws until the Commonwealth should legislate.[92] Isaacs, in turn, joined with Trenwith on this issue, and Kingston, Barton, Symon and Reid apparently agreed. Symon, however, continued to express a modicum of doubt, a doubt that Glynn seemed to share.[93]

These doubts about the nature of exclusivity and the effect of the clause that became section 108 were compounded, as has been noted, by the way in which the race power turned upon the Commonwealth deeming it necessary to legislate for a particular race.[94] In the event, such doubts, combined with a concern to preserve the powers of the states as much as possible,[95] collaborated to convince the delegates to make the race power concurrent rather than exclusive. And yet, while this clarified the meaning and operation of that specific power, it left the meaning of exclusivity and the effect of what would become section 108 in a state of confusion. As Deakin put it, the provision was not 'exclusive in the strict sense of the term'.[96] State laws would continue to operate until the Commonwealth actually legislated, and section 108 was drafted so as to leave open the argument that the states might even retain the capacity to amend or repeal their own laws until the Commonwealth entered the field.[97]

Section 108 was thus concerned not only with the saving of state laws but also with state power to legislate in fields exclusively vested in the

---

[91] *Ibid.*, 234.     [92] *Ibid.*, 236 (Trenwith, Dobson).

[93] *Ibid.*, 236 (Isaacs), 242 (Isaacs, Barton), 248 (Kingston), 249 (Symon), 254–5 (Glynn, Barton), 255 (Reid).

[94] Thus, while Kingston said that until the Commonwealth legislated state laws would continue and that the states would continue to have power to amend their laws, he explained that this derived not so much from the language of cl. 100 (the precursor of s. 108), but – as Clark had pointed out – from the way in which the race power was dependent upon the Commonwealth deeming a particular race as being apposite for legislation. See *ibid.*, 248. See, likewise, *ibid.*, 253–4 (Downer).

[95] See e.g. *ibid.*, 235–7 (Trenwith), 251 (McMillan), 252 (Cockburn), 253 (Deakin).

[96] *Ibid.*, 231.

[97] Compare *R* v. *Phillips* (1970) 125 CLR 93, 109 (Menzies J), 117–19 (Windeyer J), 133–7 (Gibbs J).

Commonwealth. When understood in this way, it becomes apparent that the displacement of state laws by the laws of the Commonwealth is regulated not only by section 109, but also in part by section 108. The two sections are primarily concerned with the relationship between Commonwealth and state legislation falling, respectively, within the exclusive and the concurrent powers of the Commonwealth.

One must wonder, then, whether the meaning and scope of section 108 might be used to help identify the meaning of 'inconsistency' in section 109. As will be argued in the final chapter, it was in section 108 – and not in section 109 – that the framers deliberately provided for the exclusion of state legislative power in particular 'fields' of operation. If this is so, it casts at least a modicum of doubt upon the proposition that 'inconsistency' in section 109 can or should extend to entire 'fields' regulated by the Commonwealth under the so-called 'covering the field' test of inconsistency first promulgated by Justice Isaacs in 1926.[98]

## The High Court of Australia

Dicey had said that the essence of a federation consists in a division of power between federal and state governments, ultimately to be adjudicated by an independent court of superior jurisdiction. The High Court of Australia was thus, on Dicey's scheme and in the minds of many of the framers, the 'keystone of the federal arch' (as Symon put it), and essential to the very 'fabric' of the Constitution.[99] While it lies beyond the scope of this book to discuss in any detail the debate (such as it was) concerning the constitution, powers and jurisdiction of the High Court (or of the debate over the exclusion of appeals to the Privy Council),[100] some general observations are in order to give an indication of the way in which the framers understood the role of the Court, particularly in the context of federation.

---

[98] *Clyde Engineering Co. Ltd* v. *Cowburn* (1926) 37 CLR 466, 489–90.

[99] See e.g. *Convention Debates, Sydney* (1891), 698 (Clark); *Convention Debates, Adelaide* (1897), 937 (Dobson), 938 (Downer), 940 (Kingston), 950–1 (Symon), 952–3 (Barton), 953 (Higgins), 956 (Downer, Cockburn); *Convention Debates, Melbourne* (1898), 268 (Barton), 271 (Symon), 272 (Kingston), 275 (Downer), 279 (Higgins), 286 (O'Connor), 289 (Isaacs) 291 (Downer). See, generally, Galligan, *Federal Republic*, ch. 7.

[100] On which, compare de Garis, 'Colonial Office'; Howell, 'Chamberlain and the Constitution Bill'; Hirst, *Sentimental Nation*, 228–9, 237–43.

The framers certainly recognised that the High Court, as the ultimate interpreter of the Constitution, would be called upon to resolve jurisdictional and other disputes between the Commonwealth and the states. This much of Dicey's interpretation of federalism – and the aspect with which James Bryce and Edward Freeman certainly agreed – was clearly reflected in the Australian scheme of federation. Barton's historic resolutions, introduced at Adelaide in 1897, included a call for a 'Supreme Federal Court, which shall also be the High Court of Appeal for each colony in the Federation'.[101] By 'Federal Court' he seems to have had in mind a court exercising jurisdiction to resolve disputes between the states in a peaceful, orderly manner, thereby avoiding the threat of secession and open warfare – an 'arbitrament of blood', as he put it.[102] But he also clearly meant, as O'Connor later pointed out, that the Court would resolve disputes between the Commonwealth and the states as to the constitutional validity of both state and federal laws.[103] Thus, in addition to a general appellate jurisdiction from the decisions of the Supreme Courts of the states, provision was made for a special constitutional jurisdiction to be conferred upon the Court by the Federal Parliament, to hear matters, among other things, 'arising under the Constitution, or involving its interpretation'.[104]

The exact foundation of the power of judicial review, under which the High Court has power to pronounce conclusively on the constitutionality of both Commonwealth and state enactments, is one that has manufactured much discussion.[105] There has nevertheless not been much doubt as to its existence, not least because it is quite clear that the framers of the Constitution envisaged the Court having this most important function.[106] Indeed, it was with this in mind that the framers decided not only to establish the High Court directly,[107] but provided for its

---

[101] *Convention Debates, Adelaide* (1897), 17. Similarly, Griffith's resolutions in 1891: *Convention Debates, Sydney* (1891), 23.

[102] *Convention Debates, Adelaide* (1897), 25. See likewise *ibid.*, 129 (Symon).

[103] *Ibid.*, 962 (Barton, referring to O'Connor's observation).

[104] Australian Constitution, s. 76(i).

[105] See James Thomson, 'Constitutional Authority for Judicial Review: A Contribution from the Founders of the Australian Constitution' in Craven, *Convention Debates*, VI.

[106] Brian Galligan, *Politics of the High Court* (1987), ch. 2. See *R* v. *Kirby; Ex parte Boilermakers' Society of Australia* (1956) 94 CLR 254, 267–8.

[107] Australian Constitution, s. 71. See *Hannah* v. *Dalgarno* (1903) 1 CLR 1.

independence from the federal government through guarantees of tenure and salary.[108]

And yet, given the immense powers and responsibilities that would be entrusted to the High Court, there were misgivings. And these misgivings led to proposals, first, to make its composition representative of both the Commonwealth and the states and, second, to make its decisions amenable to popular review. As striking as these suggestions seem to modern ears, the argument over these proposals sheds a great deal of light on the framers' understandings, not only of the High Court and its role, but of the relationship between judicial review and federalism. It is convenient to deal with each of these proposals in turn.

At Melbourne in 1898, Glynn proposed that the High Court should consist of a Chief Justice and, until Parliament otherwise provided, the Chief Justices of the several states.[109] His reasons were complex and varied. One consideration was that of economy. More significantly, though, Glynn argued that even though the state Chief Justices might be subject to certain 'prejudices', constructing a Court that was composed of judges who were representative of each of the states as well as of the Commonwealth would remedy any imbalance.[110] To argue in this way raised questions about the capacity of the Court to adjudicate in federal disputes in a manner that would be independent of the federal executive and non-partisan as between the interests of the Commonwealth and the states. Indeed, up to this point, there had been something of a consensus that the Court would operate as an independent arbiter, applying the Constitution to the cases before it without partiality or political bias. Glynn also supported the establishment of an independent and effective High Court but he recognised, on the American experience, the inherently political nature of judicial appointments as well as of constitutional interpretation.[111] He therefore argued that the Court ought to be representative both of the Commonwealth and the states in a way that would be true to the 'federal' nature of the Constitution as a whole.[112]

A number of delegates – especially Barton, Symon and Wise – resisted Glynn's proposal. They considered, on the contrary, that the High Court

---

[108] Australian Constitution, s. 72. See e.g. *Convention Debates, Adelaide* (1897), 944–5 (Glynn), 946 (Kingston), 947–9 (Isaacs), 950–1 (Symon), 951–3 (Barton).

[109] *Convention Debates, Melbourne* (1898), 265.     [110] *Ibid.*, 266–8.

[111] *Convention Debates, Adelaide* (1897), 944.

[112] *Convention Debates, Melbourne* (1898), 267–8.

ought to have a 'federal' rather than a 'provincial' character, which meant in this case that members of the Court ought to owe their allegiance to the Commonwealth as a whole and not to the states in any parochial sense.[113] Supporting Glynn's proposal, however, Gordon pointed out that one might as well expect a bias in favour of the Commonwealth if the Court were appointed by the federal government, as a bias in favour of the states if state judges were automatically appointed to the High Court.[114] Kingston agreed: the Court would be adjudicating the line between Commonwealth and state power and would be vulnerable to partiality in either direction, depending upon where the power of appointment lay, and so the Court should be representative of both the Commonwealth and the states.[115]

At the heart of Glynn's proposal was an appreciation of the politically significant role that the Court would play.[116] The response to this had to be that the role of the Court was not to protect the 'interests' of the Commonwealth or the states, but rather, as Higgins put it, 'to look at what is just and what is the law' and nothing more. If state judges were appointed to the High Court they would, he argued, tend to feel themselves to be 'delegates' of their colonies, and against this Higgins urged the delegates not to 'drag the equal representation of the states into this matter of the Judiciary'.[117]

Underlying Higgins's response to Glynn's argument was a belief (sincere or otherwise) that the Court would be capable of providing politically impartial adjudication in disputes between the Commonwealth and the states over their respective jurisdictions, powers and immunities. In this way, Higgins again showed himself to be a remarkably consistent follower of Dicey, this time in terms of his conception of the Court's role. But, as has been seen, closely aligned with this idea also lurked a nationalist conception of federalism. Thus, when Kingston replied that to give the federal government ultimate control over the composition of the Court would bias it in favour of the 'whole' as against the 'part', Isaacs replied that to favour the entire Commonwealth was

---

[113] *Convention Debates, Adelaide* (1897), 115–16, 130–1 (Wise), 369 (Barton), 946 (Wise); *Convention Debates, Melbourne* (1898), 269 (Barton), 269 (Symon).
[114] *Convention Debates, Adelaide* (1897), 117.    [115] *Convention Debates, Melbourne* (1898), 272.
[116] *Ibid.*, 273 (Kingston).    [117] *Ibid.*, 279–81.

indeed appropriate, for the Court should owe its allegiance to the good of the whole rather than the partial interests of the states.[118]

It is tempting, therefore, to say that it was a measure of the framers' adherence to the Diceyan theory that, in the event, Glynn's proposal failed by a vote of 29 to 9.[119] But apart from the views of delegates like Isaacs and Higgins, it is unlikely that this entailed any wholesale adoption of the theories of Dicey – or of Burgess, for that matter. Alongside the arguments of Higgins and Isaacs, delegates like Barton and Downer expressed concern that Glynn's proposal would have placed ultimate control over the composition of the High Court into the hands of the Commonwealth Parliament.[120] That Kingston was able to contemplate this with equanimity is perhaps a measure of Kingston's confidence in the capacity of the Senate to represent the interests of the states.[121] Indeed, Barton observed in this connection that even more essential to the federal project was the establishment of a relatively powerful Senate, in which the constituent states were to be equally represented; it was only when the Senate failed to protect the rights of the states, he said, that the High Court would be called upon to adjudicate.[122] Thus, considerations derived from sources other than Dicey's theory seem to have influenced at least some of the framers against Glynn's proposal.

In any case, while a clear majority of delegates opted for a High Court that would owe its composition to the federal government, it can at least be said that all of those who spoke to the debate about Glynn's proposal expected the Court to act as the ultimate arbiter between the Commonwealth and the states, protecting the rights and powers of each in a manner that was as true as could be to the terms and intent of the Constitution. On this much, the framers were generally agreed. And yet, misgivings about the enormous power of the High Court remained. Towards the very end of the debate at Melbourne in 1898, for example, Frederick Holder proposed that, in any case in which the High Court had declared a federal law to be *ultra vires*, the Commonwealth government ought to have power, upon the adoption of a resolution by absolute majorities of both houses of

---

[118] *Ibid.*, 283.    [119] *Ibid.*, 285.

[120] *Ibid.*, 268 (Barton), 274 (Downer). But, of course, the federal government would in any case have had the capacity to stack the Court if it wished, and thus the argument really boiled down to the view that the delegates would have to 'trust' the Commonwealth to act responsibly: *ibid.*, 281 (Higgins).

[121] *Ibid.*, 274.    [122] *Convention Debates, Adelaide* (1897), 962.

Parliament, to refer the matter to a popular referendum of the voters of the Commonwealth and of the states and that, should the referendum approve the federal law in question, the Constitution should be deemed to have been amended to the extent necessary and the law conclusively determined to be *intra vires* from the date of its enactment.[123]

Holder's argument was that although the federal allocation of power between the Commonwealth and the states required the Court to adjudicate in cases of disagreement, the Constitution ought to place the power of final appeal in the hands of the people, and not the Court. Thus, while a strong defender of the rights of the states, Holder was in this respect also a progressive democrat who wished the final say to be reserved to the people of the Commonwealth and the states, voting in referendums. He saw this as a progressive measure because he anticipated the Parliament enacting laws which might possibly involve relatively minor extensions of legislative power – enactments which would not ordinarily warrant putting the matter to referendum unless found unconstitutional and which, in view of their limited nature, would be readily approved by the people. In this way, Holder certainly envisaged the High Court having the final say on whether enactments were constitutional, but he also thought that the people (federally organised) ought to have the final say on what the Constitution actually provided.[124]

In response, while sympathetic to the concerns motivating Holder's proposal, Isaacs objected that Holder's clause would have a retrospective operation, and that this would not be desirable, particularly in the case of criminal statutes.[125] O'Connor also raised the question of what effect a successful referendum under Holder's clause would have on the scope of Commonwealth power in the future: would it empower the Commonwealth to pass a second Act similar to the previous statute?[126] And while O'Connor did not make the point explicitly, this in turn raised the additional issue of how questions of this nature could be decided in the absence of any abstract statement of the scope of the Commonwealth's extended legislative power. To these queries Holder's rather feeble response was to avoid the legal technicalities and simply to urge the convention to affirm the general principle.[127]

Symon also opposed Holder's proposal, but on the ground that, if it was merely an additional means by which the Constitution could be formally

---

[123] *Convention Debates, Melbourne* (1898), 1717–18.    [124] *Ibid.*, 1717–19.
[125] *Ibid.*, 1719, 1727–8.    [126] *Ibid.*, 1719.    [127] *Ibid.*, 1720–1.

amended, then it was unnecessary (that is, the general method of amendment was sufficient), but if it in fact amounted to an appeal to the people from a decision of the High Court, then it actually served to undermine the vital role that the High Court would play as federal arbiter and guardian of the rights of both the states and the Commonwealth.[128] Barton agreed with this, noting that Holder's clause provided that the federal law would be 'deemed' to be *intra vires*, and arguing that this suggested that the High Court's actual decision was to be reversed, an outcome that would weaken the authority of the High Court dramatically.[129]

To these objections, Holder's response was that by referring the matter to the people, the proposal merely reverted to the method by which the Constitution would be formally amended, cutting short any suggestion that the referendum would actually function as a kind of appeal from the High Court's interpretation of the Constitution. Realising, however, that the proposed clause contradicted the amendment clause, he withdrew the amendment.[130]

Given the opposition that it received, Holder's idea was not raised again. As it happened, a proposition motivated by not dissimilar concerns had been earlier raised by Gordon when he moved a clause that would have restricted the right to plead the unconstitutionality of Commonwealth and state laws to the attorneys-general of the states and the Commonwealth respectively. Arguing that individual citizens should not have the right to initiate constitutional challenges to legislation passed through democratic means, Gordon's objective was to preserve, as he put it, a 'remnant of parliamentary sovereignty' as against the powers of the courts to declare legislation unconstitutional.[131] Putting it bluntly, he insisted that 'no individual should be allowed to attack what is the will of the people', and he maintained that 'individual rights should be subordinated to the general rights of the community'.[132] Gordon also said that such a clause would allow the Commonwealth and the states some additional flexibility and relief from what he called 'the extreme rigidity of a written Constitution' by providing an alternative method of constitutional amendment 'by acquiescence'.[133]

What Gordon had in his sights here was Dicey's doctrine of the written constitution, demarcating the boundaries of Commonwealth and state

---

[128] *Ibid.*, 1723–6.  [129] *Ibid.*, 1729–30.  [130] *Ibid.*, 1730–2.  [131] *Ibid.*, 1679–82.
[132] *Ibid.*, 1683, 1690.  [133] *Ibid.*, 1684, 1689.

power, secured through a court of final jurisdiction, exercising judicial review. Gordon wished to moderate Dicey's doctrine in the direction of popular majority rule, at least to some extent. It should come as no surprise, therefore, that the immediate response of a delegate like Wise was to quote Dicey to defend the importance and efficacy of judicial review as a bulwark of federal constitutions.[134] Higgins also joined the fray, arguing that Gordon's proposal would place the rights of individuals in extreme jeopardy.[135] Such was the consensus in favour of judicial review by the High Court that Gordon's proposal was negatived, as Holder's had been, without a division and without an additional voice speaking on its behalf.[136]

In sum, then, there seems to have been little doubt about the important jurisdictional role that the High Court would play. The framers were conscious of this, so much so that some of them wished to see it made 'representative' of both the states and Commonwealth and others wished to render its decisions subject to ultimate review by the people. And while there was disagreement on the best way to secure an impartial resolution of disputes between the Commonwealth and the states, the framers were strongly united on the importance of judicial independence as a means to the end of keeping both the Commonwealth and the states within their respective spheres. As Downer put it, the High Court would exercise 'vast powers of judicial decision' in determining what would be 'the relative functions of the Commonwealth and of the States'. And he seemed to speak for many of the framers when he added that the Court would have:

> the obligation of finding out principles which are in the minds of this Convention in framing this Bill and applying them to cases which have never occurred before, and which are very little thought of by any of us. With this Supreme Court, particularly in the earlier days of the Commonwealth, rests practically the establishment on a permanent basis of the Constitution, because with them we leave it not to merely judicially assert the principles which we have undoubtedly asserted, but with them rests the application of those principles, and the discovery as to where the principles are applicable and where they are not.[137]

Such was Downer's conception, at least, of the role to be played by the High Court. No one ventured to contradict him.

---

[134] *Ibid.*, 1686–7.   [135] *Ibid.*, 1688.   [136] *Ibid.*, 1690.   [137] *Ibid.*, 275.

# 11

## Amendment procedures

We have different peoples here. This is not a homogeneous state.
My people are not necessarily thy people!

John Gordon (1897)

A central motivation of the framers of the Australian Constitution was the hope that federation might 'enlarge the powers of self-government of the people'. But for most of them this did not mean that the 'seat of sovereignty' was now to rest simply with the people of the entire nation, considered as a whole and without regard to the states into which they were organised. Having recently acquired powers of self-governance, the people of the Australian colonies were not about to acquiesce in the loss of those rights to a consolidated national government. The abiding concern remained one of local self-government, which meant the self-government of each state *vis-à-vis* the federation, as well as the self-government of the federation *vis-à-vis* the empire. There was even a hint that it might also mean the self-government of regions and localities within the states.

In strictly legal terms, local self-government did not mean self-constitution or autochthony. The colonies had derived their legal powers from the empire and the federation would come into being by force of an imperial statute. But just as federation represented an opportunity to enlarge Australian powers of local self-government, it also presented an opportunity to move towards a greater degree of constitutional self-determination through the acquisition of local powers of constitutional alteration. Thus, while there was no assertion of autochthony, full provision would be made under section 128 of the Constitution for amendment of the federal Constitution by popular referendum, a section which, as is well known, requires any proposed amendment to the Constitution to be approved by a majority of voters in a majority of states as well as a majority of voters in the nation overall. While this power did not extend, in explicit terms, to the amendment of the Commonwealth of Australia Constitution Act, it was supplemented by the further extraordinary provision that the Commonwealth Parliament, acting with the concurrence of all the state parliaments, could exercise the powers of the imperial Parliament as they related to Australia,[1] as well as a provision which enabled the states to transfer legislative powers to the Commonwealth.[2]

While a power of constitutional amendment represented an opportunity for constitutional self-determination, it also presented a potential challenge to the continuing independence of the states. By federating the states necessarily committed themselves to a joint constitutional destiny determined by a joint decision-making process. An important question, therefore, concerned how that process would be structured. In particular, would it require a majority of states or a national majority of individual voters? If the former, how would the views of the several states be ascertained? Would it be through the state legislatures, through specially elected state conventions or through referendums held in each of the states? And how far would each state retain control over its participation in the federation?

Federation meant both self-rule and shared rule. The Australian framers, as representatives of independent colonies, sought to ensure that the voices of the states in the amending processes would remain distinct and effective: that they would retain a definite share in the determination of their joint constitutional destiny. Understandings of the formative basis of the Constitution and the representative system established thereunder were therefore constantly at play during the debate about the proposed means of altering the Constitution. Indeed, as will be seen, the conventions of 1891 and 1897–8 were differently constituted, and this influenced the amending formulas ultimately adopted. The amending formula represented a commitment to a joint constitutional destiny, to a decision-making rule which presupposed that the states were bound together more tightly than they had been before. The different philosophical and institutional characteristics of the two conventions led to different amending formulas, just as they had led to different representative structures.

Further, it is important to appreciate that the framers never envisaged the formal amendment process in section 128 of the Constitution as

---

[1] Section 51(xxxviii).    [2] Section 51(xxxvii).

bearing full responsibility for the amendment of the Constitution. It has been noted that the framers provided for the exercise of imperial powers by the Commonwealth with the consent of the states concerned as well as the reference by the states of their legislative powers to the Commonwealth. Additionally, on many occasions, the framers deliberately drafted the Constitution so as to make provision 'until parliament otherwise provides' and gave the Commonwealth specific power to legislate in such cases.[3] Although the intention in respect of some of these provisions was that the Federal Parliament would have merely a 'supervisory' role to be exercised only in exceptional cases, the Commonwealth has in fact taken full advantage of them. All of these methods of constitutional alteration were vital aspects of the way in which the framers of the Constitution sought to enlarge the powers of self-government of the Australian people by securing, to the maximum extent possible, a local control over Australia's constitutional destiny.

## Amendment by state conventions

During the conventions of 1891 and 1897–8, the abiding principle was that the federal Constitution would only come into force with the consent of every participant state. The framers were steadily mindful of the formative basis of the Constitution in the unanimous agreement of the states, and of the representative structure of the proposed federation that was emerging. In 1891 the convention delegates had been nominated by the colonial legislatures and it was envisaged that senators under the Constitution would be chosen by the legislatures. The formative basis of the proposed Constitution and the representative institutions to be adopted thereunder shaped the debate about its amendment from an early stage.[4] In Griffith's draft Commonwealth Bill of 1891, the precursor of section 128 drew on the American example. It provided:

> The provisions of this Constitution shall not be altered except in the following manner:–
>
> Any law for the alteration thereof must be passed by an absolute majority of the senate and house of representatives and shall thereupon be submitted to conventions, to be elected by the electors of the several states qualified to vote for the election of members of the

---

[3] Section 51(xxxvi).    [4] See *Convention Debates, Sydney* (1891), 495–9.

house of representatives. The conventions shall be summoned, elected, and held in such manner as the parliament of the commonwealth prescribes by law, and shall, when elected, proceed to vote upon the proposed amendment. And if the proposed amendment is approved by conventions of a majority of states, it shall become law, subject nevertheless to the Queen's power of disallowance. But an amendment by which the proportionate representation of any state in either house of the parliament of the commonwealth is diminished shall not become law without the consent of the convention of that state.[5]

In providing for the alteration of the Constitution by conventions to be held in each of the states, Griffith's clause not only reflected American practice, but reflected the fact that the members of the convention of 1891 were delegates of the colonial parliaments. In these respects, both the formative basis of the Constitution and the proposed amendment clause were based on the assumption that it was appropriate that fundamental constitutional decisions of this kind be made by representative institutions such as legislatures and nominated conventions, rather than through directly elected conventions and popular referendums. In choosing between the various methods that might be used, the framers could not therefore avoid questions relating to the respective strengths and weaknesses of representative and direct democracy. Also at stake were questions concerning the relationship between democracy and federalism, the people of the nation and the peoples of the states.

An important exchange between Munro and Gillies over Griffith's clause illustrates the relationship between the formation of the Constitution and its amendment. Munro, who wanted 'the power of numbers' to have its proper 'weight', objected that this scheme gave the states two opportunities to veto proposed alterations: the requirement of an absolute majority of the Senate (itself chosen by the state legislatures) and the requirement of a majority of conventions popularly elected in each state. By contrast, he said, the 'people as a whole only get the power once', meaning through the House of Representatives.[6] Munro was therefore concerned that should an amendment pass 'inadvertently' through the

---

[5] *Ibid.*, 884. Clark's draft had required the confirmation of two-thirds of the provincial legislatures: Reynolds, 'Clark's American Sympathies', 74.
[6] *Convention Debates, Sydney* (1891), 884, 885.

House, or if the House should fail to represent its constituents properly, the people of the nation as a whole would not be able to prevent alterations passed by a majority of states but opposed by a majority of the people of the nation. Speaking favourably of the Swiss referendum as an alternative means of constitutional alteration, he indicated that he wanted 'a reference to the whole of the people of Australia in one convention'. As he later explained, 'representatives often vote against their promises', and he wanted to 'refer the question to the people!'[7]

Although Gillies's later comments appear to have confused the matter, and he certainly lost the debate in the final analysis, his immediate response to Munro's proposal is instructive:[8] he returned to the formative basis of the Constitution in order to explain its reasoning and to provide a normative and practical context in which to assess it. He pointed out:

> Each state comes into the constitution on a basis contained in the constitution to be agreed to by the various colonies, and subsequently passed by the Imperial Parliament. Any alteration of that constitution may be a very serious thing to one or more of the states, and the states would naturally contend that they had made a bargain, entered into an agreement – no part of that agreement ought to be lightly set aside, and that it ought to require the greatest consideration, not only of the majority of the people as represented in the conventions, but a majority of the state representatives as representatives . . . [N]o state ought to be compelled to submit to an amendment of the constitution when it has not a right to withdraw from that constitution, certainly not to amendments which would really press improperly upon its state rights. The committee felt every precaution ought to be taken that before an amendment . . . was permitted, the sanction should be obtained of a majority of the states which had come into the convention under a certain written agreement . . . .[9]

Gillies's manner of reasoning – to assess questions of constitutional amendment in the light of the formative basis of the Constitution – recurred frequently in the debate. The decisive point at the time, however,

---

[7] *Ibid.*, 884–6, 888.   [8] *Ibid.*, 888–90.
[9] *Ibid.*, 884–5. John Donaldson wanted to 'make the amendment of the constitution as difficult as possible', proposing a two-thirds majority in each House, plus a majority of the states. Donaldson's reasoning was similar to Gillies's, except for the more extreme conclusion: *ibid.*, 887.

was that Griffith accepted Munro's argument. Munro's concern was that where a majority of state conventions was all that was required, the four smaller states could outnumber the two larger states, even though the two larger states contained more people than the smaller states combined. He wanted a balance between small and large states, and a balance between a national majority and a national minority (the smaller states considered 'numerically'). Accepting this, Griffith proposed that the clause be changed to require approval by a majority of state conventions as well as by conventions representing a majority of the people of the Commonwealth. This followed the duality of the Swiss system but used conventions rather than referendums.[10] Griffith's intention was to meet Munro's concern that an amendment 'might be carried against the wishes of a majority of the people of Australia'. Unlike Munro, however, he did not express the problem as one of small versus large states.

Nevertheless, Griffith's solution still enabled a minority of the Australian people to obtain amendments to the Constitution. As Playford explained, if small majorities in a sufficient number of state conventions agreed to a particular change, they might represent states which contained a majority of the Australian population and thus carry the proposed amendment – even though much larger convention majorities in states which represented a minority of the Australian population might oppose the change. As a consequence, a majority of individual convention delegates in the several state conventions might actually oppose the change, but on Griffith's scheme, the proposal would be adopted. Given, moreover, that representatives within the conventions might fail to represent the people properly, it would be far better, he argued, to adopt the Swiss system. A plebiscite would be better calculated to ensure that the 'voice of the states' and the 'voice of the people' was heard.[11] Deakin confessed that he too had been considering this option, and was only concerned that it would make amendment too difficult.[12] For him, the problem was to 'adjust the balance' so that 'state rights' were protected 'in every possible way', but 'equitably' as regards the 'numerical majority'.[13]

---

[10] *Ibid.*, 890–1.   [11] *Ibid.*, 891–2.   [12] *Ibid.*, 888, cf. 891–2.

[13] *Ibid.*, 886. Deakin's felt need to qualify 'majority' by 'numerical' suggests a consciousness that the 'majority' in a federation, meaning 'the major part' or the proper ground of governmental authority, is not necessarily the numerical majority of the nation as a whole.

In this way, Griffith, Playford and Deakin had begun to conceive of a 'national people' interacting with the 'peoples of the States' over fundamental matters such as the alteration of the federal Constitution. Just as McMillan had exhorted the delegates to adopt what he called 'that mental posture in which we might imagine ourselves to be ... when we have really become one people',[14] the delegates were beginning to apprehend the existence of a federation and its relation to the states, and were not simply thinking in terms of the 'pre-federal' phenomenon of large and small colonies. But having conceded that as a matter of principle a majority of the Australian population ought to have a veto on constitutional alterations, Griffith would be hard pressed to deny Playford's argument that the Swiss referendum provided a more effective means of achieving that objective. The use of conventions would have to be defended on other grounds, such as their deliberative virtues.

For his part, Cockburn was not concerned about protecting majorities, for, as he said, they 'will always take care of themselves'. None the less he favoured the referendum because conventions, as James Bryce had argued, were devices by which the American framers had set up a barrier against the popular will. Two things are noticeable about Cockburn's position. First, he did not see any contradiction between rejecting Munro's and Playford's concern for the Australian majority and yet supporting the referendum as a direct expression of the popular will. Second, he linked his support for the referendum to the formative basis of the entire scheme of federation. His language was emphatic and prescient. Just as the people, he said, will insist on the right to 'speak directly' through referendums in the establishment of the Constitution, 'so they will in regard to any alteration of the constitution'.[15] Popular participation in the formation of the Constitution would require popular participation in its amendment. Accordingly, Cockburn proposed that the Constitution only be altered 'by a majority of the people of each state, from whom this constitution originated' and made clear that he meant 'a majority of the majority of the states'.[16]

Gillies and Griffith agreed with Cockburn that the states must agree to federation and therefore must have a distinct say on constitutional amendments, but they rejected the referendum as the appropriate means by which this might to be achieved.[17] Griffith's primary argument was that

[14] *Ibid.*, 266.   [15] *Ibid.*, 893.   [16] *Ibid.*, 894.   [17] *Ibid.*, 892–4.

an elected convention would be conducive to a better informed and more
carefully reasoned public deliberation over any proposed alteration of the
Constitution.[18] In response to this, however, Deakin pointed out that a
definite proposal would have to be submitted to the convention and that
the convention would only have the opportunity of saying 'yes or no'. The
convention would for this reason merely 'introduce between the
amendment of the constitution and the people, a body of men who are
elected to say simply yes or no, and not to exercise their reason in anyway'.
As between Parliament and the people, Deakin thought that 'the power of
general review and of general judgment should be left as far possible with
the people as it is now by our general elections', for 'we are adopting the
principle of the popular vote more and more into the present framework
of representative and responsible government'. Just as Deakin favoured
direct election for both houses of the Federal Parliament, so he preferred
the dual referendum for constitutional amendments.[19]

This last line of argument would be decisive as regards the ultimate
outcome in 1897–8, but it remained unsuccessful in 1891, by a vote of 19
to 9. The delegates of 1891 instead supported the approval of constitutional amendments by a majority of state conventions, as well as,
pursuant to Griffith's amendment, approval by conventions representing
a majority of the people of the Commonwealth.[20] And yet, throughout
the discussion in both 1891 and 1897–8, and on both sides of the debate,
the formative basis of the Constitution and the representative structures
to be adopted thereunder were thought very relevant to the question of
constitutional amendment. Having been nominated by the colonial
parliaments, the delegates of 1891 adopted a system of representation and
a mode of constitutional alteration which reflected their high regard for
the deliberative processes of an elected parliament and an elected convention. Six years later, in 1897–8, a largely directly elected convention,
accepting that the Constitution would be approved by referendums in the
several colonies, adopted instead the Swiss referendum for the alteration
of the Constitution. Yet in both 1891 and 1897–8, the delegates accepted
that constitutional alterations must be approved by both a majority of

---

[18] *Ibid.*, 894. See also *ibid.*, 896 (Baker).    [19] *Ibid.*, 895–6.
[20] *Ibid.*, 897. The 'ayes' included Baker, Clark, Downer, Forrest, Gillies, Griffith, Hackett,
McMillan, Munro and Parkes; the 'noes' included Cockburn, Deakin, Grey, Kingston and
Playford.

states and a majority in the nation as whole. This principle remained constant throughout.

It is also important to note that the earliest drafts of the amending clause made special provision in order to protect the 'proportionate representation' of each state in the Federal Parliament. In Griffith's draft clause, any such change would require the consent of the particular state or states concerned.[21] That it was the representation of each state that was specifically protected is instructive. While other changes to the Constitution, such as the expansion of the legislative powers of the Commonwealth, would necessarily affect the states, the framers were willing to allow these to be altered by a majority of states notwithstanding the opposition of a minority. Indeed, at the 1891 convention, concern was expressed whether this protective provision was sufficiently explicit as regards the 'minimum number of representatives' to which each state would be entitled. Griffith successfully proposed an amendment which extended the protective words to 'the minimum number of representatives of a state in the house of representatives'.[22] This concern to protect the state's representation in the Federal Parliament reinforced, even at this early stage, the delegates' prevailing and abiding interest in the preservation of federal representation for the states as constituent members of the federation.

Apart, however, from the special protection of federal representation, under Griffith's clause constitutional amendments would certainly be 'imposed' on dissenting states. To this extent, the framers clearly had in mind something much more than a mere 'confederation' in which each state fully retained its 'sovereign' capacity to control any future changes to the agreed basis of the arrangement. A new, federal body politic that would possess an independent capacity to alter its constitutional basis was clearly in view. At the same time, however, this capacity specially recognised the initial and ongoing constitutive function of each of the states. Neither a majority of the people of the 'nation' nor majorities in the two houses of the federal legislature could alter the Constitution without the consent of a majority of the states.

The delegates saw all of these features as 'essentials' of federation, both as a matter of theory and as an unavoidable part of the bargain upon which they were prepared to enter the federation. Notably, no firm

[21] *Ibid.*, 884.    [22] *Ibid.*, 897–8.

distinction between the theoretical and pragmatic elements was drawn. The proposed federation of the Australian colonies was instead simply understood to be a kind of compact between peoples in which, as a matter of both normative theory and pragmatic necessities, the terms of federation must be freely agreed. Each constituent state, having the capacity to decide whether to enter the federation, considered itself morally entitled to, and in fact insisted upon, certain rights and protections in terms of its representation within the Federal Parliament, the conferral of only limited powers upon the Commonwealth and, as can now be seen, a specific role in any proposed amendment to the Constitution. In 1897–8 this would be subject to yet further discussion and elaboration.

## Amendment by state referendums

At the convention of 1897–8, argument over the amending formula was again shaped by the formative basis of the Constitution and the representative structures to be adopted thereunder. This time, the direct election of representatives to the Convention and the proposed ratification of the Commonwealth Bill by popular referendum suggested that the Constitution should also be amended by referendum. This, in turn, raised the question of how 'direct democracy' (in the form of the referendum) would be integrated with 'representative democracy' (instituted in the Federal Parliament). If 'the people' would ultimately decide issues of constitutional amendment, what would be the role of Parliament? The method of amendment would somehow have to be accommodated to both the formative basis and representative structures of the proposed Constitution.

### Direct democracy versus representative democracy

It has been seen that the convention of 1897–8 was formed under the auspices of the so-called Corowa plan, pursuant to which the Constitution would be drafted by a popularly elected convention and then submitted to referendums in the several colonies.[23] Writing on the eve of the convention, Garran criticised the method of amendment of the Constitution adopted in 1891 as potentially enabling the minority to

---

[23] See ch. 6.

outvote the majority, and urged the adoption of the Swiss system. He argued:

> We are already committed to the Referendum to decide upon the acceptance of the Constitution in the first instance; and it seems equally applicable to subsequent amendments of the Constitution.[24]

This line of argument proved compelling. In the outcome, the convention of 1897–8 produced a Constitution Bill which reflected the manner of its own appointment as well as the proposed method of ratification under the Corowa plan. Clause 121 (which was to become section 128 of the Constitution) differed from the corresponding provision in the bill of 1891 essentially in the fact that it required the direct approval of amendments by the electors of the several states voting in referendums. Although the idea of a dual majority of the states and of the entire Commonwealth was retained, recourse was had to the people directly, rather than through elected conventions.[25] Indeed, the convention of 1897–8 rejected without debate a proposal by the Legislative Council of New South Wales that the referendum be replaced by a reference to the state parliaments, even though on this proposal a majority of two-thirds in each house in each state would have been required to ratify a proposed alteration.[26]

But while clause 121 introduced an element of 'direct democracy' and rejected the use of elected conventions, the draft nevertheless retained the requirement that any proposed alteration be passed (i.e. initiated) by an absolute majority of both houses of Parliament. It did not provide for popular initiative of proposed alterations, as did the Swiss Constitution,[27] even though the referendum was in other respects modelled on the Swiss precedent. The initiative would remain with the houses of Parliament, and therefore with elected politicians.

Barton understood the provision as operating in the following way. Each house of Parliament would, by absolute majority, pass a law for the alteration of the Constitution. That law, without a referendum, would not have the capacity to alter the Constitution. Because clause 121 declared that the Constitution could not be altered except in accordance

---

[24] Garran, *Coming Commonwealth*, 184; Quick and Garran, *Annotated Constitution*, 150–5, 160–5.

[25] See *Convention Debates, Adelaide* (1897), 1020–1 (Deakin).

[26] *Convention Debates, Melbourne* (1898), 765–6.

[27] Swiss Constitution, 1890 Amendment, Art. 121.

with the manner and form that it prescribed, a mere statute inconsistent with the Constitution would be *ultra vires*; only upon successful passage of the referendum would the Commonwealth law become effective.[28] In this connection, Kingston expressed concern that the provision was expressed negatively, and did not confer any power to alter the Constitution, except by implication. He proposed that an express power be inserted, but this fell on deaf ears, apparently.[29]

Supporters of direct democracy endeavoured to qualify the role of Parliament in a number of respects. At Adelaide in 1897, Deakin sought an amendment which would have reduced the initiation requirement from an absolute to an ordinary majority in the two houses of Parliament.[30] He also suggested, in passing, that a majority of the state parliaments might also have a right to initiate proposals.[31] He was not successful. Similarly, at Melbourne in 1898, the convention debated a proposal of the Legislative Assembly of Victoria, sponsored by Isaacs, that in the event of a difference between the two houses of Parliament, an amendment passed by just one of the houses be referred 'to the direct determination of the people'.[32] The proposal was debated for the better part of an entire day, but was rejected by a vote of 31 to 14.[33] But with the failure of the referendum for the ratification of the Constitution in New South Wales in 1898, the premiers' conference of 1899 agreed to amend the clause. In this way, the Victorian proposal was substantially adopted,[34] subject to the further requirement that the proposed amendment be passed twice in the house supporting the measure – reflecting Premier Reid's opinion on the matter.[35]

The debate concerning the proposals of Isaacs, Deakin and Reid was centrally concerned with the relative merits of representative democracy and direct democracy.[36] One of the persistent themes of this debate again

---

[28] *Convention Debates, Melbourne* (1898), 224.

[29] *Ibid.*, 224. Isaacs understood the introductory words of the provision as negativing the application of the deadlock-breaking mechanism to bills for the alteration of the Constitution: *ibid.*, 728–30. Deakin disagreed; Symon concurred as a matter of interpretation, but desired that they should not apply: *ibid.*, 731–2. See the discussion of s. 57 in ch. 6 above.

[30] *Convention Debates, Adelaide* (1897), 1021.

[31] *Convention Debates, Melbourne* (1898), 730–1.    [32] *Ibid.*, 716.

[33] *Ibid.*, 765; see 759 (Forrest).    [34] Quick and Garran, *Annotated Constitution*, 988.

[35] *Convention Debates, Melbourne* (1898), 736 (Reid and Isaacs), 741 (Higgins).

[36] See *ibid.*, 741 (Higgins), 742 (Cockburn). Interpreting the convention debate on this point is difficult because the side that won at the convention lost at the premiers' conference.

concerned the proposition that such questions should be resolved consistently with the means by which the Constitution would be ratified and
the system of representation adopted thereunder. For example, Glynn
had moved the following complicated alternative:

> A proposed law passed in each of two successive sessions of
> Parliament, with a periodical election of half the Senators between,
> [the proposed law being passed] in the Senate [by] a majority
> including half the members for each state, and in the House of
> Representatives [by] a majority including a third of the members for
> each state . . .[37]

But the proposal failed when Barton pointed out that the principle that
was to apply in the initial ratification of the Constitution ought also to
apply to its alteration:

> Whatever my opinions are of the referendum as an engine in the
> process of ordinary legislation, I have no doubt in my own mind that
> for the making of a Constitution, or for the alteration of that Con-
> stitution, so that it becomes in part different, it is a wise and a right
> thing that there should be a vote of the people taken. For that reason
> I think that an amendment which dispenses with the vote of the
> people in certain cases is not desirable. Granted Parliament has ful-
> filled its functions, and had the requisite majorities, then there ought
> to be in such a case a ratification by a popular vote.[38]

This form of reasoning was often repeated during the debate about the
role of Parliament and the role of the people in the alteration of the
Constitution.[39]

In supporting the Victorian proposal that one of the houses of Parliament should be able to initiate a reference to the people, Isaacs pointed
out that the convention had already accepted the principle that proposed
alterations be ratified by popular referendum. Having accepted this
principle, he argued, there was no point in distinguishing between cases
in which both houses agreed to an alteration and cases where there was a
deadlock between the two houses. If the people (through the dual

---

[37] *Ibid.*, 771, see also 738.    [38] *Ibid.*, 772.

[39] Isaacs used the same argument to reject Glynn's proposal: *ibid.*, 738; cf. 763 (Wise). Reid noted
that the convention of 1897–8 had been, for the most part, directly elected, and that the results
of that process had proved 'decidedly encouraging': *ibid.*, 735.

referendum) were to decide when the two houses agreed, then the people should also decide when the two houses could not agree.[40]

Isaacs's point was that while the convention could have decided that alterations to the Constitution would be passed by representative means, it had in fact decided on popular amendment or direct democracy. The convention had therefore conceded that ultimate recourse must be had to the 'direct voice of the people, both as a population and as states' – rather than what Symon called the 'representative voice of the people'.[41] Isaacs could therefore allege inconsistency on the part of those who objected to the referendum 'on principle', that is, on the ground that it was an appeal from 'wisdom' to 'folly', from 'the well-informed' to 'the ill-informed', and from 'knowledge' to 'ignorance'.[42] They had adopted the referendum instead of ratification by elected conventions or the state parliaments; how could they, in principle, object then to the people deciding when one house affirmed and another house rejected a proposed alteration to the Constitution? If they were to be consistent, they ought to reject the referendum altogether; but the convention had not done this.

Central to Isaacs's argument was the claim that questions of constitutional alteration ought in principle to be decided specifically, without confusion with other issues. By contrast, members of Parliament are elected 'for general purposes', he said, 'not on one particular question but on a variety of questions' and so 'the main issue is frequently obscured'. But constitutional questions are different from ordinary legislation, he maintained: they need to be addressed specifically and they need to be determined directly by the people, rather than by their representatives.[43]

Symon's response to this was that Isaacs was himself inconsistent, in that he did not support the popular initiative (as in Switzerland), but left the initiative to the houses of Parliament. If members of Parliament are only elected for general purposes, he asked, why should they control the initiation of constitutional change?[44] Symon elaborated:

---

[40] *Ibid.*, 716–24.

[41] *Ibid.*, 717, 724. Isaacs defined the issue as: 'who is to decide the question finally? Is it the house that negatives the proposal, or is it the house that affirms the proposal, or is it, as we think, neither of them, but the people themselves?' See *Ibid.*, 717.

[42] *Ibid.*, 718; cf. 761–2 (Reid).    [43] *Ibid.*, 718, 721–2.

[44] *Ibid.*, 724. Isaacs's reply was somewhat unclear: he expressed a willingness to 'hear the argument', it being a 'strong matter for debate'. However, when challenged by Braddon that he was 'abolishing Parliament', Isaacs affirmed the role of the people's agents in Parliament: *ibid.*, 724. Symon might also have objected to Isaacs's seemingly inconsistent affirmation that the

> where is the logic, where is the consistency, of having neither one nor the other, but having a reference through the Parliament, and then if there is disagreement a reference direct to the people?[45]

Symon pointed out that Isaacs had argued for a more democratic Senate, representing the people on a population rather than a state basis and, failing that, a weaker Senate.[46] Such democratic views implied that alterations ought to be ratified solely by a referendum of the people of the Commonwealth as a whole (and not as states).[47] Isaacs was, however, well aware that this was not achievable, given the dominant view that the federation was a compact formed by the peoples of the states, which could only to be altered with their consent. Symon also pointed out that the logic of Isaacs's position suggested that the government ought to have the power to initiate constitutional change, but that Isaacs had drawn back from the suggestion.[48]

In this way, considerations of fundamental principle were controlled by what had already been agreed, by what was practically achievable and by the means of formation and representation that already featured in the Constitution Bill.[49] Isaacs grounded his argument on what had already been conceded, and channelled his arguments of principle within that framework. But Symon was able likewise to point out that while the referendum had been conceded, popular initiative and national major-itarianism had been rejected. Isaacs and Symon argued from basic principles and necessarily linked their conception of representation and representative structures to the question of constitutional alteration. But neither could claim, within the practical constraints of the convention, that what they were specifically proposing was logically consistent in its entirety. For example, delegates might have grave reservations about the referendum, but their arguments could only be directed at the Victorian proposal. Likewise, delegates could not eliminate the referendum, but they could limit the circumstances in which it would come into play.[50]

---

states effectively had the capacity to initiate constitutional change through the Senate: *ibid.*, 730. Isaacs earlier seemed to be positing a discontinuity between the people and their representatives; later he apparently identified their interests.

[45] *Ibid.*, 732.    [46] *Ibid.*, 733.

[47] A proposal which was rejected at the premiers' conference in 1899: Quick and Garran, *Annotated Constitution*, 220.

[48] *Convention Debates, Melbourne* (1898), 732–3.    [49] E.g. *ibid.*, 760 (Reid), 766 (Higgins).

[50] E.g. *ibid.*, 737–9 (Glynn), 745 (O'Connor), 751 (Barton), 753–4 (Solomon), 755 (Howe).

Both sides were also constrained by the need to convince the people of the colonies to ratify the Constitution. This consideration was used particularly to caution against an excessively logical adherence to principle. In this context, the amending clause took on a strategic function: it would be easier to convince the people to ratify the Constitution if they could be assured that they could amend it easily.[51] But because the Constitution was formed on federal lines, it particularly constrained those who wished to see the Constitution take a more national democratic form. Thus, the nationalists could argue that New South Wales or Victoria might refuse to ratify if the Constitution was insufficiently democratic, while their opponents could argue that the four smaller colonies would refuse to join the federation if their rights as states were not safeguarded. Yet the relatively stronger position lay with the proponents of states' rights, because the very mechanism by which the Constitution was to be ratified required the consent of each participant state rather than the consent of a majority of individuals of the nascent Commonwealth.[52]

Higgins sought to avoid the problem posed by Isaacs and Symon by affirming his support for the referendum and the Victorian proposal, yet explaining that he also supported the deliberative processes of Parliament being engaged in the first instance. The 'advantage of representation', he said, was that 'any measure goes through the refining process first in the minds of men who have been elected for that particular responsible purpose'. In turn, the people would have 'the advantage of a long discussion before they commit themselves', that is, 'the advantage of what appears in the newspapers, and of what takes place in Parliament, and on the platform'.[53] O'Connor took a similar approach on the other side of the debate. He likewise emphasised the importance of the calm, deliberative processes of Parliament but, unlike Higgins, vividly contrasted this with the 'popular excitement[s]' that were apt to influence voters at a referendum. Therefore, the referendum 'should be adopted only under very extraordinary and special circumstances' and 'only after the fullest opportunity has been given for the Houses to exercise their opinion and their responsibility'.[54] Cockburn, on the other hand, while 'strongly in

---

[51] E.g. *ibid.*, 724, 757 (Isaacs), 760–1 (Reid), 767–8 (Higgins); but cf. 759–60 (Forrest).

[52] E.g. *ibid.*, 746 (Dobson): 'The Constitution embodies the bargain and the terms upon which the different states will enter the Federation.'

[53] *Ibid.*, 741.     [54] *Ibid.*, 745; cf. 746 (Dobson), 754 (Solomon).

favour of maintaining in every way the States House', perceived no
negative impact on the Senate at all; and the dual referendum would
sufficiently protect the interests of the states, he thought. Accordingly, the
real debate, he said, was between 'those who are in favour of the referendum and those who are altogether opposed to it'.[55] Unlike O'Connor,
Cockburn was firmly in favour of the referendum, so long as it did not
impinge on the rights of the states.

Barton, in typically conciliatory fashion, saw that deliberative processes
were presupposed by both stages of the process (i.e. the reference to
Parliament and to the people), and that both principles were fundamental
to the amendment clause as it stood. But, he continued, the first stage of
the process ought not to be undermined by the Victorian proposal. In fact,
he thought, the referendum, particularly in relation to the resolution of
deadlocks in matters of ordinary legislation, was completely subversive of
the principle of what he called 'responsible government', meaning, in this
particular context, the wider principle of government by representatives
who were responsible, through the Parliament, to the people.[56]

Isaacs responded by insisting upon the democratic credentials of the
referendum: if a deadlock between the two houses could prevent a
proposal going to the people, then Parliament would be made 'the be-all
and end-all' of the Constitution. On the contrary, the progress of
democracy had been one of a shift of power, at first from the Crown to the
Parliament, and lately, from Parliament to the people. 'The Constitution',
he concluded, 'is being made for the people, not the people for the
Constitution.'[57]

Wise's reply to Isaacs's argument was that the amendment clause must
be consistent with the 'design' of the system of representative and
responsible government provided for in the Constitution. The referendum was appropriate to enable the people to determine the terms of the
Constitution, both in its initial ratification and in its amendment, he said,
but the people ought not to be able to 'exercise their will in a manner
inconsistent with the form of government which this Constitution is
designed to provide, that is to say, constitutional government'.[58] In these
ways, and others, the representative structures adopted under the proposed Constitution were connected to the amendment formula.

---

[55] *Ibid.*, 742.    [56] *Ibid.*, 750–2; cf. 756 (Isaacs).    [57] *Ibid.*, 758–9; cf. 761 (Reid).
[58] *Ibid.*, 763, 765.

### Flexibility, rigidity and the rights of the states

Another recurring theme in the debate about the alteration of the Constitution, particularly among the supporters of the Victorian proposal,
was that the Constitution ought not to be overly rigid, as was claimed to
be the case in the United States. In this context, the strategic importance
of the amending clause was repeatedly emphasised. According to Isaacs, a
relatively easy means of constitutional alteration would curtail the control exercised by the 'dead hand of the past', so that the Constitution
might remain relevant and be adapted to the actual conditions of an
evolving society. Otherwise, the Constitution would, as John Burgess had
put it, fall into 'stagnation, retrogression, and revolution'. The reason
why the American Constitution had been overly rigid was that proposed
alterations had to pass both houses, and Burgess had criticised provisions
such as this as 'relics of confederation'.[59] Isaacs's concern was that apart
from the Victorian proposal, the Australian Constitution would not be
much easier to amend than the American. To avoid 'ill-feeling', even
'catastrophe', delegates must 'trust the people'.[60]

Against this view, Barton held that the amending clause, without the
Victorian amendment, was 'very much more easy than the American'.[61]
Cockburn similarly argued that the dual referendum merely required
majorities, whereas the American Constitution required a two-thirds vote
for initiation of proposed changes and the approval of three-quarters of
the state legislatures or state conventions.[62] Howe grounded the relative
'flexibility' of the provision on the fact that the Australian Senate, unlike
the American, would be directly and popularly elected. McMillan,
moreover, thought that the Constitution 'ought to be to a certain extent
conservative in its instincts', and opposed the Victorian proposal for this
reason.[63]

Dicey had said that federalism required a rigid Constitution as a
guarantee of the respective rights of the federal and state governments.[64]
O'Connor made clear that the issue, therefore, was not simply a matter of
rigidity and flexibility, but an issue of states' rights. The Constitution, he

---

[59] See ch. 3.    [60] *Ibid.*, 716, 718–22 (Isaacs), 735 (Reid).    [61] *Ibid.*, 750.
[62] However, Cockburn's support for the referendum and his conviction that the Victorian
    proposal did not strike at the Senate led him to support the proposal: *ibid.*, 742.
[63] *Ibid.*, 754–6 (Howe), 744 (McMillan).    [64] See ch. 3.

said, 'guarantee[d] the maintenance of the rights of every state entering the Federation'. At issue, therefore, were the representative, legislative and territorial rights of the states. It was accordingly important 'that the Constitution [. . .] not be lightly interfered with'. And '[i]t would be a derogation of that principle if we were to place the alteration of the Constitution in the hands of a majority'.[65]

Indeed, one of the most contentious of the underlying issues was whether the Victorian proposal amounted, in the terms of its opponents, to 'an insidious attack on the rights and powers of the Senate', since it enabled the House of Representatives to propose changes to the Constitution and have them ratified by the people in the face of Senate opposition.[66] When advancing this argument, Symon's fundamental concern was a systematic one: that the means of alteration of the Constitution ought not to 'do violence to the framework of the Constitution'.[67] That framework included a representative system which presupposed that 'if the constituents do not approve of the action of their representatives they have a remedy in their own hands'. Therefore, if what was in question was:

> an important fundamental amendment, one in which the constituents of the states would be so greatly interested . . . then they would take care that their representatives . . . who were adverse to that amendment would not be returned again.[68]

Behind this argument was an assumption that both houses were essential to the full and effective representation of the Australian people. Thus, the operation of the amending clause could not be divorced from the nature of the system of representation in the two houses. Other delegates made the same connection.[69] In Braddon's words:

> We have to remember that the great body of the people will be just as much represented in the Senate . . . as in the House of Representatives. Either the Senate or the House of Representatives would yield to its constituents – the whole people of Australia – and this would save any further reference of the matter to the people.[70]

---

[65] *Convention Debates, Melbourne* (1898), 745.

[66] *Ibid.*, 733 (Symon), 725 (Downer), 752 (Solomon), 759 (Forrest).

[67] *Ibid.*, 735; cf. 752–3 (Solomon). Symon foresaw that if submitted to the people by only one of the houses, a proposal would be made into a party political question: *ibid.*, 733.

[68] *Ibid.*, 734.  [69] *Ibid.*, 725 (Downer), 746 (Dobson).  [70] *Ibid.*, 744–5.

Glynn advanced the same argument against the referendum in general: 'it undermines the principle of representative government', he said. But he also accepted that the American Constitution had proved too rigid, and he feared that an activist judiciary would emerge if the Constitution were not sufficiently flexible. He therefore proposed an alternative method of constitutional alteration, requiring special majorities in the two houses, as noted earlier. He understood this suggestion to be consistent with 'the federal idea'.[71] But, as has been seen, Barton and Isaacs rejected the proposal as inconsistent with the means by which the Constitution would be ratified in the first place.

## The people or the peoples?

In this context, debate about the alteration of the Constitution persistently turned on the question of precisely how the alteration of the Constitution would be made consistent with the means by which it would be initially ratified and with the system of representative government adopted thereunder. On both sides the concern was with systemic consistency. Against the wider suspicion that the Victorian proposal was a means of strengthening the House of Representatives at the expense of the Senate, its supporters made two key arguments. First, they emphasised that the referendum would be a dual one, so that the reference would be both to the people of the Commonwealth and to the people of the constituent states.[72] For this reason, although the Senate might (fruitlessly) object to a proposed change, the people of the states would make the ultimate decision, and could defend their own interests. Second, supporters of the Victorian proposal pointed out that either house could initiate changes in the face of opposition by the other house. The proposal was therefore even handed as between the House of Representatives and the Senate.[73]

---

[71] *Ibid.*, 738–40, 771.     [72] *Ibid.*, 722, 756 (Isaacs), 762 (Reid).

[73] *Ibid.*, 717, 721, 756 (Isaacs), 735, 761 (Reid), 740 (Higgins), 748 (Kingston). The opponents of the Victorian proposal doubted whether this would be its practical effect. On the question of the House and the Senate, however, Isaacs gave away a party political concern when he claimed that the two houses would probably be 'distinctly conservative'. However, he retraced his steps: '[b]oth Houses may be democratic; both Houses may be conservative . . . I want . . . to guard against all possible eventualities': *ibid.*, 723–4. Reid and Higgins also emphasised that the proposal was not radical; that it was not a question of liberal or conservative politics: *ibid.*,

Behind these differences was a disagreement as to how 'the people' were to be understood. Isaacs said that where the two houses disagreed, the matter was to be referred directly to 'the people'. If both sides disagreed, 'it show[ed] that one side must be wrong as to what the people wish'.[74] On the other hand, Dobson, like Symon, said that disagreement between the houses indicated that 'the people [were] undecided on the point'.[75] Who, then, were 'the people', and how would their views be expressed? Isaacs was content with an expression of opinion by a majority of the people of the nation and a majority of the people of the states. By giving both houses a veto on constitutional alteration, Dobson (in his case probably with conservative motives) looked for a 'consensus' wider than mere majority vote, indeed a vote which gave weight to the opinion of the people of each state. Given the use of local electorates in the House of Representatives, the clause reinforced the need for widespread consensus among members of both houses, the people of the states and the people of the Commonwealth as a whole.

This difference as to how the people were to be understood was reflected again in a later exchange between Isaacs and Wise. At one point, Wise argued that 'if the people desire an amendment of the Constitution', the people 'will return members disposed to make that amendment', and they will return such members to both houses. Isaacs's reply was that if the people were going to agree in this way, the people needed to have only one house in which to be represented; two houses would be unnecessary. Wise did not accept this inference. Isaacs's presuppositions led him to conceive of the agreement of the people in a homogeneous or majoritarian sense. Wise, however, envisaged such agreement as involving a broader consensus consisting of multiple majorities among the people of the nation and the people organised in states as represented in both houses of Parliament.[76]

## Responsible government

Also lurking behind the issue between the two houses was the question of responsible government. The committee draft as well as the Legislative

---

735–6 (Reid), 740 (Higgins). In this context, Cockburn reiterated his view that the Senate ought not to be understood as a conservative institution: *ibid.*, 742.

[74] *Ibid.*, 723.    [75] *Ibid.*, 723, 746; see also 754 (Solomon).    [76] *Ibid.*, 757.

Council of Victoria proposal used mandatory language in providing for the reference of proposed alterations of the Constitution to referendum and also in providing for the presentation of successful bills to the governor-general for the Queen's assent.[77] Accordingly, the convention debate was generally premised on the assumption that no ministerial discretion would be involved. But, as has been mentioned, while the Victorian proposal failed at the convention, the premiers' conference of 1899 agreed to a similar provision, virtually in the terms of section 128 as it currently stands. The report from the premiers' conference recorded:

> The Premiers agree that, where there is a difference of opinion between the two Houses as to whether the people should have the opportunity of deciding if any alteration should be made in the provisions of the Constitution, one House should not have the power to prevent the question being decided by the people. They have therefore endeavoured to provide a means whereby, after full discussion and reasonable delay, the matter may be referred from either House to the electors.[78]

No mention of ministerial discretion appears here. Section 128 in its final form retains mandatory language with respect to the presentation of a successful bill to the governor-general for assent and with respect to the submission of proposed changes to the electorate consequent on passage through both houses. In the case of passage through only one house, however, the section provides that 'the Governor-General *may* submit the proposed law ... to the electors'.[79]

It would indeed be remarkable that a responsible ministry, having submitted a proposal to the electorate and having obtained the electorate's approval, would refuse to present the approved bill to the governor-general for assent or advise the governor-general to withhold assent.[80] But given the permissive language used where the proposal was passed by only one house, there is a question whether the governor-general, acting on the advice of the cabinet or prime minister, might actually refuse to

---

[77] *Convention Debates, Adelaide* (1897), 1020; *Convention Debates, Melbourne* (1898), 715, 716. See also the committee draft of 1891 and the draft bill of 1891: *Convention Debates, Sydney* (1891), 884, 963–4.

[78] Quick and Garran, *Annotated Constitution*, 220.

[79] Constitution, s. 128, para. 2 (emphasis added).

[80] See Referendum (Machinery Provisions) Act 1984 (Cth).

submit the proposal to the electorate. If such a discretion exists (it has in fact been exercised),[81] the practical effect of the paragraph is that the government – enjoying the confidence of the House of Representatives – is in a position to refuse to submit to the electors proposals which have been passed by the Senate.[82] If this interpretation is correct, the concern of states' righters that responsible government would strengthen the House of Representatives at the expense of the Senate has clearly come to fruition as regards the alteration of the Constitution, at least in this respect.

In any case, given the mandatory language before the convention, the references to the effect of responsible government were generally vague and uncomprehending of the implications of the non-mandatory words of section 128 as finally enacted – just as they were necessarily incapable of apprehending the form which responsible government would take under the federation. Downer did, however, express a suspicion that Isaacs had in view initiatives by the House and not the Senate. Downer pointed out that responsible government implied a corresponding increase in the power of the House of Representatives, and that this would make 'all the difference'.[83] He could not, however, express its full implications because no governmental discretion was specifically in view. Solomon came only a little closer to the point by referring to the executive government's control over finance. Barton, seeking to make a similar observation, could only refer vaguely to the likely effects of responsible government, and apparently assumed that the government would not stand in the way of a decision of the two houses.[84] In this context, Isaacs and Higgins could therefore ask how responsible government had anything to do with the

---

[81] See H. V. Evatt, 'Amending the Constitution' (1937) 1 *Res Judicatae* 264; Geoffrey Sawer, *Australian Federal Politics and Law 1901–1929* (Melbourne University Press, 1972), 124–5; Lumb and Moens, *Annotated Constitution*, 568–9; Harry Evans (ed.), *Odgers' Australian Senate Practice* (11th edn, Australian Government Publishing Service, Canberra, 2004), ch. 12. In fact, Constitution alteration bills passed by both houses in 1965 and 1983 were not submitted to referendum by the governor-general acting on the advice of the government of the day. Given the nature of the debate at the conventions and the mandatory language of the section, this course of proceeding was questionable, and Lumb and Moens suggest that the governor-general may have a 'reserve power' in such cases.

[82] One may speculate as to whether such a refusal might be a ground upon which the Senate might (controversially) choose to refuse to pass supply.

[83] *Convention Debates, Melbourne* (1898), 725–6, noting the coordinate powers of the two houses in Switzerland. See also *ibid.*, 740 (Dobson, in response to Higgins), 762 (Reid).

[84] *Ibid.*, 752 (Solomon), 750–1 (Barton).

question. Higgins emphatically affirmed that responsible government would make no difference because, as in Switzerland, there was 'a duty to have a change of the Constitution remitted to the states and to the people, for acceptance or rejection'.[85]

Deakin, while generally supportive of Isaacs's case, conceded that responsible government made a significant difference. Noticeably, however, he seemed to understand the ministry to be responsible to both houses. In the United States, he argued, there was 'no sufficient provision for obtaining unity of action' between the president, the House of Representatives and the Senate. In Australia, however, 'responsible government . . . will occasion an entire transformation. Both Houses are linked together by the Executive, which is made answerable to Parliament.'[86] As such, proposed alterations will always be in the hands of the ministry, which will be:

> compelled to use of its potencies – and they are many – to bring both Houses into agreement, and by the exercise of its authority secure the submission to the people of a direct issue on this question.[87]

Because Deakin seemed here to envision a ministry responsible to both houses, he expected that responsible government would generally lead to agreement between the houses on proposed alterations to the Constitution. Deakin supported the Victorian amendment because he wanted 'several means' by which the amendment process could be initiated. Yet he attributed less significance to the Victorian proposal than did Isaacs.[88]

In fact, it was only the last delegate to speak who explicitly saw the relevance of responsible government. Wise asked:

> How would this really work in practice? I cannot imagine any Ministry – depending, as a responsible government must depend, on the support of the House of Representatives – allowing an amendment of the Constitution to be moved in the House of Representatives of which they do not approve . . .[89]

Wise himself soon thereafter discounted the significance of this observation, however. In circumstances where one house had passed a bill for the amendment of the Constitution and the other house had failed to pass

[85]  *Ibid.*, 726 (Isaacs), 740–1 (Higgins).     [86]  *Ibid.*, 727.     [87]  *Ibid.*, 727–8.     [88]  *Ibid.*, 730–1.
[89]  *Ibid.*, 763.

it, Wise courageously expected that the ministry would act appropriately. In light of their 'duty' as ministers of the Crown and their 'high notions of self-respect' and 'personal honour', they would, if the amendment were one of importance, put aside their own views and dissolve the two houses, giving the people the opportunity to vote on the matter in a general election. The returned members of Parliament would then reflect the views of the people on the proposed amendment to the Constitution.[90]

## Conclusion

It has been noted that while the Victorian proposal was negatived in the convention, it was effectively reinstated at the premiers' conference. The convention of 1897–8 was part of a formative process controlled by the colonial Enabling Acts. This process involved elements of popular and legislative participation. It was based on the equality of the colonies and it presupposed the principle of unanimity as the basis of federation. The amending formula which emerged from this formative process embodied similar elements: parliamentary initiative, popular participation and equality among the states. From a nationalist perspective, the preference was for national majoritarianism, reflected in the initiative of the 'national house' and a national vote. From a fully compactual perspective, the preference would have been for state or senatorial initiative, a state-by-state vote and the retention of unanimity. The convention mediated between these two positions, settling on initiative by both houses, a dual referendum and majority rule. It was not until the premiers' conference of 1899 that passage through either house was adopted. Notably, under responsible government control over the process would remain with the ministry, enabling it to prevent a Senate proposal from advancing. As heads of responsible ministries in their respective colonies, the premiers agreed to a proposal which, in this way, tended to strengthen the federal ministry.

## Amendment by unanimous consent

Federation meant a commitment on the part of the peoples of the colonies to a joint constitutional destiny. Because federation meant shared

---

[90] *Ibid.*, 763–5.

rule, a role was given to the Senate and to the people of the several states voting in referendums. And because federation also meant a joint destiny, the House of Representatives and the people of the nation as a whole played an important role, and voting was by majority – rather than by unanimity. In these respects, the amendment process showed that something more than a confederation had been formed. A strictly 'compactual' interpretation could not easily explain features such as majority rule and the role of the people of the nation.

Federation also meant self-rule, both for the union and the individual states. Accordingly, unanimity was retained as the decision-making rule for constitutional amendment in two important respects. One of these concerned the special protection of the representative rights of the original states as constituent members of the federation. The other concerned the acquisition of constitutive self-sufficiency *vis-à-vis* the imperial Parliament. The Constitution also provided for an informal means of constitutional alteration through the reference of powers to the Commonwealth by a state or states, and this similarly presupposed the principle that the powers granted to the Commonwealth rested upon the consent of each state. Features such as these cannot easily be accommodated to a nationalist interpretation of Australian federalism.

## *Amendment by the people of each state*

It has been seen that through all of the versions of what was to become section 128, there was a provision which especially protected the representation of each original state in the Federal Parliament. Similarly, all the draft constitutions contained provisions which protected the territorial integrity of each state.[91] In sum, these provisions required the consent of a state before any change could be made to its representation in Parliament, its limits or the extent of its territory.

In 1891 the provision that became section 128 took the form of a requirement that the convention of the state concerned must 'consent' to the proposed alteration to its representation. The provisions that became sections 123 and 124 similarly required that the parliament of the state must 'consent' to and agree upon the 'terms and conditions' of any change to its limits or territory. In 1897, however, the section 128 provision

---

[91] I.e. the clauses that would become ss. 111, 123 and 124, discussed in ch. 9.

became a requirement that the 'electors of the State' must 'consent' and in 1898 this was altered to the requirement that 'the majority of electors voting in that state [must] approve the proposed law'.[92] At the premiers' conference of 1899, it was agreed to accord 'the fullest protection' to the states so that 'no alteration of territory should be made without the consent of the people as well as of the Parliament of the State affected' and an amendment to section 123 requiring the 'approval of the majority of electors' of the state was made.[93] These special provisions reflected the general shift in tenor, between 1891 and 1897–8, from representative to direct democracy. They also affirmed, as has been seen, the principle that the agreement of the states, as parties to the federal compact, would be required for fundamental changes to their territory as well.[94]

The scope of protection provided by these mechanisms was also progressively expanded. In Griffith's draft bill of 1891, the protection extended to 'the proportionate representation of any State in either House of the Parliament of the Commonwealth'. During the 1891 convention, the protection was extended to include 'the minimum number of representatives of a State in the House of Representatives'. Barton's draft bill of 1897 maintained this wording and it was approved by the convention of 1897–8 with only minor, verbal amendments. What became the fifth paragraph of section 128 was likewise agreed to at Melbourne in 1898 with relatively little debate and by a very strong majority, suggesting a broad consensus regarding its importance. Finally, the concern to accord the 'fullest protection' to the states agreed to at the premiers' conference of 1899 led to the insertion of the words 'or increasing, diminishing, or otherwise altering the limits of the State, or in any manner affecting the provisions of the Constitution in relation thereto' in section 128.[95]

Higgins objected that the fifth paragraph 'made absolutely rigid for all time the equal representation of the states' and he sought to limit its 'life' to ten or, alternatively, twenty years. He argued that making such a provision 'unchangeable' was to assume a superior wisdom in the present generation.[96] The issue here for Higgins was intergenerational parity.

---

[92] See *Convention Debates, Sydney* (1891), 884, 964; *Convention Debates, Adelaide* (1897), 1020, 1243; *Convention Debates, Melbourne* (1898), 715, 2543; Constitution, s. 128, para. 5.

[93] See Quick and Garran, *Annotated Constitution*, 216–20, 974–5; *Agreement of the Premiers*, Baker Papers; cf. *Convention Debates, Sydney* (1891), 897–8 (Griffith).

[94] See ch. 9.     [95] See Quick and Garran, *Annotated Constitution*, 216–20, 998.

[96] *Convention Debates, Melbourne* (1898), 766–9. See also Higgins, *Essays and Addresses*, 6–12, 20.

Behind the objection lay a commitment to the idea that, at least within Australia, the highest authority lying behind the Constitution was the people of the nation as a whole. Burgess had likewise said that the similar provision in Article V of the United States Constitution was a 'relic of confederation', and Quick and Garran seemed to agree.[97]

The responses to Higgins's attack on the fifth paragraph shed light on the contemporary significance of the provision. For most of the framers the issue was in fact inter-colonial, rather than intergenerational, parity. Frederick Holder's appeal, therefore, was to the formative basis of the Constitution: 'We do not assume any special wisdom; we regard this as one of the terms of a compact.' And even Reid accepted the fifth paragraph as a necessity for acquiring the agreement of the people of the colonies.[98]

The significance accorded to these protections by the convention as a whole is reflected in the vote of 34 to 2 against Higgins's proposal. Burgess could argue that such provisions were relics of confederation, but evidently a majority of the Australian framers regarded them as essential to federation. As Quick and Garran later observed:

> the people of the Commonwealth, in the majority of States, will not feel inclined to interfere with the principles of local liberty, local self-government, State autonomy, and State individuality which pervade the Constitution. They will recoil from an Imperial policy of consolidation and centralization, which would swallow up, absorb, and obliterate the States.[99]

### Amendment by the legislature of each state

Two further provisions remain to be considered. The first is section 51 (xxxvii) of the Constitution. It empowers the Commonwealth Parliament to legislate with respect to matters 'referred' to it by the state parliaments, but provides that such laws shall apply only in those States which refer the power, or which 'afterwards adopt the law'. The provision is one of a

---

[97] See ch. 3; Quick and Garran, *Annotated Constitution*, 991–2.
[98] *Convention Debates, Melbourne* (1898), 769 (Holder), 770 (Reid). Gordon also pointed out that the imperial Parliament could always intervene: *ibid.*, 769. Its continuing sovereignty meant that it legally could both create and amend the Constitution.
[99] Quick and Garran, *Annotated Constitution*, 992.

number which empower the Commonwealth to legislate 'with the consent' of a state.[100] Based on a power given to the Federal Council, as well as the Privy Council proposal of 1849,[101] the provision reflected the 'confederal' nature of the Federal Council as 'the mere creature of the colonies'. The power was only exercisable in respect of those states that requested it and, if a law enacted under the provision was to be applied to the entire Commonwealth, the states would have to concur in its exercise unanimously.

The various precursors to section 51(xxxvii) passed without discussion through the first and second conventions until the Melbourne session of 1898.[102] In Deakin's view, the power was an important and necessary one, since it enabled federal action by agreement among the states without the need for formal amendment to the Constitution.[103] Quick, however, cautioned that the provision effectively added a 'free and easy method of amending' the Constitution without reference to the people of the various states as was required for constitutional amendment under section 128. He therefore objected to the provision as a 'mischievous' means of avoiding the referendum requirement of section 128, and altering the Constitution on an *ad hoc* basis.[104] As Symon put it, the provision would enable the Parliaments to amend the Constitution 'upon the hazard of the moment'. Such a power, he said, was 'inconsistent . . . with the foundation of our Federal Government' – no matter how appropriate it may have been for the Federal Council.[105] Glynn apparently agreed, and proposed that references of jurisdiction under the provision be limited to 'specific points', rather than 'general powers'. He, like Quick, feared that it enabled the state parliaments to 'give away' the 'sovereign powers' of the people of the state without the consent of the people.[106]

---

[100] See, for example, s. 51(xxxiii), (xxxiv) of the Constitution, dealing with the acquisition of state railways and railway construction in any state.

[101] Discussed in ch. 5. See *Convention Debates, Melbourne* (1898), 215 (Deakin); Quick and Garran, *Annotated Constitution*, 648–9.

[102] *Convention Debates, Melbourne* (1898), 215–25.  [103] *Ibid.*, 217.

[104] *Ibid.*, 217–18. He called it 'the states' Constitution'.

[105] *Ibid.*, 219; see also 725 (Downer). Symon thought that the provision that was to become s. 51 (xxxviii) (discussed below) would meet the case envisaged by this precursor to s. 51(xxxvii), despite the exclusive terms of s. 128. Deakin, however, pointed out that the two provisions were concerned with very different things: *ibid.*, 220.

[106] *Ibid.*, 225

Although the characterisation of the power as an *ad hoc* means of amending the Constitution was to a degree hyperbolic, the power was indeed inconsistent with the exclusivity of section 128, with its principles of parliamentary initiative, majority rule and dual referendums. But to criticise the provision on this basis is to overlook the way in which it is consistent with the formative basis of the federation. Just as the federation depended on Enabling Acts passed by each of the colonial legislatures, so section 51(xxxvii) required the consent of the state legislatures. Moreover, just as the federation was formed upon the consent of every colony that agreed to join, so section 51(xxxvii) would only apply to those states which 'referred' the power or 'adopted' the federal law in question.

Notably, Downer thought that the provision laid down a 'comparatively easy method' – neither too easy nor too difficult – of enabling a few states to refer powers to the Commonwealth. Implicit in his argument was an answer to Symon: the provision was consistent with the 'foundation' of the Constitution because the whole idea of the Constitution was to define the powers of the Commonwealth and 'leave everything else to the states'. In turn, a few states, exercising their 'formative' powers, might consider that additional matters or specific issues need to be referred to the Commonwealth. In this context, Downer seemed to imply: why is it improper to allow the states to make such a reference?[107]

It is significant that Isaacs supported the provision. For him, it was a means of referring power to the federation without the difficulties of formal amendment. In particular, it was a means of overcoming the extra-territorial fetter that limited the legislative powers of the colonial parliaments. If the colonies had been sovereign and independent states in the fullest sense, there would have been no need for section 51(xxxvii) in the first place; they could at any time have referred the powers, without the need for imperial warrant through the Constitution Act. Despite his nationalism, therefore, Isaacs accepted that the states would continue to have the capacity to agree to refer additional matters to the Federal Parliament.[108] The provision reflected an important tension: the colonies were not 'sovereign states', yet they were self-governing bodies politic.

Probably the same considerations led Barton to understand the provision to be an 'enlargement' of the legislative powers of the states, and a power that ought to be conferred upon them 'in the spirit of

---

[107] *Ibid.*, 220–1.    [108] *Ibid.*, 222.

democracy'.[109] In this context, section 51(xxxvii) not only illustrated an important point of continuity between the formation of the Constitution and its amendment, it was a further means by which the various imperial fetters on the powers of the colonies were removed and their capacities of 'local self-government' expanded.

### Amendment by the consent of all of the state legislatures

The other so-called 'drag-net' provision, section 51(xxxviii), provides for the exercise of imperial powers by the Commonwealth and the states, acting in concert. Under the section, the Commonwealth may make laws with respect to:

> The exercise within the Commonwealth, at the request or with the concurrence of the Parliaments of all the States directly concerned, of any power which can at the establishment of this Constitution be exercised only by the Parliament of the United Kingdom or by the Federal Council of Australasia.

In 1891, Griffith was the central exponent of the clause that would become section 51(xxxviii). His comments were remarkable. Griffith believed that an adequate federation would necessarily bring to an end the need to turn to the United Kingdom for fundamental constitutional change – for both the federation and the states. In this connection, he expressed support for the 'American theory' that 'all constitutions are the act of the individual members of the community, and that they delegate their power to the legislature, and that legislature can only work within the authority given to it'. Griffith contrasted this with the 'English theory' of a 'sovereign parliament' which 'can do what it likes', 'no matter how it originated'. He acknowledged that the English approach had in fact been adopted in the Australian colonies, for the Parliaments had full power to alter their own constitutions under the Colonial Laws Validity Act 1865 (UK). He went on to explain that while 'each colony has the power within its own constitution to change that constitution', the colonies 'cannot change [their constitutions] by throwing off their allegiance to the

---

[109] *Ibid.*, 223–4. To the objection that the provision would enable an evasion of the referendum, he argued that the states did not as yet provide for referendums themselves but rather assumed that the people 'speak' through laws passed by majorities of their two houses of Parliament.

Crown; and they cannot get rid of her Majesty's representative. That would be a revolutionary act.' He nevertheless held that 'in the abstract' the American theory was 'right' and expected that the states would soon adopt the American scheme of an elected constitutional convention.[110]

Alteration of the state constitutions was, however, 'only remotely connected' with the work of drafting a federal Constitution. Griffith thus did not think it appropriate at the time to interfere with or to dictate any particular method for the alteration of the state constitutions.[111] In light of practical realities and the limited agenda of the federal convention, the achievable goal was to make the powers of the imperial Parliament available at a local, Australian level. For the present, he was content to support a provision that, at the least, transferred the existing capacities of the imperial Parliament to Australian shores – organised on a basis consistent with federalism and local self-governance. The Federal Parliament would have power, at a minimum, to undertake any constitutional changes requested by a state which at the time lay beyond the legal capacities of the colonial parliaments – the legal 'ratification' of such alterations, as he put it. But it was not intended that the Commonwealth would 'interfere' with the state legislatures. As he summarised his position:

> after the federal parliament is established anything which the legislatures of Australia want done in the way of legislation should be done within Australia, and the parliament of the commonwealth should have that power. It is not proposed by this provision to enable the parliament of the commonwealth to interfere with the state legislatures; but only, when the state legislatures agree in requesting such legislation, to pass it, so that there shall be no longer any necessity to have recourse to a parliament beyond our shores . . .[112]

---

[110] *Convention Debates, Sydney* (1891), 490. Griffith thought that such an alteration would be a 'revolutionary' act, yet appeared to support the power. This suggests that he probably had in mind a 'lawful evolution' or 'devolution' of authority from the imperial Parliament to the Australian federal and state parliaments.

[111] *Ibid.*, 491. Compare the delegates' attitude to s. 106, discussed in ch. 9. Griffith did hold that the federal Constitution 'ought to contain provisions prohibiting any state from changing its constitution under its existing powers in particular directions . . . for instance, as to make it unfit to be a member of the commonwealth of states'. This was probably inspired by the guarantee of a 'republican' form of government guarantee in the US Constitution, Art. IV, s. 4, cl. 1.

[112] *Ibid.*, 524; cf. 490.

During debate about the clause, Baker pointedly asked whether it was intended that the provision would remove the power of the imperial Parliament to legislate for Australia. Griffith shortly answered that the provision merely granted the Commonwealth the 'same powers' as that Parliament, 'in respect of certain matters'.[113] Brief as this exchange was – there was little specific discussion of what those 'matters' were – it serves to underscore the strategic role of section 51(xxxviii). If it did not 'take away' imperial powers, it certainly reproduced them.

Isaacs was later to express concern at the width of the power thus granted to the Commonwealth. Not that he had any objection to seeing 'the largest of powers given to the Federal Parliament', but he wondered whether the imperial Parliament was likely to assent to such a wide grant. '[I]t is rather a long way', he said, 'to ask the Imperial Legislature, so to speak, to place all its powers in the hands of the Federal Legislature.'[114] The provision was nevertheless agreed to in both conventions without further debate.[115]

Section 51(xxxviii) was therefore an important aspect of the movement in Australia towards local self-government and constitutional self-determination. It anticipated an emergent convention within the British empire which would culminate in the Balfour Report of 1926 and the Statute of Westminster 1931 (UK). The 1926 report stated:

> we refer to the group of self-governing communities composed of Great Britain and the Dominions. Their position and mutual relation may be readily defined. *They are autonomous Communities within the British Empire, equal in status, in no way subordinate one to another in any aspect of their domestic or external affairs, though united by a common allegiance to the Crown, and freely associated as members of the British Commonwealth of Nations.*[116]

Such principles of self-governance, autonomy and equality were reflected in different ways in both section 51 (xxxviii) of the Constitution and what

---

[113] *Ibid.*, 698.   [114] *Convention Debates, Melbourne* (1898), 226.

[115] Section 51(xxxviii) was one of the provisions about which the imperial Crown Law Office expressed concern, because it could be doubted that the Colonial Laws Validity Act 1865 (UK) would apply to laws of the Commonwealth Parliament: Quick and Garran, *Annotated Constitution*, 232, 350–2.

[116] Inter-Imperial Relations Committee, Imperial Conference 1926, *Report, Proceedings and Memoranda* (1926), 2.

became section 4 of the Statute of Westminster. Within Australia, under section 51 (xxxviii), federal legislation would extend to a state only if that state had requested and concurred in that result. Within the empire, under section 4, imperial legislation would only apply to a dominion upon its request and with its consent. When read outside of this context, and apart from the need for state concurrence, section 51 (xxxviii) seems to be a nationalising provision – it confers imperial powers upon the Commonwealth Parliament. But when read within its context, it was in fact a 'localising' and 'federalising' provision which shifted 'ultimate control' from the imperial Parliament to the Commonwealth, and was intended to leave open the full adoption of 'the American theory' of state autonomy and autochthony in Australia over the long term. As Clark later observed, as members of the drafting sub-committee of the Constitutional Committee of the 1891 convention, Griffith, Kingston and himself:

> knew what they were doing. They went to work with their eyes open; and he claimed part of the responsibility, or glory, or whatever they might call it. They told the Convention what they were doing, and it agreed with them. He had quoted Sir Samuel Griffith's words at the Convention, and surely they did not shirk the question. They did not hold anything back. They faced the position that they were going in for absolute legislative independence for Australia as far as it could possibly exist consistent with the power of the Imperial Parliament to legislate for the whole Empire when it chose.[117]

## Conclusion

The agreement of the peoples of the states to be formed into a federal commonwealth under the Constitution represented a remarkable relinquishment of control over their own constitutional destinies. Each colony agreed to join a federation the terms of which could be altered by a majority of states and thus against the wishes of an individual state. Clearly, the motive in federating and relinquishing such rights was to form a new polity having a life and destiny of its own, a destiny beyond the control of any one of its constituent elements. And yet that destiny

---

[117] Reynolds, 'Clark's American Sympathies', 66. See Neasey, 'Clark and Australian Federation', 15; Williams, 'Clark and our Republican Tradition'.

was a joint one. If the people of each colony relinquished any absolute claim to autonomy, they at the same time preserved to themselves an equal share in the determination of that destiny through the dual referendum provided for in section 128.

In this context, sections 51(xxxvii) and (xxxviii) and the fifth paragraph of section 128 are more important than is sometimes recognised, for here the constitutional destiny of the federation remained, in certain vital although limited respects, in the hands of each constituent state considered individually. In this sense, while the act of federation called a new and independent body politic into being, the federation continued in specific respects to recognise the individuality and autonomy of the several states. In this sense, the principles of shared rule and self-rule are presupposed by the amending processes: shared rule is embodied in the normal process envisaged by section 128, self-rule in the special provisions of the fifth paragraph and section 51 (xxxvii) and (xxxviii).

This casts a distinct light on the concern that the Constitution is difficult to amend and ought not to be shackled by the 'dead hand' of the past. Where constitutions are entrenched by way of special majorities, say of 66 or 75 per cent, the 'dead hand' argument has particular force. Where, however, the amending formula adopts a simple majority as its decision-making rule, but requires a majority of voters in a majority of states, or even a majority of voters in every state, the 'dead hand' objection only has force if it is presupposed that the only legitimate locus of authority is the people of the federation as a whole. But if it is understood that the ultimate loci of legitimate authority are the peoples of the several original states, the anomaly lies with an amending formula that merely requires a simple 'national' majority. In such cases, the 'national' majority is in the position to force its will on a relevantly independent body politic against the will of a majority of its own members. The question, therefore, is ultimately one of 'size' and 'boundaries'. Where is the locus of ultimate authority: in the federation, or in the states, or both?

Under the influence of nationalist and compactual theories which presuppose the necessity of a unitary locus of sovereignty, many have held that in federal systems ultimate sovereignty must somehow be vested in either the constituent states or in the people of the federation as a whole. Systems which exhibit both characteristics are 'monstrosities', it is said, and provisions which require the consent of individual states are to

be disregarded as 'relics of confederation'.[118] Considerations such as
these led Isaacs and Higgins to seek to moderate the amending formula in
the direction of national democracy. Higgins thought that 'just as we go
by a majority of heads in Victoria for Victorian purposes, we must go by
a majority of heads in Australia for Australian purposes'. But he was
consistently met with the kind of response given by Holder, who spoke
for most, when he simply replied that 'we regard this as one of the terms
of a compact'.[119]

Two very different conceptions of the formative basis of the Constitution were at work here; and these conceptions dictated contradictory
approaches to the amending processes adopted in the Constitution. Is the
federation based on a 'compact' deriving from constituent states or is it
based on a 'constitution' deriving from some ultimate locus of sovereignty, whether that be the imperial Parliament or the people of the
nation as a whole? The framers of the Australian Constitution, operating
within a specific institutional and philosophical context, held that the
terms of the federation did indeed derive from the agreement of the
peoples of the several constituent states, but they also understood that
through such agreement the states had consented to being integrated into
a new body politic and a joint constitutional destiny. However, this
compacting agreement did not involve a complete absorption of the
states into a consolidated nation-state but, instead, the formation of a
'federal commonwealth' in which the peoples of each state would retain a
distinct identity and constitutional status. In this way, the formative basis
of the Australian Constitution dictated many of the specific terms
therein, not only in terms of the representative structures and the specific,
limited legislative powers that were conferred on the Commonwealth, but
also in respect of the various ways in which the Constitution provided for
its own amendment.

---

[118] See Burgess, *Political Science*, I, 90, 107, 142–5, 151–4; II, 49, 115; Quick and Garran,
*Annotated Constitution*, 415–16.

[119] *Convention Debates, Melbourne* (1898), 768. It is significant that Higgins had earlier accepted
that, if 'the states, and the people of the states, are coming into a deed of partnership, that
deed of partnership . . . ought not to be altered without at least the consent of a majority of
the states': *Convention Debates, Sydney* (1897), 684. See, however, H. B. Higgins, 'The Rigid
Constitution' (1905) 20 *Political Science Quarterly* 203, where Higgins completely fails to
acknowledge, let alone address, this contrary line of argument.

# PART IV

## Conclusions

# 12

# A federal commonwealth

A federal constitution is the last and final product of political intellect and constructive ingenuity; it represents the highest development of the possibilities of self-government among peoples scattered over a large area. To frame such a constitution is a great task for any body of men.

Alfred Deakin (1898)

Democracy demanded that government should be carried on within the sight and hearing of the people. Any form of union adopted must have as its object the safeguarding and not the supplanting of the right to local self-government. It must come not to destroy but to fulfill their autonomy. Fortunately this was just what federation was intended to effect; it was a device by which the individual existence of a State could be ensured without the surrender of sovereign powers of self-control.

John Cockburn (1901)

## Federative logic

The Commonwealth of Australia is in substance an integrative federation in the sense that the terms of the Australian Constitution were almost wholly determined by the representatives and electors of several mutually independent bodies politic, the self-governing colonies of Australia. As such, the Australian Constitution presents a particular kind of federating logic which makes it comparable, in varying degrees, with other covenanted associations, particularly other integrative federations, such as Switzerland and the United States, the two decisive models for the Australian framers. Since the terms and structure of the Australian Constitution were determined in this manner, it seems reasonable to suppose that a theory of the Constitution will not effectively account for the textual detail and structural relationships contained therein unless it interprets these in the light of the federating logic that shaped the deliberations of the 1890s.

The particular kind of federating logic that prevailed when the Australian Constitution was drafted was informed by both its institutional and philosophical context. The federation of the Australian colonies was understood to be part of a movement from the autocratic, unitary and subordinate patterns of government characteristic of the convict era, towards a scheme of representative government, local government and constitutional self-determination. The central thrust of that movement was an 'enlargement' of 'the powers of self-government of the people'.[1] But this did not mean that sovereignty was now to rest with the people of the entire nation without regard to the states into which they were organised. Having recently acquired powers of local self-governance, the peoples of the colonies were not about to acquiesce in the loss of those rights to a consolidated national government. Instead, the objective was to enlarge the powers of self-government of each colony, and to participate in the self-governing powers of the Commonwealth within the British empire. While self-constituting autochthony was not secured, federation was a means of enhancing the constitutional self-determination and self-government of the colonies.

The basic assumption of Australian federation, therefore, was the original, mutual independence of the colonies. As a consequence, federation could only be founded on the unanimous agreement of the constituent states. The formative process by which the federal Constitution came into being thus reflected the fundamental principle of unanimity in its structuring, drafting and ratifying dimensions. The calling of the federal conventions, the choice of delegates and the inter-colonial agreement embodied in the Commonwealth Bill were predicated on the consent of each participant colony, its representatives and its people. Only at the point of deliberation within the conventions did something other than unanimity prevail: delegates did not vote on instructions or as blocs, and voting was by majority. Yet even in this respect, the deliberative processes were under the ultimate control of the several colonial legislatures. The colonies were equally represented at the conventions and the Commonwealth Bill ultimately faced the test of a

---

[1] *Convention Debates, Adelaide* (1897), 17 (Barton's resolutions).

plebiscite in each colony. Only the colonies that agreed to federate would be included in and bound by the proposed federal Constitution.

This formative context operated as a presupposition in the deliberations of the framers so that the structure of the formative process shaped the particular representative structures, configurations of power and amending formulas that were ultimately adopted. In the first place, the colonial legislatures controlled the process, and this orientation to parliamentary deliberation was reflected in several ways. Thus, even though there were submissions to the contrary, the Constitution provided for a federal legislature unchecked in its ordinary law-making function by a popular or direct initiative or veto by way of referendum.[2]

Similarly, the framers rejected the referendum as a means of resolving deadlocks between the houses of Parliament.[3] They looked to the deliberative processes of the two houses and the pressure of public opinion to resolve disputed issues; and they consciously chose not to insert an extended catalogue of individual rights into the Constitution.[4] The framers also required parliamentary initiative for constitutional amendments, and they provided that the Federal Parliament would have power to exercise the powers of the imperial Parliament within Australia with the consent of the legislatures of the states concerned.[5]

Second, in each of the colonies a system of responsible government was in operation. The conventions of responsible government effectively focus authority on a small group of ministers of the Crown, responsible to Parliament. This orientation to cabinet government was generally reflected in the hesitating adoption of responsible government at a federal level, as well as the movement toward a greater degree of national majority rule. In particular, it was decided at the convention of 1897–8 that federal ministers would be required to hold seats in Parliament.[6] However, responsible government had to be adapted to federalism. Traditionally conceived, responsible government meant responsibility to the lower, popular house of Parliament, an accountability secured by the power over government finance enjoyed by that house. But for the framers, federalism meant the equal representation of the states in a powerful Senate.[7] The question, therefore, was how federalism and

---

[2] Constitution, ss. 51, 52.    [3] Constitution, s. 57.
[4] *Convention Debates, Melbourne* (1898), 688–90; La Nauze, *Making of the Constitution*, 227, 229.
[5] Constitution, ss. 51(xxxviii), 128.    [6] Constitution, s. 64.    [7] Constitution, s. 7.

responsible government could be harmonised. At the convention of 1891 the uneasy compromise was that the Senate would have power to reject (but not initiate or amend) money bills. Despite the move towards responsible government in the bill of 1897–8, the compromise of 1891 was ultimately retained, leaving open the possibility that a federal ministry could be called to account in the Senate as well as in the House.[8]

Nevertheless, delegates to the convention of 1897–8 were directly elected and the Commonwealth Bill ultimately faced popular referendums held in each of the colonies. This orientation to popular ratification in the formative process was reflected in the democratic features of the House of Representatives, the direct election of senators, the relatively greater powers and larger size of the House of Representatives, and in the dual referendum required for the amendment of the Constitution.[9] Once again, however, there were limits to the extent to which the popular principle was embodied in the Constitution. Proposals to elect the executive directly and to resolve deadlocks between the houses by referendum were decisively rejected in favour of parliamentary responsible government, the double dissolution and the joint sitting.[10]

The ultimate ground of federation was unanimous agreement among the original states, considered as equals. The idea that the federation derived its origin from the states was expressed in the 'delegation' or 'surrender' of limited powers to the Commonwealth, with the 'continuing' states retaining to themselves all powers not specifically transferred.[11] Equality between the states was most clearly reflected in the equal representation of each state in the Senate and the guaranteed minimum representation of each state in the House of Representatives.[12] The foundation of the federation in the unanimous agreement of every state was reflected in the control each state retained over any proposed changes to its boundaries or its representation in the Federal Parliament.[13] Power was conferred on the Federal Parliament to exercise the powers of the imperial Parliament, but the principle of unanimity also meant that the Federal Parliament would not be able to exercise this power without the consent of the legislature of any state affected thereby.[14] Moreover, particular colonies were potentially in a position to

---

[8] Constitution, s. 53.    [9] Constitution, ss. 7, 24, 128.    [10] Constitution, ss. 57, 61, 64.
[11] Constitution, ss. 51, 52, 106–9.    [12] Constitution, ss. 7, 24.    [13] Constitution, s. 128.
[14] Constitution, s. 51(xxxviii).

negotiate special arrangements or concessions as a condition of their agreement to federate and the 'hold-out' colonies of Queensland and Western Australia particularly took advantage of this opportunity.[15] The Constitution recognised the constitutive status of the states in these and a number of other ways.

By the same token, the formation of the Australian federation involved the integration of mutually independent political communities into a wider or larger body politic. If unanimity was the basic presupposition of federation, the decision to federate entailed a commitment to unity and a joint constitutional destiny, and this involved a movement towards majority rule. Such a movement was already evident in the rules for deliberation and decision-making within the federal conventions of the 1890s. It culminated in the adoption of majority rule within the House of Representatives, the Senate and the amendment processes of section 128.[16] However, majority rule was implemented within the context of the 'continuing' states represented therein. There was majority rule within the Senate, but it was a Senate in which the peoples of the states were equally represented. Decisions in the Senate would therefore represent the views of a majority of peoples, not a majority of the people of the federation considered as a whole. Similarly, the amending process of section 128 embodied majority rule, but it was a dual majority of peoples of the states and of the nation as a whole. Neither political community or grouping of 'people' was treated as more legitimate than the other.

In ultimate legal terms, the federation was created by royal proclamation made under the authority of the imperial Parliament.[17] The Constitution of the Commonwealth of Australia was, and still is, contained in a statute of the British Parliament. In orthodox legal terms, therefore, Australian federation was the result of an exercise of imperial sovereignty. Even so, as Joseph Chamberlain, Secretary of State for the Colonies, recognised when introducing the Commonwealth Bill into the House of Commons, the Australians understood themselves to have secured a 'complete independent self-governing existence', and therefore 'worked alone without inviting or desiring any assistance from outside'. In contrast to the Canadians, they 'created a federation for distinctly definite and limited objects of a number of independent states, and state rights

[15] Constitution, ss. 7, 95.    [16] Constitution, ss. 23, 40, 128.
[17] Commonwealth of Australia Constitution Act 1900 (UK), s. 3.

have throughout been jealously preserved'. Accordingly, he urged, the imperial Parliament should 'accept every point . . . every word, every line, every clause, which deals exclusively with the interests of Australia'.[18] The Australians believed that they were creating a federation along the lines of the American and Swiss Constitutions, notwithstanding the imperial factor. As Patrick Glynn observed in 1897, '[t]he comparative weakness of the Canadian Federation is due to its being too much impregnated with the monarchical element'. Following Edward Freeman, he noted:

> On the whole, the general teaching of history is to show that, though a monarchical Federation is by no means theoretically impossible, yet a republican Federation is far more likely to exist as a permanent and flourishing system. We may, therefore, in the general course of comparison, practically assume that a Federal State will also be republican State.[19]

According to Glynn, this observation did 'not tell against our Federation, because we really set up a crowned republic'.[20]

What theory of Australian federalism emerges? Compactual theories of federalism define the concept primarily by reference to an agreement or treaty between sovereign states or sovereign peoples. These approaches treat federations like confederations or alliances, noting that they are formed on the basis of the consent of each constituent member. As a consequence, federal constitutions can be interpreted, amended and dissolved unilaterally by such members, as an exercise of sovereign will – ignoring the commitment to interpretive and amendment processes which depart from unanimity. By contrast, nationalist theories of federalism define the idea of federalism primarily by reference to a particular kind of system of government, called 'federal government'. Such theories, in so far as they address the formative basis of federations, treat them like unitary states, positing an original unitary 'sovereign power' which distributes its powers among central and regional government units. The conception is one of a unitary state with a 'dual system of government'.

---

[18] United Kingdom, *Commonwealth of Australia Constitution Bill: Reprint of the Debates in Parliament, The Official Correspondence with the Australian Delegates, and Other Papers* (London: Wyman and Sons, 1900), House of Commons, 14 May 1900, 10–12.

[19] Freeman, *Federal Government*, 77, quoted by Glynn: *Convention Debates, Adelaide* (1897), 173.

[20] *Convention Debates, Adelaide* (1897), 173.

Both the compactual and nationalist theories are counterfactual. The operative assumption of both approaches is that there must be a unitary locus of sovereignty in some definite institution or political community: either the constituent states or the federation as a whole. Neither approach can accurately account for all of the specific institutional features of extant federations, in their formative basis, representative structures, configuration of power and amendment procedures. The nationalist and compactual theories adopt dichotomist, extreme positions between 'unity' and 'diversity' and between the role of 'individuals' and 'groups' in the formation of federal political societies. Compactualism overplays unanimity in the formative process; nationalism overplays majority rule in the representative structures and amendment procedures and treats the division of power as definitive.

Though some of the framers of the Australian Constitution were influenced by nationalist and compactual conceptions of federation, radical proposals premised on the sovereignty of either the states or the Commonwealth consistently failed. Australian federation, like the models on which it was based, did not allow for a concentration of sovereignty in any particular community. The formative basis of Australian federation, as well as the ideals embodied in the Swiss and American models,[21] led the Australians to agree on a federal Constitution which is better explained by reference to a mediating, covenantal interpretation. Such an approach has a superior capacity to explain both the formative (compactual) and representational (national) features of the Constitution in a coherent fashion. Such an approach seeks to account for all of the inter-individual and inter-communal features of the Australian Constitution without making one aspect determinative. It seeks to capture the descriptive merits of both the national and compactual approaches without falling into their respective pitfalls.

While it might be argued that the detailed features of the Australian Constitution are best explained as a compromise between the nationalist and compactual approaches,[22] most of the Australian framers understood

---

[21] See e.g. *Convention Debates, Sydney* (1891), 197 (Cockburn), distinguishing integrative and disintegrative federalism as embodied in the United States, Switzerland and Canada respectively, and favouring the former.

[22] Cf. Hugh Collins, 'Political Ideology in Australia: The Distinctiveness of a Benthamite Society', in Steven R. Graubard (ed.), *Australia: The Daedalus Symposium* (Sydney: Angus and Robertson, 1985), 152.

the Constitution to be something significantly more than a mere compromise. For many, while negotiation and compromise were of the
essence of federalism, the Madisonian 'partly national, partly federal'
balance of 'state representation' in the Senate and 'national representation' in the House of Representatives was its cardinal principle. At the
least, it was widely accepted that the only viable form of union would be
a 'federal' one, and indeed the colonial Enabling Acts charged the conventions with the task of constructing this particular kind of union. But
most of the framers insisted that the peoples of each state were independent, self-governing bodies politic as a matter of right, and that as a
matter of principle federation could only be formed with their consent as
to its terms. It followed that federation must be based on the autonomy
of the several colonies and must serve to enhance and extend their
capacities of local self-government and constitutional self-determination.
It was therefore a matter of right and principle that the original states be
equally represented in the Senate, for example.

In this context, the federal Constitution was certainly about 'government by the people', but this did not mean national majoritarian government. Many of the framers had learned from political experience to
value the ideals of self-government and local autonomy, and the writings
of Bryce and Freeman served to reinforce this value system. In contrast to
nationalist approaches, these values implied that a federation constructed
out of several independent states must form a matrix of partly independent, partly interdependent political communities. If a theory of
popular sovereignty is presupposed by the federal constitutional system,
it is a theory that contemplates local, provincial and national 'peoples'
constituting their governments in their varying capacities, and being
represented in the wider governments which they have formed. The
Senate is the house of the peoples of the States; the House of Representatives is the national house, but it is also the house of locality.

Moreover, each state continues to govern itself and control its own
Constitution. The powers of each state are, indeed, liable to be curtailed
as legislation is progressively passed by the Federal Parliament and as the
federal Constitution is amended. Yet at the same time, the people of each
state and their representatives participate in the enactment of federal
legislation and the passage of constitutional amendments. Indeed, the
consent of the people of each state or their representatives are required in
a number of respects, including the transfer of state powers, the exercise

of imperial powers by the Federal Parliament and the passage of constitutional amendments altering state representation in the Parliament. Australian federation has meant in these and other ways a joint destiny in which elements of both self-rule and shared rule operate concurrently.

In sum, the Australian federation is a political community made up of political communities. The Commonwealth of Australia is a political community in which there are multiple loci of authority bound together by a common legal framework which has been adopted by covenant.[23] The Constitution of Australia is, indeed, the constitution of a federal commonwealth.

## Interpretive implications

Reasons of space make it impossible to detail the many interpretive implications of the account of the making and the meaning of the Australian Constitution that has been advanced in this book. By way of conclusion, however, there may be value in indicating in very schematic terms some of the general implications of the argument in its various theoretical and practical dimensions.

### *Formation*

One of the most intriguing and apparently insoluble questions that has entertained scholars in recent years has to do with the source, authority and bindingness of the Australian Constitution, particularly following the cessation of the legislative authority of the UK Parliament over Australia affected by the Australia Acts 1986 (UK) and (Cth). The question, it can be acknowledged, is primarily theoretical. But, as Sir Owen Dixon long ago pointed out:

> An inquiry into the source whence the law derives its authority in a community, if prosecuted too far, becomes merely metaphysical. But if a theoretical answer be adopted by a system of law as part of its principles, it will not remain a mere speculative explanation of juristic facts. It will possess the capacity of producing rules of law.[24]

---

[23] Griffith, *Draft Commonwealth Bill*, 8.
[24] Dixon, 'The Statute of Westminster' in *Jesting Pilate*, 82.

A theoretical answer concerning the source of authority adopted by a system of law can have practical implications in a number of ways. Where there has been a 'devolution' of constitutive power, as from the United Kingdom to Australia, there may possibly be gaps in the totality of powers explicitly devolved, or the powers conferred on different institutions may apparently overlap, leading to potential conflict. An answer to the theoretical inquiry to which Sir Owen referred may indicate the location of unallocated residual power in the system (filling any 'gaps') and specify the hierarchy of constitutional design (resolving any 'overlap'). Identifying the locus of ultimate authority (if one exists) may also suggest a certain view of the 'nature' of the Constitution and indicate a general approach to its interpretation.

After the passage of the Australia Acts, it seems, the way is open to interpret the Constitution in light of its local sources and, in particular, in terms of what is often referred to as 'popular sovereignty'. Commentators and judges of the High Court have discussed this possibility at length and argued about the specific legal conclusions which might follow.[25] All too often these discussions have overlooked the fact that the Australian Constitution is the constitution of a federal commonwealth in the sense explained and defended in this book. While the account of the making and meaning of the Constitution here advanced does not answer all of the many technical legal and theoretical issues associated with questions of bindingness, authority and legitimacy, it does underscore certain features of the constitutional system which must be taken into account in any theory that seeks to address those questions.

The ultimate sovereignty of the Australian people is advanced as an alternative foundation for the bindingness of the Constitution on a number of different empirical grounds.[26] First, there is the role of registered voters in the ratification of the Constitution through the referendums held between 1898 and 1900. Second, there is the role of the voters in the amendment of the Constitution through the process prescribed in section 128 of the Constitution. Third, although less clearly, there is the role of the people in the election of members of the

---

[25] See Lindell, 'Why is Australia's Constitution Binding?'; George Winterton, 'Popular Sovereignty and Constitutional Continuity' (1998) 26 *Federal Law Review* 1; Simon Evans, 'Why is the Constitution Binding? Authority, Obligation and the Role of the People' (2004) 25 *Adelaide Law Review* 103.

[26] See Lindell, 'Why is Australia's Constitution Binding?', 37.

Commonwealth Parliament. And, fourth, there is the 'acquiescence' of the Australian population to the exercise of governmental power under the Constitution.

There are serious problems with each of these grounds, both theoretical and factual.[27] For a start, there are numerous theoretical questions concerning the precise meaning of, as well as the relationship between, the ideas of 'legal', 'political' and 'ultimate' sovereignty as used in the popular sovereignty literature. To speak of the sovereignty of the people, even when presented as an explanation of why the Constitution is legally binding, unavoidably carries with it a whole host of normative associations having to do with democracy, social contract theory, and the like. It comes as no surprise, therefore, that much of the critical discussion has focused upon the significant gap that existed at the time the Constitution came into force between 'the people' and the limited number of registered voters who were in fact legally entitled to participate in the ratifying referendums of the 1890s.[28] Indeed, the role reserved for 'the people' in terms of original ratification, subsequent amendment and the election of parliamentary representatives was reserved to qualified electors as defined by applicable legislation enacted by the relevant legislatures. In what sense, then, is it meaningful to ascribe 'sovereignty' to the people, even in the limited sense of 'legal sovereignty', when the identity of the people for these purposes was and is dependent upon an exercise of legislative power? An account of the Australian constitutional system that seeks to explain it in terms of its local sources must therefore take account of the role of the relevant Parliaments in enacting the relevant electoral laws which define what 'the people' means in precise legal terms.

For the sake of argument, however, these kinds of problems can be put aside and the view that it is meaningful to speak of 'the people' can be accepted. For their part, the framers of the Australian Constitution were willing to refer to 'the people' as having 'agreed to unite' under the Constitution and to stipulate that the House of Representatives and Senate would be composed of members 'chosen by the people', as well as to provide for the amendment of the Constitution with the 'approval' of

---

[27] See Evans, 'Why is the Constitution Binding?', 125–31.

[28] See e.g. Anne Twomey, 'The Constitution: 19th Century Colonial Office Document or a People's Constitution?' Parliamentary Library Background Paper no. 15 (Canberra: Department of the Parliamentary Library, Australian Government Publishing Service, 1994).

those qualified to vote in elections for the House of Representatives.[29] What, then, is the role of 'the people' as understood by the framers and embodied in the text and structure of the Constitution? It is at this point that the account of the making and meaning of the Australian Constitution developed in this book is particularly relevant.

There are, indeed, theories of the federal state which, as has been seen, would interpret the Australian Constitution as resting upon a sovereign act of a national people. While not advanced as a theory of Australian federalism (and this is itself part of the problem), relatively recent claims by several members of the High Court of Australia that the Constitution rests on the sovereignty of the people fall precisely into this category.[30] Thus, members of the Court have held that because the Constitution rests upon the consent of the people of the nation conceived as an aggregate of individuals, the Constitution necessarily implies that Australian citizens are entitled to certain rights which facilitate their participation in a democracy, and that the responsibility for defining and protecting these rights is cast upon the courts.[31] The problem with this account is that the federative process by which the Constitution came into being has meant that the fundamental role of the people was as much the role of the peoples organised into their respective colonies, deciding as autonomous bodies politic whether to federate or not. Accordingly, the popular ratification of the Constitution – in so far as the process was 'popular' – rested upon the unanimous agreement of a plurality of constituent peoples, rather than an agreement, by majority, of a unitary people understood in national terms.

Justice Michael McHugh, for example, has affirmed that 'the political and legal sovereignty of Australia now resides in the people of Australia' and, adopting a dictum of James Bryce, has maintained that 'ultimate sovereignty resides in the body which made and can amend the Constitution'.[32] Although it has been one of the burdens of this book to

---

[29] Australian Constitution, preamble, ss. 7, 24, 128.

[30] *Nationwide News Pty Ltd* v. *Wills* (1992) 177 CLR 1, 70 (Deane and Toohey JJ); *Australian Capital Television Pty Ltd* v. *Commonwealth of Australia (No.2)* (1992) 177 CLR 106, 136 (Mason CJ), 210–1 (Gaudron J).

[31] Nicholas T. Aroney, *Freedom of Speech in the Constitution* (Sydney: Centre for Independent Studies, 1998), ch. 4.

[32] *McGinty* v. *Western Australia* (1996) 186 CLR 140, 230, 236–7, citing Bryce, *History and Jurisprudence*, II, 57.

underscore the important influence that Bryce had on the framers of the Australian Constitution, the dictum and its use by Justice McHugh provides a particularly clear example of the way in which theories of 'sovereignty' are liable to distort our understandings of federal systems. Even if it were possible to say that there was a sense in which the people of Australia (however understood) somehow 'made' the Constitution, closer analysis makes clear that the body that created the Constitution is certainly not identical to the body that has authority, under its terms, to 'amend' it. Rather, consistent with the federal theory underlying the Constitution, while the formative basis of the Constitution looked to a unanimous agreement among the peoples, the amendment formula shifted the decision-making rule decisively towards determination by majority rule, albeit the dual majorities of the Australian electors as a whole and the electors of the several states.

Does this mean that, if sovereignty is to be ascribed to some determinate institution or body within Australia, the best candidates are the several states? At first sight, it would seem that a 'compactual' account of the Australian Constitution does much better justice to the role of the peoples as well as the colonial legislatures in the formation of the Constitution. The problem with the compact theory, however, is again its emphasis on 'sovereignty' – a status which, by its very definition, must subsist indefinitely in a particular person or institution until divested by virtue of a revolutionary transfer of sovereignty to some other agent. If sovereignty subsists until transferred, the compact theory of federalism leads to the conclusion that the original sovereignty of the states must continue until and unless a revolution occurs. And, in the absence of any such revolution, it would seem to follow that the states retain the right to exercise ultimate sovereignty through such extreme measures as nullification of 'unconstitutional' federal laws and secession from the federation altogether.

Less radically, as has been seen, the theory also suggests that the states must enjoy all of the immunities and privileges associated with sovereignty, and a doctrine of the immunity of state instrumentalities also naturally follows.[33] But again, the problem lies at the foundation of the theory. The formation of the Australian Constitution, understood in local

---

[33] See *Federated Amalgamated Governmental Railway and Tramway Service Association* v. *NSW Railway Traffic Employees Association* (1906) 4 CLR 488.

terms, indeed rested upon the unanimous agreement of the several colonies, expressed through their representative governments and legislatures as well as through direct referendums. However, the representative
structures and amendment processes agreed to under the Constitution, as
well as the constitutionally defined configuration of legislative power
ultimately adjudicated by the High Court, belie the idea that the states
(or, indeed, the Commonwealth) may be regarded straightforwardly as
'sovereign'. Simple majorities suffice in both houses of the Commonwealth Parliament for the enactment of legislation and the amendment
formula in section 128 also turns on majority rule. Moreover, the legislative and executive powers of the Commonwealth and the states are
clearly limited by the Constitution in a way that reflects the federating
logic of the system as a whole. The intention was to create an 'indissoluble' federal commonwealth, foreclosing the possibility of unilateral
secession, and the intention was to make the High Court the ultimate
arbiter of disputes concerning the constitutional validity of government
action and legislation, foreclosing the possibility of state-determined
nullification of federal laws.

A more fruitful way to conceptualise the Australian constitutional
system, therefore, is to recognise the extent to which we are dealing with
the constitution of a federal commonwealth, a political community in
which the idea of sovereignty is simply out of place, whether this sovereignty be ascribed to the people, the states or the Commonwealth. In
the introduction to this book attention was given to certain observations
made by Justice William Gummow in *McGinty* v. *Western Australia*
relating to claims about the location of 'ultimate sovereignty' in the
Australian constitutional system.[34] The interpretation of the Australian
federal system advanced in this book is very much based upon the features of the Constitution which his Honour said must be taken into
account in addressing this issue. Among them, Justice Gummow
underscored the fact that the formal amendment of the Constitution
depends not only upon 'a majority of all the electors' within Australia,
but also upon 'a majority of the electors in a majority of states'. He also
noted that the initiative lies with Parliament and that there is provision
for resolution of deadlocks between the houses, as well as the special
provision in the fifth paragraph of section 128 for safeguarding each

---

[34] *McGinty* v. *Western Australia* (1996) 186 CLR 140, 274–5.

state's representation in Parliament and its territorial boundaries. Moreover, his Honour concluded by drawing attention to the fact that none of the Australia Acts followed approval at a referendum, but were enacted through the processes envisaged by the Statute of Westminster 1931 (UK) on the one hand, and section 51(xxxviii) of the Constitution on the other (both of which leave the decision to the Parliaments of the United Kingdom and Australia, acting in concert), as well as the fact that in section 15 thereof, the Australia Acts provide their own mechanism for amendment or repeal through legislation unanimously agreed upon by the Commonwealth and state parliaments.[35]

Arguments about 'sovereignty' and the 'bindingness' of the Constitution raise deep theoretical issues many of which lie beyond the scope of this book. What the present study serves to underscore is that any theory about sovereignty or bindingness must take account of the factors to which Justice Gummow rightly drew attention. Each of these factors can be traced to certain specific conceptions of what it means for Australia to be a federal commonwealth, conceptions which profoundly shaped the deliberations of the framers and thereby left indelible marks upon the text and structure of the Constitution. A simplistic incantation of 'the sovereignty of the people' is, for these reasons, bound to provide an inadequate explanation of Australia's Constitution, in part because it overlooks the role of 'the peoples', and in part because it uncritically assumes that 'sovereignty' is a concept capable of explaining the Australian Constitution.

## Amendment

All of this leads very naturally into a consideration of several specific and as yet largely unanswered questions regarding available mechanisms for fundamental constitutional change. Again, the questions are so fundamental that they are liable to be regarded as essentially theoretical rather than practical in nature. The 1999 referendum to amend the Constitution

---

[35] *Ibid.*, 275. Intriguingly, when summarising the fifth paragraph of s. 128, Gummow J referred to the final aspect as concerning 'proposed alterations . . . (iii) "in any manner" affecting the provisions of the Constitution in relation to a State' (*ibid.*, 275). In fact, the paragraph is worded 'in any manner affecting the provisions of the Constitution in relation thereto', an expression which has usually been understood to refer to representation in Parliament and the limits of the state, rather than referring to the state Constitutions in general.

in order to replace the Queen with a president (and thus make Australia a republic, so it was argued) illustrated the way in which at least some of these issues can indeed arise in practice.[36]

The proposal to make Australia a presidency involved, not only the removal of the Queen from the system of government but also the adoption of a new preamble to the Constitution.[37] The debate about an Australian republic was thus largely concerned with two basic matters, the first a very substantial set of questions about constitutional design, the second concerning a series of less substantial but equally prominent questions about the symbolism of an Australian republic.

As far as the proposal for a new preamble was concerned, the objectives were almost entirely symbolic. It was thought that the existing preamble was outdated in a number of respects, particularly in so far as it clearly acknowledged Australia's colonial status and the imperial origins of the Constitution. And so it was proposed that a new preamble, expressing a set of values said to be quintessentially Australian, ought to be inserted into the Constitution. While the preamble referendum, as well as the presidency referendum, famously failed, the limited terms in which the preamble referendum was couched reflected, whether deliberately or not, a profound doubt that exists to this day concerning the available mechanism for amending the preamble and covering clauses of the Commonwealth of Australia Constitution Act 1900 (UK).[38]

Notably, the preamble proposal was merely to insert a new preamble into the Commonwealth Constitution,[39] rather than amend or replace the existing preamble, or else insert a new preamble immediately after the existing one within the Commonwealth of Australia Constitution Act. If national symbolism was a central motivation for the proposal, why not replace the existing preamble, or amend it, or else supplement it by a second preamble right at the beginning of the Constitution Act? While the reasons for the limited terms of the preamble referendum were certainly complicated and various, doubt about the capacity to alter or

---

[36] See Nicholas T. Aroney, 'A Public Choice: Federalism and the Prospects of a Republican Preamble' (1999) 21 *University of Queensland Law Journal* 205.

[37] Constitution Alteration (Establishment of Republic) 1999 (Cth); Constitution Alteration (Preamble) 1999 (Cth).

[38] Although, see Parliament of Australia, Senate, Constitution Alteration (Establishment of Republic) 1999, Revised Explanatory Memorandum, para. 1.8.

[39] Constitution Alteration (Preamble) 1999 (Cth), s. 3.

replace the existing preamble by referendum under section 128 appears to have been an important factor.

This question about the appropriate legal mechanism for amending or repealing the preamble and covering clauses of the Commonwealth of Australia Constitution Act is one of a number of ways in which there is continuing uncertainty about the conditions of fundamental constitutional change in Australia. Questions such as these concern problems of unallocated residual power and the hierarchy of constitutional design. Two such further questions are whether the general amending power in section 128 of the Constitution can be used to alter the fifth paragraph of section 128 without the consent of the electors in all the states concerned, and whether the procedure in section 128 can be used to amend the Constitution as a means of conferring the power to alter, repeal or insert a new provision into the state Constitution Acts? It is convenient to address each of these questions in turn. Necessarily, the discussion must be brief.

### Amending the preamble and covering clauses

Elsewhere I have argued that section 128 does not extend to the alteration of the preamble and covering clauses of the Constitution Act.[40] While the matter is not without doubt, I have argued that to place the issue beyond question as a matter of law and to ensure that the process is politically legitimate, the appropriate mechanism ought to involve the joint and unanimous action of the state parliaments, the Federal Parliament and the people of every state voting in referendums. It is not argued that this is the most minimally sufficient legal process that might possibly pass constitutional muster, but that it is safest and the most legitimate. Without repeating all of the arguments here, it may be worth explaining them at least to the extent necessary to show how they cohere with the inquiry undertaken in this book.

Briefly put, the argument is founded upon the fundamental proposition that the Australian federation involves a plurality of communities and authorities in which no particular community or authority is sovereign. The Commonwealth was built upon an agreement among 'continuing' states, each conceived as a mutually independent, self-governing body politic. Putting aside the supervening authority of the imperial Parliament, the Commonwealth of Australia is an integrative federation

---

[40] See Aroney, 'A Public Choice'.

of states. The formation of the federation adhered to the principle of unanimity as between the peoples of the colonies and the legal control of the process by their representative legislatures. The peoples of the several colonies certainly agreed to a degree of consolidation in the majoritarian and nationalist aspects of section 128. However, restrictions on the scope of section 128 were deliberately imposed. By its terms section 128 is limited to the amendment of the 'Constitution' – an expression that does not include the preamble and covering clauses of the Constitution Act.[41] Moreover, in section 51(xxxviii), the residual powers of the imperial Parliament were deliberately vested in the federal and state legislatures acting unanimously. This last provision later served as the local source of authority pursuant to which the Australia Act 1986 (Cth) was enacted, severing the residual authority of the Parliament at Westminster over Australia. Maintaining the same principle, section 15(1) of the Australia Acts in turn provided that the power to amend the Australia Acts (and the Statute of Westminster) would henceforth require the unanimous agreement of the state and Commonwealth legislatures. Unanimity in this sense therefore continues to be one of the ultimate decision-making rules undergirding the entire federation and, in my opinion, the most fundamental one. Thus, where there is an apparent silence concerning the authority to amend the Constitution Act, the principle of unanimity provides the key.

Now, it is true that, just as the scope of section 128 is limited to the amendment of the Constitution, so section 15 is limited to the amendment of the Australia Acts and the Statute of Westminster, and section 51(xxxviii) remains 'subject to' the Constitution. It would in each of these cases involve a kind of 'bootstrapping' for any one mechanism to be used to enact a law which enabled that same mechanism to transcend those limitations so as to amend the preamble and covering clauses of the Commonwealth of Australia Constitution Act.[42] It is contrary to the fundamentals of constitutional law, said Sir Owen Dixon, for a stream to be induced to rise above its source.[43] And yet, to suggest that the

---

[41] See Commonwealth of Australia Constitution Act 1900 (UK), ss. 1 and 9.

[42] But see the Constitution (Requests) Bill 1999 (Vic.), which presupposed that the Commonwealth Parliament could be empowered to amend the Constitution Act at the request of the State Parliaments under the Australia Acts 1986. The assumptions underlying this presupposition are critically assessed in Aroney, 'A Public Choice'.

[43] Dixon, 'The Statute of Westminster' in *Jesting Pilate*, 96.

preamble and covering clauses simply cannot be amended by any legally available means seems at least extraordinary, if not unthinkable.[44] Accordingly, while the matter is not without doubt and depends, ultimately, on one's conception of the fundamental principles involved, the safest and most legitimate way to amend the Constitution Act, it is submitted, is to secure the unanimous agreement of the state and Commonwealth parliaments as well as a majority of voters in all of the states.[45]

## State boundaries, state representation and state constitutions

The fifth paragraph of section 128 especially prevents the constitutional alteration of the representation and boundaries of a state without the consent of the people of that state.[46] It has been seen in previous chapters that the provision carries the formative basis of the federation (unanimity among the states) into the amending procedure. Moreover, the general power in section 128 extends to the alteration of 'this Constitution', literally including section 128. But does this include the fifth paragraph itself?

The inquiry into the drafting of section 128 undertaken in this book suggests that section 128 cannot be used to amend the fifth paragraph without the consent of the states concerned.[47] The territorial boundaries of the states and their representation in the Parliament were matters of sustained attention and concern. To suggest that the guarantee secured in the fifth paragraph of section 128 might be nullified by a mere majority of states runs deeply counter to the fundamental principle of the entire Constitution.

Now it has to be conceded that the amendment process provided for by section 128 has certainly been used to amend aspects of section 128 itself.[48] However, the additional words 'or in any manner affecting the provisions of the Constitution in relation thereto' contained in the fifth paragraph were added to accord 'the fullest protection' to the states. Read literally, the fifth paragraph is itself part of the 'Constitution' which 'relates' to the representation and 'limits' of the states. This suggests that, consistent with the formative basis of the Constitution, section 128

---

[44] *Polyukhovich v. Commonwealth* (1991) 172 CLR 501, 638 (Dawson J); *Final Report of the Constitutional Commission* (1988), I, 120, para. 3.104.

[45] For the full argument, see Aroney, 'A Public Choice'.

[46] See Twomey, *Constitution of New South Wales*, 788ff. 796ff.

[47] See, likewise, Moore, *Constitution of the Commonwealth*, 604, who considered that the general power in s. 128 could not be used to alter the fifth paragraph unless the requirements of the fifth paragraph were met.

[48] Constitution Alteration (Referendums) Act 1977 (Cth).

cannot be used to alter the fifth paragraph in order to enable section 128 to amend the representation or boundaries of a state without the consent of the people of that state.

The formative basis of the federation also serves to confirm an interpretation of section 128 that would limit the extent to which the provision can be used to amend the state Constitution Acts and other state laws, particularly those of a fundamental nature. The people of the Australian colonies agreed to form a federal system in which the powers of the state legislatures would be curtailed in a number of ways. There can be no doubt that amendments of the Constitution under section 128 may further curtail state powers, since the state constitutions are continued 'subject to' the Federal Constitution. But can this power be used to alter the state Constitution Acts and other state laws directly?[49]

It has been one of the central objectives of this book to show how the formative basis of the Australian federation (this involving the unanimous consent of the states) decisively influenced the representative institutions and amendment procedures adopted thereunder. The Constitution thus treats the original states as the fundamental constituents of the federation. The states are foundational, continuing and self-governing bodies politic in the formation, representative structures and amending formula of the federal Constitution. It is inconsistent with this to suggest that the power to amend the federal Constitution might extend to the direct amendment of the state constitutions and other state laws. The framers clearly agreed that there should be no federal 'interference' with the state constitutions, although they differed about the extent to which provision should be made for the state constitutions within the federal Constitution. Some sought to confirm in the Constitution the states' control over their individual constitutional destinies; others opposed even this as an unnecessary interference. But they were agreed that the states should determine for themselves their own separate constitutional destinies.

In 1901 Quick and Garran drew attention to the dominating idea that the states 'continued' within the federation, noting that the 'pre-existing colonies' were 'converted into states', and that their constitutions were 'confirmed and continued by the Federal Constitution, not created

---

[49] See *Attorney-General (WA)* v. *Marquet* (2003) 217 CLR 545, 571, 613–16, discussed in Twomey, *Constitution of New South Wales*, 294; and cf. Twomey, *Constitution of New South Wales*, 775ff., 801ff.

thereby'. Moreover, in the light of the 'supreme and absolute sovereignty of the Empire', they suggested that the state constitutions had been 'incorporated into the new Constitution'.[50] In recent times some judges and commentators have adopted this view.[51] However, the framers drew a firm distinction between 'continuation' and 'establishment', as Quick and Garran also noted. Certainly, new states might be 'formed' and 'established' out of territories of the Commonwealth or a state, but this could only occur with that state's consent. Moreover, the original states, upon which the federation was built, were not 'established' by the federal Constitution, but rather 'continued'. Certainly, the transformation of the original colonies into states derived from the Commonwealth Constitution, and their continuing status as self-governing colonies within the empire was confirmed thereby. But this status derived from the imperial Parliament and not from the Constitution itself. The termination of imperial authority over Australia did not materially alter this logic. Indeed, the two versions of the Australia Acts were enacted, respectively, under the authority of the imperial Parliament and all seven Australian legislatures acting unanimously and the amending provision in section 15(1) preserved their separate, though joint, status. It would be inconsistent with this if the state constitutions could be altered directly through section 128 of the federal Constitution. Section 128 confers a power to alter the Commonwealth Constitution. It is not a power to amend, or to confer the power to amend, the constitutions of the several states.

## Representation

### Equality of voting power and the House of Representatives

In two cases heard by the High Court of Australia it has been argued that the Constitution by implication requires that electoral districts be of

[50] Quick and Garran, *Annotated Constitution*, 343–4, 927–8, 930. Compare Bryce, *History and Jurisprudence*, I, 494–5.

[51] Most clearly in *New South Wales* v. *Commonwealth* (1976) 135 CLR 337, 372; *Bistricic* v. *Rokov* (1976) 135 CLR 552, 566. But see *Western Australia* v. *Wilsmore* [1981] WAR 179, 181–4. See also Geoffrey Sawer, 'The British Connection' (1973) 47 *Australian Law Journal* 113, 113–14; R. D. Lumb, 'Fundamental Law and the Processes of Constitutional Change in Australia' (1978) 9 *Federal Law Review* 148, 162–3, 182–3; Gregory Craven, 'A Few Fragments of State Constitutional Law' (1990) 20 *University of Western Australia Law Review* 353, 368–72; N. F. Douglas, 'The Western Australian Constitution: Its Source of Authority and Relationship with Section 106 of the Australian Constitution' (1990) 20 *University of Western Australia Law Review* 340.

substantially the same size, so that individual voters enjoy a kind of 'equality of voting power' in both federal and state elections.[52] The argument that equality of voting power is a necessary implication of the Constitution rests on the provision in sections 7 and 24 of the Constitution that members of Parliament are to be 'chosen ... by the people'. The inquiry undertaken in this book underscores, however, a number of features of the Constitution which militate against any such implication. In the first place, the equal representation of the states in the Senate is a definite contradiction of any general principle of equality of voting power enjoyed by all voters within the federation. Moreover, while many framers understood the House of Representatives to be the 'popular' or 'national' house, just as many thought it to be the house in which 'localities' would especially be represented. Certainly, several framers observed that 'individuals' would be represented in the House, in proportion to population. But proportionality to population was guaranteed to each state, not each electorate, again reflecting the view that the states were the constituent parties to the Constitution. Furthermore, the smaller states were additionally protected by a guarantee of a minimum representation in the House, further qualifying the principle of proportionality.

At one point during the debate the size of the House of Representatives was defined by reference to a fixed ratio of voters to representatives for each electorate (which, read out of context, could possibly suggest an implication of equality). However, this was ultimately replaced by a prescribed nexus between the size of the two houses, conceived as a means of protecting the Senate and the rights of the states. Indeed, as has been seen, despite their differences on many other matters, the framers explicitly decided that no guarantee of equal voting power should be provided for or implied by the Constitution. Rather, when specifically considering the issue, the framers decided in section 29 to leave the determination of federal electorates to the state parliaments, with a protective, supervisory role reserved to the Federal Parliament. In so doing, the framers consciously decided to make the Federal Parliament the custodian of the integrity of the electoral process and the definition of federal electorates.

---

[52] See *Attorney-General (Cth); Ex rel McKinlay* v. *Commonwealth* (1975) 135 CLR 1 and *McGinty* v. *Western Australia* (1996) 186 CLR 140, discussed in Nicholas T. Aroney, 'Democracy, Community and Federalism in Electoral Apportionment Cases: The United States, Canada and Australia in Comparative Perspective' (2008) 58 *University of Toronto Law Journal* 421.

These considerations support the High Court's decisions in *McKinlay* and *McGinty* denying the existence of an implied guarantee of equal voting power in federal elections. They also substantiate the focus on the entrenchment of the nexus in *McKinlay* and the focus on the 'adaptation of democracy to federalism' in *McGinty*. During the convention debates, O'Connor pointed out that the only thing that section 24 entrenched was the nexus, leaving ultimate control over all other matters to Parliament.[53] In *McGinty*, Justice Gummow similarly pointed out that the matters that were entrenched in section 24 were concerned with federalism, not national democracy.[54]

## Responsible government and the Senate

The inquiry undertaken in this book has served to underscore a difficult tension in the Constitution between federalism and responsible government. This tension concerns a series of related issues concerning the role of the Senate as a states' house, the function of political parties in the Parliament, the powers of the Senate over revenue and appropriation bills and the practical operation of responsible government.

In the first place, it is often said that the Senate has failed to operate as a states' house because divisions in the Senate have reflected party politics, rather than the interests or rights of particular states or the state governments as distinct from the Commonwealth government. The operation of party government under the federation was foreseen by Macrossan, Deakin and others, and it is often thought that the framers who nevertheless insisted on the equality of representation of the states in a powerful Senate were misguided.

While Macrossan's prediction has proven correct in so far as divisions on the floor of the Senate are concerned,[55] the inquiry undertaken in this book renders the attitudes of the framers much more comprehensible than would first appear. In the first place, it is not so clear that the

---

[53] *Convention Debates, Sydney* (1897), 429.

[54] *McGinty* v. *Western Australia* (1996) 186 CLR 140, 276–7.

[55] Divisions within the party rooms are much more likely to be influenced by the regional interests with which local members and senators are associated. See Percy E. Joske, *Australian Federal Government* (3rd edn, Sydney: Butterworths, 1976), 75–7. Howell argues that overlooking this has led to the erroneous view that the Senate has altogether failed as a states' house: Peter Howell, 'The Strongest Delegation: The South Australians at the Constitutional Convention of 1897–98' (1998) 1 *The New Federalist* 11, 16.

framers expected the Senate to protect states' 'interests', nor that these would be protected by votes on the floor of the Senate. For many of them, equal representation of the people of the states was itself a 'right' to which the people of each state were entitled, rather than a means of protecting states' interests. Equal representation was thus conceived to be a principle fundamental to the idea of a 'compound' political community. In an associated way, a number of framers did not expect that the 'success' of the Senate would be evidenced by divisions on state lines. Rather, they hoped, the Senate would be a means by which the peoples of the states might be integrated and that the success of the Senate would be measured by its capacity to unite the peoples into one people. As Hackett observed:

> [T]he main function of the Senate . . . [is] to cement these isolated communities together, to make a dismembered Australia into a single nation . . . to convert the popular will into the federal will . . . to give full voice to the wishes of the populace, but, at the same time, to take care before that voice issues forth as the voice of Australia that it shall be clothed with all the rights and duties of the federal will.[56]

In the second place, there was a strong resistance to party government among the framers. Many of them positively hoped that strict party discipline would not operate in the Federal Parliament. A substantial number recognised that party discipline was closely associated with responsible government and many were opposed to responsible government. Some, like Baker, positively supported the Swiss model of an executive responsible to both houses of Parliament. Others, like Griffith, observed that responsible government was a relatively recent institution and that the Constitution should not be too prescriptive, but instead leave the issue open for further evolution.

Responsible government, it was understood, turned on the powers of the two houses of the Federal Parliament, particularly over money bills, since, as Henry Wrixon had pointed out, 'finance is government and government is finance, and under the English system of government one or other house must appoint the executive'.[57] Those who favoured responsible government and a dominant 'popular' house, sought to eliminate or limit substantially the powers of the Senate over money bills. Those who favoured the Swiss model or wished to leave the matter open,

---

[56] *Convention Debates, Sydney* (1891), 280.    [57] *Ibid.*, 214.

argued in the opposite direction. The consequence in 1891 was a compromise: the Senate would be equal with the House except that it could not initiate or amend money bills – but it could reject them. Even though in 1897–8 a majority of framers supported responsible government, the compromise of 1891 was preserved, the only significant difference being the requirement that ministers must hold seats in either house of Parliament.

When read in this context, it is clear that the silence in section 53 as regards rejection of financial bills implies that a legal power of rejection exists. The delegates clearly drew a distinction between amendment and rejection; the decision to limit the powers of the Senate only in respect of amendment meant that a power of rejection was intended.[58] In 1891 Griffith convinced Downer that the power of veto in whole was the significant power.[59] In 1898 Reid objected to the resulting inconsistency with responsible government, but admitted that the power of rejection was 'a real living power'.[60] Even Higgins admitted that the Senate would be able to delay supply bills indefinitely, reject supply and force Ministers to 'yield'.[61] Indeed, Bryce himself foresaw the possibility, and was keen to observe its practical outworking.[62]

The possibility was vividly demonstrated in 1975. The Senate exercised its legal power to deny supply to an executive government which had the confidence of the House of Representatives. It is often argued that there is a convention of responsible government that the Senate, as an upper house, should not reject or fail to pass supply or should only do so when 'state interests' are at stake.[63] From the perspective of the convention debates, however, it was certainly not understood that the powers while formally conferred were not to be exercised in practice. Nor were 'state

---

[58] See *Victoria v. Commonwealth* (1975) 134 CLR 81, 121, 143, 168, 185; Geoffrey Sawer, *Federation under Strain* (Melbourne University Press, 1977), 107–17; Galligan and Warden, 'Design of the Senate'.

[59] *Convention Debates, Sydney* (1891), 442–4.

[60] Reid, 'Yes-No Speech'; cf. Quick and Garran, *Annotated Constitution*, 214, 216–17, 673.

[61] Higgins, *Essays and Addresses*, 16–17; cf. 18–19.

[62] Bryce, *History and Jurisprudence*, I, 515–18.

[63] See Colin Howard and Cheryl Saunders, 'The Blocking of the Budget and Dismissal of the Government', in Gareth Evans (ed.), *Labor and the Constitution 1972–1975* (Melbourne: Heinemann Educational, 1977) and LJM Cooray, *Conventions, the Australian Constitution and the Future* (Sydney: Legal Books, 1979), ch. 4; cf. Sawer, *Federation under Strain*, 121–7; Lumb and Moens, *Annotated Constitution*, 311–13 and see Winterton, *Parliament, Executive and Governor-General*, 144–9.

interests' conceived to be the only basis for the composition and powers of the Senate; many understood it to be a matter of 'right' or a 'principle'. While many delegates in 1897–8 felt that the federal government ought to be responsible to the House, in giving the Senate a legal power to reject financial bills, a majority were prepared to give the Senate the power to withhold supply, fully aware that the exercise of such power could bring a government to its knees.

## Configuration of power

The Australian Constitution is constructed on the assumption that the several original states were pre-existing, independent bodies politic, whose respective constitutions, territorial integrity and governmental powers would continue within the federation – a status which contrasted sharply with that of the Commonwealth, whose juridical personality and powers would be established by the Constitution.[64] That the several states continued, whereas the Commonwealth was established, had important implications not only for the Commonwealth and state constitutions, but also for the allocation of powers between the Commonwealth and the states.

It was clearly the general intention of the framers to establish a genuinely federal government fully equipped with all of the necessary institutions and powers necessary to enable it to function as a sovereign nation within its sphere. The federation would be much more than a 'glorified' council of constituent states. It would be governed by a national executive having full capacity to execute federal laws against its citizens without having to depend upon the state governments.[65] Moreover, the powers to be vested in the Commonwealth would be expressed in wide and general terms, and would include extensive powers over matters such as defence, external affairs, taxation and public borrowing, as well as all necessary powers incidental to the fulfilment of such responsibilities.

While wide and extensive powers were to be conferred upon the Commonwealth, the consensus remained that the Federal Parliament was to be a legislature of enumerated and limited powers. The possibility that

---

[64] Compare Commonwealth of Australia Constitution Act 1900 (Cth), ss. 3, 4, 6; Commonwealth Constitution, ss. 106, 107.
[65] *Convention Debates, Melbourne* (1898), 202.

the Commonwealth might seek to expand its powers beyond those intended was something to be guarded against. Indeed, there was general agreement that the limited terms in which federal powers were conferred implied a prohibition on the Commonwealth and a reservation of powers to the states.[66] Thus, while several provisions originally expressing the prohibition and reservation explicitly were redrafted into positive affirmations of power without any explicit limitation, this, it appears, was done solely to simplify the drafting and not to negative the implied prohibition and reservation that was intended. Great care was taken in the drafting, the concern being expressed that if the responsibilities cast upon the federation were too numerous or too wide, this could seriously undermine the capacity of the people of each state to govern themselves.

The 'reserved powers' doctrine subsequently developed by Samuel Griffith, Edmund Barton and Richard O'Connor as justices of the High Court was largely an outworking of this understanding of the meaning and effect of the Constitution. On this approach, the limited nature of the powers conferred upon the Commonwealth in section 51, together with the preservation of the powers of the states pursuant to section 107, were taken to imply a reservation to the states of an exclusive capacity to regulate all matters deemed to fall within their 'domestic' affairs. More precisely, the doctrine regarded the silences and omissions in particular heads of federal power to be as significant as the explicit prohibitions.[67] Thus, the fact that the Commonwealth was granted under section 51(i) power to legislate with respect to 'trade and commerce with other countries, and among the States', implied a limitation on the capacity of the Commonwealth to legislate under other heads of power in a way that would interfere with trade and commerce solely within the territorial limits of a particular state.[68]

Alongside the reserved powers doctrine, the early High Court also developed a doctrine of implied inter-governmental immunities which prohibited both the Commonwealth and the states from validly enacting a law which would in any way interfere with or regulate each other. The theory here was that both the Commonwealth and the states were to be

---

[66] See e.g. *ibid.*, 502–4, 596–7, 600, 1008–10 (Barton), 504–5 (Symon), discussed in chs. 9 and 10.

[67] See Nicholas T. Aroney, 'Constitutional Choices in the Work Choices Case, or What Exactly is Wrong with the Reserved Powers Doctrine?' (2008) 32 *Melbourne University Law Review* 1.

[68] *Attorney-General (NSW)* v. *Brewery Employees Union of NSW* (1908) 6 CLR 469.

regarded as 'sovereign' within their respective spheres and that sovereignty implied an absolute immunity from external interference. This
meant that a federal law could not constitutionally 'fetter, control, or
interfere with' any of the 'instrumentalities' through which the states
executed their various governmental functions, and the states could not
do the same to the Commonwealth.[69]

Space does not permit a detailed explanation of this doctrine, or of the
approach to constitutional interpretation which later supplanted it, or of
the respective strengths and weaknesses of each approach. It must suffice
to say that each approach rests, in part, upon a different conception of
the nature of the Australian federal system, neither of which fully does
justice to the conception of a federal commonwealth which animated the
framers and shaped the text and structure of the Constitution. Indeed, it
should come as no surprise that Isaacs and Higgins, so often in the
minority during the convention debates, as justices of the High Court
adopted approaches to the interpretation of the Constitution radically
divergent from those taken by Griffith, Barton and O'Connor. The
famous *Engineers* case of 1920, in which the reserved powers and implied
communities doctrines were eclipsed, is often said to have rested upon an
approach to interpretation which emphasises the literal text of the
Constitution over against the intentions and original understandings of
the framers.[70] A close reading of the majority judgment – a judgment
generally ascribed to Justice Isaacs – suggests, however, that it was dictated not only by a commitment to textual literalism, but also by a theory
of Australian federalism which understood the Constitution as being
founded most immediately upon the authority of the Australian
people as a whole and ultimately upon the sovereignty of the imperial
Parliament.[71]

The reserved powers doctrine has been widely criticised on the ground
that it reverses the correct order of inquiry. The Constitution provides us
with explicit guidance about the specific powers conferred upon the

---

[69] *D'Emden* v. *Pedder* (1904) 1 CLR 91; *Federated Amalgamated Government Railway and Tramway Service Association* v. *NSW Railway Traffic Employees Association* (1906) 4 CLR 488; *Baxter* v. *Commissioners of Taxation (NSW)* (1907) 4 CLR 1087.

[70] *Amalgamated Society of Engineers* v. *Adelaide Steamship Co Ltd* (1920) 28 CLR 129.

[71] See Nicholas T. Aroney, 'The Griffith Doctrine: Orthodoxy and Heresy', in Michael White and Aladin Rahemtula (eds.), *Queensland Judges on the High Court* (Brisbane: Supreme Court of Queensland Library, 2003).

Commonwealth and says nothing about the particular topics that are supposedly reserved to the states. The starting point of the inquiry, it is therefore said, must be with the express terms in which Commonwealth jurisdiction is defined; these words must be interpreted as widely as the words allow; and whatever is left over (the residue) is that which is reserved to the states, and nothing more. The reserved powers doctrine, it is argued, reverses this, in that it begins with an assumption about particular topics reserved to the states, and proceeds to interpret federal heads of power narrowly so as to ensure that they do not extend into those reserved topics. In other words, the reserved powers doctrine begins with an assumption that has no textual basis in the Constitution (it is an inference from silence) and proceeds to read down the natural meaning of the words actually used to define the legislative powers conferred upon the Commonwealth.

The critique of the reserved powers doctrine, thus presented, seems logical and compelling. But is it as simple is this? As formulated by the early High Court, the reserved powers doctrine rested not simply upon the reservation of legislative powers under section 107, but also upon the deliberately limited terms in which federal legislative powers were defined. Notably, although the critique of the reserved powers doctrine has dominated the High Court ever since the *Engineers* case, the High Court has recognised that in at least some instances – for example, the banking, insurance and acquisition powers – the limited terms in which federal power is conferred must cut down, at least to some extent, the scope of other heads of federal power.[72] Although there is to some degree textual warrant for interpreting these particular heads of power in this special way, none the less these decisions represent an important qualification of the *Engineers* doctrine. This is not to suggest that the limited terms of the interstate trade and commerce power should be read as an absolute prohibition upon Commonwealth legislation regulating or interfering with intra-state trade and commerce under some other head of power. But it is to suggest an alternative approach to the terms and structure of the Constitution as far as the configuration of legislative power is concerned. The legislative powers of the Commonwealth were specifically enumerated not in order to give them interpretive priority,

---

[72] See e.g. *W. H. Blakeley Co* v. *Commonwealth* (1953) 87 CLR 501, 521; *Attorney General (Cth)* v. *Schmidt* (1961) 105 CLR 361, 371–2; *Bourke* v. *State Bank of NSW* (1990) 170 CLR 276, 286–9.

but to ensure that the Commonwealth would remain a legislature of limited powers.[73] The words of any legal instrument will always be open to alternatively wider or narrower interpretations. The overall structure of the Constitution – the general configuration of power as between the Commonwealth and the states – suggests that where a such a choice presents itself, there is good reason for the Court to avoid the wider interpretation so as to leave ample room for the exercise of the continuing powers and self-governing responsibilities of the states.[74]

On the other hand, the immunity of instrumentalities doctrine as developed by the early High Court was founded upon a conception of the Commonwealth and the states as 'sovereign' within their respective spheres, a status which implied a virtually absolute immunity from any form of interference. As has been argued in this book, however, the idea of sovereignty provides an inadequate conceptual framework for understanding the federation of the Australian colonies. To this extent, the Court was on solid ground in rejecting the immunity doctrine in its near absolute form in the *Engineers* case. At the same time, federalism for the framers of the Constitution certainly meant that the states as well as the Commonwealth should continue to function as instruments of popular self-government in their respective spheres, and it is a legitimate inference to be drawn from the terms and structure of the Constitution that neither the Commonwealth nor the states can validly prevent the other from functioning as such. Such was the reasoning of the High Court in its famous decision in *Melbourne Corporation* v. *Commonwealth* in 1947.[75] There is every good reason for the Court to continue to uphold the modified doctrine of inter-governmental immunity as established in that case.

In sum the configuration of legislative power in the Constitution reflected not so much a Diceyan 'division of powers' between the Commonwealth and the states,[76] but a transfer of limited powers to the Commonwealth by the states. This is not to deny the undoubted fact that the Australian Constitution would derive its legal force from its

---

[73] See *Attorney-General (Cth)* v. *Colonial Sugar Refining Company Ltd* (1913) 17 CLR 644, 651–6.

[74] In its recent *Workchoices* decision, the High Court has chosen to persevere with *Engineers*. See *New South Wales* v. *Commonwealth* (2006) 229 CLR 1.

[75] *Melbourne Corporation* v. *Commonwealth* (1947) 74 CLR 31. Compare the recent statement in *Austin* v. *Commonwealth* (2003) 215 CLR 185.

[76] See Dicey, *Law of the Constitution*, 130–55, 410–13, discussed in ch. 3.

enactment by the imperial Parliament at Westminster, so that, legally speaking, the powers of both the Commonwealth and the states were ultimately derived from the United Kingdom and 'divided' among them in this sense.[77] But it is to assert that the structural logic of the Constitution was shaped not by the legally defined origin of the Constitution, but by its political origin: the peoples, the representative legislatures and the elected governments of the several colonies. The political origin of the Constitution meant that legislative power was conceived as originating with the states, with limited and mostly overlapping or concurrent powers being conferred upon the Commonwealth.[78]

Dicey had also said that the 'division' of power between federal and state governments was in a federation ultimately adjudicated by an independent court of superior jurisdiction. And in this respect there is little doubt that the framers of the Australian Constitution followed Dicey (and with him Bryce and Freeman). Symon went so far as to call the High Court the 'keystone of the federal arch'.[79] Indeed, despite misgivings about the inherently political nature of the decisions the Court would be called upon to make which led to proposals to make the Court more representative and its decisions subject to popular review, a majority of the framers insisted that members of the Court be appointed by the federal government in its unfettered discretion. Part of the reason for this was that the Court was to be an organ of the Commonwealth and not just of the states, but just as vital in the deliberations was a concern to secure the independence of the Court from both the Commonwealth and the states.

It is a moot question whether the framers were naïve in expecting that the High Court would operate as a independent arbiter, conscientiously seeking to discover and apply the fundamental principles which they, as framers, 'had in mind' in designing the Constitution. Certainly, Downer envisaged the Court operating in this manner, and it seems that he expressed the general view.[80] It is also a moot question, strictly beyond the scope of this book, whether the Court ought to interpret the Constitution in a way that takes into consideration the intentions or understandings of the framers, to the extent that these can be ascertained.

---

[77] See Quick and Garran, *Annotated Constitution*, 380, discussed in ch. 4.
[78] Constitution, s. 51.
[79] *Convention Debates*, Sydney (1891), 950–1 (Symon), discussed in ch. 10.
[80] *Convention Debates*, Melbourne (1898), 275 (Downer).

Remarkably, it was Griffith, Barton and O'Connor who, as original members of the High Court, excluded the citation of the convention debates in argument before the Court,[81] whereas it has only been in more recent years that the debates have been admitted to shed light on the meaning of the words used as well as 'the nature and objectives of the movement towards federation'.[82] While some of the framers looked primarily to the High Court, and others placed more emphasis and reliance upon what have been called 'the political safeguards of federalism' (the role of the people of the states in the composition of the Federal Parliament and executive government),[83] what actually emerged from the convention debates was a Constitution in which both safeguards – the political and the judicial – were regarded as vital to the integrity of the federal system.

## Final remarks

If a 'federal theory' can be identified in the Australian Constitution, it is summed up in the aphorism of John Alexander Cockburn that 'local government, self government and government by the people are analogous terms'.[84] As such, the Constitution was certainly about 'government by the people', and perhaps even 'popular sovereignty'. But popular government did not exclusively mean national majoritarian government. The idea of local self-government implied that there were numerous configurations of 'the people': in localities, in states and in the federation as a whole. In this context, Barton's recognition that parliamentary representation was founded in something like Freeman's federative principle, 'from mark, to hundred, to shire' takes on an additional significance.[85] If a theory of 'popular sovereignty' is presupposed by the federal constitutional system, it is a theory which contemplates varying configurations of the 'people' and the 'peoples' constituting their

---

[81] *Tasmania* v. *Commonwealth* (1904) 1 CLR 329, 333–4, 338–40 (Griffith CJ), 346–50 (Barton J), 358–60 (O'Connor J).

[82] *Cole* v. *Whitfield* (1988) 165 CLR 360, 385.

[83] Herbert Wechsler, 'The Political Safeguards of Federalism: The Role of the States in the Composition and Selection of the National Government' (1954) 54 *Columbia Law Review* 543; Larry Kramer, 'Putting the Politics Back into the Political Safeguards of Federalism' (2000) 100 *Columbia Law Review* 215; but cf. Ernest Young, 'The Rehnquist Court's Two Federalisms' (2004) 83 *Texas Law Review* 1.

[84] *Convention Debates, Adelaide* (1897), 338–9.     [85] *Ibid.*, 388.

governments in their distinct capacities, as sections 51(xxxviii) and 128 especially envisage. Local self-government, within the context of federalism, meant both self-rule and shared rule. It meant a political community in which there are multiple loci of authority bound together by a common legal framework which has been adopted by covenant. It meant a 'non-centralised matrix', or, as Montesquieu put it, an 'assemblage of societies' which is itself a society.[86]

A second aspect of the theory of federalism underlying the Constitution is to be discerned in Deakin's point of departure from Higgins's rationalism: that 'it is a question between equal contracting parties, as to the terms and conditions on which they will enter the Federation'.[87] Presupposing that federalism is indeed akin to a covenant or a treaty, it is to be expected that the parties will make historically conditioned choices. Accordingly, the abstract philosopher will no doubt find plenty to quibble about in the result, but in so doing, the philosopher may well be wishing for something other than federalism. Even the federalist may express concern about the consistency or the expediency of those choices and ask whether too much might have been conceded by one or other of the parties. But federalism must always involve choice, and with commitment to the federal principle goes a fundamental respect for the historically conditioned choices which the parties have negotiated and recorded in the Constitution.

As a consequence, federalism, for the framers, was centrally concerned with formative processes, structures of federal representation and amendment procedures. Only after 1901 did the 'division of powers' come to be widely regarded as the very essence of federal government. This has led many to overlook the relationship between formation, representation and amendment within the Australian Constitution. It has been the objective of this book to recover this relationship and to show how central it was to the framers' theory of federalism. In the words of James Bryce, the framers created 'a Commonwealth of commonwealths, a Republic of republics, a State which, while one, is nevertheless composed of other States even more essential to its existence than it is to theirs'.[88] In other words: the Constitution of a federal commonwealth.

---

[86] Montesquieu, *Spirit of Laws*, 183–4.   [87] *Convention Debates, Adelaide* (1897), 650.
[88] Bryce, *American Commonwealth*, I, 12–15, 332.

SELECT PROVISIONS

**Commonwealth of Australia Constitution Act 1900 (UK)**

63 & 64 Victoria, c. 12
An Act to constitute the Commonwealth of Australia

*Preamble*

WHEREAS the people of New South Wales, Victoria, South Australia, Queensland, and Tasmania, humbly relying on the blessing of Almighty God, have agreed to unite in one indissoluble Federal Commonwealth under the Crown of the United Kingdom of Great Britain and Ireland, and under the Constitution hereby established:

And whereas it is expedient to provide for the admission into the Commonwealth of other Australasian Colonies and possessions of the Queen:

Be it therefore enacted by the Queen's most Excellent Majesty, by and with the advice and consent of the Lords Spiritual and Temporal, and Commons, in this present Parliament assembled, and by the authority of the same, as follows:–

Section 1 Short title

This Act may be cited as the Commonwealth of Australia Constitution Act.

Section 2 Act to extend to the Queen's successors

The provisions of this Act referring to the Queen shall extend to Her Majesty's heirs and successors in the sovereignty of the United Kingdom.

### Section 3 Proclamation of Commonwealth

It shall be lawful for the Queen, with the advice of the Privy Council, to declare by proclamation that, on and after a day therein appointed, not being later than one year after the passing of this Act, the people of New South Wales, Victoria, South Australia, Queensland, and Tasmania, and also, if Her Majesty is satisfied that the people of Western Australia have agreed thereto, of Western Australia, shall be united in a Federal Commonwealth under the name of the Commonwealth of Australia. But the Queen may, at any time after the proclamation, appoint a Governor-General for the Commonwealth.

### Section 4 Commencement of Act

The Commonwealth shall be established, and the Constitution of the Commonwealth shall take effect, on and after the day so appointed. But the Parliaments of the several colonies may at any time after the passing of this Act make any such laws, to come into operation on the day so appointed, as they might have made if the Constitution had taken effect at the passing of this Act.

### Section 5 Operation of the constitution and laws

This Act, and all laws made by the Parliament of the Commonwealth under the Constitution, shall be binding on the courts, judges, and people of every State and of every part of the Commonwealth, notwithstanding anything in the laws of any State; and the laws of the Commonwealth shall be in force on all British ships, the Queen's ships of war excepted, whose first port of clearance and whose port of destination are in the Commonwealth.

### Section 6 Definitions

'The Commonwealth' shall mean the Commonwealth of Australia as established under this Act.

'The States' shall mean such of the colonies of New South Wales, New Zealand, Queensland, Tasmania, Victoria, Western Australia, and South Australia, including the northern territory of South Australia, as for the time being are parts of the Commonwealth, and such colonies or territories as may be admitted into or established by the Commonwealth as States; and each of such parts of the Commonwealth shall be called 'a State.'

'Original States' shall mean such States as are parts of the Commonwealth at its establishment.

. . .

## Section 9 Constitution

The Constitution of the Commonwealth shall be as follows: –

. . .

### Chapter I The Parliament

#### Part I General

**Section 1 Legislative Power**

The legislative power of the Commonwealth shall be vested in a Federal Parliament, which shall consist of the Queen, a Senate, and a House of Representatives, and which is hereinafter called 'The Parliament', or 'The Parliament of the Commonwealth.'

**Section 2 Governor-General**

A Governor-General appointed by the Queen shall be Her Majesty's representative in the Commonwealth, and shall have and may exercise in the Commonwealth during the Queen's pleasure, but subject to this Constitution, such powers and functions of the Queen as Her Majesty may be pleased to assign to him.

. . .

#### Part II The Senate

**Section 7 The Senate**

The Senate shall be composed of senators for each State, directly chosen by the people of the State, voting, until the Parliament otherwise provides, as one electorate.

But until the Parliament of the Commonwealth otherwise provides, the Parliament of the State of Queensland, if that State be an Original State, may make laws dividing the State into divisions and determining the number of senators to be chosen for each division, and in the absence of such provision the State shall be one electorate.

Until the Parliament otherwise provides there shall be six senators for each Original State. The Parliament may make laws increasing or diminishing the number of senators for each State, but so that equal representation of the several Original States shall be maintained and that no Original State shall have less than six senators.

The senators shall be chosen for a term of six years, and the names of the senators chosen for each State shall be certified by the Governor to the Governor-General.

. . .

## Part III The House of Representatives

### Section 24 Constitution of House of Representatives

The House of Representatives shall be composed of members directly chosen by the people of the Commonwealth, and the number of such members shall be, as nearly as practicable, twice the number of the senators.

The number of members chosen in the several States shall be in proportion to the respective numbers of their people, and shall, until the Parliament otherwise provides, be determined, whenever necessary, in the following manner:–

(i) A quota shall be ascertained by dividing the number of the people of the Commonwealth, as shown by the latest statistics of the Commonwealth, by twice the number the senators:

(ii) The number of members to be chosen in each State shall be determined by dividing the number of the people of the State, as shown by the latest statistics of the Commonwealth, by the quota; and if on such division there is a remainder greater than one-half of the quota, one more member shall be chosen in the State.

But notwithstanding anything in this section, five members at least shall be chosen in each Original State.

. . .

### Section 29 Electoral divisions

Until the Parliament of the Commonwealth otherwise provides, the Parliament of any State may make laws for determining the divisions in each State for which members of the House of Representatives may be chosen, and the number of members to be chosen for each division. A division shall not be formed out of parts of different States.

In the absence of other provision, each State shall be one electorate.

. . .

Part V Powers of the Parliament

### Section 51 Legislative powers of the Parliament
The Parliament shall, subject to this Constitution, have power to make laws for the peace, order and good government of the Commonwealth with respect to:–

. . .

(xxxvi) Matters in respect of which this Constitution makes provision until the Parliament otherwise provides:

(xxxvii) Matters referred to the Parliament of the Commonwealth by the Parliament or Parliaments of any State or States, but so that the law shall extend only to States by whose Parliaments the matter is referred, or which afterwards adopt the law:

(xxxviii) The exercise within the Commonwealth, at the request or with the concurrence of the Parliaments of all the States directly concerned, of any power which can at the establishment of this Constitution be exercised only by the Parliament of the United Kingdom or by the Federal Council of Australasia:

(xxxix) Matters incidental to the execution of any power vested by this Constitution in the Parliament or in either House thereof, or in the Government of the Commonwealth, or in the Federal Judicature, or in any department or officer of the Commonwealth.

### Section 52 Exclusive powers of the Parliament
The Parliament shall, subject to this Constitution, have exclusive power to make laws for the peace, order, and good government of the Commonwealth with respect to:–

(i) The seat of government of the Commonwealth, and all places acquired by the Commonwealth for public purposes:

(ii) Matters relating to any department of the public service the control of which is by this Constitution transferred to the Executive Government of the Commonwealth:

(iii) Other matters declared by this Constitution to be within the exclusive power of the Parliament.

### Section 53 Powers of the Houses in respect of legislation

Proposed laws appropriating revenue or moneys, or imposing taxation, shall not originate in the Senate. But a proposed law shall not be taken to appropriate revenue or moneys, or to impose taxation, by reason only of its containing provisions for the imposition or appropriation of fines or other pecuniary penalties, or for the demand or payment or appropriation of fees for licenses, or fees for services under the proposed law.

The Senate may not amend proposed laws imposing taxation, or proposed laws appropriating revenue or moneys for the ordinary annual services of the Government.

The Senate may not amend any proposed law so as to increase any proposed charge or burden on the people.

The Senate may at any stage return to the House of Representatives any proposed law which the Senate may not amend, requesting, by message, the omission or amendment of any items or provisions therein. And the House of Representatives may, if it thinks fit, make any of such omissions or amendments, with or without modifications.

Except as provided in this section, the Senate shall have equal power with the House of Representatives in respect of all proposed laws.

### Section 54 Appropriation Bills

The proposed law which appropriates revenue or moneys for the ordinary annual services of the Government shall deal only with such appropriation.

### Section 55 Tax Bill

Laws imposing taxation shall deal only with the imposition of taxation, and any provision therein dealing with any other matter shall be of no effect.

Laws imposing taxation, except laws imposing duties of customs or of excise, shall deal with one subject of taxation only; but laws imposing duties of customs shall deal with duties of customs only, and laws imposing duties of excise shall deal with duties of excise only.

### Section 56 Recommendation of money votes

A vote, resolution, or proposed law for the appropriation of revenue or moneys shall not be passed unless the purpose of the appropriation has in the same session been recommended by message of the Governor-General to the House in which the proposal originated.

## Section 57 Disagreement between the Houses

If the House of Representatives passes any proposed law, and the Senate rejects or fails to pass it, or passes it with amendments to which the House of Representatives will not agree, and if after an interval of three months the House of Representatives, in the same or the next session, again passes the proposed law with or without any amendments which have been made, suggested, or agreed to by the Senate, and the Senate rejects or fails to pass it, or passes it with amendments to which the House of Representatives will not agree, the Governor-General may dissolve the Senate and the House of Representatives simultaneously. But such dissolution shall not take place within six months before the date of the expiry of the House of Representatives by effluxion of time.

If after such dissolution the House of Representatives again passes the proposed law, with or without any amendments which have been made, suggested, or agreed to by the Senate, and the Senate rejects or fails to pass it, or passes it with amendments to which the House of Representatives will not agree, the Governor-General may convene a joint sitting of the members of the Senate and of the House of Representatives.

The members present at the joint sitting may deliberate and shall vote together upon the proposed law as last proposed by the House of Representatives, and upon amendments, if any, which have been made therein by one House and not agreed to by the other, and any such amendments which are affirmed by an absolute majority of the total number of the members of the Senate and House of Representatives shall be taken to have been carried, and if the proposed law, with the amendments, if any, so carried is affirmed by an absolute majority of the total number of the members of the Senate and House of Representatives, it shall be taken to have been duly passed by both Houses of the Parliament, and shall be presented to the Governor-General for the Queen's assent.

. . .

### Chapter II The Executive Government

### Section 61 Executive Power

The executive power of the Commonwealth is vested in the Queen and is exercisable by the Governor-General as the Queen's representative, and extends to the execution and maintenance of this Constitution, and of the laws of the Commonwealth.

. . .

### Section 64 Ministers of State

The Governor-General may appoint officers to administer such departments of State of the Commonwealth as the Governor-General in Council may establish. Such officers shall hold office during the pleasure of the Governor-General. They shall be members of the Federal Executive Council, and shall be the Queen's Ministers of State for the Commonwealth.

...

## Chapter III The Judicative

### Section 71 Judicial power and Courts

The judicial power of the Commonwealth shall be vested in a Federal Supreme Court, to be called the High Court of Australia, and in such other federal courts as the Parliament creates, and in such other courts as it invests with federal jurisdiction. The High Court shall consist of a Chief Justice, and so many other Justices, not less than two, as the Parliament prescribes.

...

## Chapter IV Finance and Trade

### Section 81 Consolidated Revenue Fund

All revenues or moneys raised or received by the Executive Government of the Commonwealth shall form one Consolidated Revenue Fund, to be appropriated for the purposes of the Commonwealth in the manner and subject to the charges and liabilities imposed by this Constitution.

...

### Section 83 Money to be appropriated by law

No money shall be drawn from the Treasury of the Commonwealth except under appropriation made by law.

...

## Chapter V The States

### Section 106 Saving of Constitutions

The Constitution of each State of the Commonwealth shall, subject to this Constitution, continue as at the establishment of the Commonwealth, or as at the admission or establishment of the State, as the case may be, until altered in accordance with the Constitution of the State.

## Section 107 Saving of Power of State Parliaments

Every power of the Parliament of a Colony which has become or becomes a State, shall, unless it is by this Constitution exclusively vested in the Parliament of the Commonwealth or withdrawn from the Parliament of the State, continue as at the establishment of the Commonwealth, or as at the admission or establishment of the State, as the case may be.

## Section 108 Saving of State laws

Every law in force in a Colony which has become or becomes a State, and relating to any matter within the powers of the Parliament of the Commonwealth, shall, subject to this Constitution, continue in force in the State; and until provision is made in that behalf by the Parliament of the Commonwealth, the Parliament of the State shall have such powers of alteration and of repeal in respect of any such law as the Parliament of the Colony had until the Colony became a State.

## Section 109 Inconsistency of laws

When a law of a State is inconsistent with a law of the Commonwealth, the latter shall prevail, and the former shall, to the extent of the inconsistency, be invalid.

. . .

### Chapter VI New States

### Section 121 New States may be admitted or established

The Parliament may admit to the Commonwealth or establish new States, and may upon such admission or establishment make or impose such terms and conditions, including the extent of representation in either House of the Parliament, as it thinks fit.

### Section 122 Government of territories

The Parliament may make laws for the government of any territory surrendered by any State to and accepted by the Commonwealth, or of any territory placed by the Queen under the authority of and accepted by the Commonwealth, or otherwise acquired by the Commonwealth, and may allow the representation of such territory in either House of the Parliament to the extent and on the terms which it thinks fit.

### Section 123 Alteration of limits of States

The Parliament of the Commonwealth may, with the consent of the Parliament of a State, and the approval of the majority of the electors of the State voting upon the question, increase, diminish, or otherwise alter the limits of the State, upon such terms and conditions as may be agreed on, and may, with the like consent, make provision respecting the effect and operation of any increase or diminution or alteration of territory in relation to any State affected.

### Section 124 Formation of new States

A new State may be formed by separation of territory from a State, but only with the consent of the Parliament thereof, and a new State may be formed by the union of two or more State or parts of States, but only with the consent of the Parliaments of the States affected.

...

*Chapter VIII Alteration of the Constitution*

### Section 128 Mode of altering the Constitution

This Constitution shall not be altered except in the following manner:–

The proposed law for the alteration thereof must be passed by an absolute majority of each House of the Parliament, and not less than two nor more than six months after its passage through both Houses the proposed law shall be submitted in each State and Territory to the electors qualified to vote for the election of members of the House of Representatives.

But if either House passes any such proposed law by an absolute majority, and the other House rejects or fails to pass it, or passes it with any amendment to which the first-mentioned House will not agree, and if after an interval of three months the first-mentioned House in the same or the next session again passes the proposed law by an absolute majority with or without any amendment which has been made or agreed to by the other House, and such other House rejects or fails to pass it or passes it with any amendment to which the first-mentioned House will not agree, the Governor-General may submit the proposed law as last proposed by the first-mentioned House, and either with or without any amendments subsequently agreed to by both Houses, to the electors in each State and Territory qualified to vote for the election of the House of Representatives.

When a proposed law is submitted to the electors the vote shall be taken in such manner as the Parliament prescribes. But until the qualification of electors of members of the House of Representatives becomes uniform throughout the Commonwealth, only one-half the electors voting for and against the proposed law shall be counted in any State in which adult suffrage prevails.

And if in a majority of the States a majority of the electors voting approve the proposed law, and if a majority of all the electors voting also approve the proposed law, it shall be presented to the Governor-General for the Queen's assent.

No alteration diminishing the proportionate representation of any State in either House of the Parliament, or the minimum number of representatives of a State in the House of Representatives, or increasing, diminishing, or otherwise altering the limits of the State, or in any manner affecting the provisions of the Constitution in relation thereto, shall become law unless the majority of the electors voting in that State approve the proposed law.

In this section 'Territory' means any territory referred to in section one hundred and twenty-two of this Constitution in respect of which there is a law in force allowing its representation in the House of Representatives.

## Statute of Westminster 1931 (UK)

### 22 George V, c. 4

An Act to give effect to certain resolutions passed by Imperial Conferences held in the years 1926 and 1930.

WHEREAS the delegates to His Majesty's Governments in the United Kingdom, the Dominion of Canada, the Commonwealth of Australia, the Dominion of New Zealand, the Union of South Africa, the Irish Free State and Newfoundland, at Imperial Conferences holden at Westminster in the years of our Lord nineteen hundred and twenty-six and nineteen hundred and thirty did concur in making the declarations and resolutions set forth in the Reports of the said Conference:

AND WHEREAS it is meet and proper to set out by way of preamble to this Act that, inasmuch as the Crown is the symbol to the free association of the members of the British Commonwealth of Nations, and as they are united by a common allegiance to the Crown, it would be in accord with the established constitutional position of all the members of the Commonwealth in relation to one another that any alteration in the law touching the Succession to the Throne or the Royal Style and Titles shall hereafter require the assent as well of the Parliaments of all the Dominions as of the Parliament of the United Kingdom:

AND WHEREAS it is in accord with the established constitutional position that no law hereafter made by the Parliament of the United Kingdom shall extend to any of the said Dominions as part of the law of that Dominion otherwise than at the request and with the consent of that Dominion:

AND WHEREAS it is necessary for the ratifying, confirming and establishing of certain of the said declarations and resolutions of the said Conferences that a law be made and enacted in due form by authority of the Parliament of the United Kingdom:

AND WHEREAS the Dominion of Canada, the Commonwealth of Australia, the Dominion of New Zealand, the Union of South Africa, the Irish Free State and Newfoundland have severally requested and consented to the submission of a measure to the Parliament of the United Kingdom for making such provision with regard to the matters aforesaid as is hereafter in this Act contained:

NOW, THEREFORE, be it enacted by the King's Most Excellent Majesty by and with the advice and consent of the Lords Spiritual and Temporal, and Commons, in this present Parliament assembled, and by the authority of the same, as follows:–

### Section 1 Meaning of 'Dominion' in this Act

In this Act the expression 'Dominion' means any of the following Dominions, that is to say, the Dominion of Canada, the Commonwealth of Australia, the Dominion of New Zealand, the Union of South Africa, the Irish Free State and Newfoundland.

*Section 2 Validity of laws made by Parliament of a*
*Dominion 28 & 29 Vict c. 63*

(1) The Colonial Laws Validity Act, 1865, shall not apply to any law made after the commencement of this Act by the Parliament of a Dominion.

(2) No law and no provision of any law made after the commencement of this Act by the Parliament of a Dominion shall be void or inoperative on the ground that it is repugnant to the law of England, or to the provisions of any existing or future Act of Parliament of the United Kingdom, or to any order, rule, or regulation made under any such Act, and the powers of the Parliament of a Dominion shall include the power to repeal or amend any such Act, order, rule or regulation in so far as the same is part of the law of the Dominion.

. . .

*Section 4 Parliament of United Kingdom not to legislate*
*for Dominion except by its consent*

No Act of Parliament of the United Kingdom passed after the commencement of this Act shall extend or be deemed to extend, to a Dominion as part of the law of that Dominion, unless it is expressly declared in that Act that that Dominion has requested, and consented to, the enactment thereof.

. . .

*Section 8 Saving for Constitution Acts of Australia and New Zealand*

Nothing in this Act shall be deemed to confer any power to repeal or alter the Constitution or the Constitution Act of the Commonwealth of Australia or the Constitution Act of the Dominion of New Zealand otherwise than in accordance with the law existing before the commencement of this Act.

*Section 9 Saving with respect to States of Australia*

(1) Nothing in this Act shall be deemed to authorize the Parliament of the Commonwealth of Australia to make laws on any matter within the authority of the States of Australia, not being a matter within the authority of the Parliament or Government of the Commonwealth of Australia.

(2) Nothing in this Act shall be deemed to require the concurrence of the Parliament or Government of the Commonwealth of Australia, in any law made by the Parliament of the United Kingdom with respect to any matter within the authority of the States of Australia, not being a matter within the authority of the Parliament or Government of the Commonwealth of Australia, in any case where it would have been in accordance with the constitutional practice existing before the commencement of this Act that the Parliament of the United Kingdom should make that law without such concurrence.

(3) In the application of this Act to the Commonwealth of Australia the request and consent referred to in section four shall mean the request and consent of the Parliament and Government of the Commonwealth.

*Section 10 Certain sections of Act not to apply to Australia,
New Zealand or Newfoundland unless adopted*

(1) None of the following sections of this Act, that is to say, sections two, three, four, five and six, shall extend to a Dominion to which this section applies as part of the law of that Dominion unless that section is adopted by the Parliament of the Dominion, and any Act of that Parliament adopting any section of this Act may provide that the adoption shall have effect either from the commencement of this Act or from such later date as is specified in the adopting Act.

(2) The Parliament of any such Dominion as aforesaid may at any time revoke the adoption of any section referred to in subsection (1) of this section.

(3) The Dominions to which this section applies are the Commonwealth of Australia, the Dominion of New Zealand and Newfoundland.

. . .

**Australia Act 1986 (Cth)**

An Act to bring constitutional arrangements affecting the Commonwealth and the States into conformity with the status of the Commonwealth of Australia as a sovereign, independent and federal nation.

WHEREAS the Prime Minister of the Commonwealth and the Premiers of the States at conferences held in Canberra on 24 and 25 June 1982 and 21 June 1984 agreed on the taking of certain measures to bring constitutional arrangements affecting the Commonwealth and the States into conformity with the status of the Commonwealth of Australia as a sovereign, independent and federal nation:

AND WHEREAS in pursuance of paragraph 51 (xxxviii) of the Constitution the Parliaments of all the States have requested the Parliament of the Commonwealth to enact an Act in the terms of this Act:

BE IT THEREFORE ENACTED by the Queen, and the Senate and the House of Representatives of the Commonwealth of Australia, as follows:

### Section 1 Termination of power of Parliament of United Kingdom to legislate for Australia

No Act of the Parliament of the United Kingdom passed after the commencement of this Act shall extend, or be deemed to extend, to the Commonwealth, to a State or to a Territory as part of the law of the Commonwealth, of the State or of the Territory.

### Section 2 Legislative powers of Parliaments of States

(1) It is hereby declared and enacted that the legislative powers of the Parliament of each State include full power to make laws for the peace, order and good government of that State that have extra-territorial operation.

(2) It is hereby further declared and enacted that the legislative powers of the Parliament of each State include all legislative powers that the Parliament of the United Kingdom might have exercised before the commencement of this Act for the peace, order and good government of that State but nothing in this subsection confers on a State any capacity that the State did not have immediately before the commencement of this Act to engage in relations with countries outside Australia.

### Section 3 Termination of restrictions on legislative powers of Parliaments of States

(1) The Act of the Parliament of the United Kingdom known as the Colonial Laws Validity Act 1865 shall not apply to any law made after the commencement of this Act by the Parliament of a State.

(2) No law and no provision of any law made after the commencement of this Act by the Parliament of a State shall be void or inoperative

on the ground that it is repugnant to the law of England, or to the provisions of any existing or future Act of the Parliament of the United Kingdom, or to any order, rule or regulation made under any such Act, and the powers of the Parliament of a State shall include the power to repeal or amend any such Act, order, rule or regulation in so far as it is part of the law of the State.

. . .

### Section 5 Commonwealth Constitution, Constitution Act and Statute of Westminster not affected

Sections 2 and 3 (2) above –

(a) are subject to the Commonwealth of Australia Constitution Act and to the Constitution of the Commonwealth; and
(b) do not operate so as to give any force or effect to a provision of an Act of the Parliament of a State that would repeal, amend or be repugnant to this Act, the Commonwealth of Australia Constitution Act, the Constitution of the Commonwealth or the Statute of Westminster 1931 as amended and in force from time to time.

### Section 6 Manner and form of making certain state laws

Notwithstanding sections 2 and 3(2) above, a law made after the commencement of this Act by the Parliament of a State respecting the constitution, powers or procedure of the Parliament of the State shall be of no force or effect unless it is made in such manner and form as may from time to time be required by a law made by that Parliament, whether made before or after the commencement of this Act.

### Section 7 Powers and functions of Her Majesty and Governors in respect of States

(1) Her Majesty's representative in each State shall be the Governor.
(2) Subject to subsections (3) and (4) below, all powers and functions of Her Majesty in respect of a State are exercisable only by the Governor of the State.
(3) Subsection (2) above does not apply in relation to the power to appoint, and the power to terminate the appointment of, the Governor of a State.

(4) While Her Majesty is personally present in a State, Her Majesty is not precluded from exercising any of Her powers and functions in respect of the State that are the subject of subsection (2) above.

(5) The advice to Her Majesty in relation to the exercise of the powers and functions of Her Majesty in respect of a State shall be tendered by the Premier of the State.

### Section 8 State laws not subject to disallowance or suspension of operation

An Act of the Parliament of a State that has been assented to by the Governor of the State shall not, after the commencement of this Act, be subject to disallowance by Her Majesty, nor shall its operation be suspended pending the signification of Her Majesty's pleasure thereon.

### Section 9 State laws not subject to withholding of assent or reservation

(1) No law or instrument shall be of any force or effect in so far as it purports to require the Governor of a State to withhold assent from any Bill for an Act of the State that has been passed in such manner and form as may from time to time be required by a law made by the Parliament of the State.

(2) No law or instrument shall be of any force or effect in so far as it purports to require the reservation of any Bill for an Act of a State for the signification of Her Majesty's pleasure thereon.

### Section 10 Termination of responsibility of United Kingdom Government in relation to State matters

After the commencement of this Act Her Majesty's Government in the United Kingdom shall have no responsibility for the government of any State.

. . .

### Section 15 Method of repeal or amendment of this Act or Statute of Westminster

(1) This Act or the Statute of Westminster 1931, as amended and in force from time to time, in so far as it is part of the law of the

Commonwealth, of a State or of a Territory, may be repealed or amended by an Act of the Parliament of the Commonwealth passed at the request or with the concurrence of the Parliaments of all the States and, subject to subsection (3) below, only in that manner.

(2) For the purposes of subsection (1) above, an Act of the Parliament of the Commonwealth that is repugnant to this Act or the Statute of Westminster 1931, as amended and in force from time to time, or to any provision of this Act or of that Statute as so amended and in force, shall, to the extent of the repugnancy, be deemed an Act to repeal or amend the Act, Statute or provision to which it is repugnant.

(3) Nothing in subsection (1) above limits or prevents the exercise by the Parliament of the Commonwealth of any powers that may be conferred upon that Parliament by any alteration to the Constitution of the Commonwealth made in accordance with section 128 of the Constitution of the Commonwealth after the commencement of this Act.

# BIBLIOGRAPHY

## Primary Australian materials

### Official records

*Official Record of the Proceedings and Debates of the Australasian Federation Conference, Melbourne* (Melbourne: Government Printer, 1890).

*Official Report of the National Australasian Convention Debates, Sydney, 2 March to 9 April, 1891* (Sydney: Acting Government Printer, 1891; reprinted Sydney: Legal Books, 1986).

*Official Report of the Federation Conference Held in the Court-House, Corowa, on Monday 31st July, and Tuesday, 1ˢᵗ August, 1893* (Corowa: James C. Leslie, 1893).

*Proceedings of the People's Federal Convention at Bathurst* (Sydney: Gordon and Gotch, 1897).

*Official Report of the National Australasian Convention Debates, Adelaide, March 22 to May 5, 1897* (Adelaide: Government Printer, 1897; reprinted Sydney: Legal Books, 1986).

*Official Record of the Debates of the National Australasian Convention, Second Session: Sydney, 2nd to 24th September 1897* (Sydney: Government Printer, 1897; reprinted Sydney: Legal Books, 1986).

*Official Record of the Debates of the National Australasian Convention, Third Session: Melbourne, 20th January to 17th March, 1898*, 2 vols. (Melbourne: Government Printer, 1898; reprinted Sydney: Legal Books, 1986).

*Australian Federal Convention Papers 1897–1898*, no. 1 (MF47); no. 2 (MF48); no. 3 (MF49), MS8871, GRG72, State Library of Victoria (cited as *Australian Federal Convention Papers* (1897–8)).

Parliament of the United Kingdom, *Commonwealth of Australia Constitution Bill: Reprint of the Debates in Parliament, The Official Correspondence with the Australian Delegates, and Other Papers* (London: Wyman and Sons, 1900).

Inter-Imperial Relations Committee, Imperial Conference 1926, *Report, Proceedings and Memoranda*, E (IR/26) series (1926).

*Private papers*

Papers of Sir Richard Chaffey Baker, State Library of South Australia, Adelaide (cited as Baker Papers).

Papers of Sir Edmund Barton, Australian National Library, Canberra (cited as Barton Papers).

Papers of Sir Charles Gavan Duffy, La Trobe Collection, State Library of Victoria, Melbourne (cited as Duffy Papers).

Papers of Sir Samuel Walker Griffith, Dixson Collection, State Library of New South Wales, Sydney (cited as Griffith Papers).

Papers of Charles Henry Pearson, La Trobe Collection, State Library of Victoria, Melbourne (cited as Pearson Papers).

Papers of Bernhard Ringrose Wise, Australian National Library, Canberra (cited as Wise Papers).


*Collections of documents*

Anderson, Hugh (ed.), *Tocsin: Contesting the Constitution 1897–1900* (Melbourne: Red Rooster Press, 2000).

Bennett, John M. and Alex C. Castles (eds.), *A Source Book of Australian Legal History* (Sydney: Law Book Co., 1979).

Bennett, Scott (ed.), *The Making of the Commonwealth* (Melbourne: Cassell, 1971).

*Federation* (Melbourne: Cassell, 1975).

Clark, C. M. H. (ed.), *Select Documents in Australian History 1851–1900* (Sydney: Angus and Robertson, 1955).

Craven, Gregory J. (ed.), *The Convention Debates 1891–1898: Commentaries, Indices and Guide* (Sydney: Legal Books, 1986).

Foster, Stephen G., Susan Marsden and Roslyn Russell (eds.), *Federation: The Guide to Records* (Canberra: National Archives of Australia, 1998).

State Library of South Australia, *Collected Pamphlets on Australian Federation* [1862–1900], 2 vols. (Adelaide: State Library of South Australia, no date).


*Contemporary Australian works*

Baker, Richard Chaffey, *A Manual of Reference to Authorities for the use of the Members of the National Australasian Convention which will assemble at Sydney on March 2, 1891, for the Purpose of Drafting a Constitution for the Dominion of Australia* (Adelaide: E. A. Petherick and Co., 1891).

*The Executive in a Federation* (Adelaide: C. E. Bristow, Government Printer, 1897).

*Federation* (Adelaide: Scrymgour and Sons, 1897).

'Sir Richard Baker at Norwood', *The Register*, 1 March 1901 (Baker Papers, series 1, vol. 7 ('Election speeches')).

Barton, George Burnett (ed.), *The Draft Bill to Constitute the Commonwealth of Australia as Adopted by the Convention of 1891* (Sydney: Acting Government Printer, 1891).

Clark, Andrew Inglis, 'Australian Federation (Confidential)' (Hobart: Attorney-General's Office, 1891) (Wise Papers, MS1708).

*A Bill for the Federation of the Australasian Colonies* [1891] (in Samuel Walker Griffith, *Successive Stages of the Constitution of the Commonwealth of Australia* (1891); reproduced in John Reynolds, 'A. I. Clark's American Sympathies and his Influence on Australian Federation' (1958) 32 *Australian Law Journal* 62; White, Michael and Aladin Rahemtula (eds.), *Samuel Griffith: The Law and the Constitution* (Sydney: Law Book Co., 2002), appendix 1).

*Studies in Australian Constitutional Law* (1st edn, Melbourne: Maxwell, 1901; reprinted Sydney: Legal Books, 1997).

'The Supremacy of the Judiciary under the Constitution of the United States, and under the Constitution of the Commonwealth of Australia' (1903) 17 *Harvard Law Review* 1.

Cockburn, John Alexander, *Australian Federation* (London: Horace Marshall and Son, 1901).

Deakin, Alfred, 'Federal Council of Australasia' (February 1895) *Review of Reviews* 154.

*The Federal Story: The Inner History of the Federal Cause*, Herbert Brooks (ed.) (Melbourne: Melbourne University Press, 1944).

*Federated Australia: Selections from Letters to the Morning Post 1900–1910*, John A. La Nauze (ed.) (Melbourne: Melbourne University Press, 1968).

Duffy, Charles Gavan, *My Life in Two Hemispheres* (London: Fisher Unwin, 1898).

Garran, Robert Randolph, *The Coming Commonwealth: An Australian Handbook of Federal Government* (Sydney: Angus and Robertson, 1897).

*Commentaries on the Constitution of the Commonwealth of Australia* (Sydney: Angus and Robertson, 1901).

'The Federation Movement and the Founding of the Commonwealth', *Cambridge History of the British Empire*, vol. VII, pt I (Cambridge: Cambridge University Press, 1933).

*Prosper the Commonwealth* (Sydney: Angus and Robertson, 1958).

Griffith, Samuel Walker, *Successive Stages of the Constitution of the Commonwealth of Australia* [1891] (Griffith Papers, MS Q198, CY221).

*Notes on Australian Federation: Its Nature and Probable Effects* (Brisbane: Government Printer, 1896).

*Some Conditions of Australian Federation* (Brisbane: Government Printer, 1896).

*Notes on the Draft Federal Constitution Framed by the Adelaide Convention of 1897* (A Paper Presented to the Government of Queensland by the Honourable Sir Samuel Walker Griffith, G.C.M.G., Chief Justice of that Colony) (*Australian Federal Convention Papers* (1897–8), no. 1, MS8871, MF47, GRG72, series 1/20, item 6; reprinted *Queensland Legislative Council, Journal* (1897), vol. 47, pt 1).

*Australian Federation and the Draft Commonwealth Bill: A Paper Read before the Members of the Queensland Federation League* (Brisbane: Government Printer, 1899).

Hearn, William Edward, *The Theory of Legal Duties and Rights: An Introduction to Analytical Jurisprudence* (Melbourne: Government Printer, 1883).

*The Government of England, its Structure and Development* (2nd edn, Melbourne: Robertson, 1886).

Higgins, Henry Bournes, *Essays and Addresses on the Australian Commonwealth Bill* (Melbourne: Atlas Press, 1900).

'The Rigid Constitution' (1905) 20 *Political Science Quarterly* 203.

Isaacs, Isaac, *Australian Democracy and our Constitutional System* (Melbourne: Horticultural Press, 1939).

Jefferis, James, *Australia Confederated* (Sydney: Woods and Co., 1880).

Jenks, Edward, *The Government of Victoria* (London: Macmillan, 1891).

Just, Thomas C., *Leading Facts connected with Federation Compiled for the Information of the Tasmanian Delegates to the Australasian Federal Convention 1891, on the Order of the Government of Tasmania* (Hobart: The Mercury Office, 1891).

Kingston, Charles Cameron, *A Bill for an Act for the Union of the Australian Colonies* [1891] (in Samuel Walker Griffith, *Successive Stages of the Constitution of the Commonwealth of Australia* (1891); reproduced in Michael White and Aladin Rahemtula (eds.), *Samuel Griffith: The Law and the Constitution* (Sydney: Law Book Co., 2002), appendix 2).

*The Democratic Element in Australian Federation* (Adelaide: J. L. Bonython and Co., 1897).

Kirwan, John, *My Life's Adventure* (London: Eyre and Spottiswoode, 1936).

Lang, John Dunmore, *The Coming Event, or Freedom and Independence for the Seven United Provinces of Australia* (Sydney: J. L. Sherriff, 1870).

Moore, William Harrison, *The Constitution of the Commonwealth of Australia* (1st edn, London: John Murray, 1902; 2nd edn, Melbourne: Maxwell, 1910; reprinted Sydney: Legal Books, 1997).

Parkes, Henry, *Fifty Years in the Making of Australian History* (London: Longmans, Green and Co., 1892).

Pearson, Charles Henry, *The Struggle for Separation* (Manuscript, n.d.) (Pearson Papers, MS7129, box 434/2).

Piddington, Albert Bathurst, *Popular Government and Federalism* (Sydney: Angus and Robertson, 1898).

Quick, John, *A Digest of Federal Constitutions* (Bendigo: J. B. Young, 1896).

*Legislative Powers of the Commonwealth and the States of Australia with Proposed Amendments* (Melbourne: Maxwell, 1919).

Quick, John and Robert Randolph Garran, *The Annotated Constitution of the Australian Commonwealth* (Sydney: Angus and Robertson, 1901; reprinted Sydney: Legal Books, 1976).

Spence, Catherine Helen, 'Side-lights on federation', *The Register*, 11 January 1897.

'Federal Convention Elections and Effective Voting' (Eildon, St Peters, 16 March 1897).

Willoughby, Howard, *Australian Federation: Its Aims and Its Possibilities: With a Digest of the Proposed Constitution, Official Statistics, and a Review of the National Convention* (Melbourne: Sands and McDougall Ltd, 1891).

Wise, Bernhard Ringrose, *The Commonwealth of Australia* (London: Isaac Pitman, 1909).

*The Making of the Australian Commonwealth 1889–1890: A Stage in the Growth of Empire* (London: Longmans, Green and Co., 1913).

## Primary comparative materials

### Collections of documents and debates

Ajzenstat, Janet, Paul Romney and Ian Gentles (eds.), *Canada's Founding Debates* (Toronto: University of Toronto Press, 2003).

Bailyn, Bernard (ed.), *The Debate on the Constitution: Federalist and Antifederalist Speeches, Articles, and Letters During the Struggle over Ratification*, 2 vols. (New York: Library of America, 1993).

Browne, G. P. (ed.), *Documents on the Confederation of British North America* (Toronto: McClelland and Stewart, 1969).

Elliot, Jonathan (ed.), *The Debates in the Several State Conventions, on the Adoption of the Federal Constitution, as Recommended by the General Convention at Philadelphia in 1787*, 4 vols. (2nd edn, Washington: Jonathan Elliot, 1836).

*Eternal Bond of Brothers Between Uri, Schwyz and Unterwalden* [1291], R. Hacken (trans.) (Provo: Harold B. Lee Library, Brigham Young University, n.d.).

Farrand, Max (ed.), *The Records of the Federal Convention of 1787* (New Haven: Yale University Press, 1911).

Jensen, Merrill, J. P. Kaminski and G. J. Saladino (eds.), *The Documentary History of the Ratification of the Constitution*, 29 vols. (Madison: State Historical Society of Wisconsin, 1976–).

Lutz, Donald S. (ed.), *Colonial Origins of the American Constitution: A Documentary History* (Indianapolis: Liberty Fund, 1998).

Madison, James, *Notes of Debates in the Federal Convention of 1787* [1840], Adrienne Koch (ed.) (New York: W. W. Norton and Co., 1966).

Storing, Herbert J. (ed.), *The Anti-Federalist: Writings by the Opponents of the Constitution, An Abridgment by Murray Dry, of The Complete Anti-Federalist* (Chicago: University of Chicago Press, 1985).

### Contemporary works and earlier sources

Adams, Francis O. and C. D. Cunningham, *The Swiss Confederation* (London: Macmillan, 1889).

Althusius, Johannes, *An Abridged Translation of Politics Methodically Set Forth and Illustrated with Sacred and Profane Examples*, Frederick S. Carney (trans.) (Indianapolis: Liberty Fund, 1995) (translation of *Politica methodice digesta atque exemplis sacris et profanis illustrata* (3rd edn, 1614), Carl Friedrich (ed.) (New York: Arno Press, 1979)).

Austin, John, *The Province of Jurisprudence Determined* (London: John Murray, 1832; reprinted London: Weidenfeld and Nicolson, 1954).

*Lectures on Jurisprudence, or, the Philosophy of Positive Law*, R. Campbell (ed.) (4th edn, London: John Murray, 1879).

Bagehot, Walter, *The English Constitution* (1st edn, London: Chapman and Hall, 1867; 2nd edn, London: Henry S. King, 1872; reprinted London: Fontana, 1963).

Baker, Andrew Jackson, *Annotated Constitution of the United States* (Chicago: Callaghan and Company, 1891).

Blackstone, William, *Commentaries on the Laws of England* (Oxford: Oxford University Press, 1765).

Bluntschli, Johann K., *The Theory of the State*, D. G. Ritchie, P. E. Matheson and R. Lodge (trans.) (Oxford: Clarendon Press, 1885) (translation of *Lehre vom modernen Staat*. Pt I: *Allgemeine Staatslehre* [1875]).

Bodin, Jean, *Six Livres de la République* [1576] in J. H. Franklin (ed. and trans.), *On Sovereignty, Four Chapters from The Six Books of the Commonweale* (Cambridge: Cambridge University Press, 1992).

Borgeaud, Charles, *Adoption and Amendment of Constitutions in Europe and America*, C. D. Hazen (trans.) (New York: Macmillan, 1895).

Bourinot, John G., *A Manual of the Constitutional History of Canada* (Montreal: Dawson, 1888).

*Federal Government in Canada* (Baltimore: Johns Hopkins University, 1889).

Bryce, James, *The American Commonwealth*, 2 vols. (2nd edn, London: Macmillan, 1889; new edn, London: Macmillan, 1914).

*The Holy Roman Empire* (4th edn, London: Macmillan, 1895).

*Studies in History and Jurisprudence*, 2 vols. (Oxford: Clarendon Press, 1901).

*Modern Democracies* (London: Macmillan, 1921).

Burgess, John W., *Political Science and Comparative Constitutional Law*, 2 vols. (Boston: Ginn and Co., 1890).

'The Ideal American Commonwealth' (1895) 10 *Political Science Quarterly* 404.

*Recent Changes in American Constitutional Theory* (New York: Columbia University Press, 1923).

Calhoun, John C., *A Discourse on the Constitution and Government of the United States* [1853], in R. M. Lence (ed.), *Union and Liberty: The Political Philosophy of John C. Calhoun* (Indianapolis: Liberty Fund, 1992).

Clarke, William M. A., 'Edward Augustus Freeman' (1892) 12(5) *The New England Magazine* 607.

Cooley, Thomas M., *A Treatise on the Constitutional Limitations which rest upon the Legislative Power of the States of the American Union* (Boston: Little, Brown and Co., 1868; reprinted New York: Da Capo Press, 1972).

Dicey, Albert Venn, 'Federal Government' (1885) *Law Quarterly Review* 80.

*Introduction to the Study of the Law of the Constitution* (4th edn, London: Macmillan, 1893; 5th edn, London: Macmillan, 1897; 8th edn, London: Macmillan, 1920).

*Lectures on the Relation between Law and Public Opinion in England During the Nineteenth Century* (London: Macmillan, 1905).

Durham, John George, First Earl of Lambton, *Lord Durham's Report* [1839], C. P. Lucas (ed.), 3 vols. (Oxford: Clarendon Press, 1912).

Fiske, John, 'Edward Augustus Freeman' (1893) 71(423) *The Atlantic Monthly* 99.

Ford, Henry Jones, *The Rise and Growth of American Politics: A Sketch of Constitutional Development* (London: Macmillan, 1898; reprinted New York: Da Capo Press, 1967).

Freeman, Edward A., *The History of the Norman Conquest of England*, 6 vols. (3rd edn, Oxford: Clarendon Press, 1867–79).

'Presidential Government' in *Historical Essays*, first series (4th edn, London: Macmillan, 1886).

*History of Federal Government in Greece and Italy* (2nd edn, London: Macmillan, 1893).

*The Growth of the English Constitution from the Earliest Times* (3rd edn, London: Macmillan, 1898).

Gierke, Otto von, *The Development of Political Theory*, Bernard Freyd (trans.) (New York: Howard Fertig, 1966) (translation of *Johannes Althusius und die*

*Entwicklung der natturrechtliclzen Staatstheorien; zugleich ein Beitrag zur Geschichte der Rechtssytematik* [1880]).

*Political Theories of the Middle Age*, F. W. Maitland (trans.) (Cambridge University Press, 1968) (translation of *Die publicistischen Lehren des Mittelalters*, in *Das deutsche Genossenschaftsrecht*, vol. III [1881]).

Hare, Thomas, *A Treatise on the Election of Representatives, Parliamentary and Municipal* (new edn, London: Longman, Brown, Green, Longmans and Roberts, 1861).

Harrington, James, *The Commonwealth of Oceana* [1656], J. G. A. Pocock (ed.) (Cambridge: Cambridge University Press, 1992).

Hamilton, Alexander, James Madison and John Jay, *The Federalist Papers*, Clinton Rossiter (ed.) (New York: New American Library of World Literature, 1961).

Hobbes, Thomas, *Leviathan* [1651], Richard Tuck (ed.) (Cambridge University Press, 1991).

Hume, David, 'The Idea of a Perfect Commonwealth' [1777], in *Essays, Moral, Political, and Literary*, Eugene F. Miller (ed.) (Indianapolis: Liberty Fund, 1987).

Jellinek, Georg, *Die Lehre von den Staatenverbindungen* (Vienna: Alfred Holder, 1882).

*Allgemeine Staatslehre* (1st edn, Berlin: O. Häring, 1900; 3rd edn, Berlin: O. Häring, 1914).

Johnson, Samuel, *A Dictionary of the English Language in which Words are Deduced from their Originals* (10th edn, London: Rivington *et al.*, 1810).

Kent, James, *Commentaries on American Law* (7th edn, New York: James Kent, 1851).

Locke, John, *Two Treatises of Government* [1690], Peter Laslett (ed.) (Cambridge: Cambridge University Press, 1992).

Maine, Henry Sumner, *Ancient Law: Its Connection with the Early History of Society, and its Relation to Modern Ideas* (London: John Murray, 1861).

May, Thomas Erskine, *A Treatise on the Law, Privileges, Proceedings, and Usage of Parliament* (6th edn, London: Butterworths, 1868).

Mill, John Stuart, *Utilitarianism, On Liberty and Considerations on Representative Government* [1863, 1859, 1861], H. B. Acton (ed.) (London: Dent, 1983).

Montesquieu, Charles-Louis de Secondat, Baron de, *The Spirit of Laws* [1748], T. Nugent (trans.) (New York: Hafner, 1949).

Proudhon, Pierre-Joseph, *The Principle of Federation*, Richard Vernon (ed.) (Toronto: University of Toronto Press, 1979) (translation of *Du principe Fédératif et de la Nécessité de Reconstituer le Parti de la Révolution* [1863]).

Sidgwick, Henry, *Elements of Politics* (1st edn, London: Macmillan, 1891; 2nd edn, London: Macmillan, 1897).

Stephens, Alexander H., *A Constitutional View of the Late War between the States; Its Causes, Character, Conduct And Results*, 2 vols. (Philadelphia: National Publishing Co., 1868).

Story, Joseph, *Commentaries on the Constitution of the United States with a Preliminary Review of the Constitutional History of the Colonies and States before the Adoption of the Constitution*, M. M. Bigelow (ed.), 3 vols. (5th edn, Boston: Little, Brown and Co., 1891).

Smith, Goldwin, *Canada and the Canadian Question* (London: Macmillan, 1891).

Syme, David, *Representative Government in England: Its Faults and Failures* (London: Kegan Paul, Trench and Co., 1881).

Taylor, John, *Construction Construed, and Constitutions Vindicated* (Richmond: Shepherd and Pollard, 1820; reprinted New York: Da Capo Press, 1970).

Tocqueville, Alexis de, *Democracy in America* [1835–43], Henry Steele Commager (ed.) (London: Oxford University Press, 1959).

Todd, Alpheus, *Parliamentary Government in the British Colonies* (London: Longmans, Green and Co., 1880).

Tucker, St George (ed.), *Blackstone's Commentaries: With Notes of Reference, to the Constitution and Laws, of the Federal Government of the United States; And of the Commonwealth of Virginia*, 5 vols. (Philadelphia: Birch and Small, 1803); Notes of reference republished in C. N. Wilson (ed.), *View of the Constitution of the United States With Selected Writings* (Indianapolis: Liberty Fund, 1999).

Willoughby, Westel Woodbury, *An Examination of the Nature of the State: A Study in Political Philosophy* (New York: Macmillan, 1896).

Wilson, Woodrow, *The State: Elements of Historical and Practical Politics* (Boston: Heath, 1898).

## Secondary materials

### Biographies

Bolton, Geoffrey, *Edmund Barton* (Sydney: Allen and Unwin, 2000).

Cowen, Zelman, *Isaac Isaacs* (Brisbane: University of Queensland Press, 1993).

Crisp, Leslie F., *Federation Fathers*, J. Hart (ed.) (Melbourne University Press, 1990).

Crowley, Frank, *Big John Forrest 1847–1918: A Founding Father of the Commonwealth of Australia*, 2 vols. (Perth: University of Western Australia Press, 2000).

Ely, Richard (ed.), *A Living Force: Andrew Inglis Clark and the Ideal of Commonwealth* (Hobart: Centre for Tasmanian Historical Studies, University of Tasmania, 2001).

Francis, Noel, *The Gifted Knight: Sir Robert Garran, GCMG, QC: First Common-wealth Public Servant, Poet, Scholar, and Lawyer* (Canberra: Australian National University Press, 1983).

Glass, Margaret, *Charles Cameron Reid: Federation Father* (Melbourne: Melbourne University Press, 1997).

Gunnar, Peter M., *Good Iron Mac: The Life of Australian Federation Father Sir William McMillan* (Sydney: Federation Press, 1995).

Haward, Marcus and James Warden (eds.), *An Australian Democrat: The Life, Work and Consequences of Andrew Inglis Clark* (Hobart: Centre for Tasmanian Historical Studies, University of Tasmania, 1995).

Headon, David and John Williams (eds.), *Makers of Miracles: The Cast of the Federation Story* (Melbourne: Melbourne University Press, 2000).

Joyce, Roger B., *Samuel Walker Griffith* (Brisbane: University of Queensland Press, 1984).

La Nauze, John A., *Alfred Deakin: A Biography*, 2 vols. (Melbourne: Melbourne University Press, 1965).

Martin, A. W., *Henry Parkes: A Biography* (Melbourne: Melbourne University Press, 1980).

McMinn, W. G., *George Reid* (Melbourne: Melbourne University Press, 1989).

Reynolds, John, *Edmund Barton* (Sydney: Angus and Robertson, 1948; reprinted Melbourne: Bookman Press, 1999).

Rickard, John, *H. B. Higgins: Rebel as Judge* (Sydney: Allen and Unwin, 1984).

Ward, John M., *Earl Grey and the Australian Colonies, 1846–1857* (Melbourne: Melbourne University Press, 1958).

White, Michael and Aladin Rahemtula, *Samuel Griffith: The Law and the Constitution* (Sydney: Law Book Co., 2002).

*General scholarship*

Aroney, Nicholas T., *Freedom of Speech in the Constitution* (Sydney: Centre for Independent Studies, 1998).

'A Public Choice: Federalism and the Prospects of a Republican Preamble' (1999) 21 *University of Queensland Law Journal* 205.

'The Griffith Doctrine: Orthodoxy and Heresy', in Michael White and Aladin Rahemtula (eds.), *Queensland Judges on the High Court* (Brisbane: Supreme Court of Queensland Library, 2003).

'Constitutional Choices in the Work Choices Case, or What Exactly is Wrong with the Reserved Powers Doctrine?' (2008) 32 *Melbourne University Law Review* 1.

'Democracy, Community and Federalism in Electoral Apportionment Cases: The United States, Canada and Australia in Comparative Perspective' (2008) 58 *University of Toronto Law Journal* 421.

Aubert, Jean-François, *Traité de Droit Constitutionnel Suisse* (Neuchâtel: Ides et Calendes, 1967).

Aulich, Chris and Rebecca Pietsch, 'Left on the Shelf: Local government and the Australian Constitution' (2002) 61 *Australian Journal of Public Administration* 14.

Bailyn, Bernard, *The Ideological Origins of the American Revolution* (Cambridge: Belknap Press, 1967).

Barendt, Eric M., *An Introduction to Constitutional Law* (Oxford: Oxford University Press, 1998).

Bartelson, Jens, *A Genealogy of Sovereignty* (Cambridge: Cambridge University Press, 1995).

Beer, Samuel, *To Make a Nation: The Rediscovery of American Federalism* (Cambridge: Belknap Press, 1993).

Bennett, Walter H., *American Theories of Federalism* (Tuscaloosa: University of Alabama Press, 1964).

Berger, Adolf, *Encyclopedic Dictionary of Roman Law* (Philadelphia: American Philosophical Society, 1953).

Berger, Raoul, *Federalism: The Founders' Design* (Norman: University of Oklahoma Press, 1987).

Birch, Antony H., 'Approaches to the Study of Federalism' (1966) 14(1) *Political Studies* 15.

Birrell, Bob, *Federation: The Secret Story* (Sydney: Duffy and Snellgrove, 2001).

Blainey, Geoffrey, 'The Role of Economic Interests in Australian Federation' (1950) 4(15) *Historical Studies, Australia and New Zealand* 224.

Bogdanor, Vernon, 'Federalism and the Nature of the European Union', in Kalypso Nicolaidis and Stephen Weatherill (eds.), *Whose Europe? National Models and the Constitution of the European Union* (Papers of a Multi-Disciplinary Conference, European Studies at Oxford, Oxford University Press, 2003).

Botsman, Peter, *The Great Constitutional Swindle: A Citizen's View of the Australian Constitution* (Sydney: Pluto Press, 2000).

Bradford, Melvin E., *Original Intentions on the Making and Ratification of the United States Constitution* (Athens: University of Georgia Press, 1993).

Brown, A. J., 'One Continent, Two Federalisms: Rediscovering the Original Meanings of Australian Federal Ideas' (2004) 39(3) *Australian Journal of Political Science* 485.

Brown, Bernard E., *American Conservatives: The Political Thought of Francis Lieber and John W. Burgess* (New York: Columbia University Press, 1951).

Buchanan, James M. and Gordon Tullock, *The Calculus of Consent: Logical Foundations of Constitutional Democracy* (Ann Arbor: University of Michigan Press, 1962).

Burgess, Michael, *Comparative Federalism: Theory and Practice* (London: Routledge, 2006).

Cairns, Alan, 'The Politics of Constitution-Making: The Canadian Experience', in Keith Banting and Richard Simeon (eds.), *Redesigning the State: The Politics of Constitutional Change in Industrial Nations* (Toronto: University of Toronto Press, 1985).

Canaway, Arthur P., *The Failure of Federalism in Australia* (London: Oxford University Press, 1930).

Castles, Alex C., 'The Reception and Status of English Law in Australia' (1963) 2 *Adelaide Law Review* 1.

    *An Australian Legal History* (Sydney: Law Book Co., 1982).

    'Two Colonial Democrats: Clark and Kingston and the Draft Constitution of 1891', in Marcus Haward and James Warden (eds.), *An Australian Democrat: The Life, Work and Consequences of Andrew Inglis Clark* (Hobart: Centre for Tasmanian Historical Studies, University of Tasmania, 1995).

Chretian, Jean, *The Role of the United Kingdom in the Amendment of the Canadian Constitution* (Ottawa: Government of Canada, 1981).

Clark, Manning, *A History of Australia, Vol. V: The People Make Laws 1888–1915* (Melbourne: Melbourne University Press, 1981).

Cochrane, Peter, *Colonial Ambition: Foundations of Australian Democracy* (Melbourne: Melbourne University Press, 2006).

Collins, Hugh, 'Political Ideology in Australia: The Distinctiveness of a Benthamite Society', in Stephen R. Graubard (ed.), *Australia: The Daedalus Symposium* (Sydney: Angus and Robertson, 1985).

Constitutional Commission, *Final Report of the Constitutional Commission*, 2 vols. (Canberra: Australian Government Publishing Service, 1988).

Cooray, L. J. M., *Conventions, the Australian Constitution and the Future* (Sydney: Legal Books, 1979).

Cosgrove, Richard A., *The Rule of Law: Albert Venn Dicey, Victorian Jurist* (London: Macmillan, 1980).

Craven, Gregory J., *Secession: The Ultimate States Right* (Melbourne: Melbourne University Press, 1986).

    'A Few Fragments of State Constitutional Law' (1990) 20 *University of Western Australia Law Review* 353.

Crawford, James, 'Amendment of the Constitution', in Gregory J. Craven (ed.), *Australian Federation: Towards the Second Century* (Melbourne: Melbourne University Press, 1992).

Crisp, Leslie F., *Australian National Government* (5th edn, Melbourne: Longman Chesire, 1967).

Crommelin, Michael, 'The Federal Model', in Gregory J. Craven (ed.), *Australian Federation: Towards the Second Century* (Melbourne University Press, 1992).

Cronne, H. A., 'Edward Augustus Freeman, 1823–1892' (1943) 28 *History* 78.

Dahl, Robert A., 'Federalism and the Democratic Process', in *Democracy, Liberty and Equality* (Oslo: Norwegian University Press, 1986).

Davidson, Alistair, *The Invisible State: The Formation of the Australian State 1788–1901* (Cambridge: Cambridge University Press, 1991).

Davis, S. Rufus, 'The "Federal Principle" Revisited', in D. P. Crook (ed.), *Questioning the Past: A Selection of Papers in History and Government* (Brisbane: University of Queensland Press, 1972).

    *The Federal Principle: A Journey through Time in Quest of a Meaning* (Berkeley: University of California Press, 1978).

    *Theory and Reality: Federal Ideas in Australia, England and Europe* (Brisbane: University of Queensland Press, 1995).

Detmold, Michael J., *The Australian Commonwealth: A Fundamental Analysis of its Constitution* (Sydney: Law Book Co., 1985).

Diamond, Martin, '*The Federalist*'s View of Federalism', in G. S. C. Benson *et al.* (eds.), *Essays in Federalism* (Claremont: Institute for Studies in Federalism, 1961).

    'What the Framers meant by Federalism', in R. A. Goldwin (ed.), *A Nation of States* (2nd edn, Chicago: Rand McNally, 1974).

Dikshit, Ramesh D., *The Political Geography of Federalism* (New York: Halstead Press, 1975).

Dixon, Owen, *Jesting Pilate and Other Papers and Addresses* (Melbourne: Law Book Co., 1965).

Dooyeweerd, Herman, 'The Contest over the Concept of Sovereignty', in D. F. M. Strauss (ed.), *Essays in Legal, Social and Political Philosophy*, series B, vol. II, *The Collected Works of Herman Dooyeweerd* (Lewiston: Edwin Mellen Press, 1997).

Douglas, N. F., 'The Western Australian Constitution: Its Source of Authority and Relationship with Section 106 of the Australian Constitution' (1990) 20 *University of Western Australia Law Review* 340.

Duchacek, Ivo, *Comparative Federalism: The Territorial Dimension of Politics* (New York: Holt, Rinehart and Winston, 1970).

    'Consociational Cradle of Federalism' (1985) 15(2) *Publius: The Journal of Federalism* 35.

Elazar, Daniel J., *American Federalism: A View from the States* (2nd edn, New York: Thomas Crowell, 1972).

    'Republicanism, Representation and Consent in the Founding Era' (1979) 9 *Publius* 1.

    *Exploring Federalism* (Tuscaloosa: University of Alabama Press, 1991).

    *Covenant and Commonwealth: From Christian Separation through the Protestant Reformation* (New Brunswick: Transaction Publishers, 1996).

Elazar, Daniel J. (ed.), *Federal Systems of the World: A Handbook of Federal, Confederal and Autonomy Arrangements* (2nd edn, Harlow: Longman Group, 1994).

Else-Mitchell, Rae, 'The Establishment in 1885 of the Federal Council of Australasia' (1985) 59 *Australian Law Journal* 666.

Evans, Simon, 'Why is the Constitution Binding': Authority, Obligation and the Role of the People' (2004) 25 *Adelaide Law Review* 103.

Evatt, Herbert Vere, 'Amending the Constitution' (1937) 1 *Res Judicatae* 264.

'The Legal Foundations of New South Wales' (1938) 11 *Australian Law Journal* 409.

Evans, Harry (ed.), *Odgers' Australian Senate Practice* (11th edn, Australian Government Publishing Service, Canberra, 2004).

Figgis, John N., *Studies of Political Thought from Gerson to Grotius 1414–1625* (Cambridge: Cambridge University Press, 1923).

Finer, S. E., Vernon Bogdanor and Bernard Rudden, *Comparing Constitutions* (Oxford: Clarendon Press, 1995).

Finnis, John, 'Revolutions and Continuity of Law', in A. W. B. Simpson (ed.), *Oxford Essays in Jurisprudence*, second series (Oxford: Clarendon Press, 1973).

Fisher, H. A. L., *James Bryce*, 2 vols. (London: Macmillan, 1927).

Fleiner, Thomas, 'Federalism in Australia and in Other Nations', in Gregory J. Craven (ed.), *Australian Federation: Towards the Second Century* (Melbourne: Melbourne University Press, 1992).

'The Initiative and Referendum in Switzerland', in Kenneth Wiltshire (ed.), *Direct Democracy: Citizens Initiated Referendums* (Melbourne: Constitutional Centenary Foundation, 1996).

Ford, Trowbridge H., *Albert Venn Dicey, the Man and his Times* (Chichester: Barry Rose Publishers, 1985).

Fraser, Andrew, *The Spirit of the Laws: Republicanism and the Unfinished Project of Modernity* (Toronto: University of Toronto Press, 1990).

Frenkel, Max, *Federal Theory* (Canberra: Centre for Research on Federal Financial Relations, Australian National University, 1986).

Friedrich, Carl J., *Trends of Federalism in Theory and Practice* (London: Pall Mall Press, 1968).

'Introduction', Johannes Althusius, *Politica Methodice Digesta* (New York: Arno Press, 1979).

Galligan, Brian, *Politics of the High Court* (Brisbane: University of Queensland Press, 1987).

*A Federal Republic: Australia's Constitutional System of Government* (Cambridge: Cambridge University Press, 1995).

Galligan, Brian and Cliff Walsh, 'Federalism – Yes or No?', in Gregory J. Craven (ed.), *Australian Federation: Towards the Second Century* (Melbourne: Melbourne University Press, 1992).

Galligan, Brian and James Warden, 'The Design of the Senate', in Gregory J. Craven (ed.), *The Convention Debates 1891–1898: Commentaries, Indices and Guide* (Sydney: Legal Books, 1986).

Garis, Brian K. de, 'The Colonial Office and the Commonwealth Constitution Bill' in A. W. Martin (ed.), *Essays in Australian Federation* (Melbourne: Melbourne University Press, 1969).

'How Popular was the Popular Federation Movement?', *Papers on Parliament* no. 21 (Canberra: Department of the Senate, 1993).

Gibbs, Harry, 'The Decline of Federalism' (1994) 18 *University of Queensland Law Journal* 1.

Gilbert, Christopher D., *Australian and Canadian Federalism 1867–1984* (Melbourne: Melbourne University Press, 1986).

Greaves, H. R. G., *Federal Union in Practice* (London: George Allen and Unwin, 1940).

Greene, Jack P., *Peripheries and Center: Constitutional Development in the Extended Politics of the British Empire and the United States, 1607–1788* (Athens: University of Georgia Press, 1986).

*Negotiated Authorities: Essays in Colonial Political and Constitutional History* (Charlottesville: University Press of Virginia, 1994).

Greenwood, Gordon, *The Future of Australian Federalism* (2nd edn, Melbourne: Melbourne University Press, 1976).

Grodzins, Morton and Daniel J. Elazar, 'Centralization and Decentralization in the American Federal System', in R. A. Goldwin (ed.), *A Nation of States* (2nd edn, Chicago: Rand McNally, 1974).

Hall, Mark, *The Political and Legal Philosophy of James Wilson 1742–1798* (Columbia: University of Missouri Press, 1997).

Haller, Walter and Alfred Kölz, *Allgemeines Staatsrecht* (Basel: Helbing und Lichtenhahn, 1999).

Henkin, Louis, *International Law: Politics and Values* (Dordrecht: Martinus Nijhoff, 1995).

Hinsley, F. H., *Sovereignty* (2nd edn, Cambridge, Cambridge University Press, 1986).

Hirst, John, *The Sentimental Nation: The Making of the Australian Commonwealth* (Oxford: Oxford University Press, 2000).

Hogg, Peter W., *Constitutional Law of Canada* (3rd edn, Toronto: Carswell, 1992).

Holcombe, Randall G., 'Constitutions as Constraints: A Case Study of Three American Constitutions' (1991) 2 *Constitutional Political Economy* 303.

Howard, Colin and Cheryl Saunders, 'The Blocking of the Budget and Dismissal of the Government', in Gareth Evans (ed.), *Labor and the Constitution 1972-1975* (Melbourne: Heinemann Educational, 1977).

Howell, Peter A., 'The Strongest Delegation: The South Australians at the Constitutional Convention of 1897–98' (1998) 1 *The New Federalist* 44.

'Joseph Chamberlain and the Amendment of the Australian Constitution Bill' (2001) 7 *The New Federalist* 16.

Hueglin, Thomas O., *Early Modern Concepts for a Late Modern World: Althusius on Community and Federalism* (Waterloo: Wilfrid Laurier University Press, 1999).

'Federalism at the Crossroads: Old Meanings, New Significance' (2003) 36 *Canadian Journal of Political Science* 275.

Hueglin, Thomas O. and Alan Fenna, *Comparative Federalism: A Systematic Inquiry* (Toronto: Broadview Press, 2006).

Hughes, Christopher J., *The Federal Constitution of Switzerland* (Oxford: Clarendon Press, 1954).

*Switzerland* (New York: Praeger, 1975).

Hunt, Erling M., *American Precedents in Australian Federation* (New York: AMS Press, 1963).

Hutson, James H., *The Sister Republics: Switzerland and the United States from 1776 to the Present* (Washington: Library of Congress, 1991).

Ions, Edmund, *James Bryce and American Democracy, 1870–1922* (London: Macmillan, 1968).

Irving, Helen, 'Fair Federalists and Founding Mothers', in *A Woman's Constitution? Gender and History in the Australian Commonwealth* (Sydney: Hale and Iremonger, 1996).

*To Constitute a Nation: A Cultural History of Australia's Constitution* (Cambridge: Cambridge University Press, 1997).

'New South Wales', *The Centenary Companion to Australian Federation* (Cambridge: Cambridge University Press, 1999).

Jensen, Merrill, *The Articles of Confederation: An Interpretation of the Social-Constitutional History of the American Revolution 1774–1781* (Madison: University of Wisconsin Press, 1940).

Joske, Percy E., *Australian Federal Government* (3rd edn, Sydney: Butterworths, 1976).

Kammen, Michael, *Deputyes & Liberties: The Origins of Representative Government in Colonial America* (New York: Knoff, 1969).

Kay, Richard S., 'The Illegality of the Constitution' (1987) 4 *Constitutional Commentary* 57.

Kincaid, John and G. Alan Tarr (eds.), *A Global Dialogue on Federalism*. Vol. I: *Constitutional Origins, Structure, and Change in Federal Countries* (Montreal: McGill-Queen's University Press, 2005).

King, Preston, *Federalism and Federation* (Baltimore: Johns Hopkins University Press, 1982).

Koch, Hannsjoachim W., *A Constitutional History of Germany* (London: Longman, 1987).

Kramer, Larry, 'Putting the Politics Back into the Political Safeguards of Federalism' (2000) 100 *Columbia Law Review* 215.

Kunkel, Wofgang, *An Introduction to Roman Legal and Constitutional History*, J. M. Kelly (trans.) (2nd edn, Oxford: Clarendon Press, 1973).

La Nauze, John A., 'A Little Bit of Lawyers' Language: The History of "Absolutely Free", 1890-1900', in A. W. Martin (ed.), *Essays in Australian Federation* (Melbourne: Melbourne University Press, 1969).

   *The Making of the Australian Constitution* (Melbourne: Melbourne University Press, 1972).

Lane, Patrick H., *The Australian Federal System with United States Analogues* (Sydney: Law Book Co., 1972).

   *Lane's Commentary on the Australian Constitution* (Sydney: Law Book Co., 1986).

   *An Introduction to the Australian Constitution* (4th edn, Sydney: Law Book Co., 1987).

Larcombe, Frederick A., *The Development of Local Government in New South Wales* (Melbourne: Cheshire, 1961).

Larsen, Jakob A. O., *Greek Federal States* (Oxford: Oxford University Press, 1968).

Laski, Harold J., 'The Obsolescence of Federalism' (1939) 98 *New Republic* 367.

   *Studies in the Problem of Sovereignty* (London: Allen and Unwin, 1968).

Latham, Richard T. E., 'The Law and the Commonwealth', in W. K. Hancock (ed.), *Survey of British Commonwealth Affairs* (London: Oxford University Press, 1937).

Lenaerts, Koen, 'Constitutionalism and the Many Faces of Federalism' (1990) 38 *American Journal of Comparative Law* 205.

Lijphart, Arendt, *Democracies: Patterns of Majoritarian and Consensus Government in Twenty-one Countries* (New Haven: Yale University Press, 1984).

Lindell, Geoffrey, 'Why is Australia's Constitution Binding? The Reasons in 1900 and Now, and the Effect of Independence' (1986) 16 *Federal Law Review* 29.

Linder, Wolf, *Swiss Democracy: Possible Solutions to Conflict in Multicultural Societies* (New York: St Martin's Press, 1994).

Livingston, Donald, *Philosophical Melancholy and Delirium: Hume's Pathology of Philosophy* (Chicago: University of Chicago Press, 1999).

   'The Founding and the Enlightenment: Two Theories of Sovereignty', in Gary L. Gregg (ed.), *Vital Remnants: America's Founding and the Western Tradition* (Wilmington: ISI Books, 1999).

Livingston, William S., *Federalism and Constitutional Change* (Oxford: Clarendon Press, 1956).

Loveday, Peter, 'The Federal Convention, an Analysis of the Voting' (1972) 18(2) *Australian Journal of Politics and History* 169.

Lumb, R. D., 'Fundamental Law and the Processes of Constitutional Change in Australia' (1978) 9 *Federal Law Review* 148.

*Australian Constitutionalism* (Sydney: Butterworths, 1983).

'The Bicentenary of Australian Constitutionalism: The Evolution of Rules of Constitutional Change' (1988) 15 *University of Queensland Law Journal* 1.

*The Constitutions of the Australian States* (5th edn, Brisbane: University of Queensland Press, 1992).

Lumb, R. D. and Gabriel A. Moens, *The Constitution of the Commonwealth of Australia Annotated* (5th edn, Sydney: Butterworths, 1995).

Lumb, R. D. and Kevin W. Ryan, *The Constitution of the Commonwealth of Australia Annotated* (Sydney: Butterworths, 1974).

Lutz, Donald S., *The Origins of American Constitutionalism* (Baton Rouge: Louisiana State University Press, 1988).

Macintyre, Stuart, 'Corowa and the Voice of the People', *The People's Conventions: Corowa (1893) and Bathurst (1896)*, Papers on Parliament no. 32 (Canberra: Department of the Senate, 1998).

Maitland, Frederic W., *The Constitutional History of England* (Cambridge: Cambridge University Press, 1955).

Martin, A. W., 'Economic Influences in the "New Federation Movement"' (1953) 6(21) *Historical Studies, Australia and New Zealand* 64.

'Parkes and the 1890 Conference', *Papers on Parliament* no. 9 (Canberra: Department of the Senate, 1990).

Martin, A. W. (ed.), *Essays in Australian Federation* (Melbourne: Melbourne University Press, 1969).

Martin, Jed, *Australia, New Zealand and Federation, 1883–1901* (London: Menzies Centre for Australian Studies, 2001).

'Explaining the Sentimental Utopia: Historians and the Centenary of Australian Federation' (2003) 18(1) *Australian Studies* 211.

McCloskey, Robert G. (ed.), *The Works of James Wilson* (Cambridge: Harvard University Press, 1967).

McConnel, Katherine, '"Separation is from the Devil while Federation is from Heaven": The Separation Question and Federation in Queensland' (1999) 4 *The New Federalist* 14.

McDonald, Forrest, *Novus Ordo Seclorum: The Intellectual Origins of the Constitution* (Lawrence: University Press of Kansas, 1985).

*States' Rights and the Union: Imperium in Imperio, 1776–1876* (Lawrence: University Press of Kansas, 2000).

McDonald, G. W., 'The Eighty Founding Fathers' (1968) 1 *Queensland Historical Review* 38.

McKenna, Mark, 'Sir Richard Chaffey Baker – the Senate's First Republican', in *The Constitution Makers, Papers on Parliament* no. 30 (Canberra: Department of the Senate, 1997).

McMinn, W. G., *A Constitutional History of Australia* (Melbourne: Oxford University Press, 1979).

*Nationalism and Federalism in Australia* (Melbourne: Oxford University Press, 1994).

McNair, Arnold Duncan, *Law of Treaties* (Oxford: Clarendon Press, 1961).

Meale, David 'The History of the Federal Idea in Australian Constitutional Jurisprudence: A Reappraisal' (1992) 8 *Australian Journal of Law and Society* 25.

Melbourne, A. C. V., *Early Constitutional Development in Australia* (Brisbane: University of Queensland Press, 1963).

Mogi, Sobei, *The Problem of Federalism: A Study in the History of Political Theory* (London: Allen and Unwin, 1931).

Neal, David, *The Rule of Law in a Penal Colony: Law and Power in Early New South Wales* (Cambridge: Cambridge University Press, 1991).

Neasey, Frank M., 'Andrew Inglis Clark Senior and Australian Federation' (1969) 15(2) *Australian Journal of Politics and History* 1.

Norris, Ronald, *The Emergent Commonwealth: Australian Federation: Expectations and Fulfilment 1889–1910* (Melbourne: Melbourne University Press, 1975).

Onuf, Peter S., *The Origins of the Federal Republic: Jurisdictional Controversies in the United States, 1775–1787* (Philadelphia: University of Pennsylvania Press, 1983).

'Reflections on the Founding: Constitutional Historiography in Bicentennial Perspective' (1989) 46(2) *William and Mary Quarterly* 341.

Ostrom, Vincent, *The Meaning of American Federalism: Constituting a Self-Governing Society* (San Francisco: San Francisco Institute for Contemporary Studies, 1991).

Patterson, P. A., 'Federal Electorates and Proportionate Distribution' (1968) 42 *Australian Law Journal* 127.

Parker, R. S., 'Australian Federation: The Influence of Economic Interests and Political Pressures' (1949) 4(13) *Historical Studies, Australia and New Zealand* 1.

Pole, Jack R., *Political Representation in England and the Origins of the American Republic* (New York: Macmillan, 1966).

Rakove, Jack N., 'The Great Compromise: Ideas, Interests, and the Politics of Constitution Making' (1987) 44 *William and Mary Quarterly* 424.

'The First Phases of American Federalism', in Mark Tushnet (ed.), *Comparative Constitutional Federalism: Europe and America* (New York: Greenwood Press, 1990).

Rakove, Jack N., *Original Meanings: Politics and Ideas in the Making of the Constitution* (New York: Alfred A. Knopf, 1996).

Reynolds, John, 'A. I. Clark's American Sympathies and his Influence on Australian Federation' (1958) 32 *Australian Law Journal* 62.

Riker, William H., *Federalism: Origin, Operation, Significance* (Boston: Little, Brown and Co., 1964).

*The Development of American Federalism* (Boston: Kluwer, 1987).

'The Lessons of 1787' (1987) 55 *Public Choice* 5.

Riley, Patrick, 'Three 17th Century German Theorists of Federalism: Althusius, Hugo and Leibniz' (1976) 5(3) *Publius: The Journal of Federalism* 7.

Roe, Michael, 'The Federation Divide Among Australia's Liberal Idealists: Contexts for Clark', in Marcus Haward and James Warden (eds.), *An Australian Democrat: The Life, Work and Consequences of Andrew Inglis Clark* (Hobart: Centre for Tasmanian Historical Studies, University of Tasmania, 1995).

Rossiter, Clinton (ed.), *The Federalist Papers* (New York: New American Library of World Literature, 1961).

Sackville, Ronald, 'The Doctrine of Immunity of Instrumentalities in the United States and Australia: A Comparative Analysis' (1969) 7 *Melbourne University Law Review* 15.

Sampford, Charles J. G., 'Responsible Government and the Logic of Federalism: an Australian Paradox?' (1990) *Public Law* 90.

Saunders, Cheryl, 'The Hardest Nut to Crack: The Financial Settlement in the Commonwealth Constitution', in Gregory J. Craven (ed.), *The Convention Debates 1891–1898: Commentaries, Indices and Guide* (Sydney: Legal Books, 1986).

Sawer, Geoffrey, *Australian Federalism in the Courts* (Melbourne: Melbourne University Press, 1967).

*Modern Federalism* (London: Watts, 1969).

*Australian Federal Politics and Law 1901–1929* (Melbourne: Melbourne University Press, 1972).

'The British Connection' (1973) 47 *Australian Law Journal* 113.

*The Australian Constitution* (Canberra: Australian Government Publishing Service, 1975).

'Foreword', John Quick and Robert Garran, *The Annotated Constitution of the Australian Commonwealth* (Sydney: Legal Books, 1976).

*Federation under Strain* (Melbourne: Melbourne University Press, 1977).

Searle, Geoffrey, 'The Victorian Government's Campaign for Federation, 1883–1889' in A. W. Martin (ed.), *Essays in Australian Federation* (Melbourne: Melbourne University Press, 1969).

Sharman, Campbell, 'Australia as a Compound Republic' (1990) 25(1) *Politics* 1.

Simpson, J. A. and E. S. C. Weiner (eds.), *The Oxford English Dictionary* (2nd edn, Oxford: Clarendon Press, 1989).

Skinner, Quentin, *The Foundations of Modern Political Thought*, 2 vols. (Cambridge: Cambridge University Press, 1978).

Stepan, Alfred, *Arguing Comparative Politics* (Oxford: Oxford University Press, 2001).

Sweetman, Edward, *Australian Constitutional Development* (Melbourne: Macmillan and Co., 1925).

Thomson, James A., 'The Australian Constitution: Statute, Fundamental Document or Compact' (1985) 59 *Law Institute Journal* 1199.

'Andrew Inglis Clark and Australian Constitutional Law', in Marcus Haward and James Warden (eds.), *An Australian Democrat: The Life, Work and Consequences of Andrew Inglis Clark* (Hobart: Centre for Tasmanian Historical Studies, University of Tasmania, 1995).

Tierney, Brian, *Religion, Law and the Growth of Constitutional Thought* (Cambridge: Cambridge University Press, 1982).

Tulloch, Hugh, *James Bryce's 'American Commonwealth': The Anglo–American Background* (Woodbridge, Suffolk: Boydell Press, 1988).

Twomey, Anne, 'The Constitution: 19th century Colonial Office document or a People's Constitution?', Parliamentary Library Background Paper no. 15 (Canberra: Department of the Parliamentary Library, Australian Government Publishing Service, 1994).

*The Constitution of New South Wales* (Sydney: Federation Press, 2004).

Van den Hoom, R., 'Richard Chaffey Baker: A South Australian Conservative and the Federal Conventions of 1891 and 1897–8' (1980) 7 *Journal of the Historical Society of South Australia* 24.

Vile, Maurice J. C., *The Structure of American Federalism* (London: Oxford University Press, 1961).

Ward, John M., *The State and the People: Australian Federation and Nation-making, 1870–1901* (Sydney: Federation Press, 2001).

Warden, James, *Federal Theory and the Formation of the Australian Constitution* (unpublished doctoral thesis, Australian National University, 1990).

'Federalism and the Design of the Australian Constitution' (1992) 27 *Australian Journal of Political Science* 143.

Watts, Ronald, *Comparing Federal Systems* (2nd edn, Montreal: McGill-Queens University Press, 1999).

Wechsler, Herbert, 'The Political Safeguards of Federalism: The Role of the States in the Composition and Selection of the National Government' (1954) 54 *Columbia Law Review* 543.

Wheare, Kenneth C., *Modern Constitutions* (Oxford: Oxford University Press, 1951).

*Federal Government* (4th edn, New York: Oxford University Press, 1967).

Williams, John M., '"With Eyes Open": Andrew Inglis Clark and our Republican Tradition' (1995) 23 *Federal Law Review* 149.

Wiltshire, Kenneth, *Planning and Federalism: Australian and Canadian Experience* (Brisbane: University of Queensland Press, 1986).

Winterton, George, *Parliament, the Executive and the Governor-General: A Constitutional Analysis* (Melbourne University Press, 1983).

'Popular Sovereignty and Constitutional Continuity' (1998) 26 *Federal Law Review* 1.

Winterton, George, H. P. Lee, Arthur Glass and James A. Thomson, *Australian Federal Constitutional Law* (Sydney: LBC Information Services, 1999).

Wood, Gordon S., *The Creation of the American Republic, 1776–1787* (New York: W. W. Norton and Co, 1993).

Yarbrough, Jean, 'Rethinking "*The Federalist*'s View of Federalism"' (1985) 15 *Publius: The Journal of Federalism* 31.

Young, Ernest, 'The Rehnquist Court's Two Federalisms' (2004) 83 *Texas Law Review* 1.

Zagarri, Rosemarie, *The Politics of Size: Representation in the United States, 1776–1850* (Ithaca: Cornell University Press, 1987).

Zines, Leslie, 'The Commonwealth', in Gregory J. Craven (ed.), *Australian Federation: Towards the Second Century* (Melbourne: Melbourne University Press, 1992).

Zuckert, Michael, 'Federalism and the Founding: Toward a Reinterpretation of the Constitutional Convention' (1986) 48 *Review of Politics* 166.

# INDEX